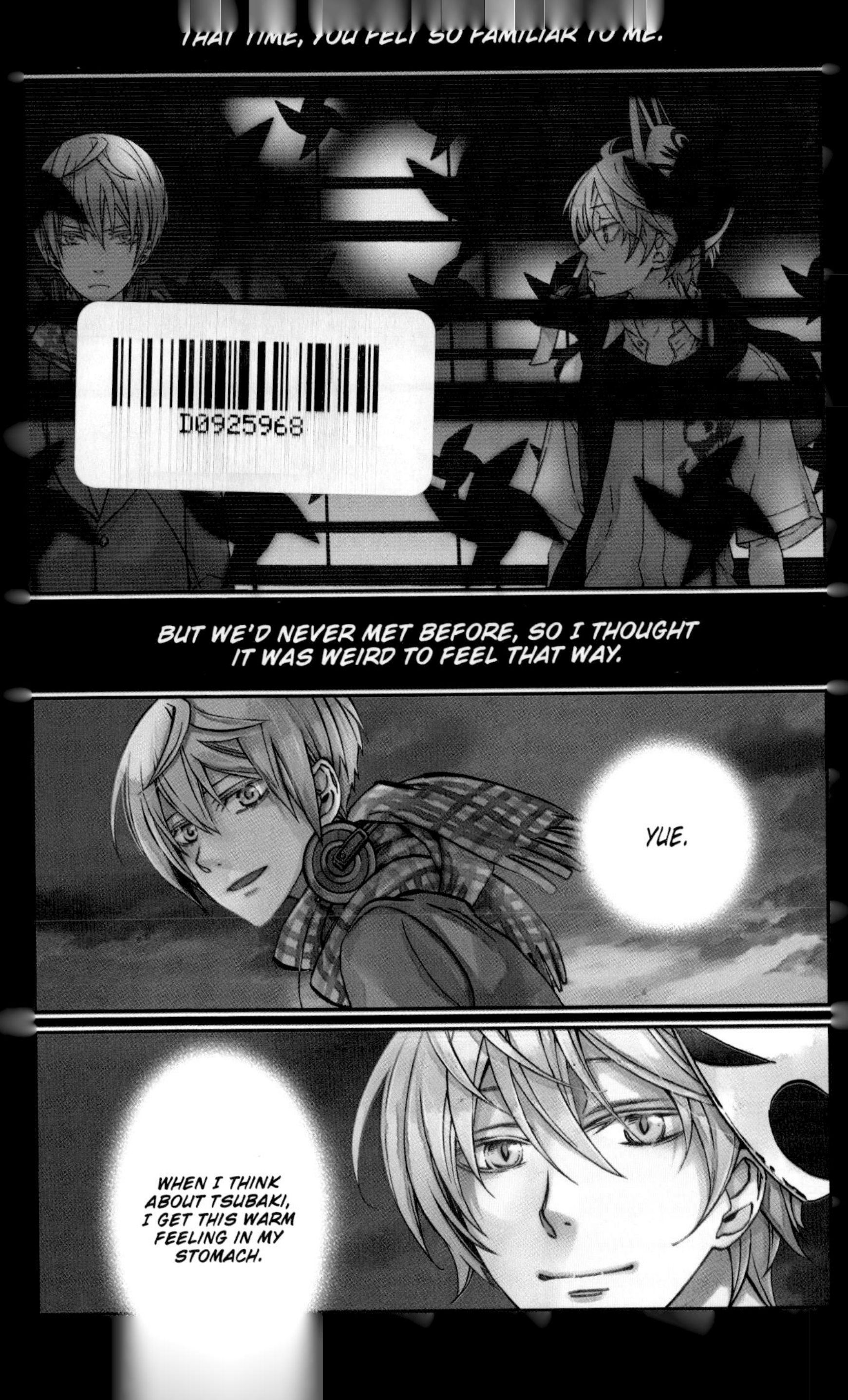
THAT TIME, YOU FELT SO FAMILIAR TO ME.
BUT WE'D NEVER MET BEFORE, SO I THOUGHT IT WAS WEIRD TO FEEL THAT WAY.
YUE.
WHEN I THINK ABOUT TSUBAKI, I GET THIS WARM FEELING IN MY STOMACH.

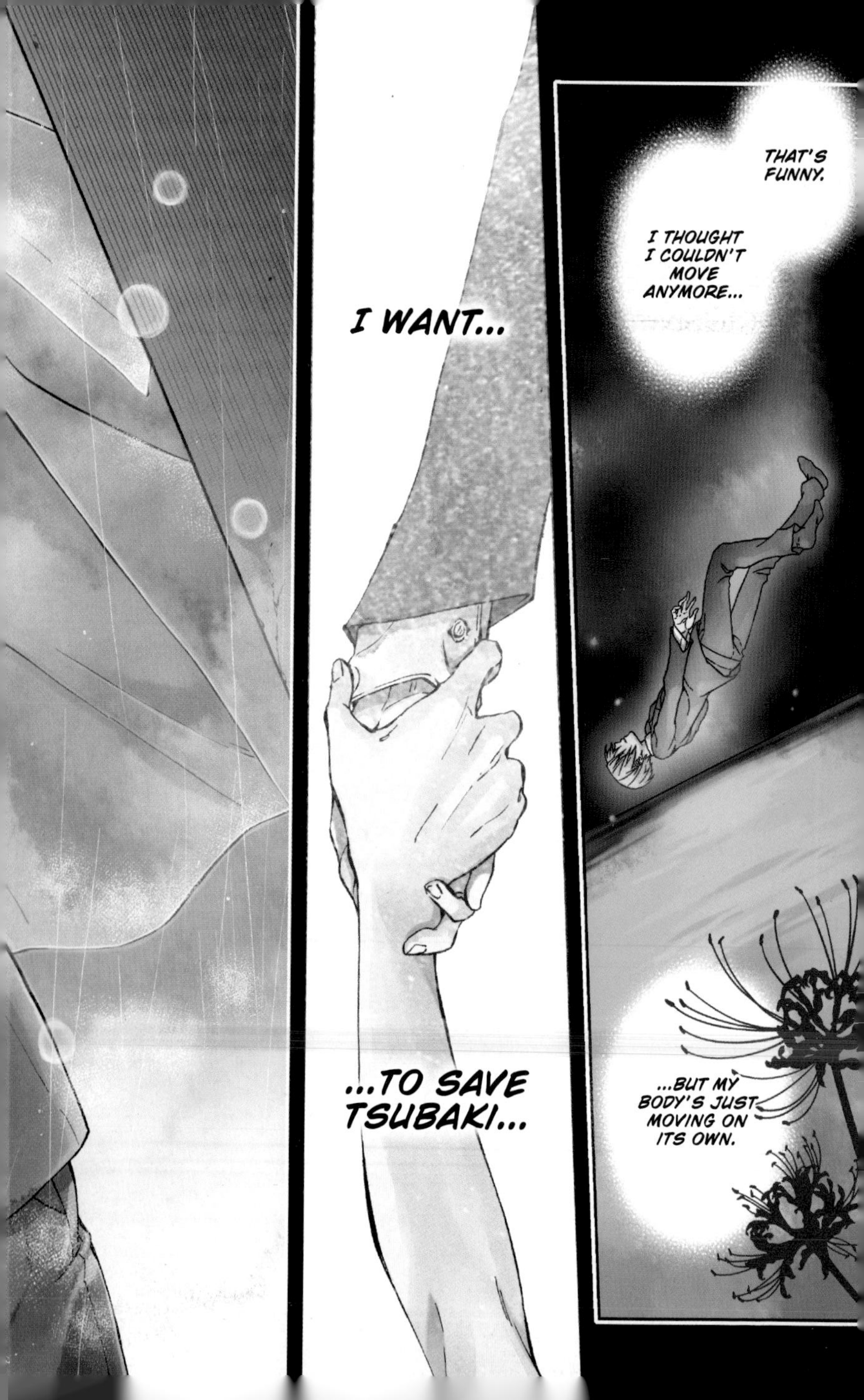
THAT'S FUNNY.
I THOUGHT I COULDN'T MOVE ANYMORE...
...BUT MY BODY'S JUST MOVING ON ITS OWN.
I WANT...
...TO SAVE TSUBAKI...

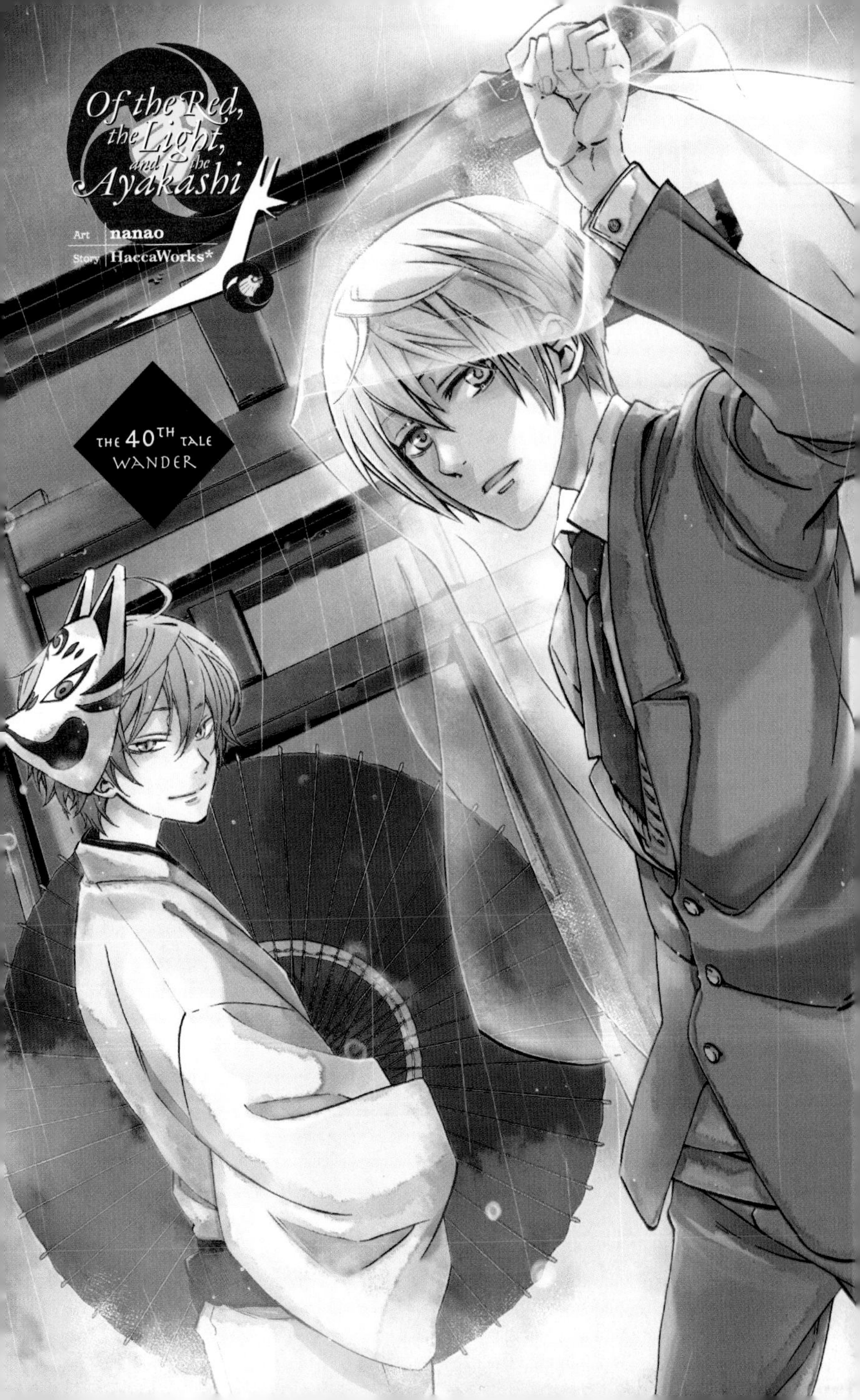

Of the Red, the Light, and the Ayakashi
Art nanao
Story HaccaWorks*
THE 40TH TALE
WANDER

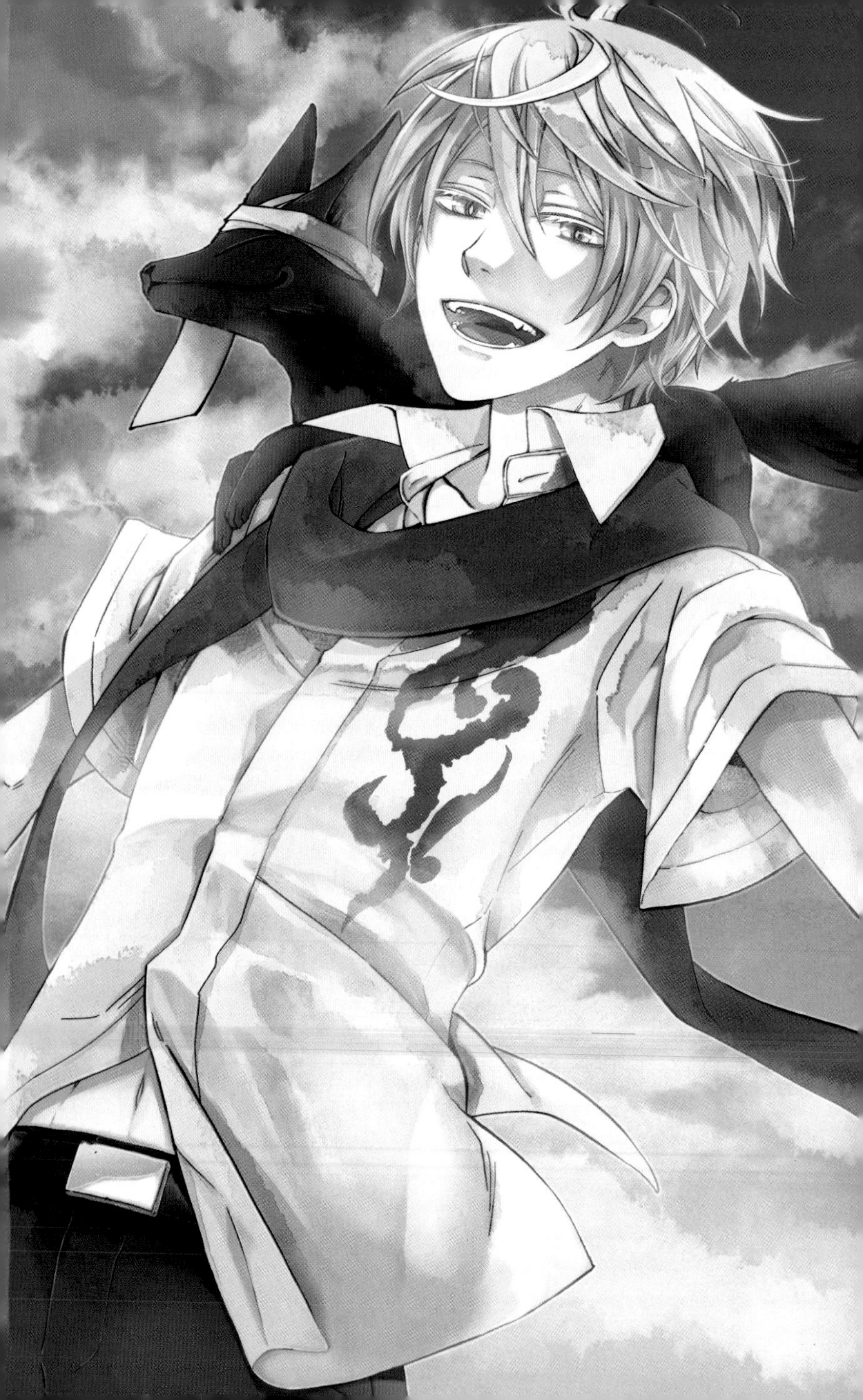

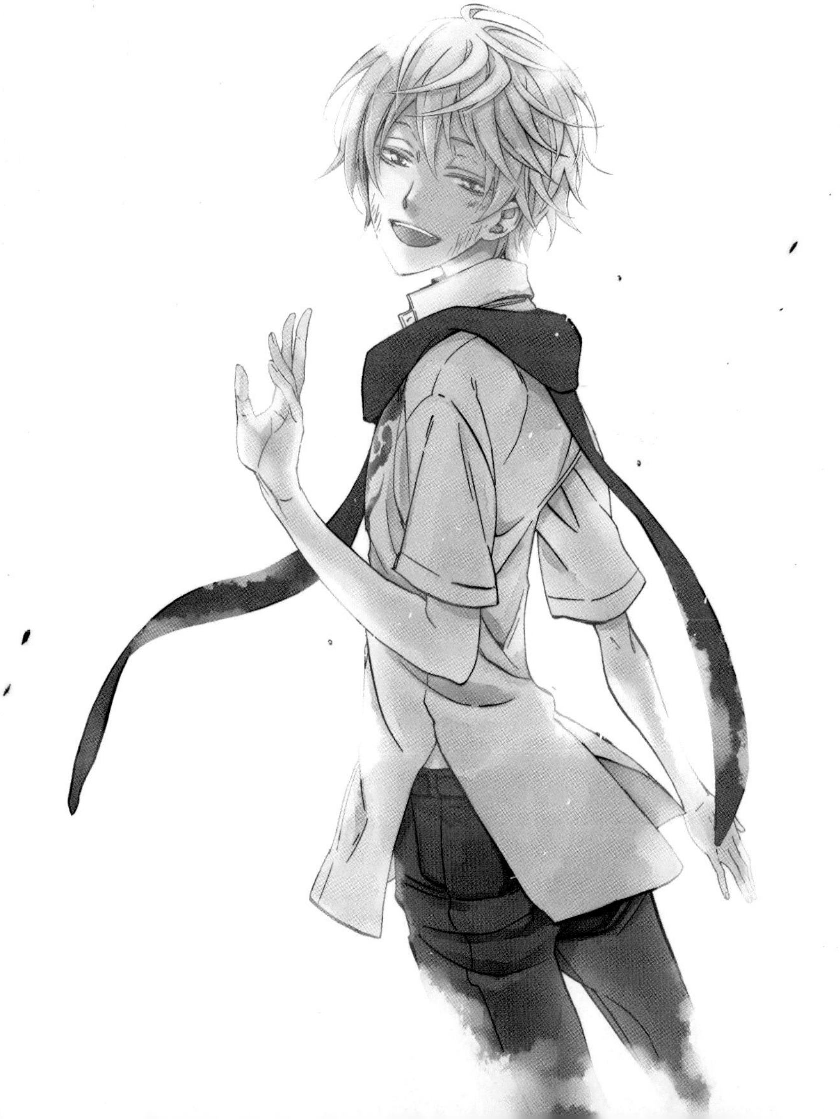

CONTENTS

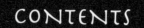

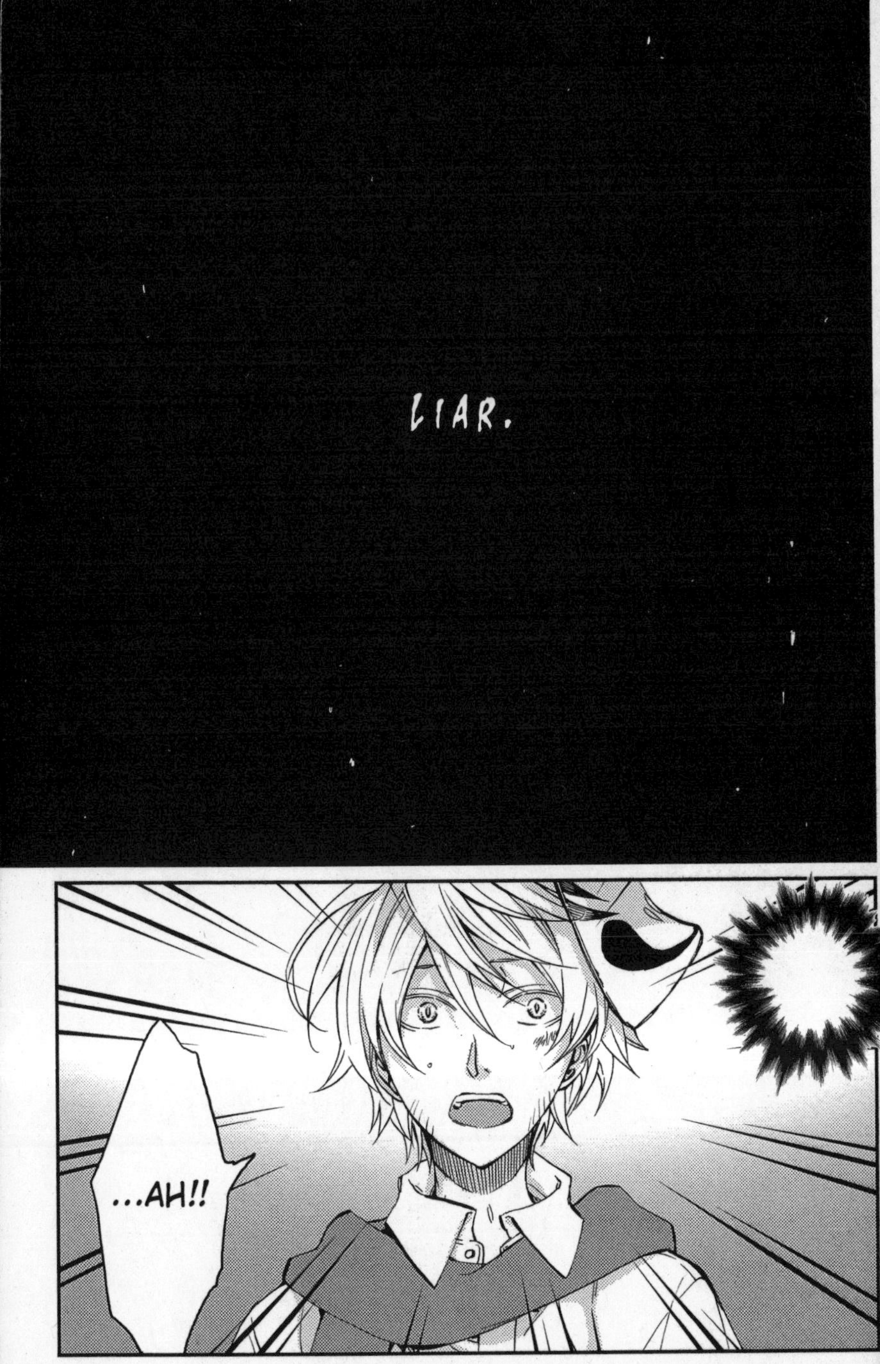
LIAR.
...AH!!

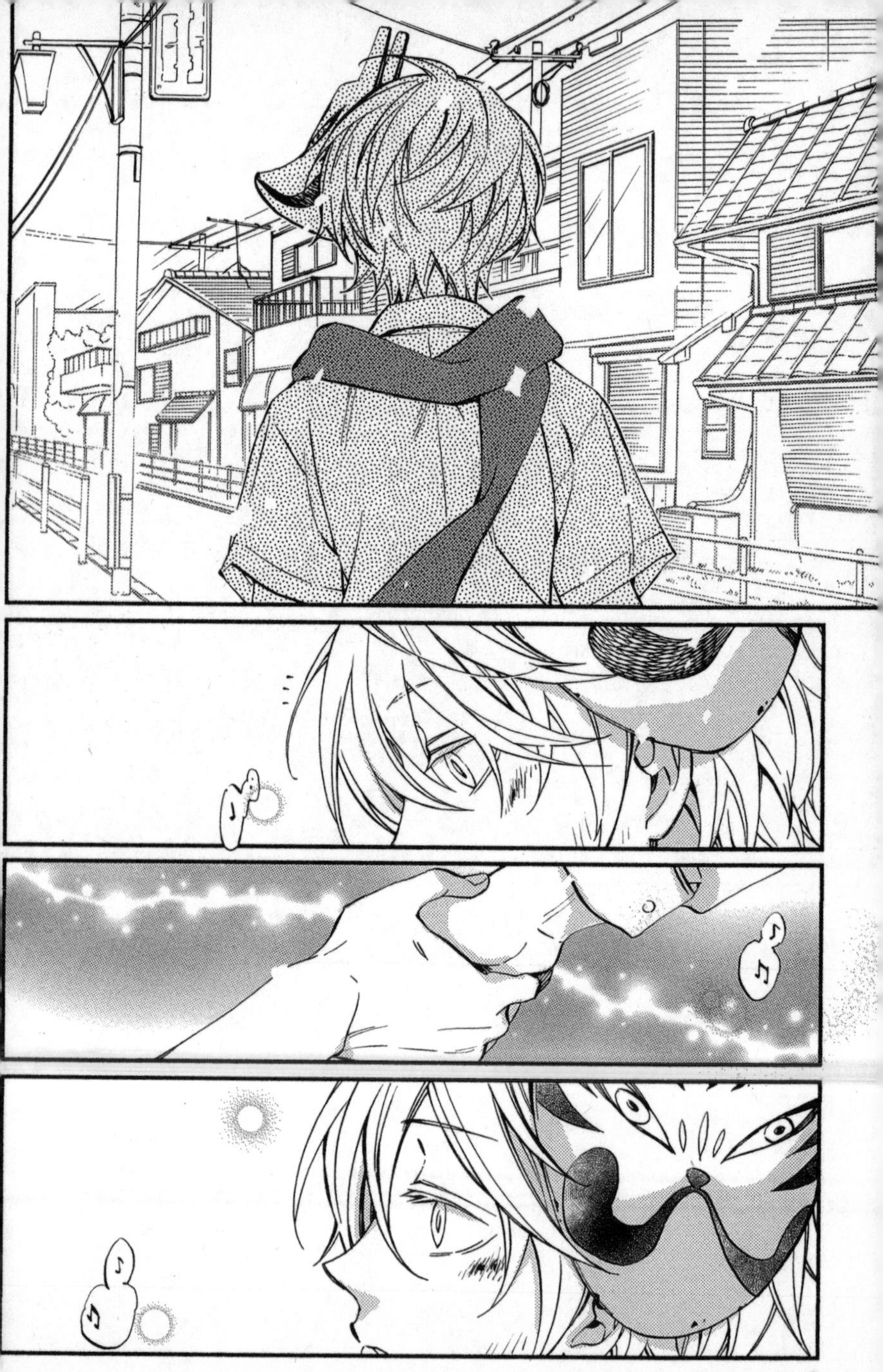

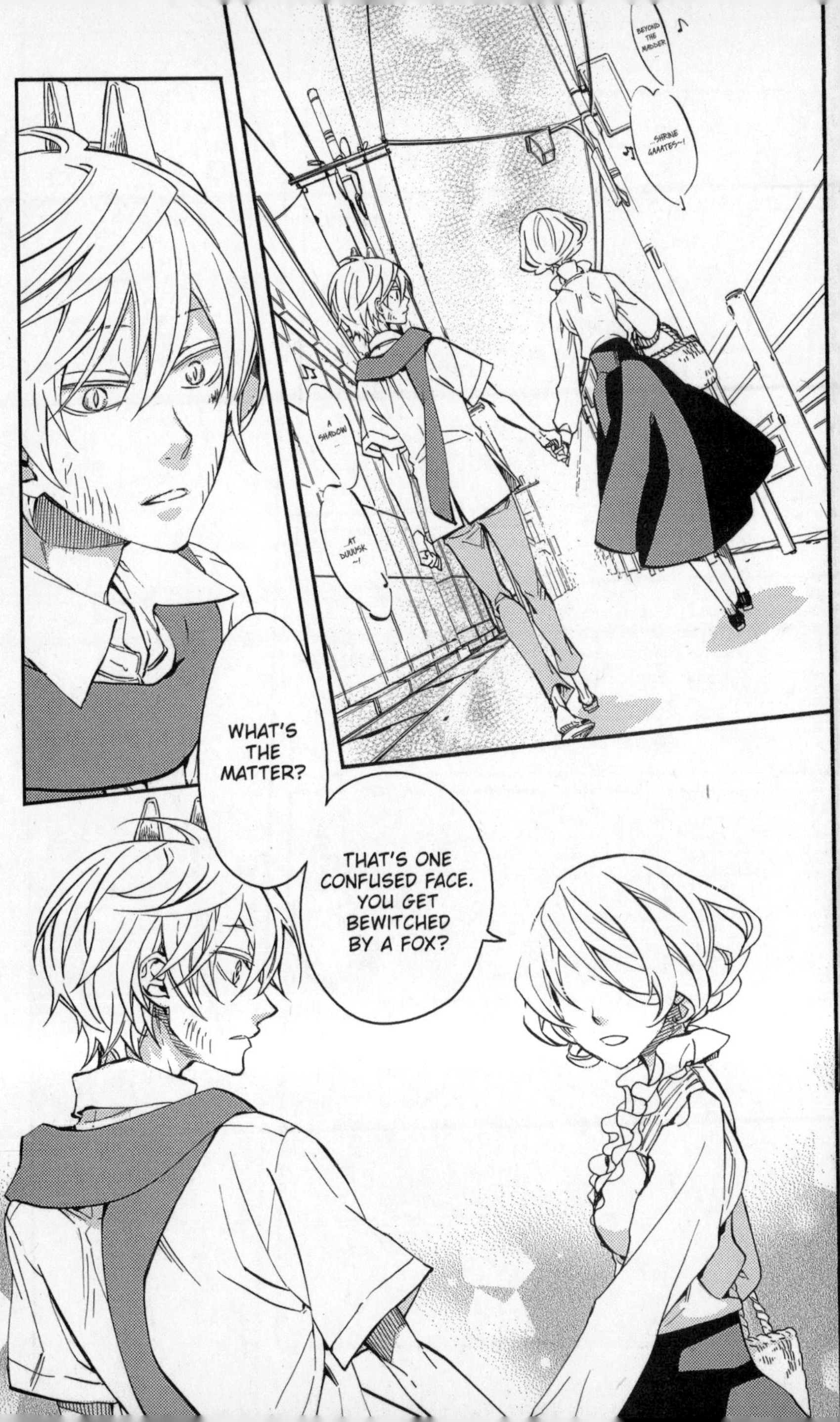
BEYOND THE MADDER...
...SHRINE GAAATES~!
A SHADOW...
...AT DUUUSK~!
WHAT'S THE MATTER?
THAT'S ONE CONFUSED FACE. YOU GET BEWITCHED BY A FOX?

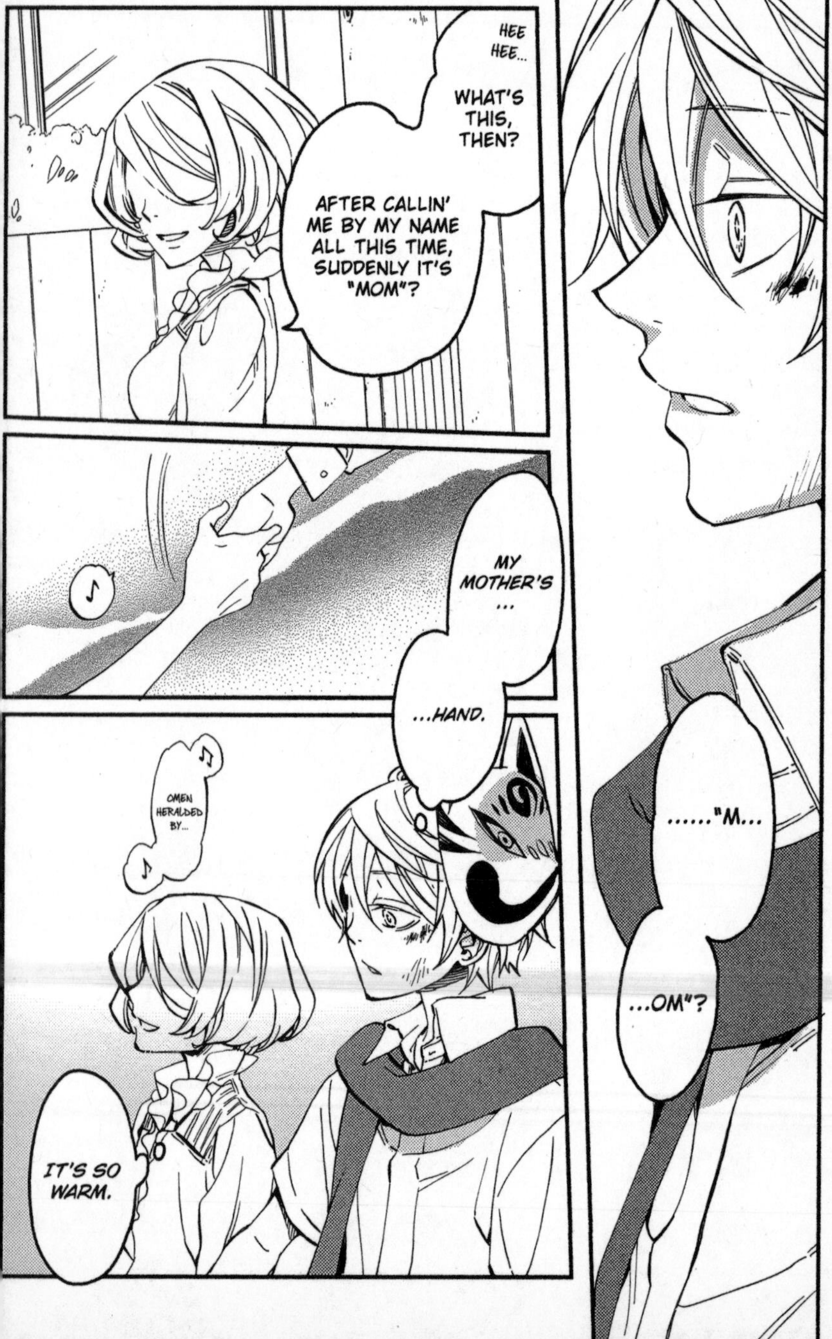
......"M...
...OM"?
HEE HEE...
WHAT'S THIS, THEN?
AFTER CALLIN' ME BY MY NAME ALL THIS TIME, SUDDENLY IT'S "MOM"?
MY MOTHER'S ...
...HAND.
OMEN HERALDED BY...
IT'S SO WARM.

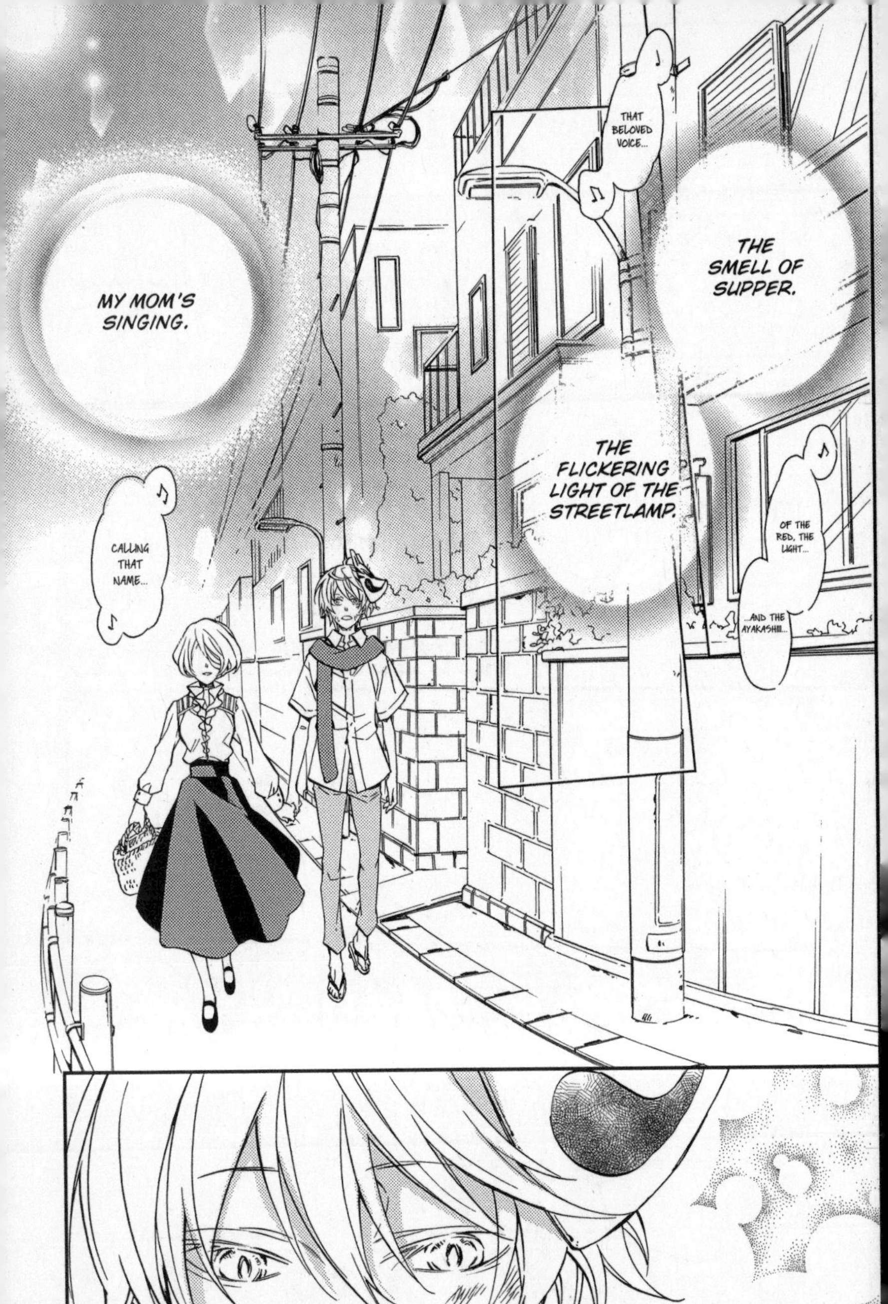
THAT BELOVED VOICE...
THE SMELL OF SUPPER.
THE FLICKERING LIGHT OF THE STREETLAMP.
OF THE RED, THE LIGHT...
...AND THE AYAKASHIII...
MY MOM'S SINGING.
CALLING THAT NAME...

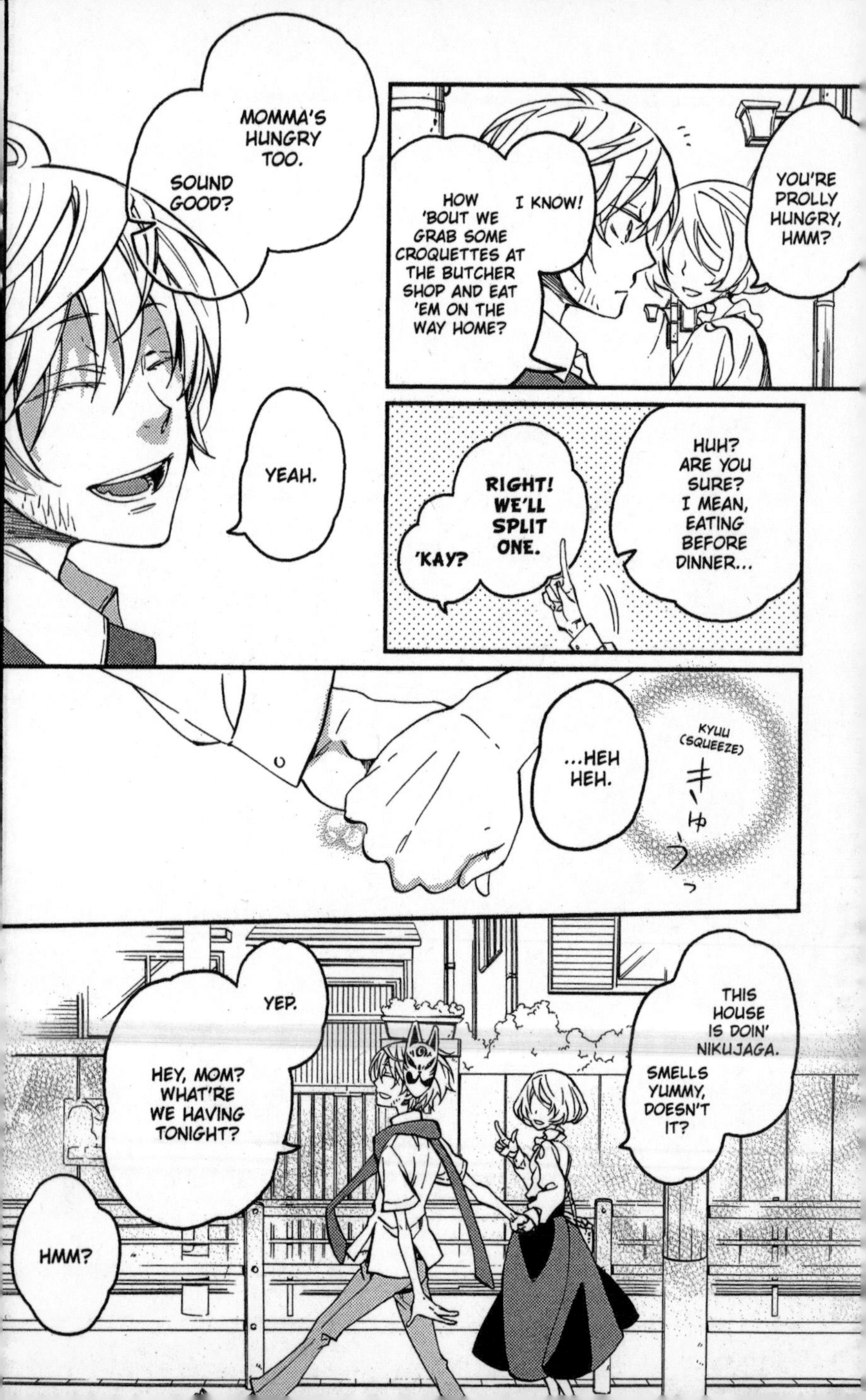
YOU'RE PROLLY HUNGRY, HMM?
I KNOW!
HOW 'BOUT WE GRAB SOME CROQUETTES AT THE BUTCHER SHOP AND EAT 'EM ON THE WAY HOME?
HUH? ARE YOU SURE? I MEAN, EATING BEFORE DINNER...
RIGHT! WE'LL SPLIT ONE.
'KAY?
MOMMA'S HUNGRY TOO.
SOUND GOOD?
YEAH.
KYUU (SQUEEZE)
...HEH HEH.
THIS HOUSE IS DOIN' NIKUJAGA.
SMELLS YUMMY, DOESN'T IT?
YEP.
HEY, MOM? WHAT'RE WE HAVING TONIGHT?
HMM?

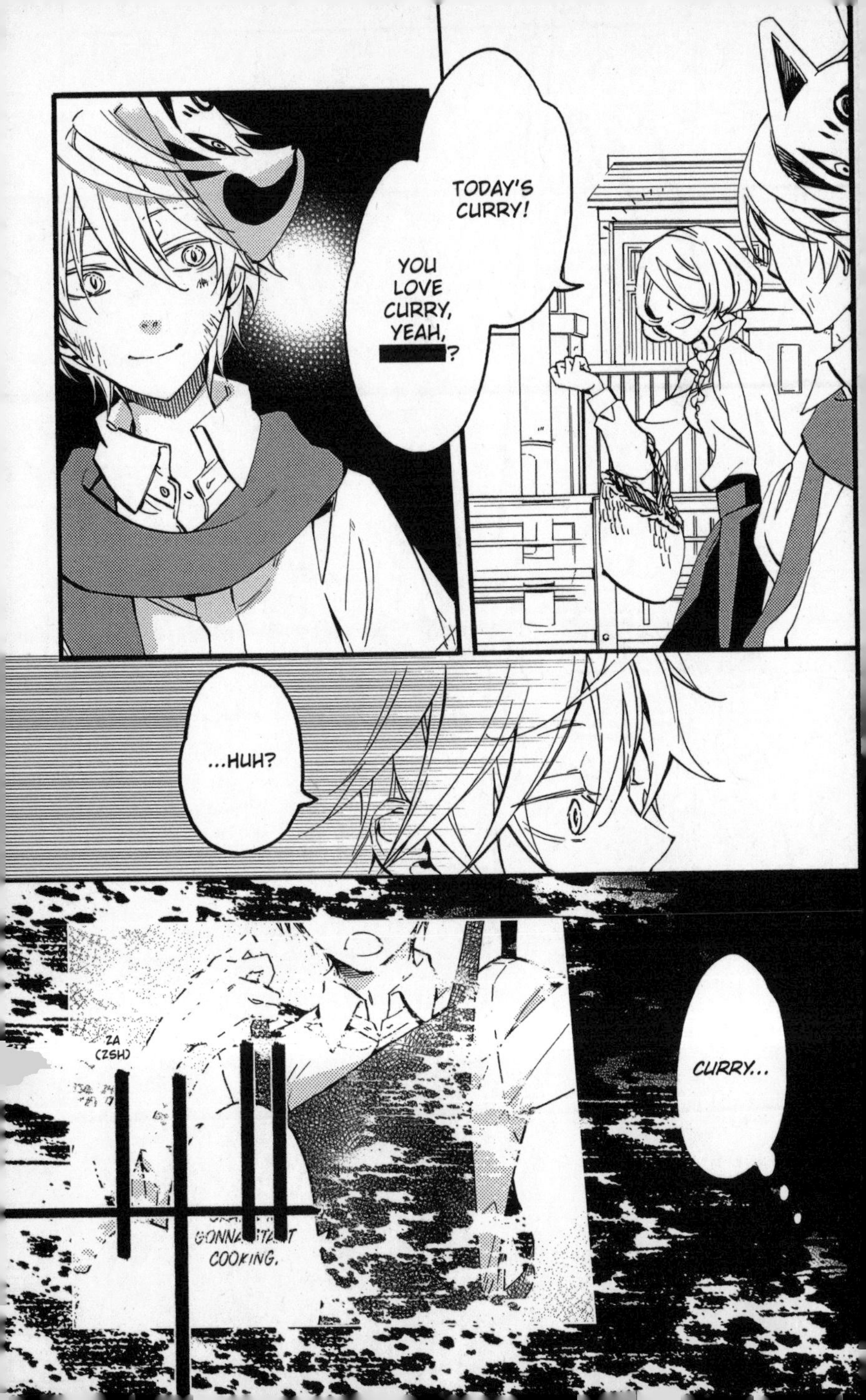
TODAY'S CURRY!
YOU LOVE CURRY, YEAH, [redacted]?
...HUH?
CURRY...
ZA (ZSH)
GONNA
COOKING.

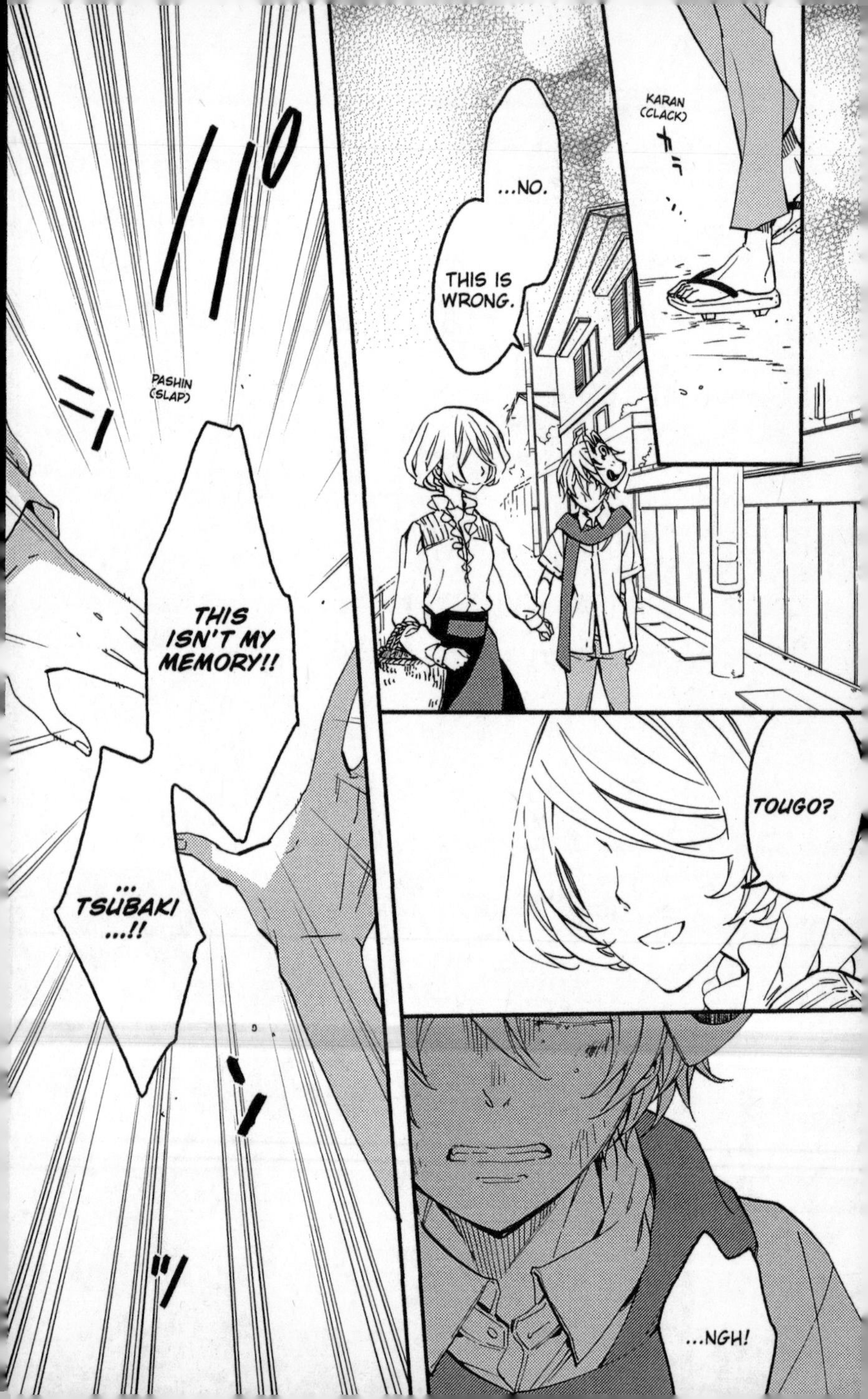
KARAN (CLACK)
...NO.
THIS IS WRONG.
TOUGO?
...NGH!
PASHIN (SLAP)
THIS ISN'T MY MEMORY!!
...TSÜBAKI...!!

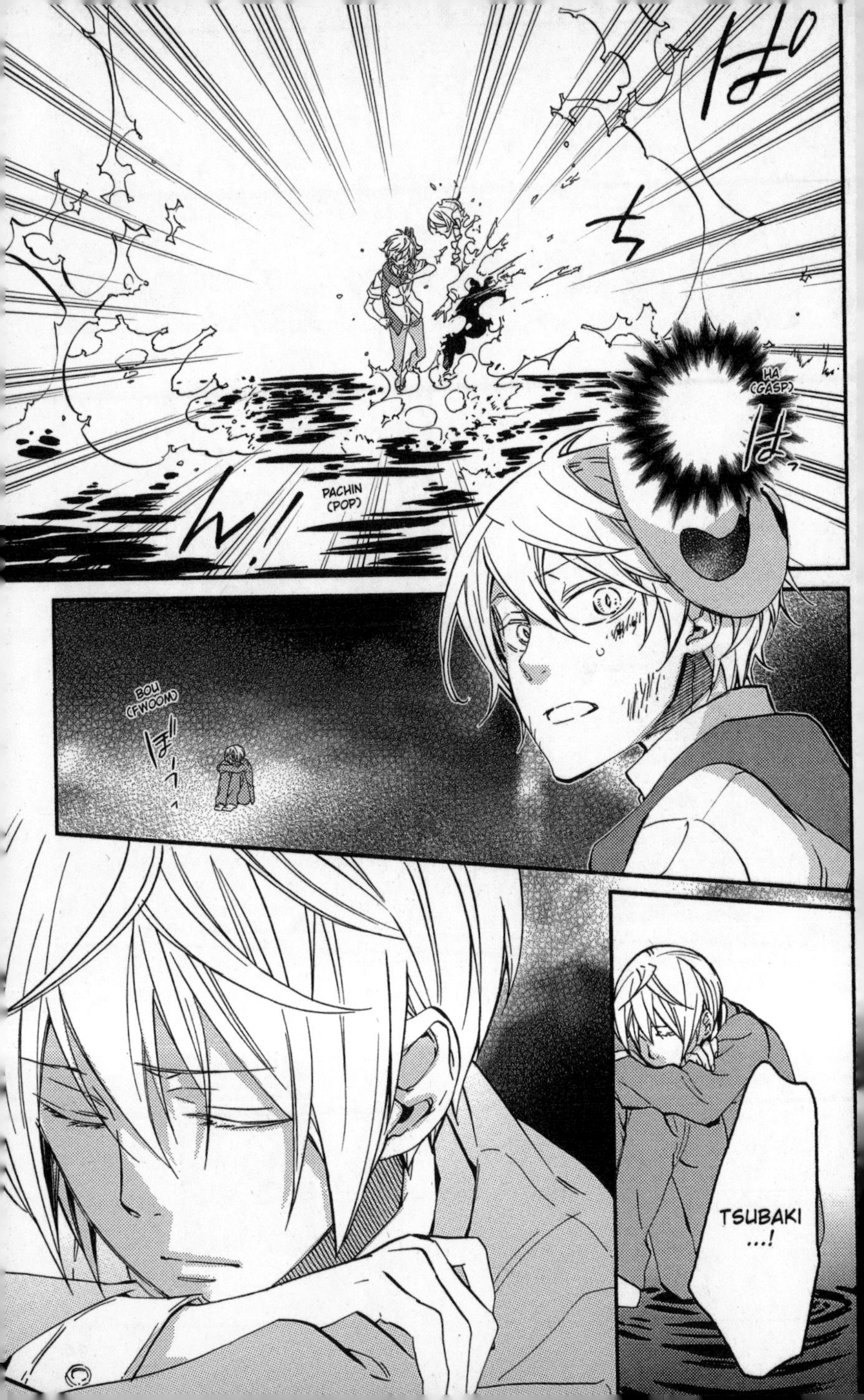
ぱちん!
PACHIN (POP)
HA (GASP)
はっ
BOU (FWOOM)
ぼーっ
TSUBAKI ...!

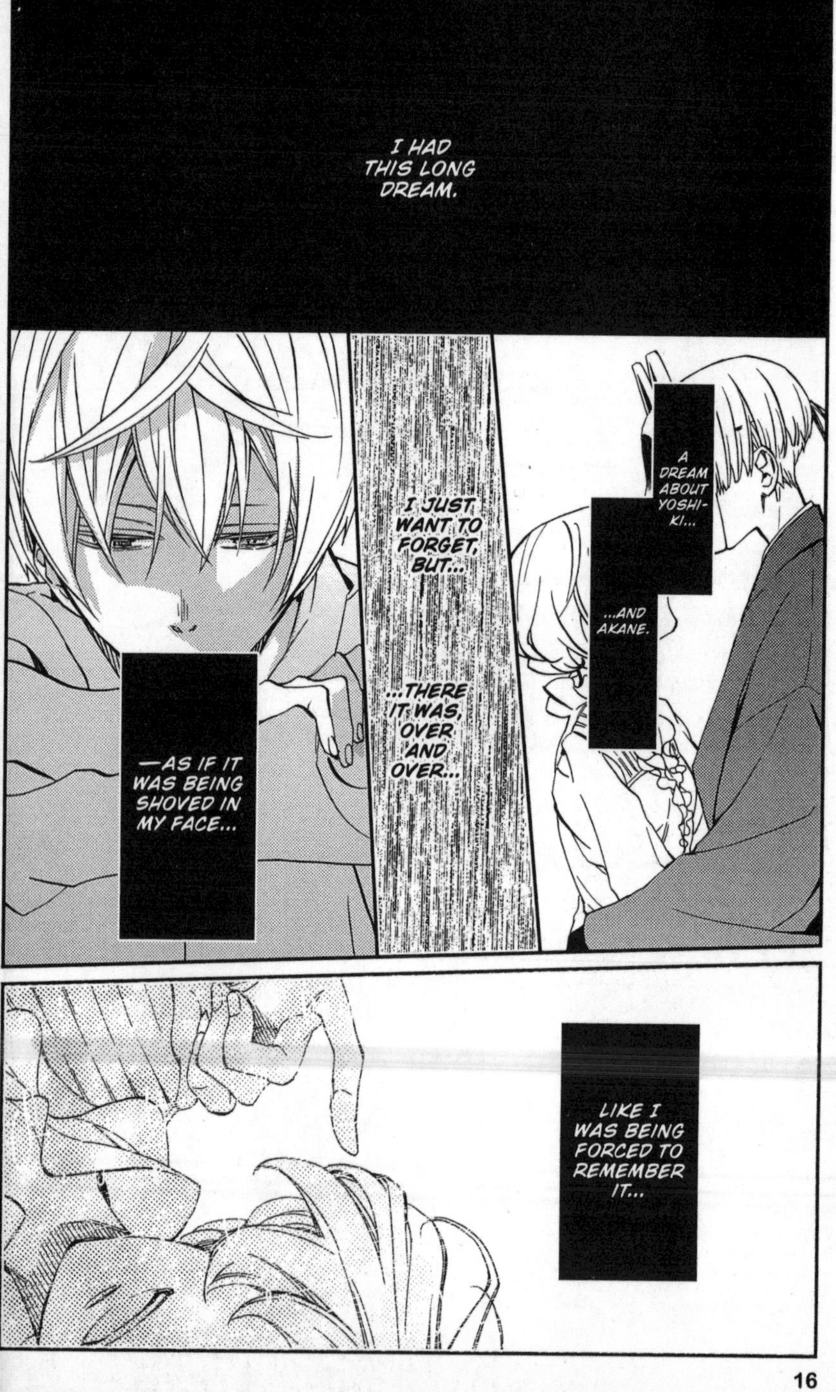
I HAD THIS LONG DREAM.
A DREAM ABOUT YOSHI-KI...
...AND AKANE.
I JUST WANT TO FORGET, BUT...
...THERE IT WAS, OVER AND OVER...
—AS IF IT WAS BEING SHOVED IN MY FACE...
LIKE I WAS BEING FORCED TO REMEMBER IT...

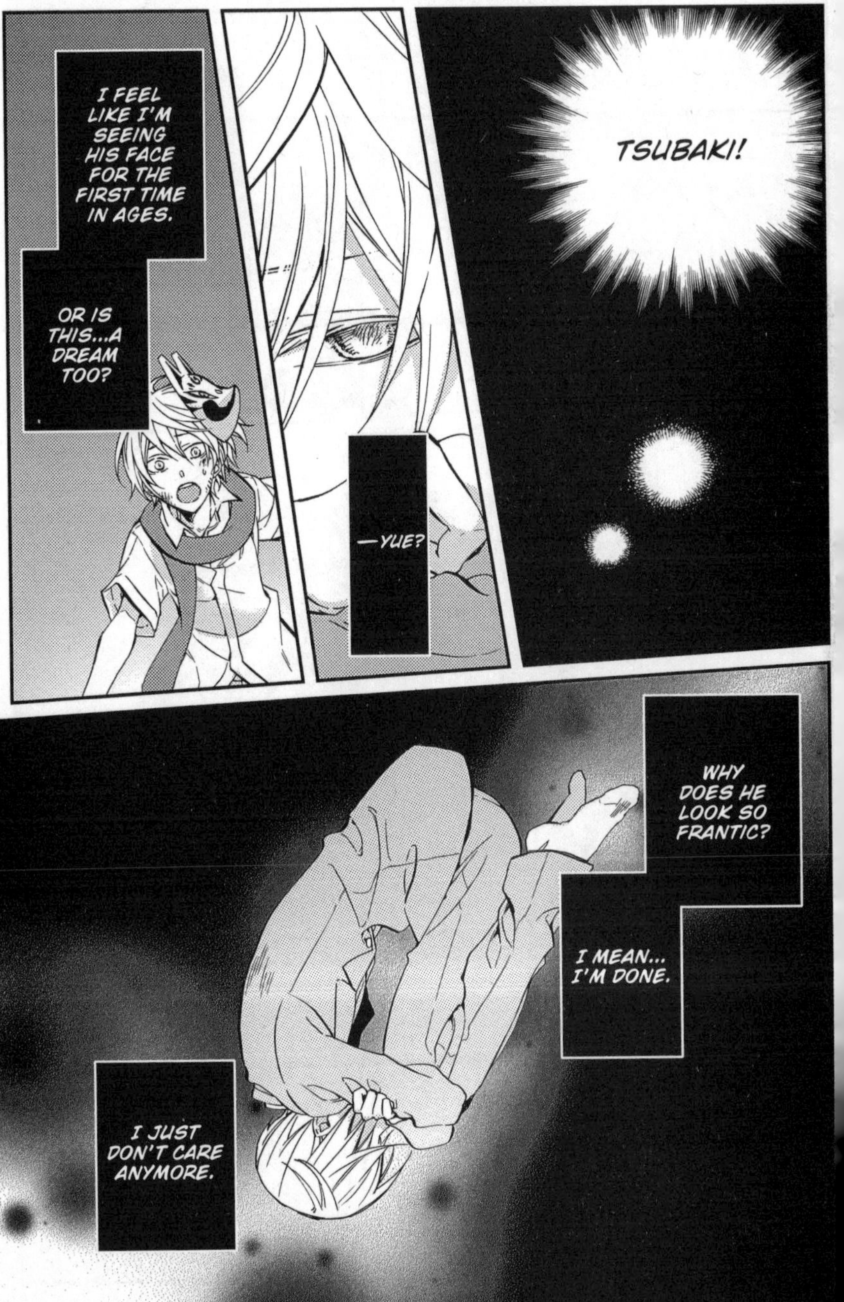
TSUBAKI!
—YUE?
I FEEL LIKE I'M SEEING HIS FACE FOR THE FIRST TIME IN AGES.
OR IS THIS...A DREAM TOO?
WHY DOES HE LOOK SO FRANTIC?
I MEAN... I'M DONE.
I JUST DON'T CARE ANYMORE.

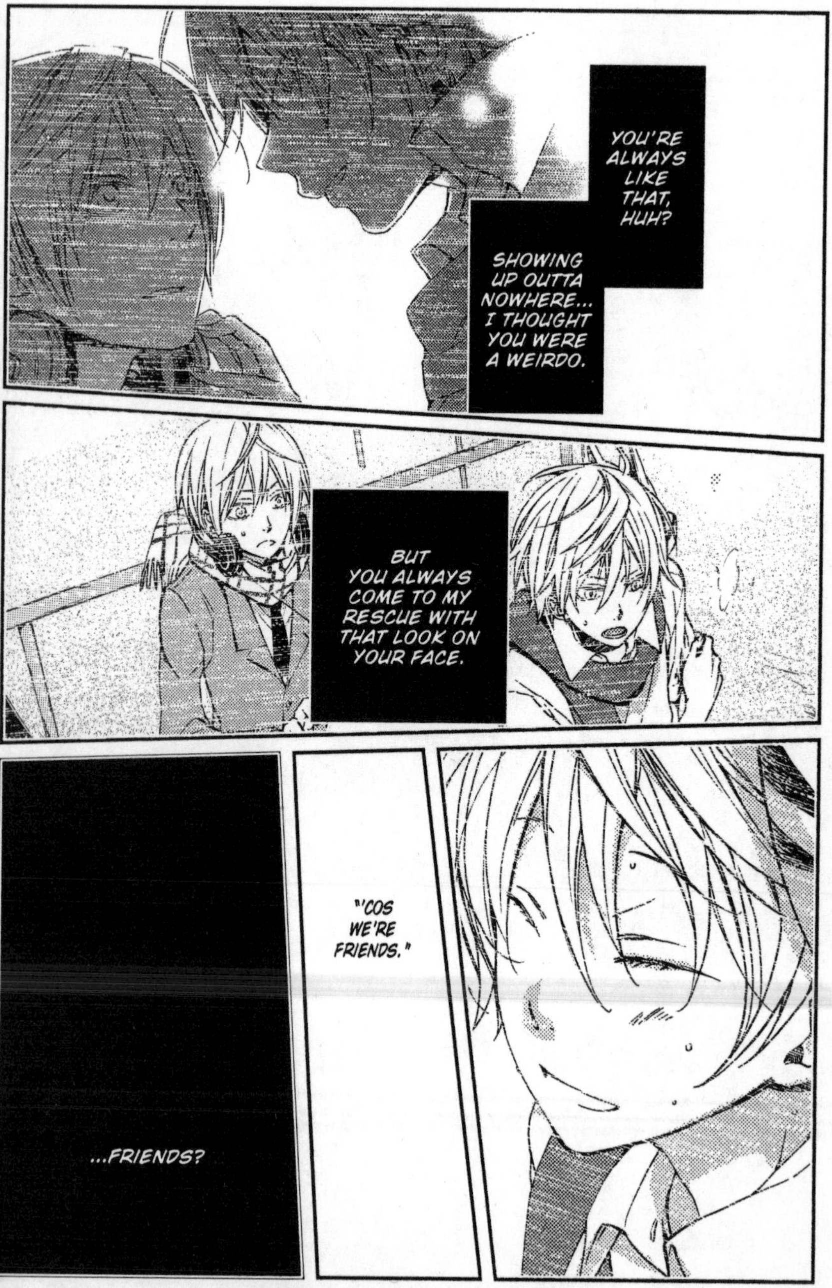
YOU'RE ALWAYS LIKE THAT, HUH?
SHOWING UP OUTTA NOWHERE... I THOUGHT YOU WERE A WEIRDO.
BUT YOU ALWAYS COME TO MY RESCUE WITH THAT LOOK ON YOUR FACE.
"'COS WE'RE FRIENDS."
...FRIENDS?

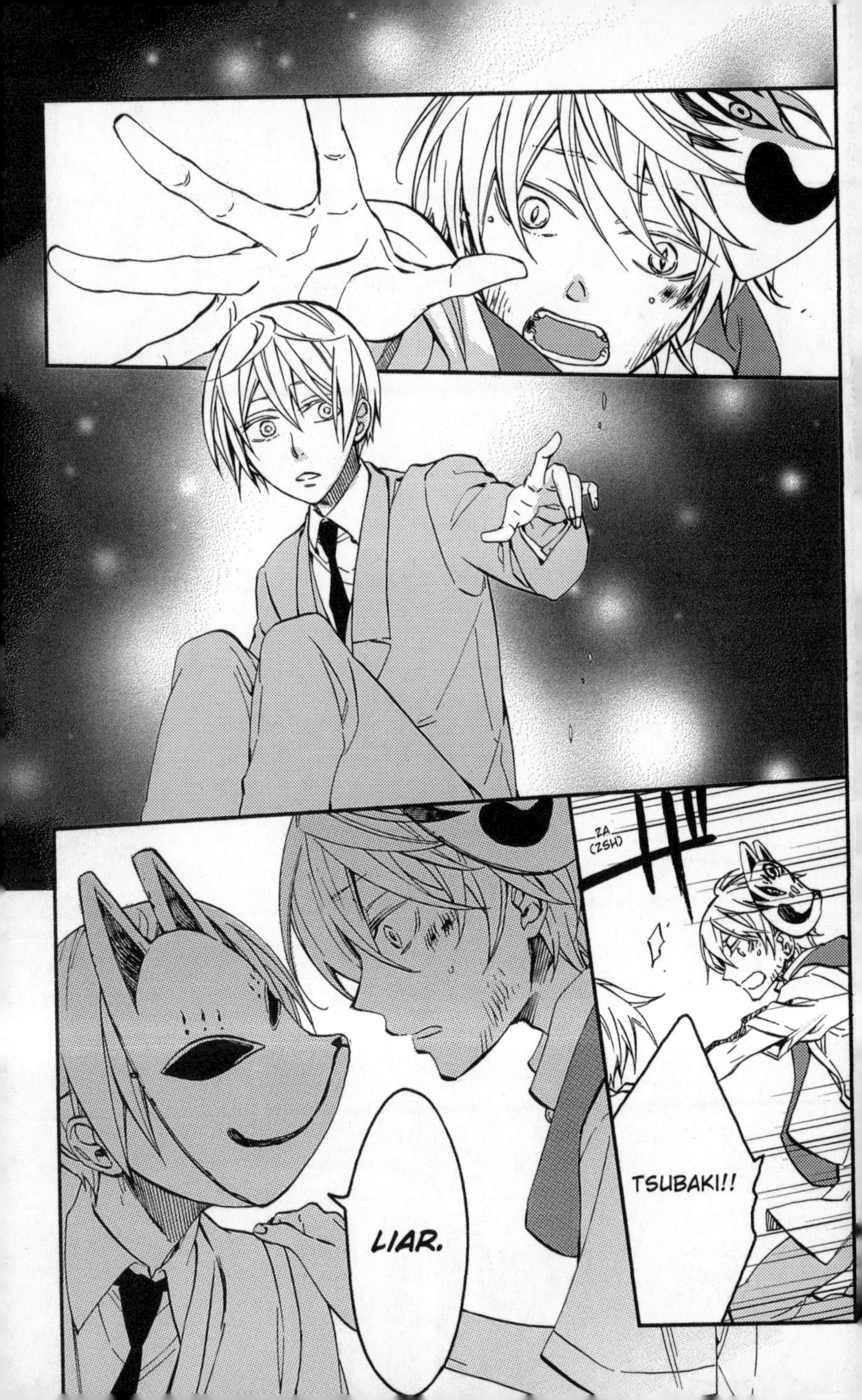
ZA
(ZSH)
TSUBAKI!!
LIAR.

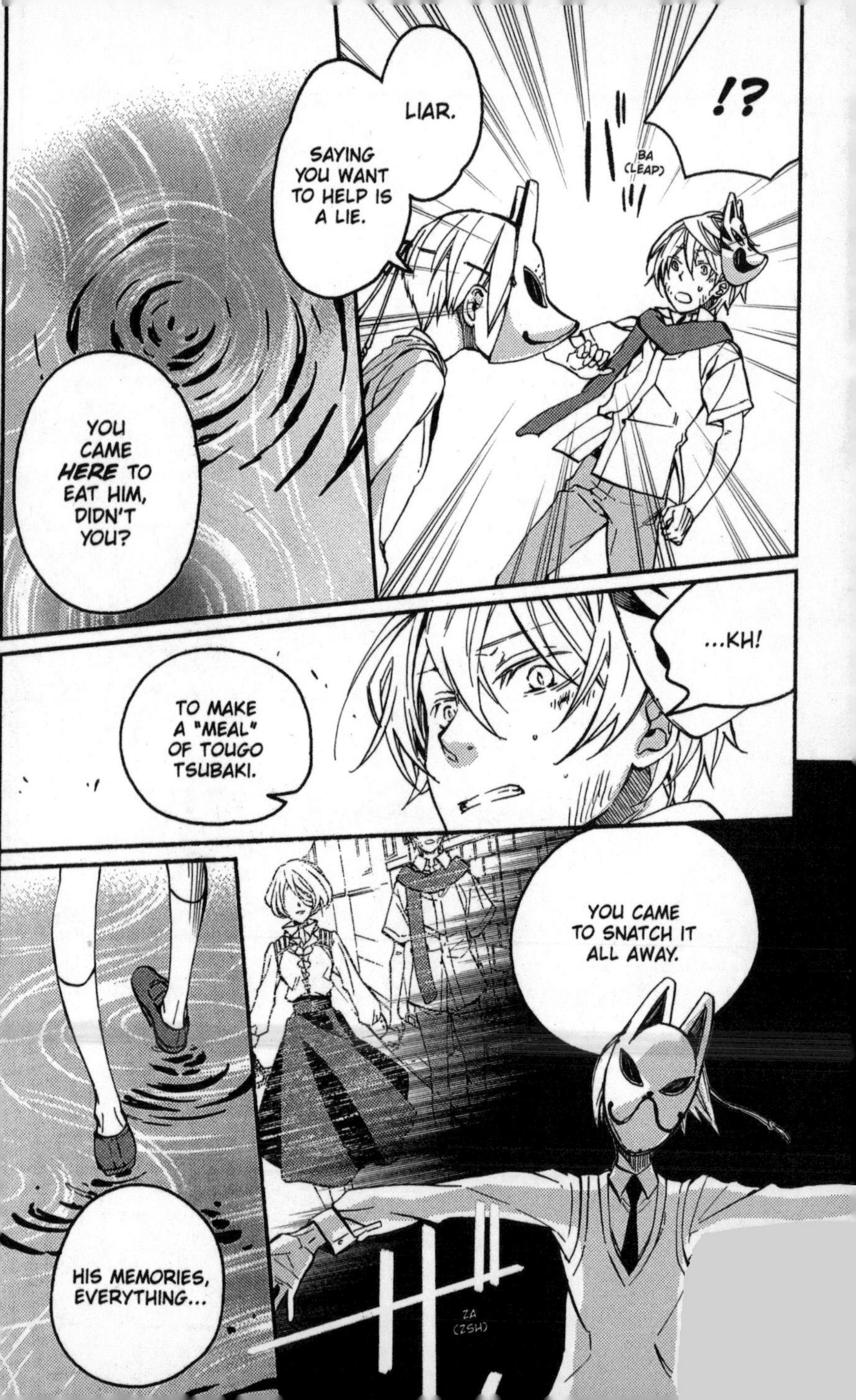
!?
BA (LEAP)
LIAR.
SAYING YOU WANT TO HELP IS A LIE.
YOU CAME HERE TO EAT HIM, DIDN'T YOU?
...KH!
TO MAKE A "MEAL" OF TOUGO TSUBAKI.
YOU CAME TO SNATCH IT ALL AWAY.
ZA (ZSH)
HIS MEMORIES, EVERYTHING...

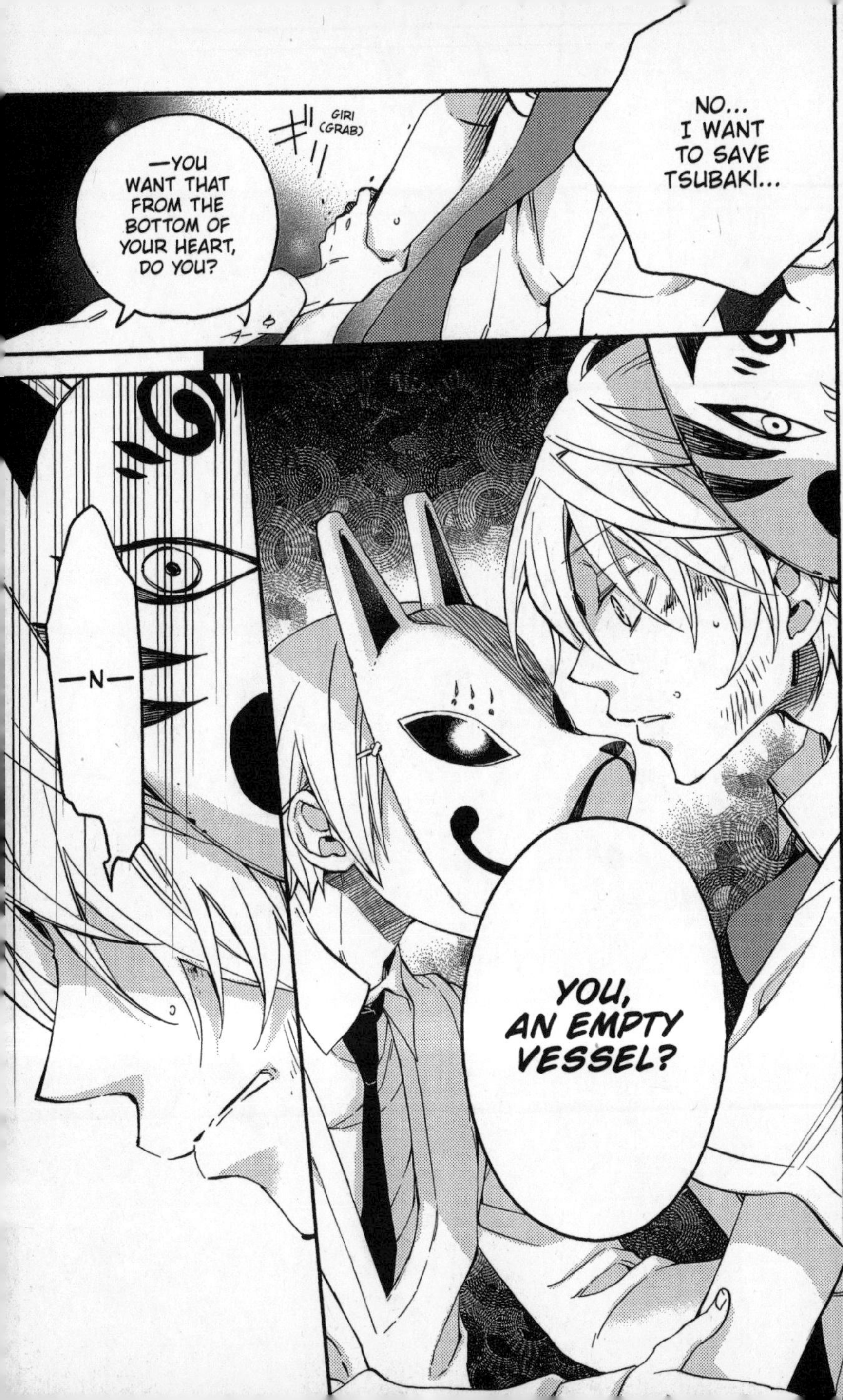
NO... I WANT TO SAVE TSUBAKI...
GIRI (GRAB)
—YOU WANT THAT FROM THE BOTTOM OF YOUR HEART, DO YOU?
YOU, AN EMPTY VESSEL?
—N—

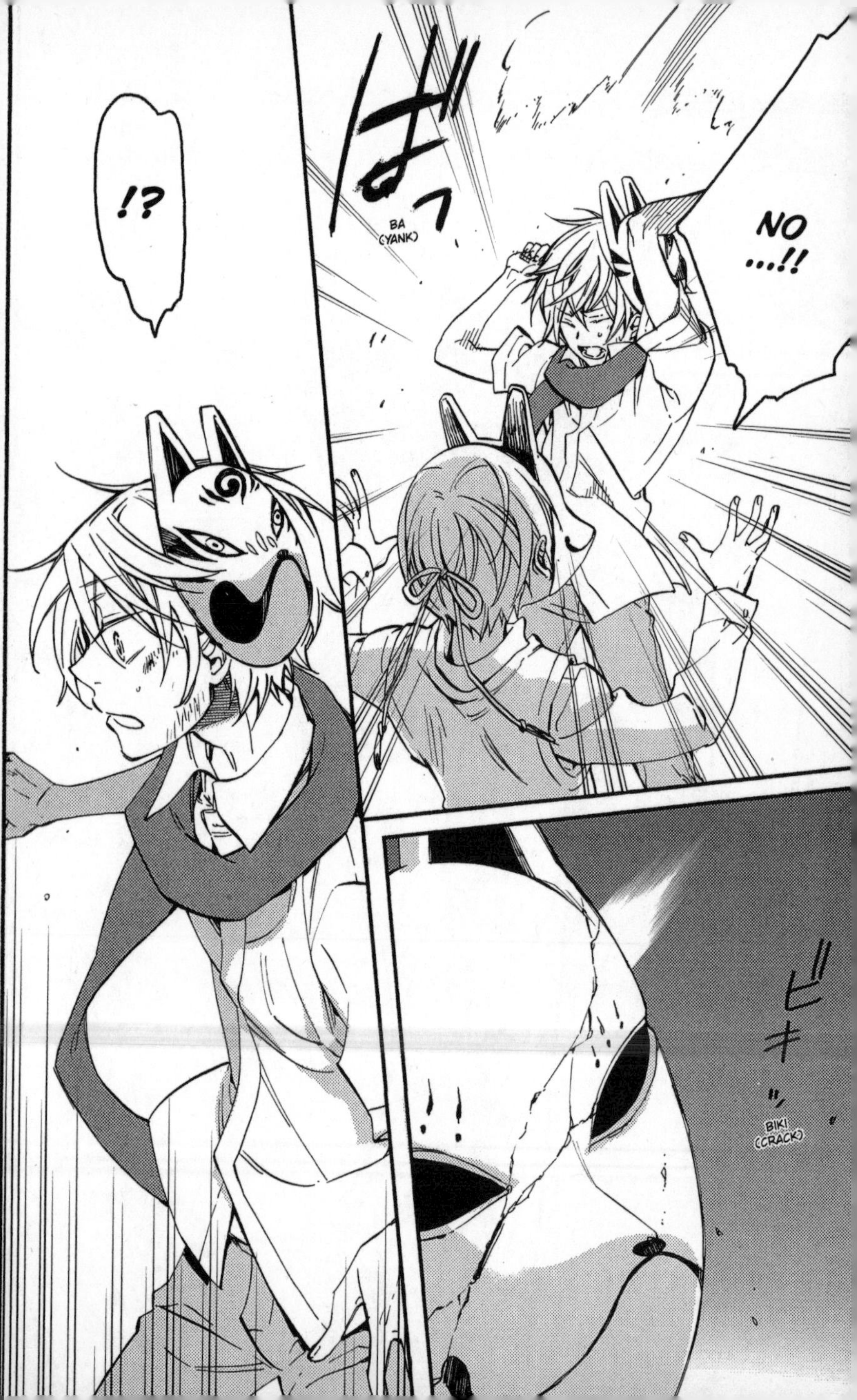

ばっ
BA (YANK)
NO ...!!
ビキッ
BIKI (CRACK)
!?

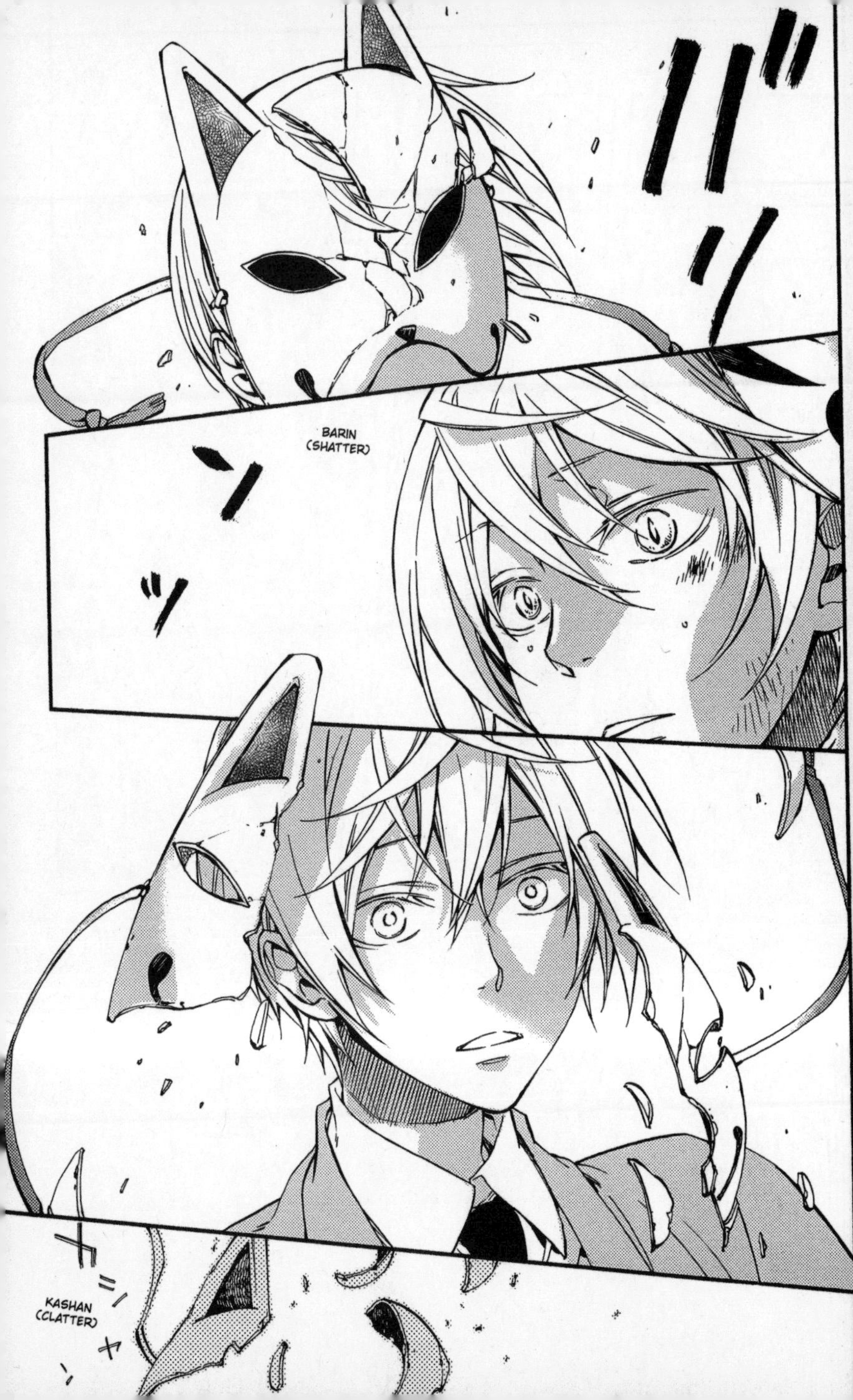
BARIN (SHATTER)
KASHAN (CLATTER)

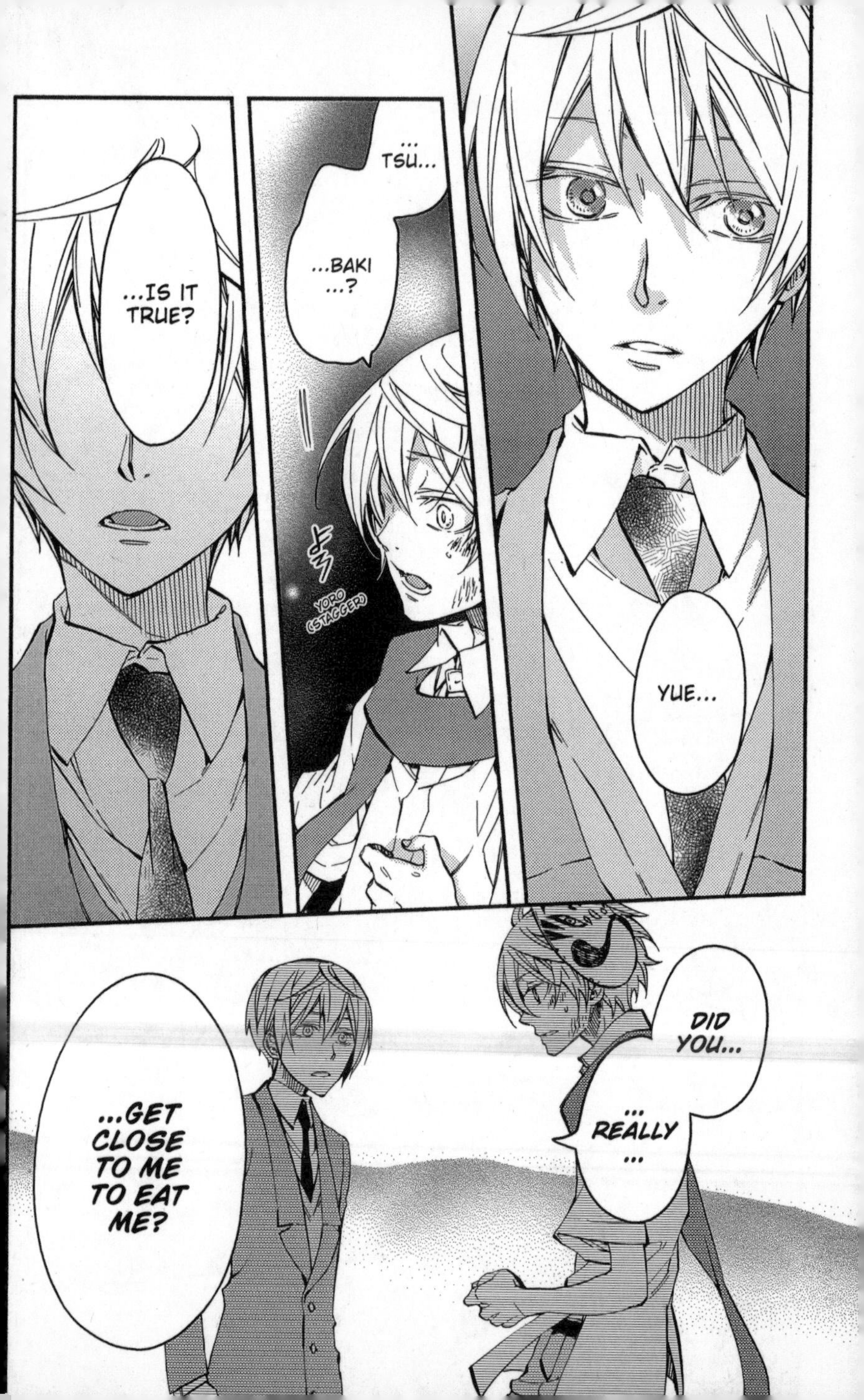

YUE...
... TSU...
...BAKI ...?
よろ
YORO (STAGGER)
...IS IT TRUE?
DID YOU...
... REALLY ...
...GET CLOSE TO ME TO EAT ME?

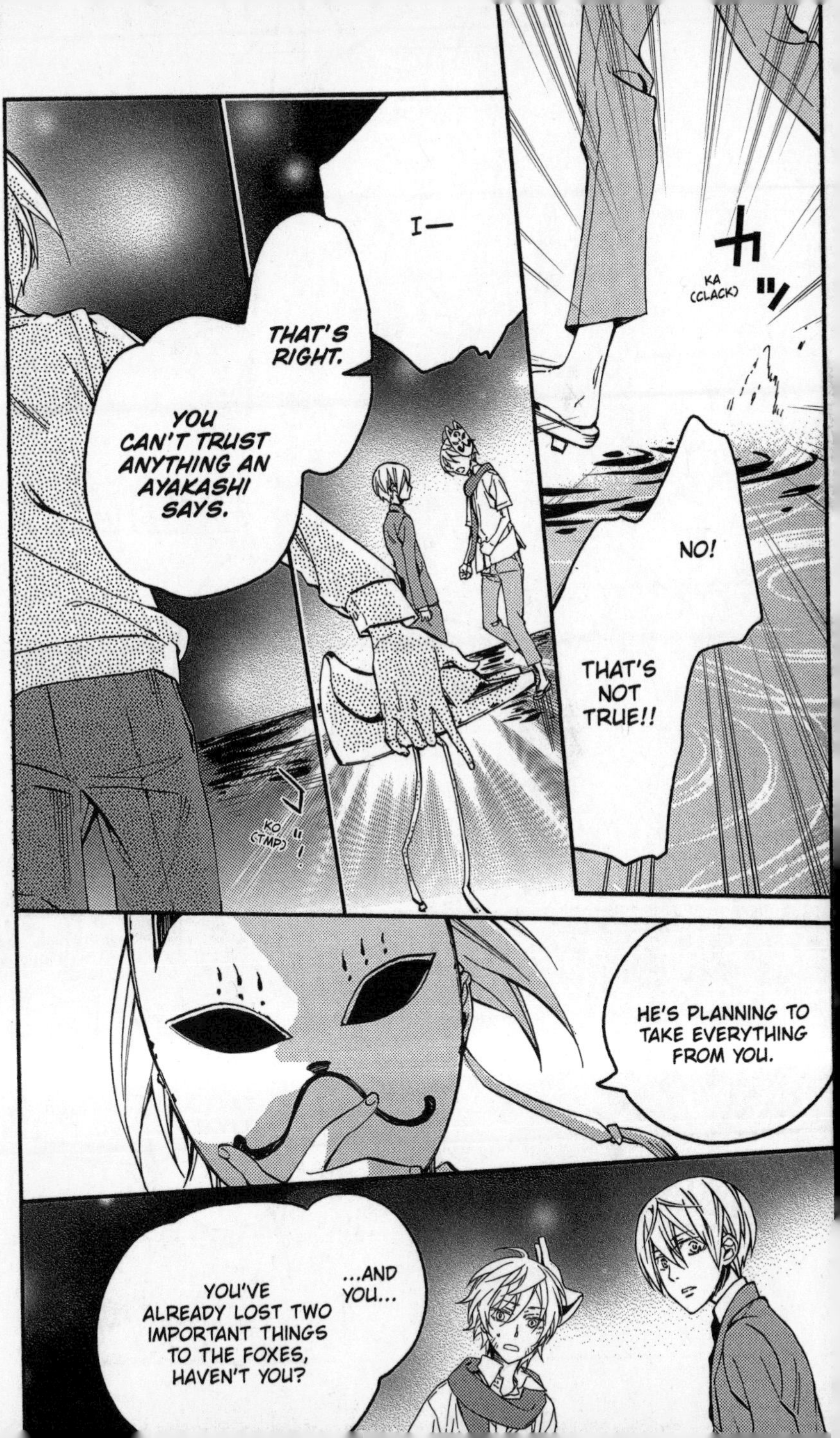
KA (CLACK)
NO!
THAT'S NOT TRUE!!
I—
THAT'S RIGHT.
YOU CAN'T TRUST ANYTHING AN AYAKASHI SAYS.
KO (TMP)
HE'S PLANNING TO TAKE EVERYTHING FROM YOU.
...AND YOU...
YOU'VE ALREADY LOST TWO IMPORTANT THINGS TO THE FOXES, HAVEN'T YOU?

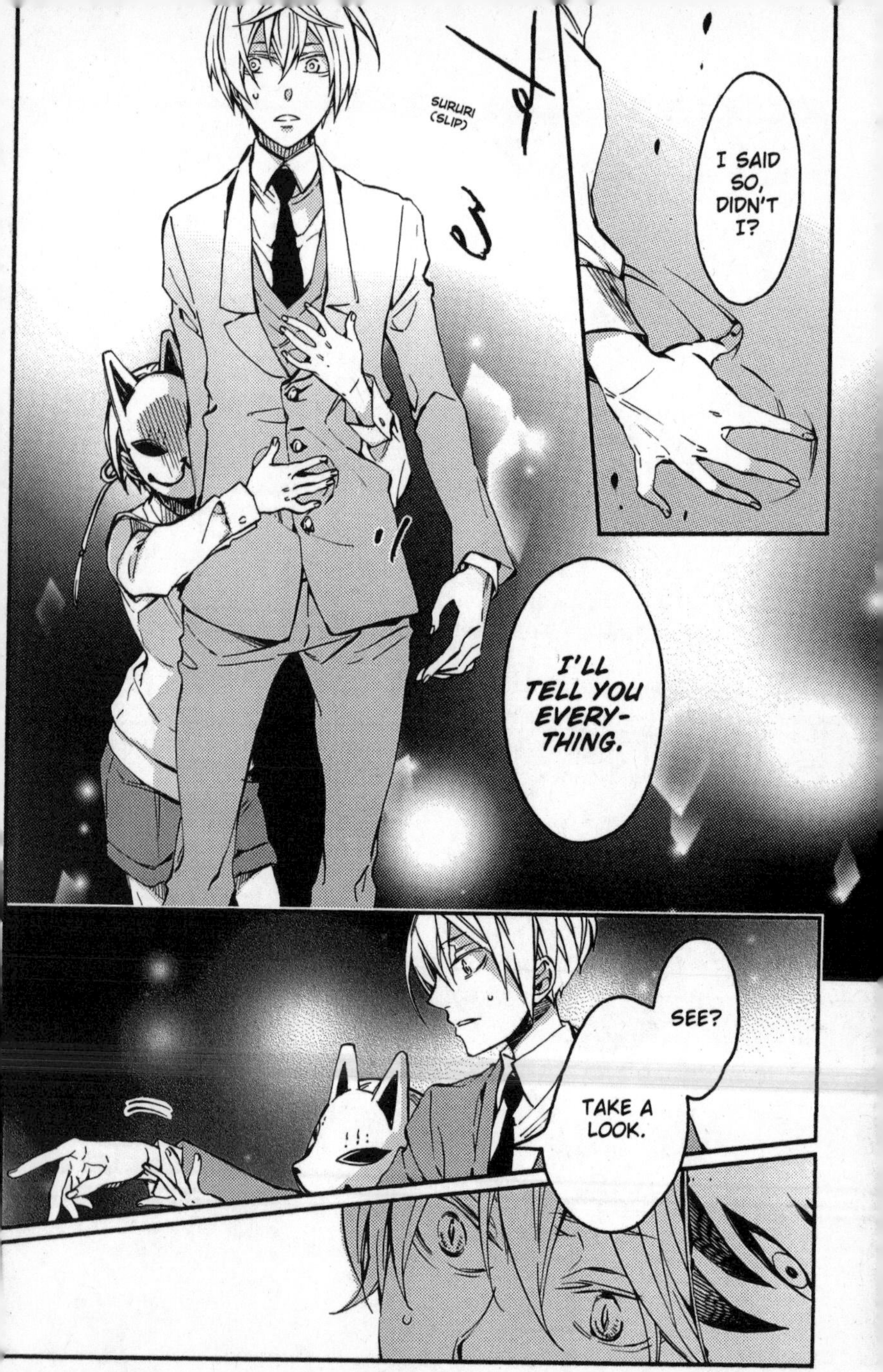
I SAID SO, DIDN'T I?
SURURI (SLIP)
I'LL TELL YOU EVERY-THING.
SEE?
TAKE A LOOK.

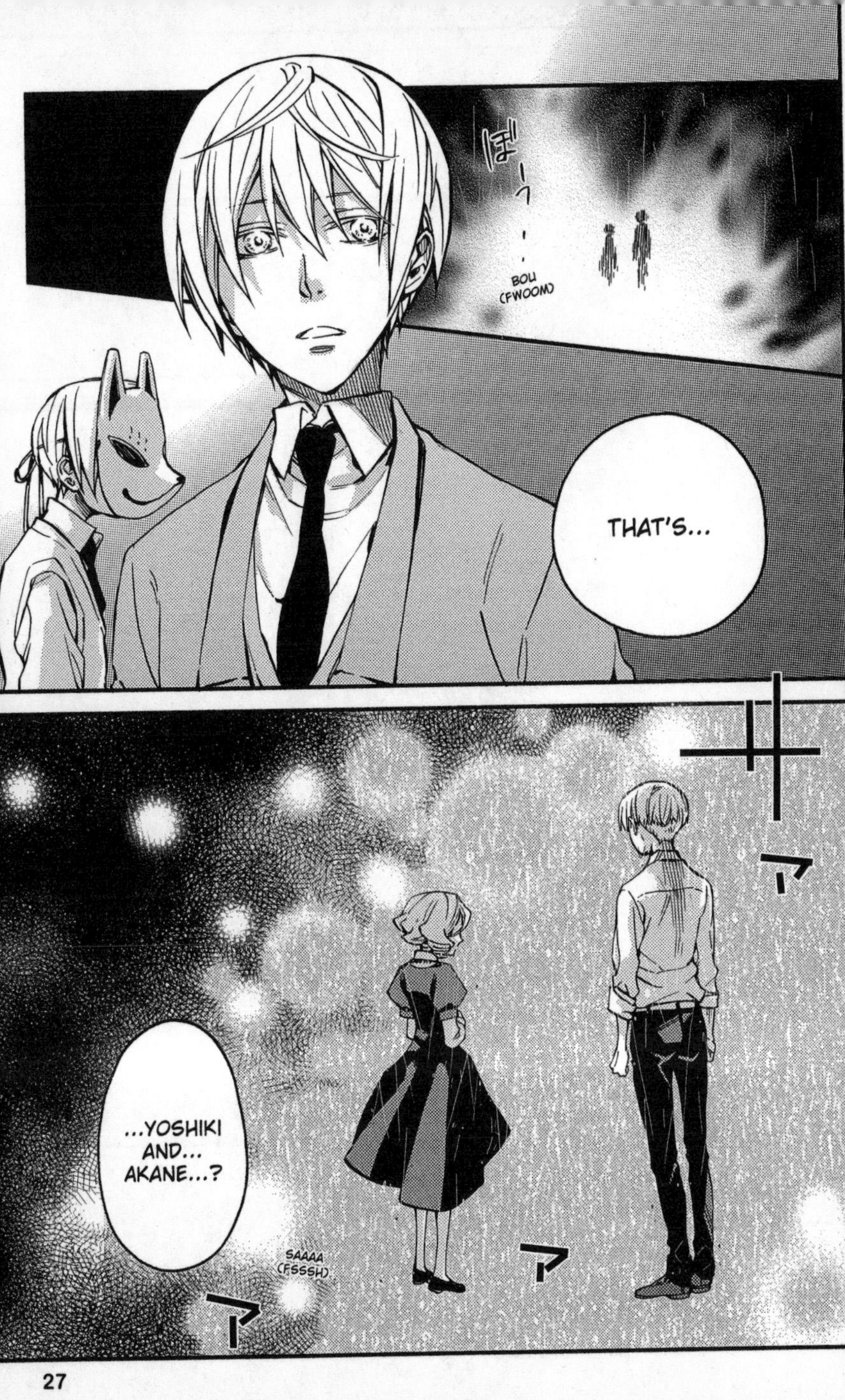
BOU (FWOOM)
THAT'S...
...YOSHIKI AND... AKANE...?
SAAAA (FSSSH)

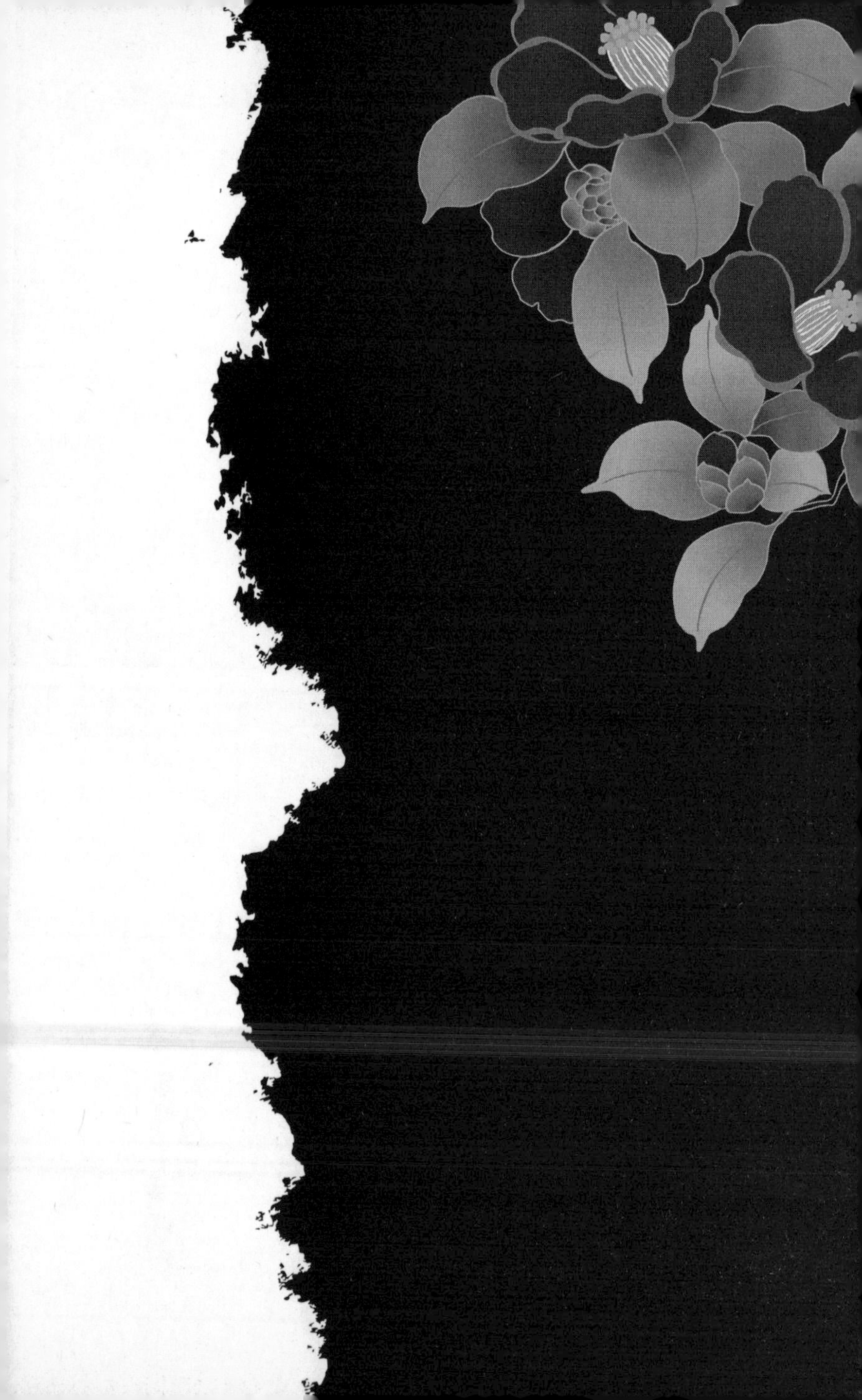

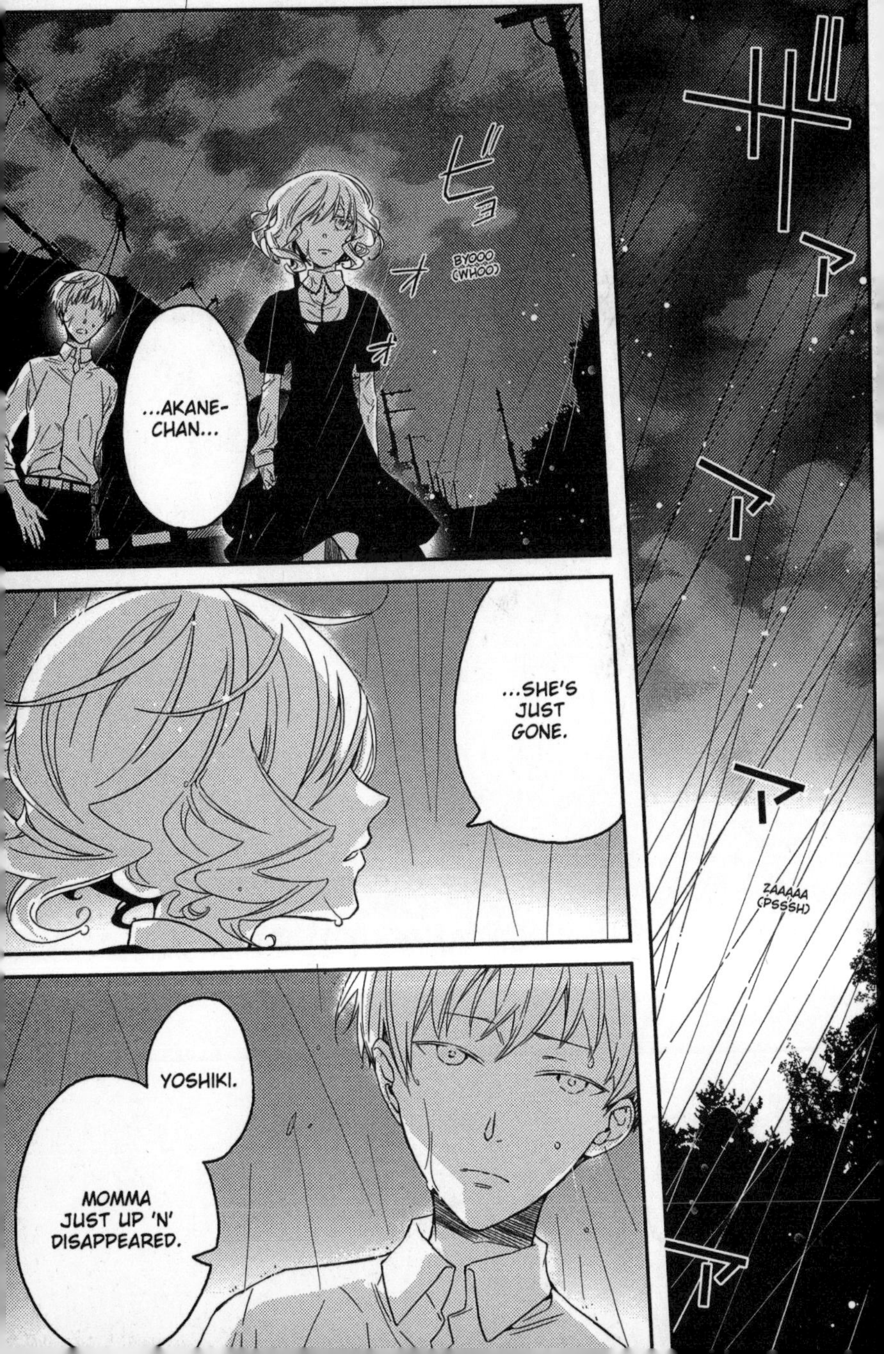
ザァァァァ
ZAAAAA (PSSSH)
ビョォォ
BYOOO (WHOO)
...AKANE-CHAN...
...SHE'S JUST GONE.
YOSHIKI.
MOMMA JUST UP 'N' DISAPPEARED.

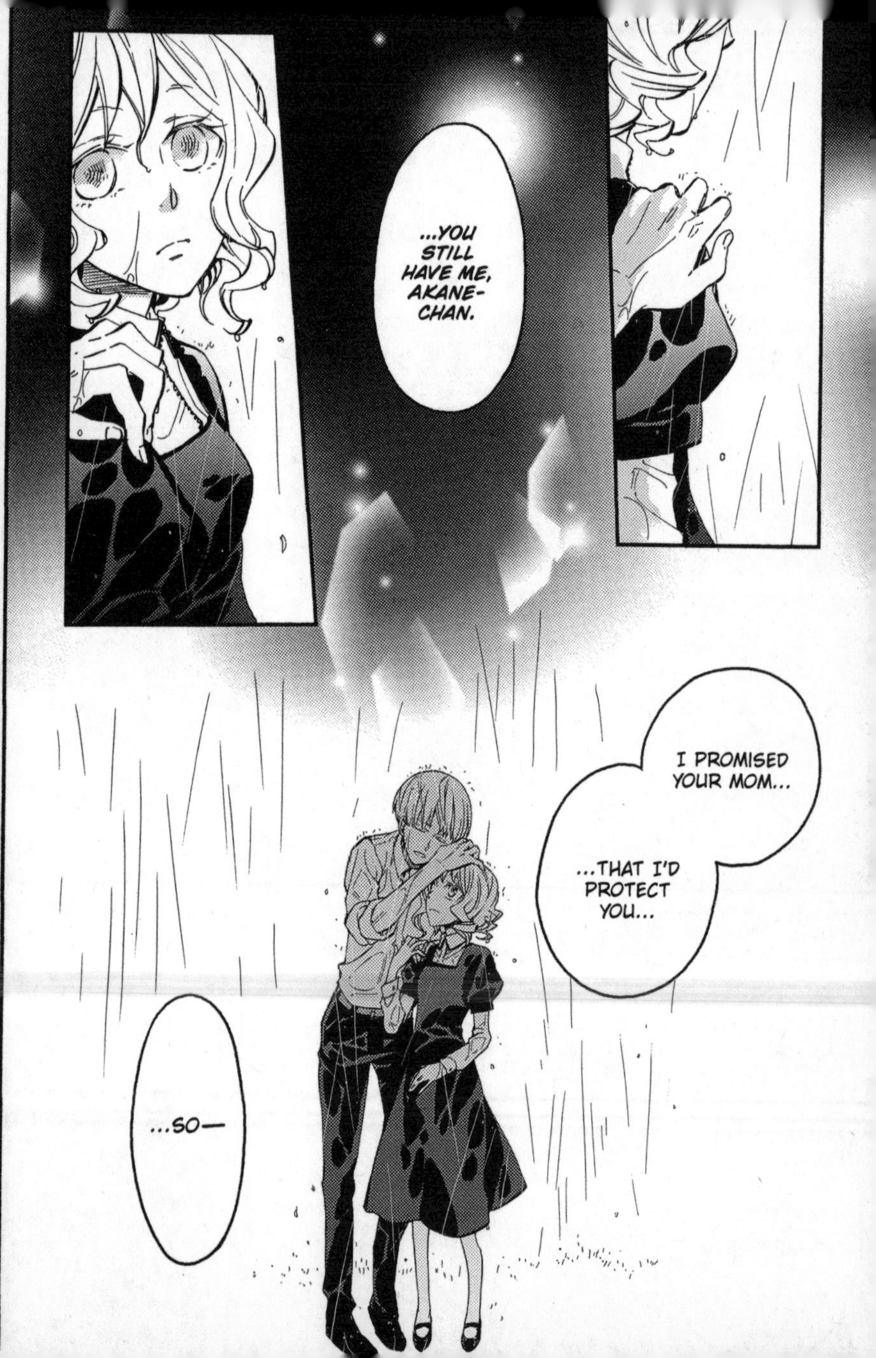
...YOU STILL HAVE ME, AKANE-CHAN.
I PROMISED YOUR MOM...
...THAT I'D PROTECT YOU...
...SO—

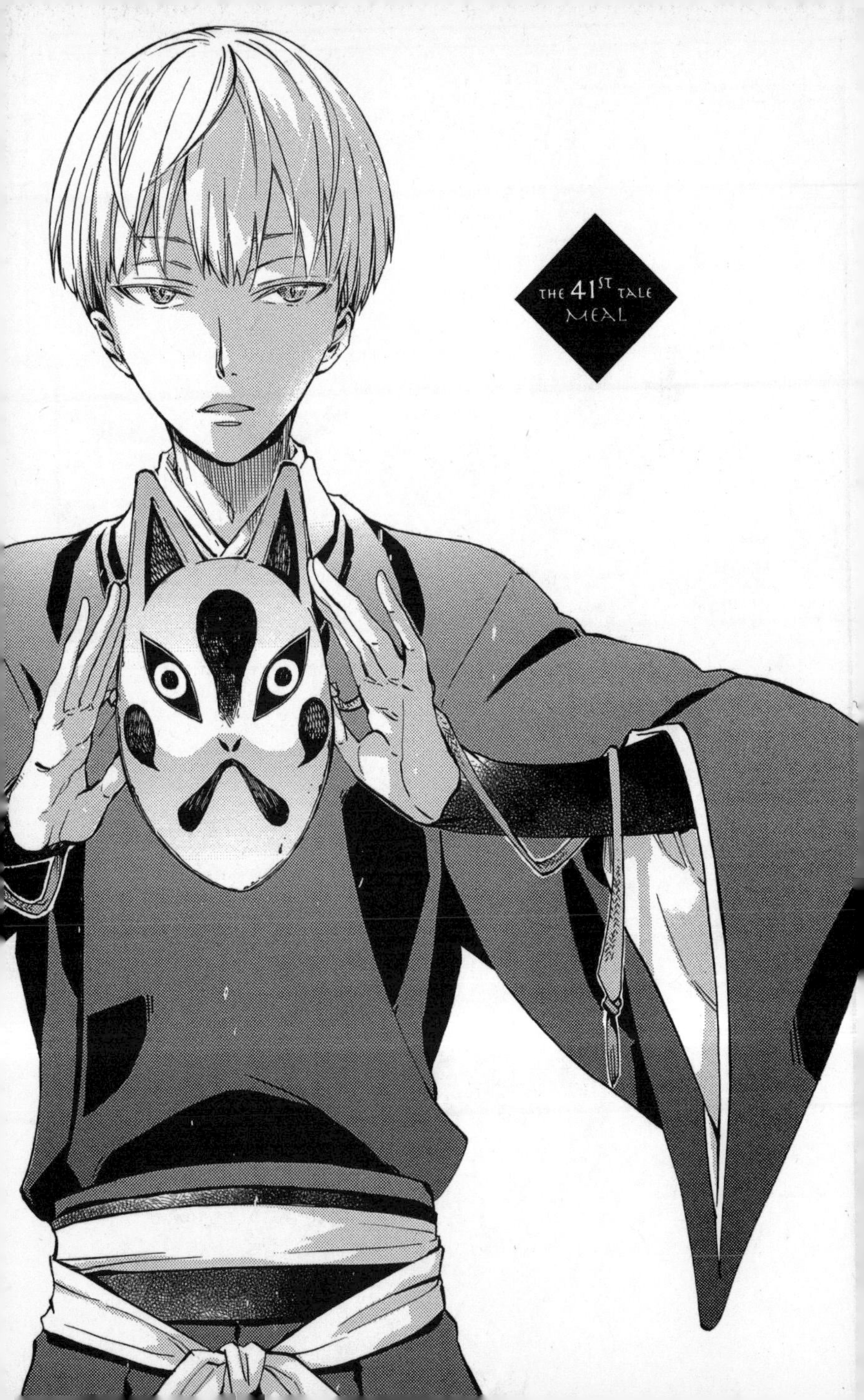
THE 41ST TALE
MEAL

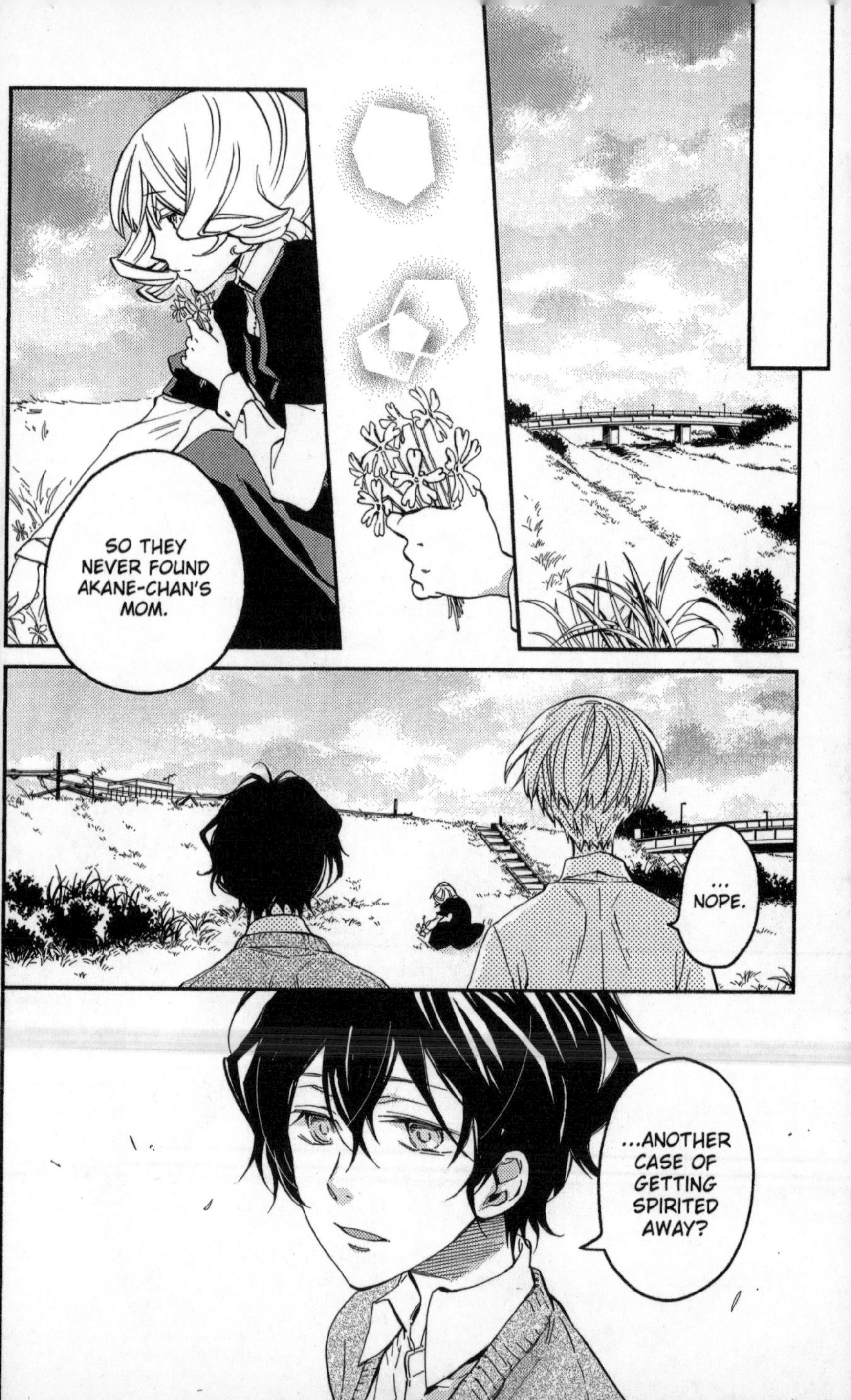
SO THEY NEVER FOUND AKANE-CHAN'S MOM.
...NOPE.
...ANOTHER CASE OF GETTING SPIRITED AWAY?

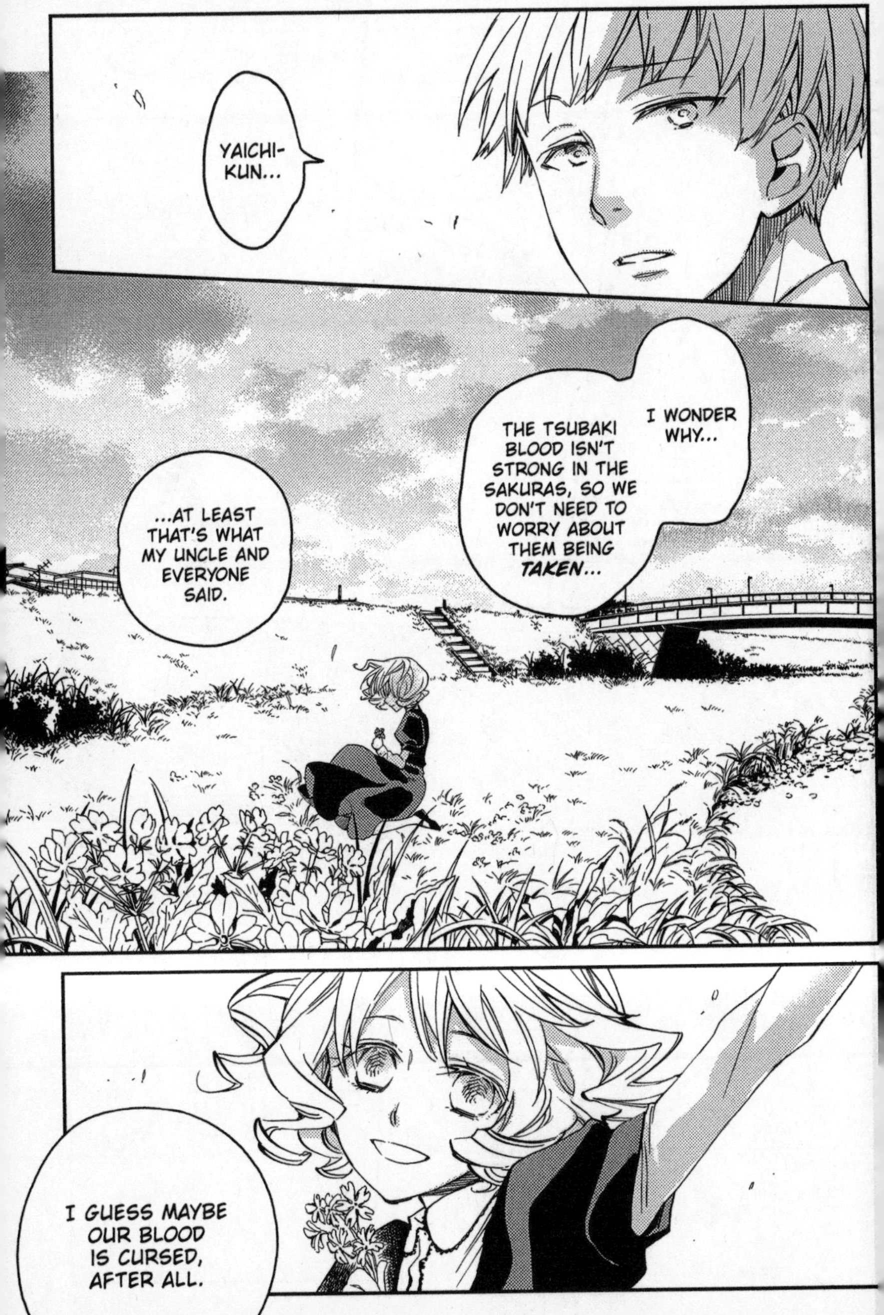
YAICHI-KUN...
I WONDER WHY...
THE TSUBAKI BLOOD ISN'T STRONG IN THE SAKURAS, SO WE DON'T NEED TO WORRY ABOUT THEM BEING *TAKEN*...
...AT LEAST THAT'S WHAT MY UNCLE AND EVERYONE SAID.
I GUESS MAYBE OUR BLOOD IS CURSED, AFTER ALL.

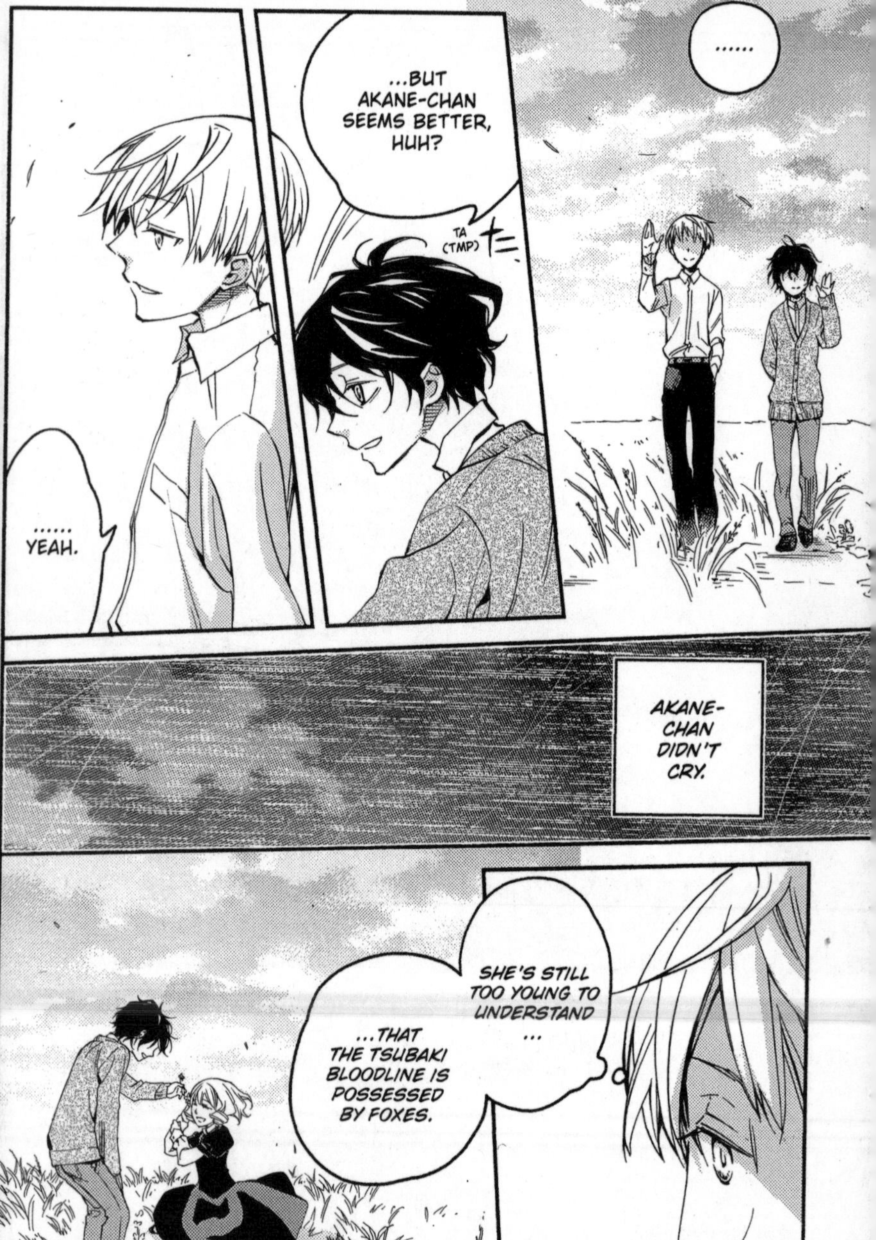
......
...BUT AKANE-CHAN SEEMS BETTER, HUH?
TA (TMP)
...... YEAH.
AKANE-CHAN DIDN'T CRY.
SHE'S STILL TOO YOUNG TO UNDERSTAND ...
...THAT THE TSUBAKI BLOODLINE IS POSSESSED BY FOXES.

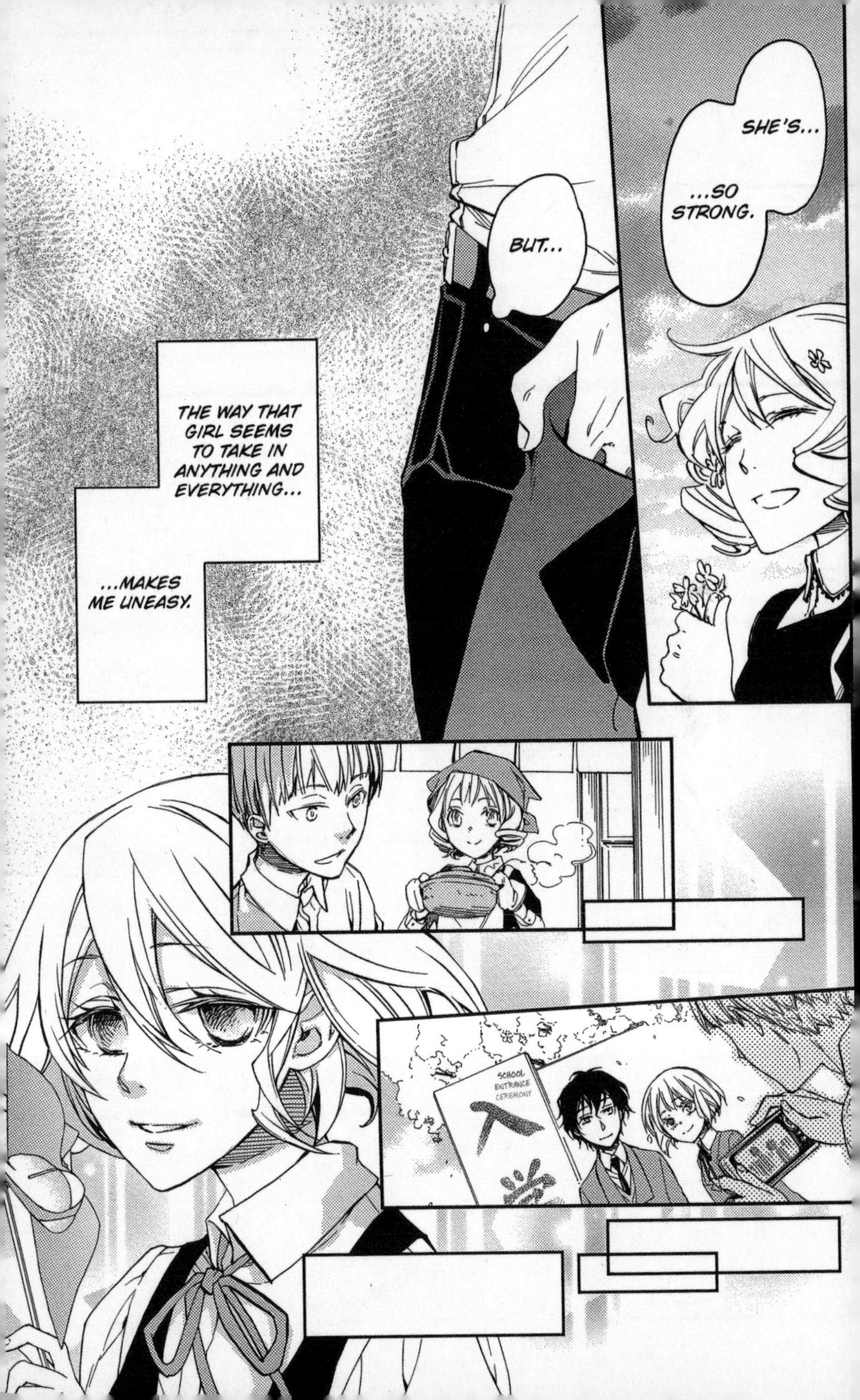
SHE'S...
...SO STRONG.
BUT...
THE WAY THAT GIRL SEEMS TO TAKE IN ANYTHING AND EVERYTHING...
...MAKES ME UNEASY.
SCHOOL ENTRANCE CEREMONY

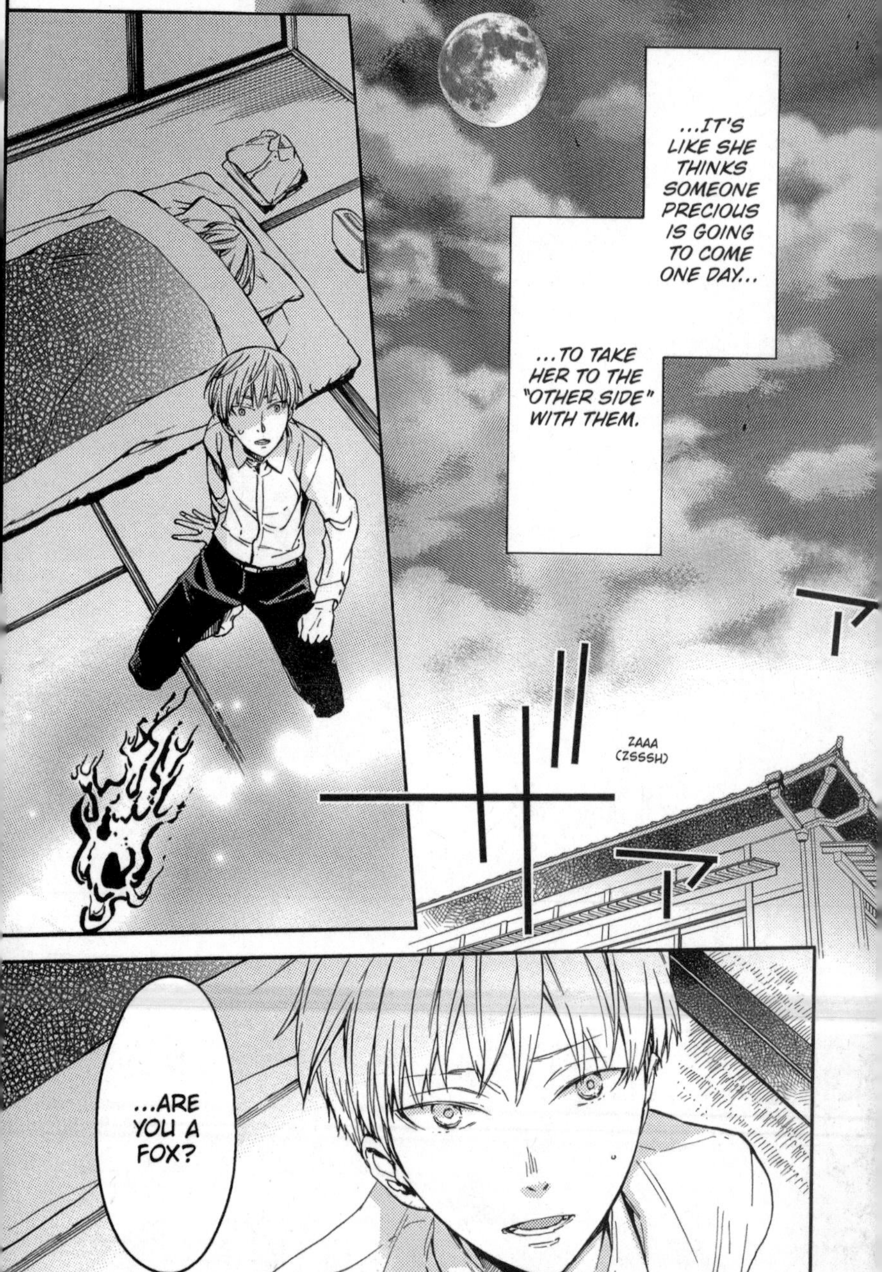
...IT'S LIKE SHE THINKS SOMEONE PRECIOUS IS GOING TO COME ONE DAY...
...TO TAKE HER TO THE "OTHER SIDE" WITH THEM.
ZAAA (ZSSSH)
...ARE YOU A FOX?

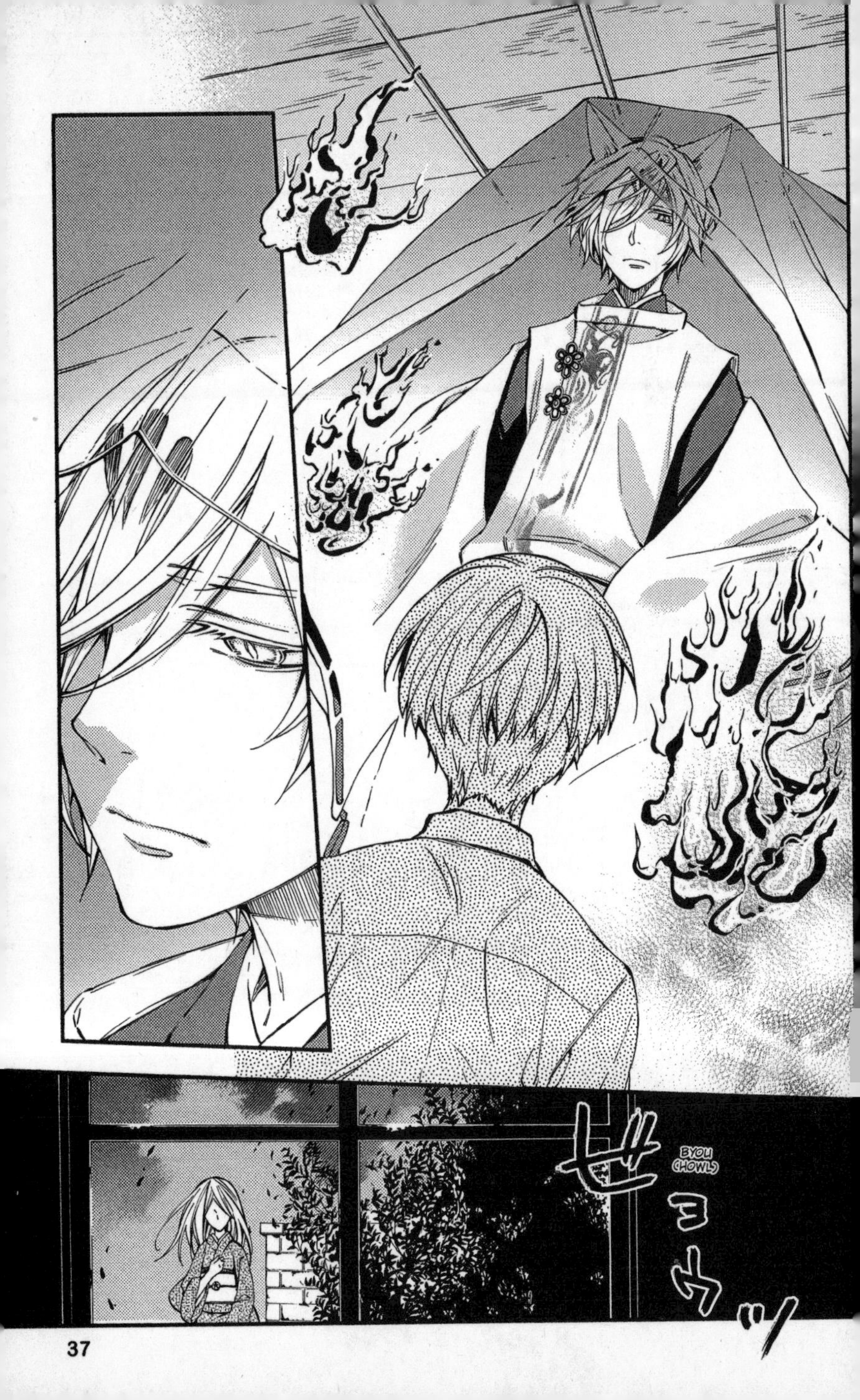
ビョウッ
BYOU
(HOWL)

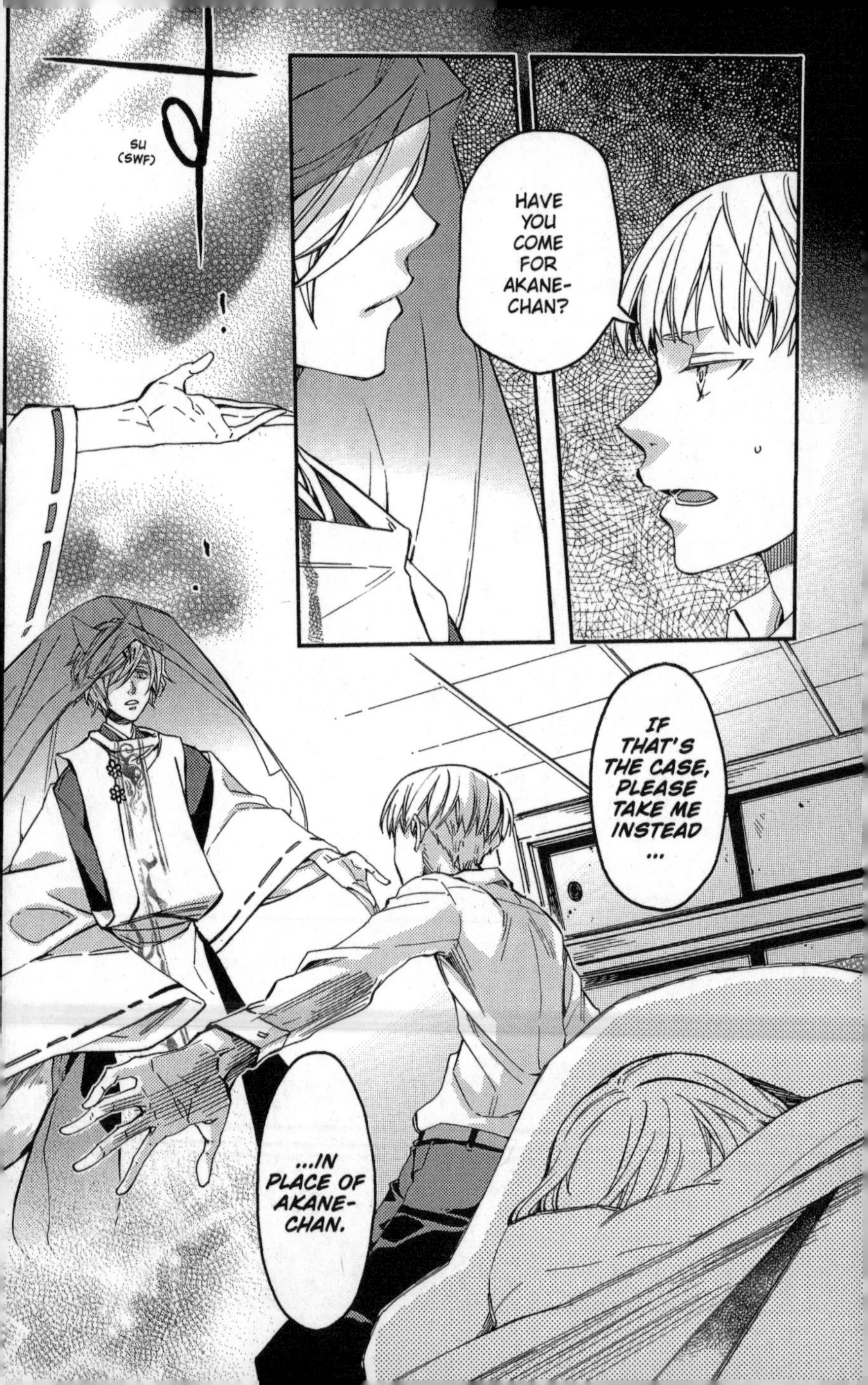
HAVE YOU COME FOR AKANE-CHAN?
SU (SWF)
IF THAT'S THE CASE, PLEASE TAKE ME INSTEAD ...
...IN PLACE OF AKANE-CHAN.

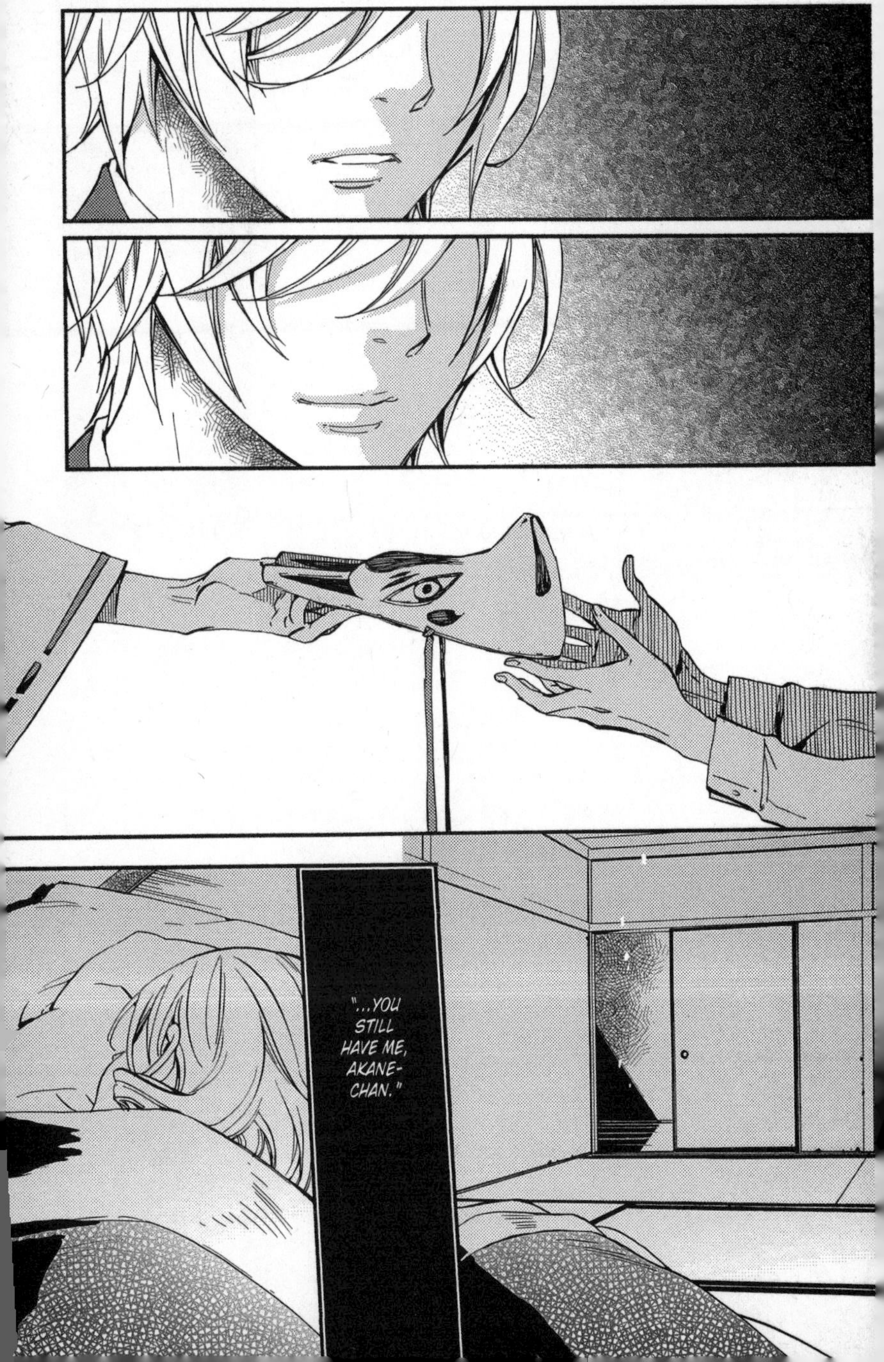
"...YOU STILL HAVE ME, AKANE-CHAN."

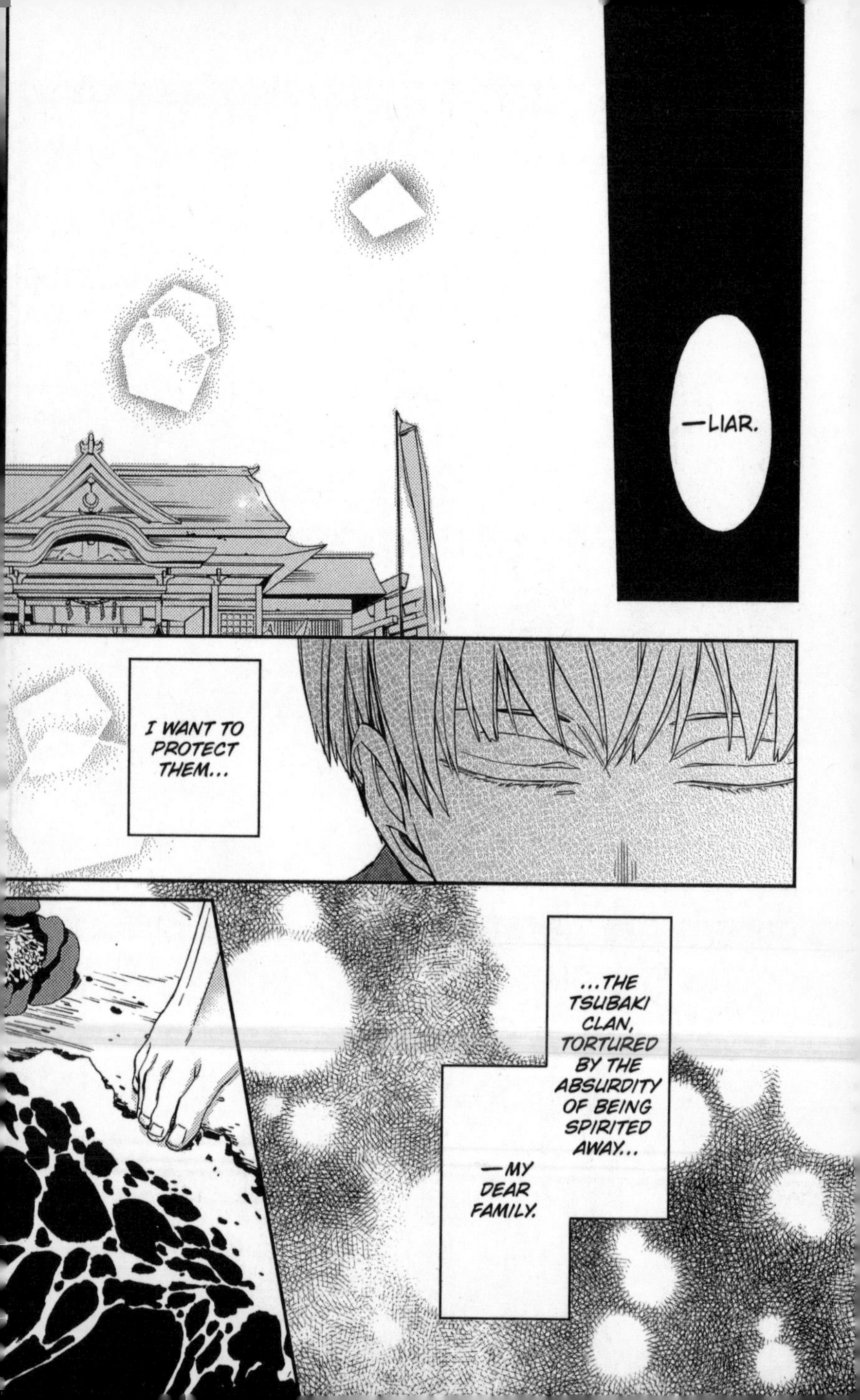
—LIAR.
I WANT TO PROTECT THEM...
...THE TSUBAKI CLAN, TORTURED BY THE ABSURDITY OF BEING SPIRITED AWAY...
—MY DEAR FAMILY.

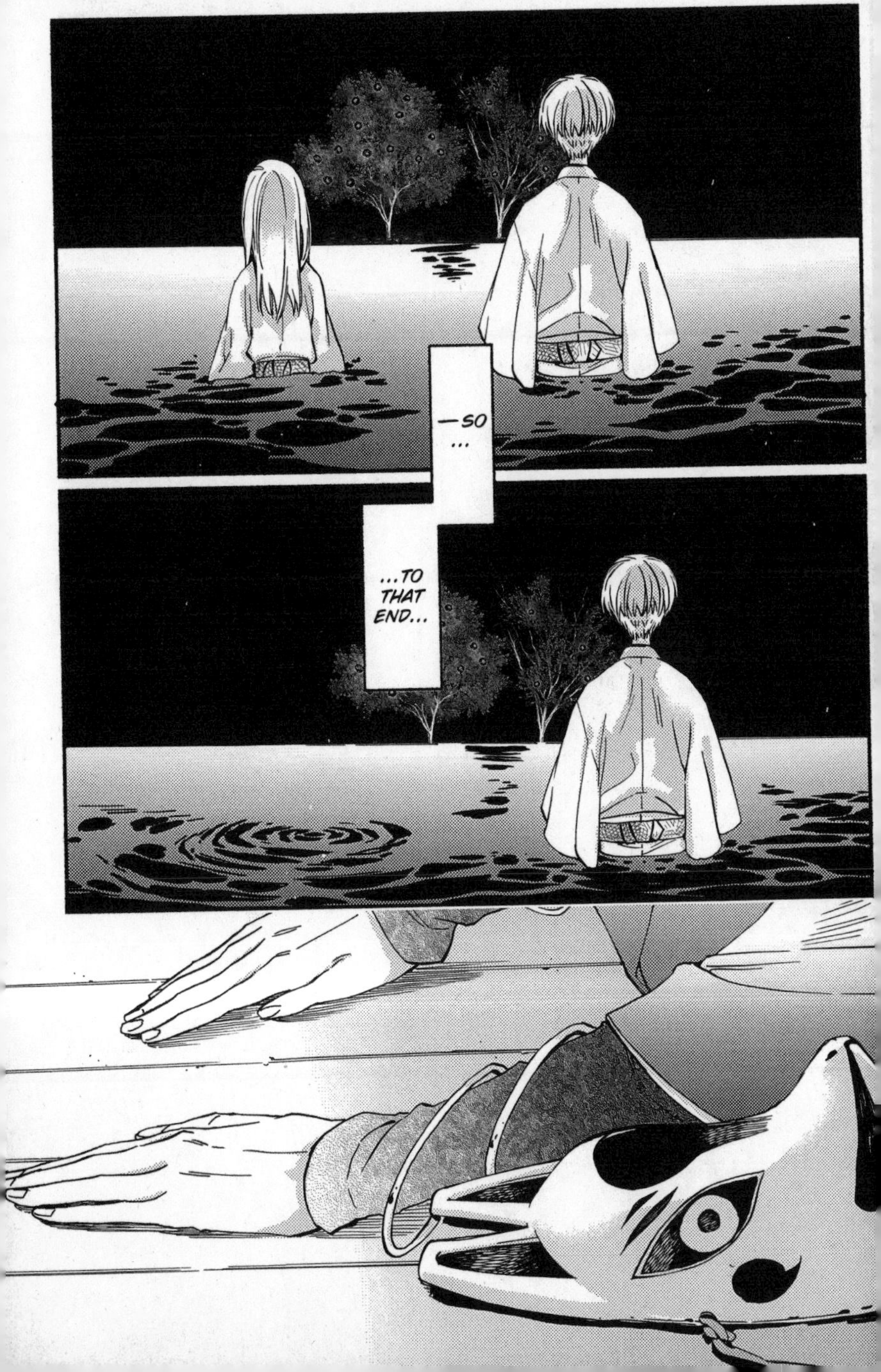
—SO
...
...TO
THAT
END...

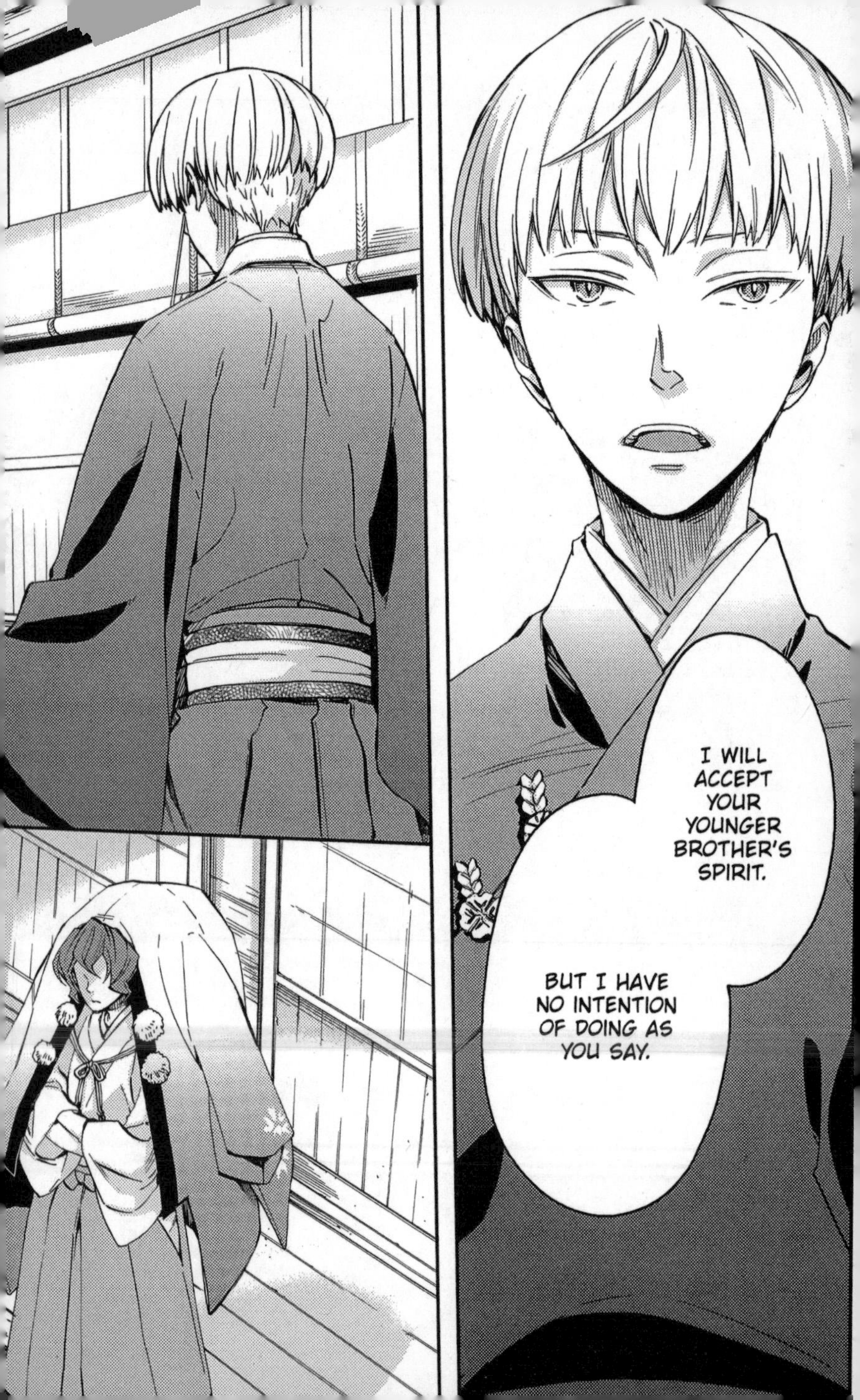
I WILL ACCEPT YOUR YOUNGER BROTHER'S SPIRIT.
BUT I HAVE NO INTENTION OF DOING AS YOU SAY.

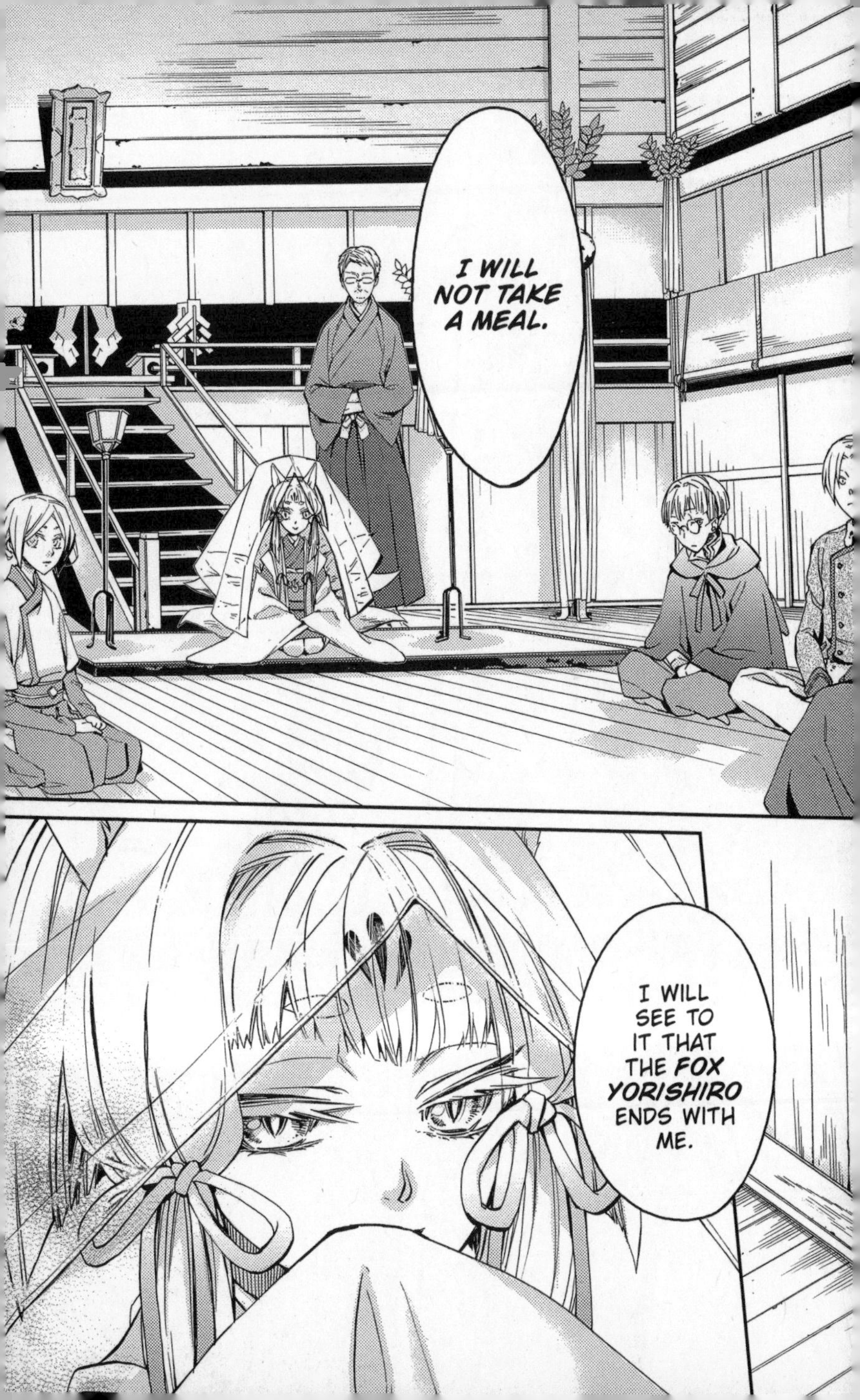
I WILL NOT TAKE A MEAL.
I WILL SEE TO IT THAT THE FOX YORISHIRO ENDS WITH ME.

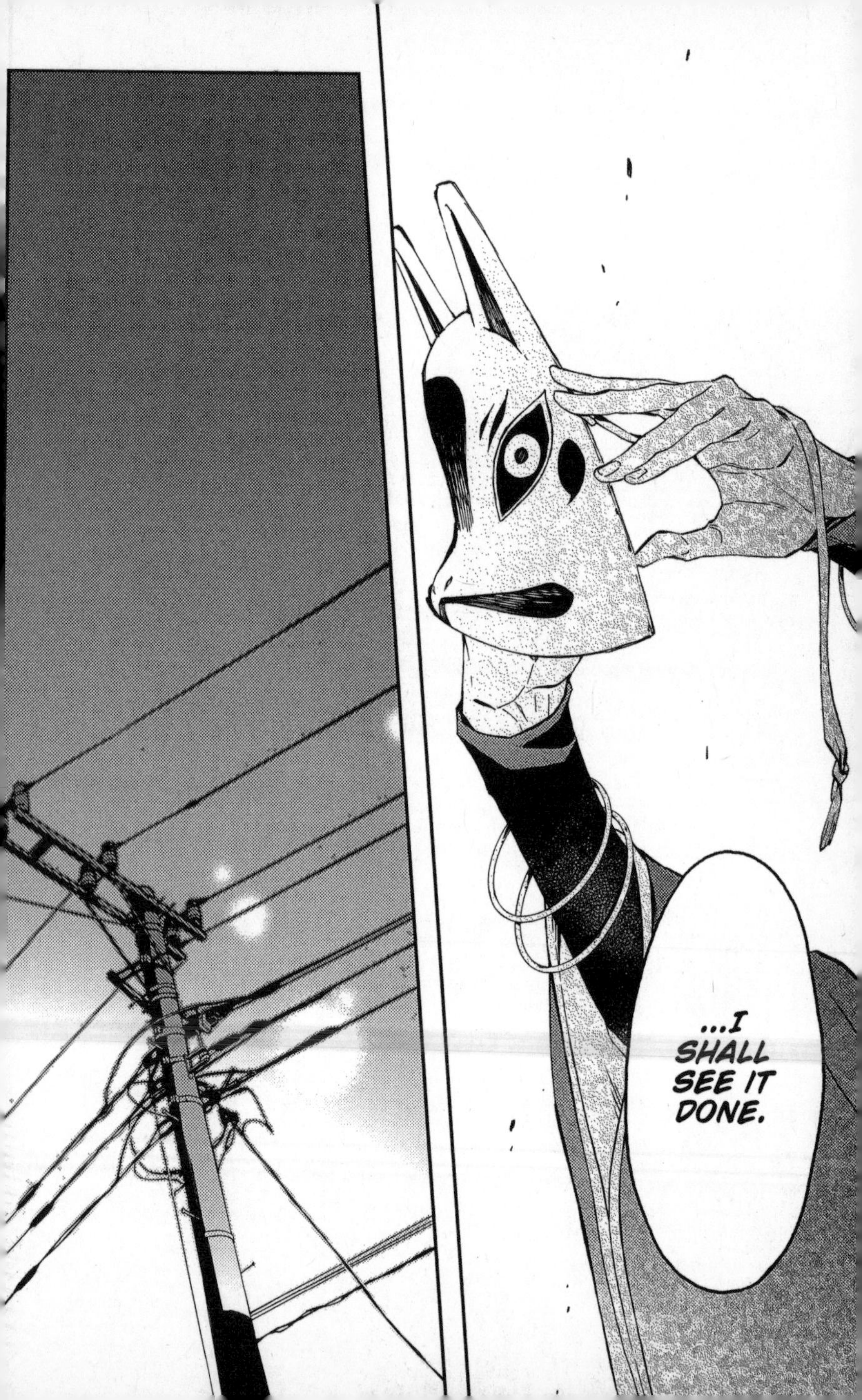
...I SHALL SEE IT DONE.

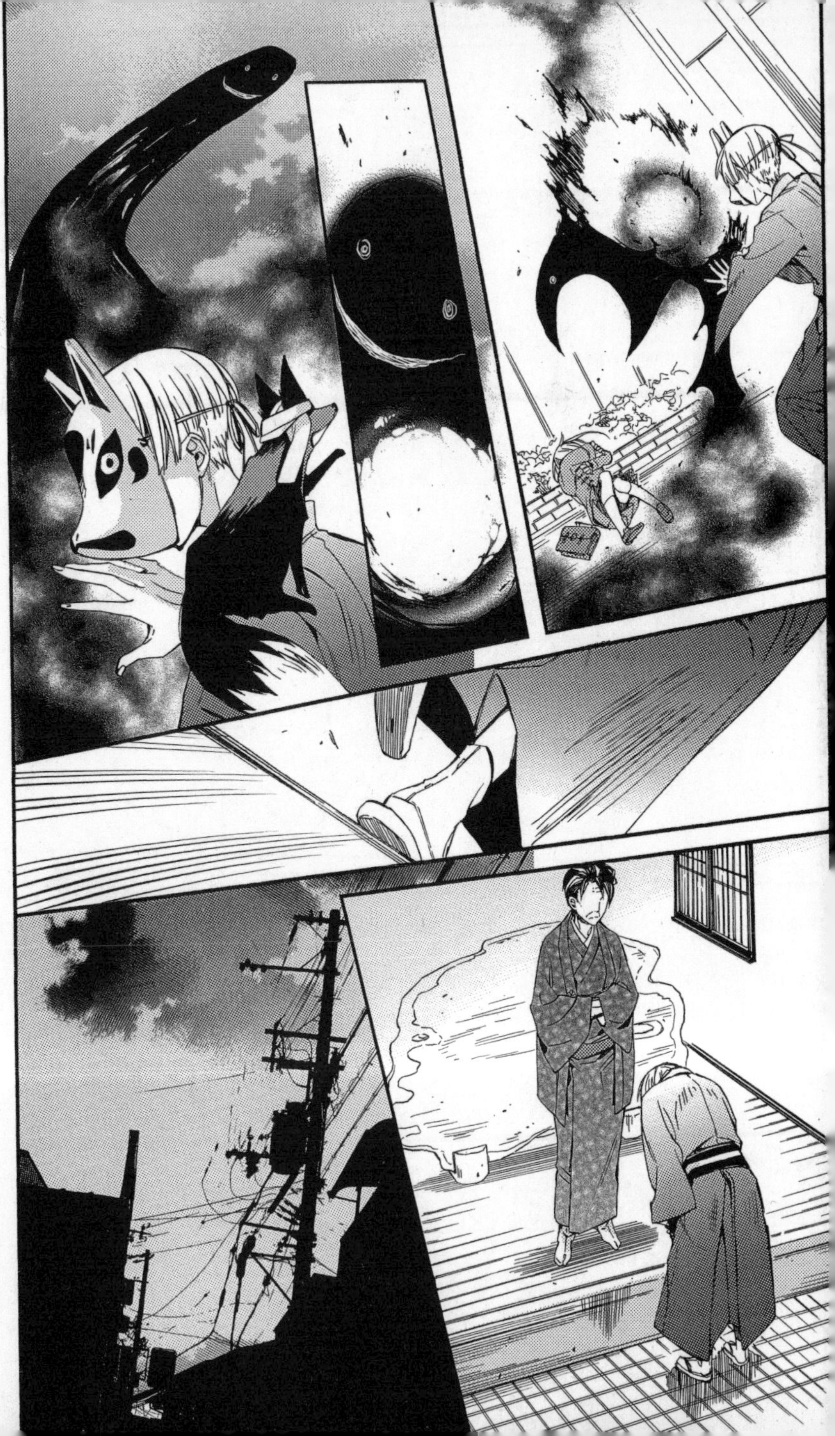

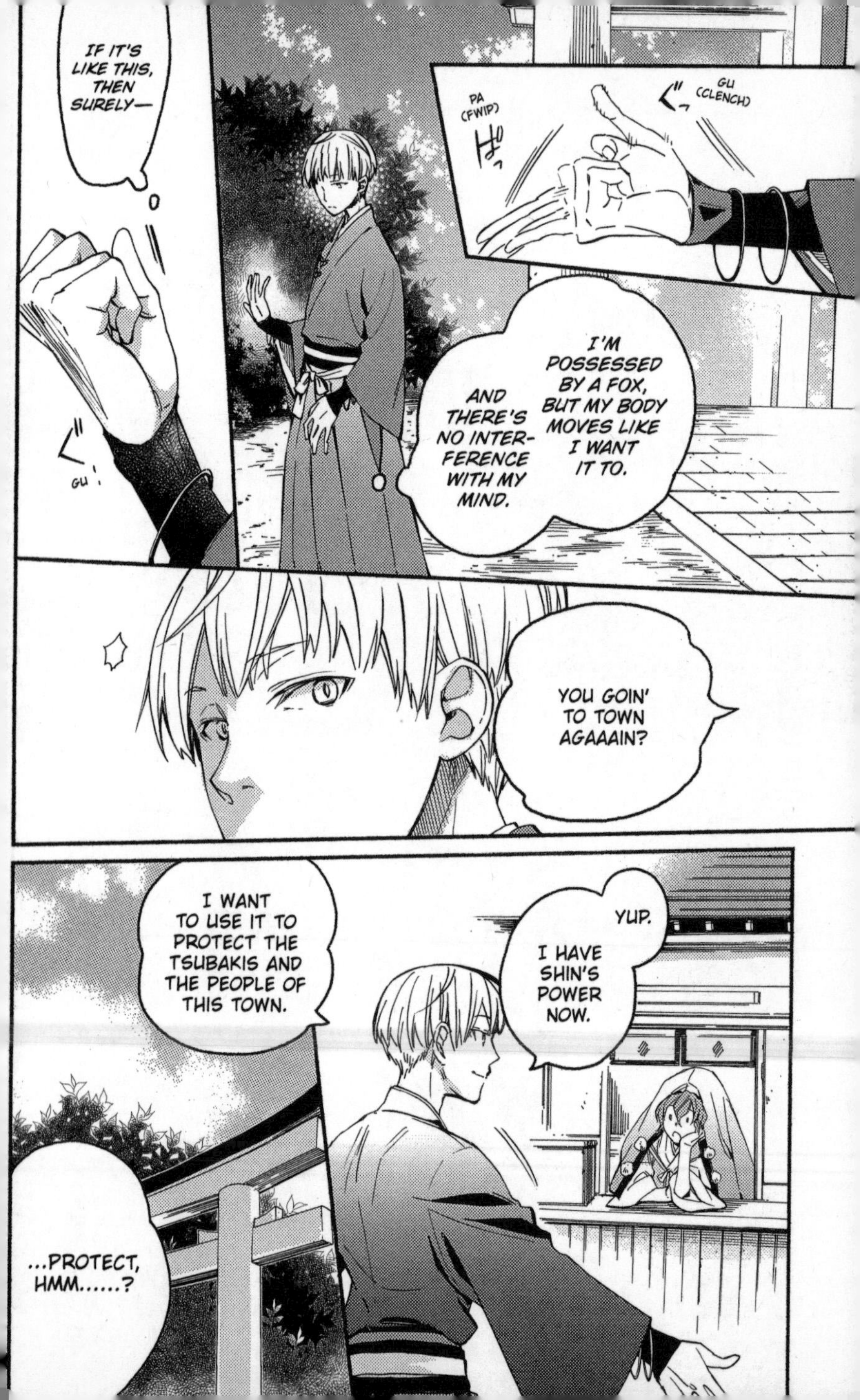
GU (CLENCH)
PA (FWIP)
I'M POSSESSED BY A FOX, BUT MY BODY MOVES LIKE I WANT IT TO.
AND THERE'S NO INTER-FERENCE WITH MY MIND.
IF IT'S LIKE THIS, THEN SURELY—
GU
YOU GOIN' TO TOWN AGAAAIN?
YUP.
I HAVE SHIN'S POWER NOW.
I WANT TO USE IT TO PROTECT THE TSUBAKIS AND THE PEOPLE OF THIS TOWN.
...PROTECT, HMM......?

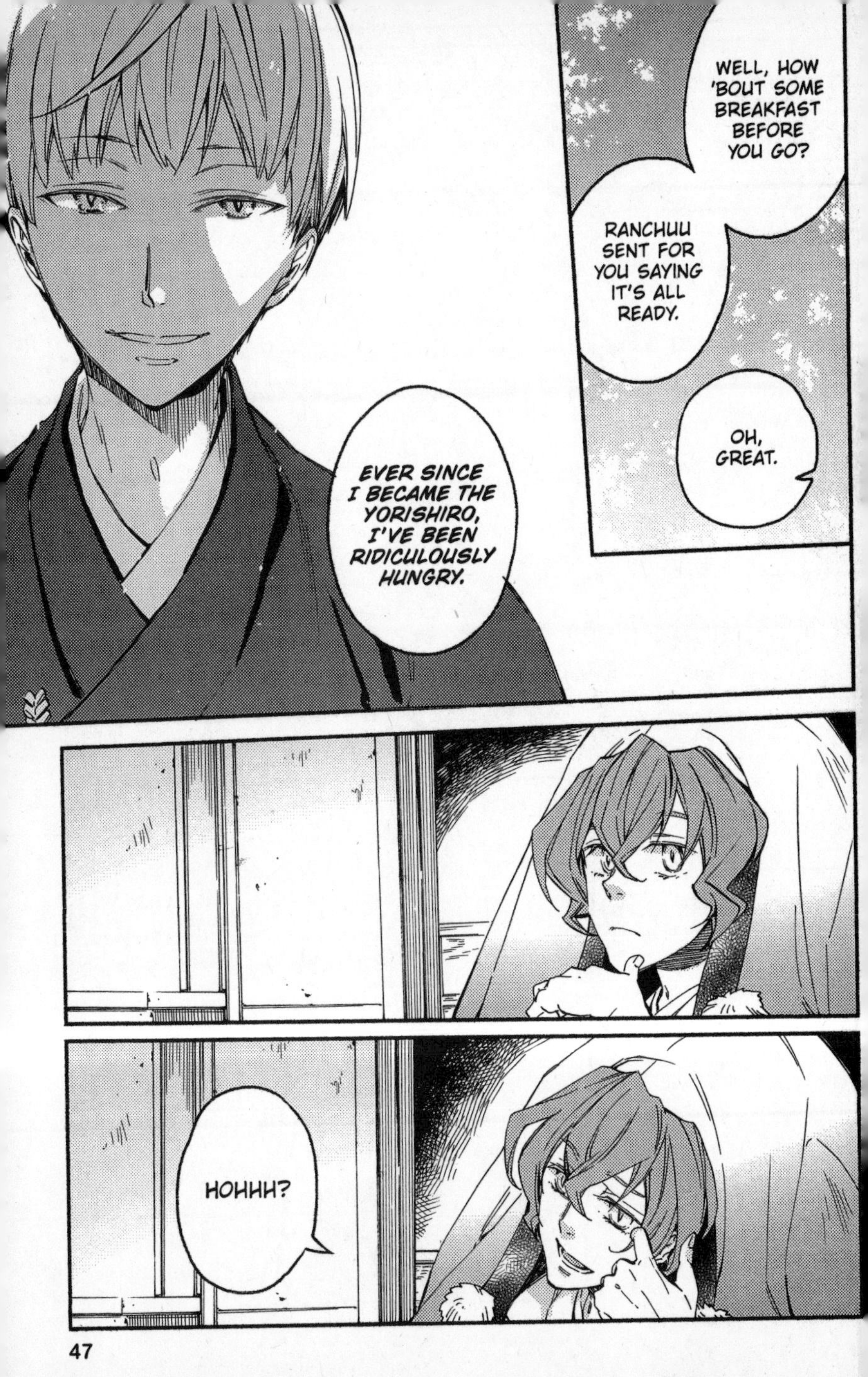
WELL, HOW 'BOUT SOME BREAKFAST BEFORE YOU GO?
RANCHUU SENT FOR YOU SAYING IT'S ALL READY.
OH, GREAT.
EVER SINCE I BECAME THE YORISHIRO, I'VE BEEN RIDICULOUSLY HUNGRY.
HOHHH?

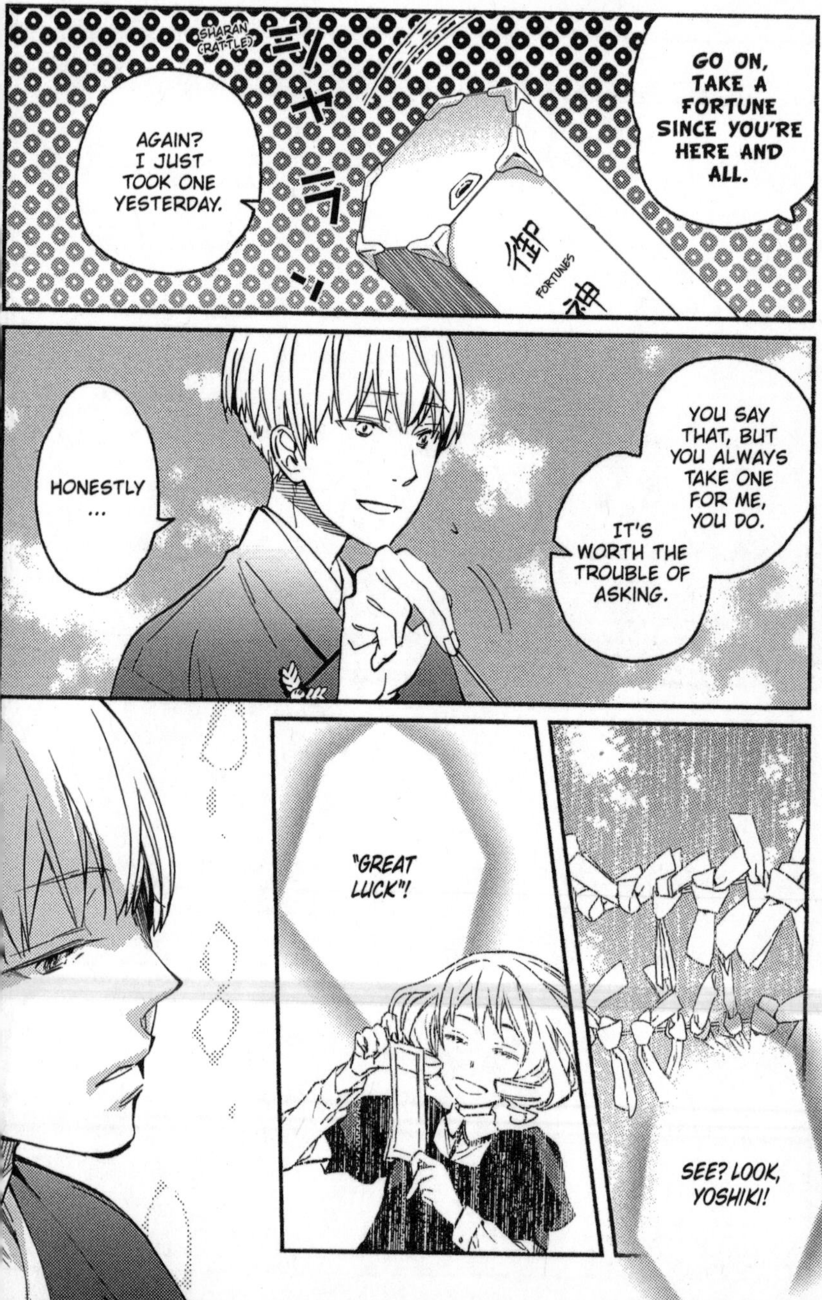
GO ON, TAKE A FORTUNE SINCE YOU'RE HERE AND ALL.
SHARAN (RATTLE)
FORTUNES
AGAIN? I JUST TOOK ONE YESTERDAY.
YOU SAY THAT, BUT YOU ALWAYS TAKE ONE FOR ME, YOU DO.
IT'S WORTH THE TROUBLE OF ASKING.
HONESTLY ...
SEE? LOOK, YOSHIKI!
"GREAT LUCK"!

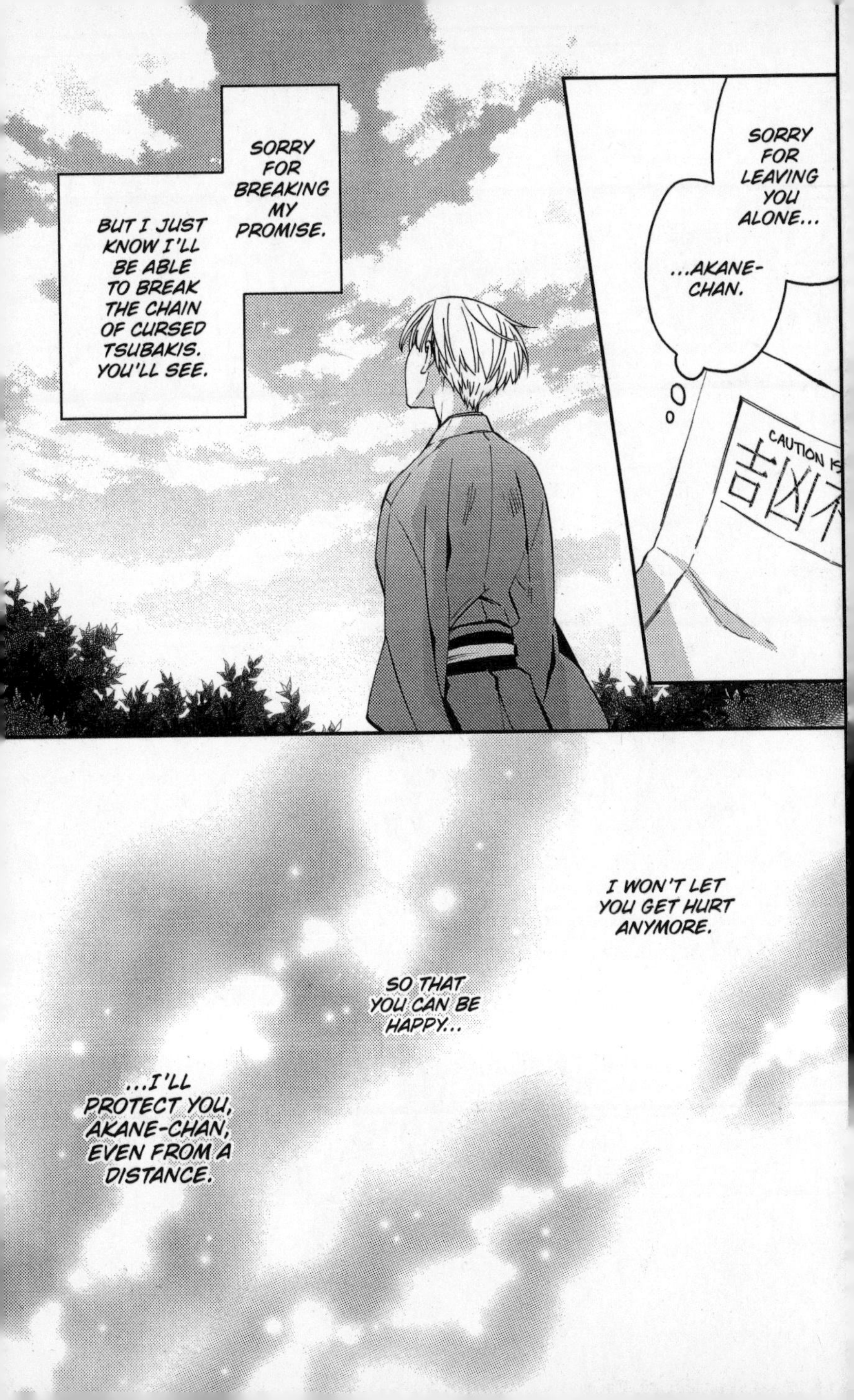
SORRY FOR LEAVING YOU ALONE...
...AKANE-CHAN.
CAUTION IS
吉凶不
SORRY FOR BREAKING MY PROMISE.
BUT I JUST KNOW I'LL BE ABLE TO BREAK THE CHAIN OF CURSED TSUBAKIS. YOU'LL SEE.
I WON'T LET YOU GET HURT ANYMORE.
SO THAT YOU CAN BE HAPPY...
...I'LL PROTECT YOU, AKANE-CHAN, EVEN FROM A DISTANCE.

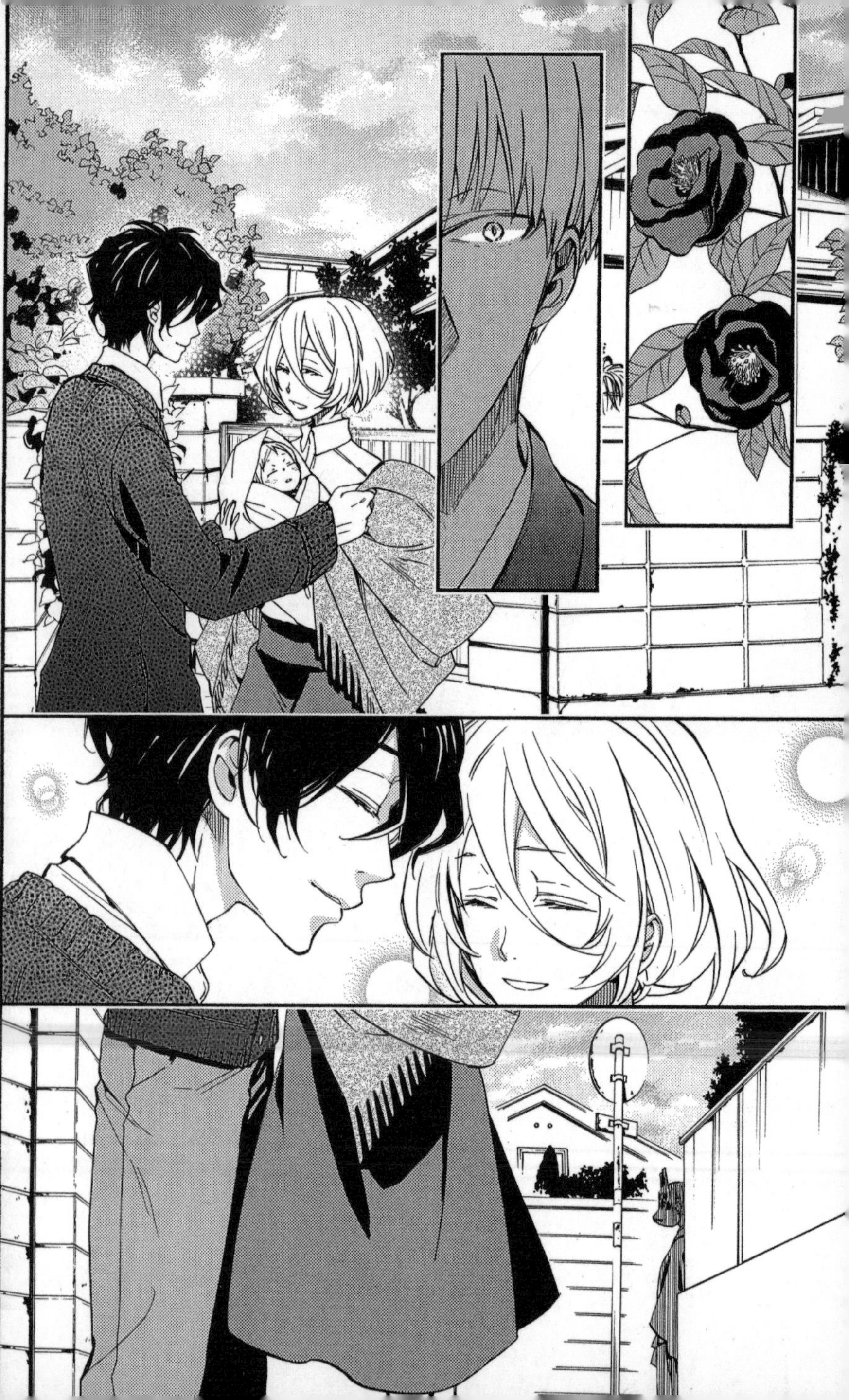

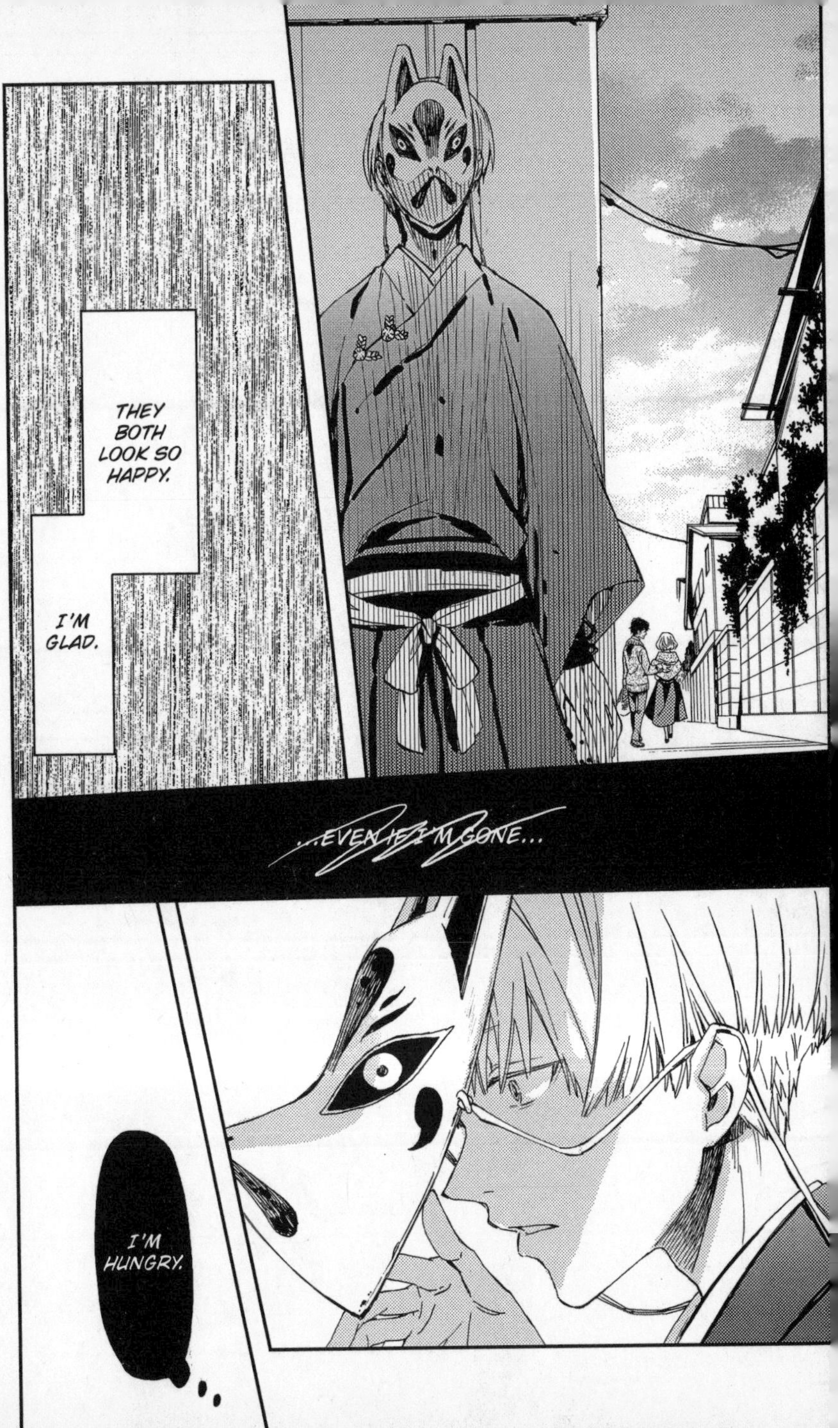
THEY BOTH LOOK SO HAPPY.
I'M GLAD.
...EVEN IF I'M GONE...
I'M HUNGRY...

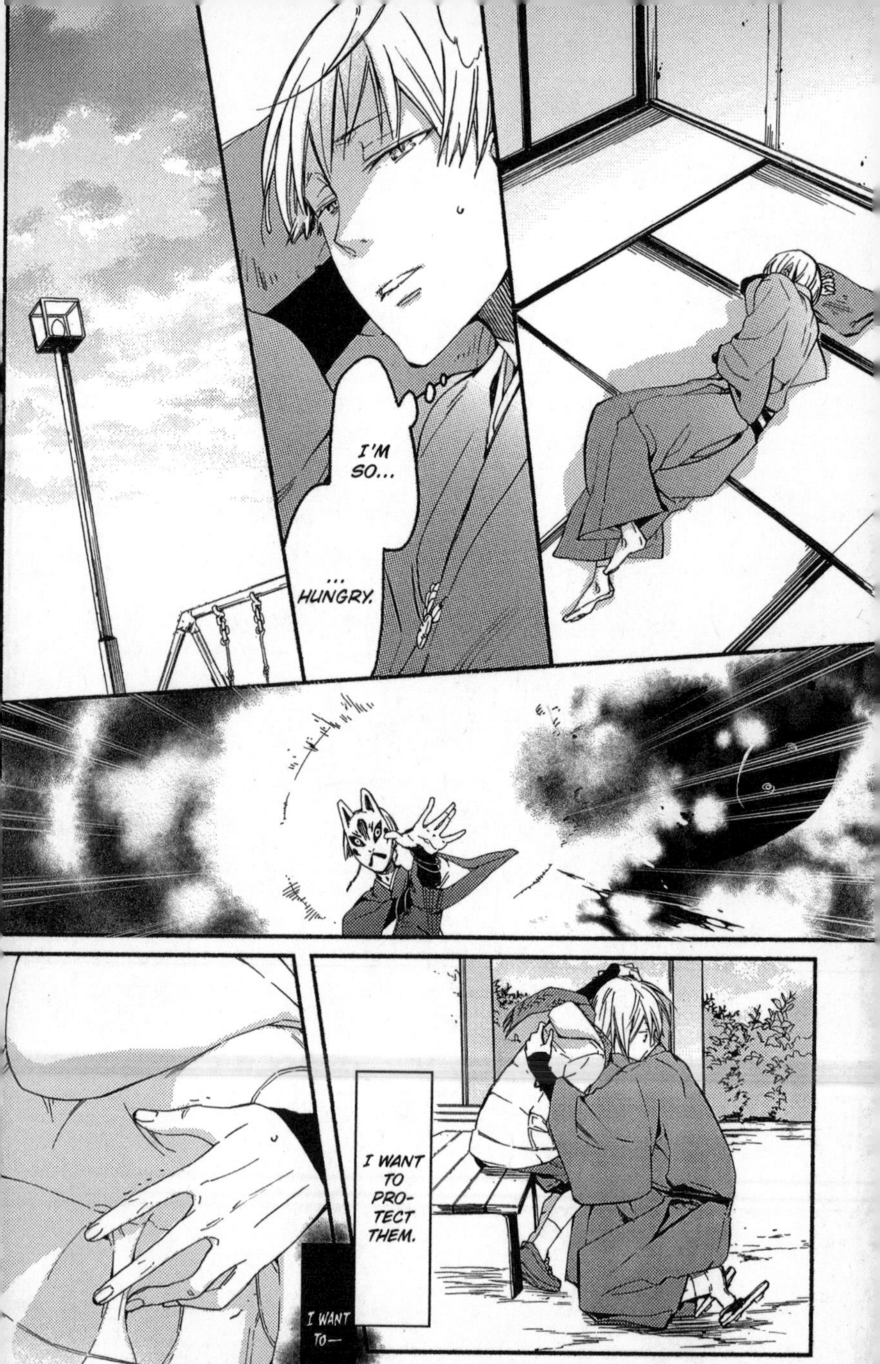
I'M SO...
...HUNGRY.
I WANT TO PRO-TECT THEM.
I WANT TO—

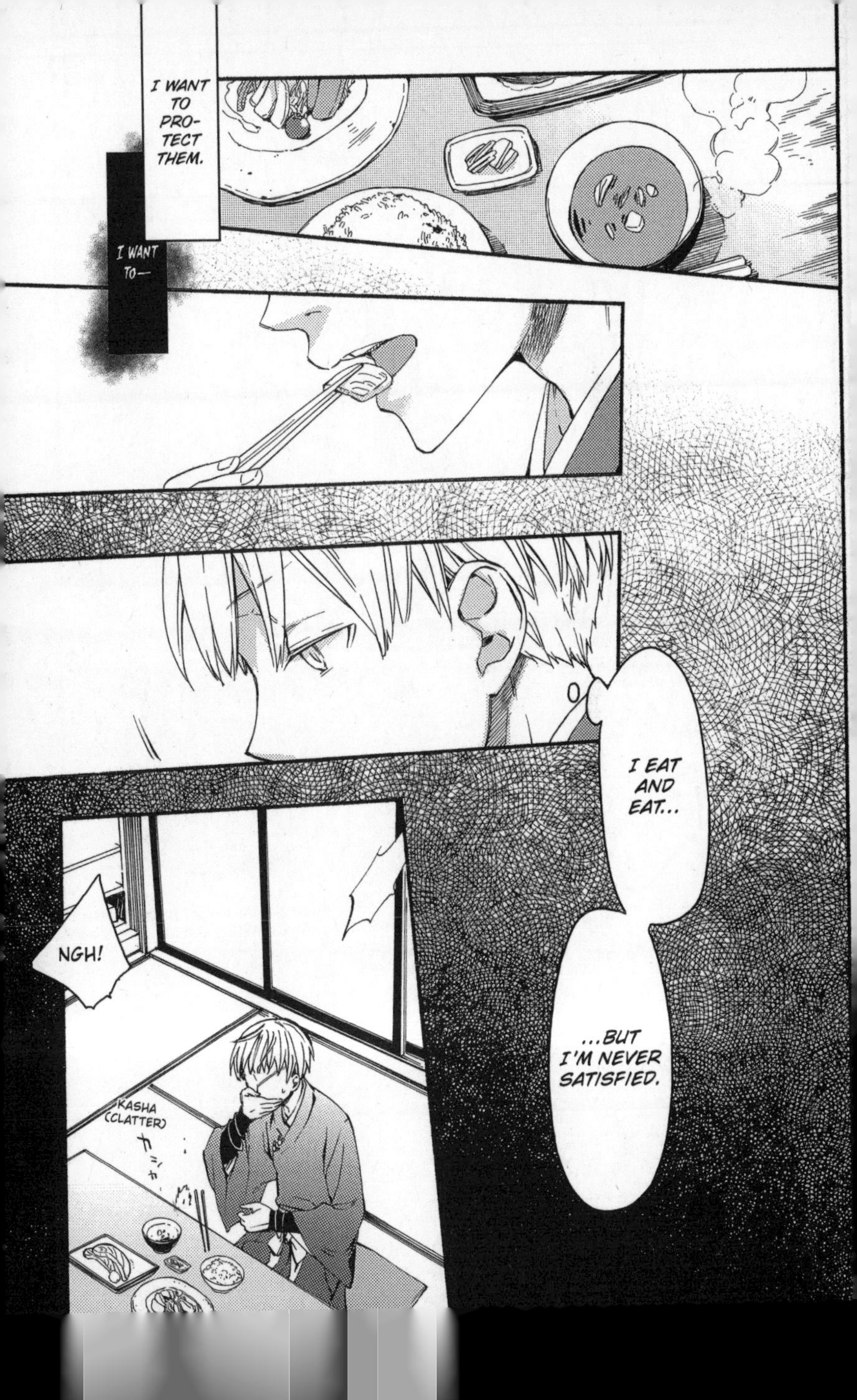
I WANT TO PRO-TECT THEM.
I WANT TO—
I EAT AND EAT...
...BUT I'M NEVER SATISFIED.
NGH!
KASHA (CLATTER)

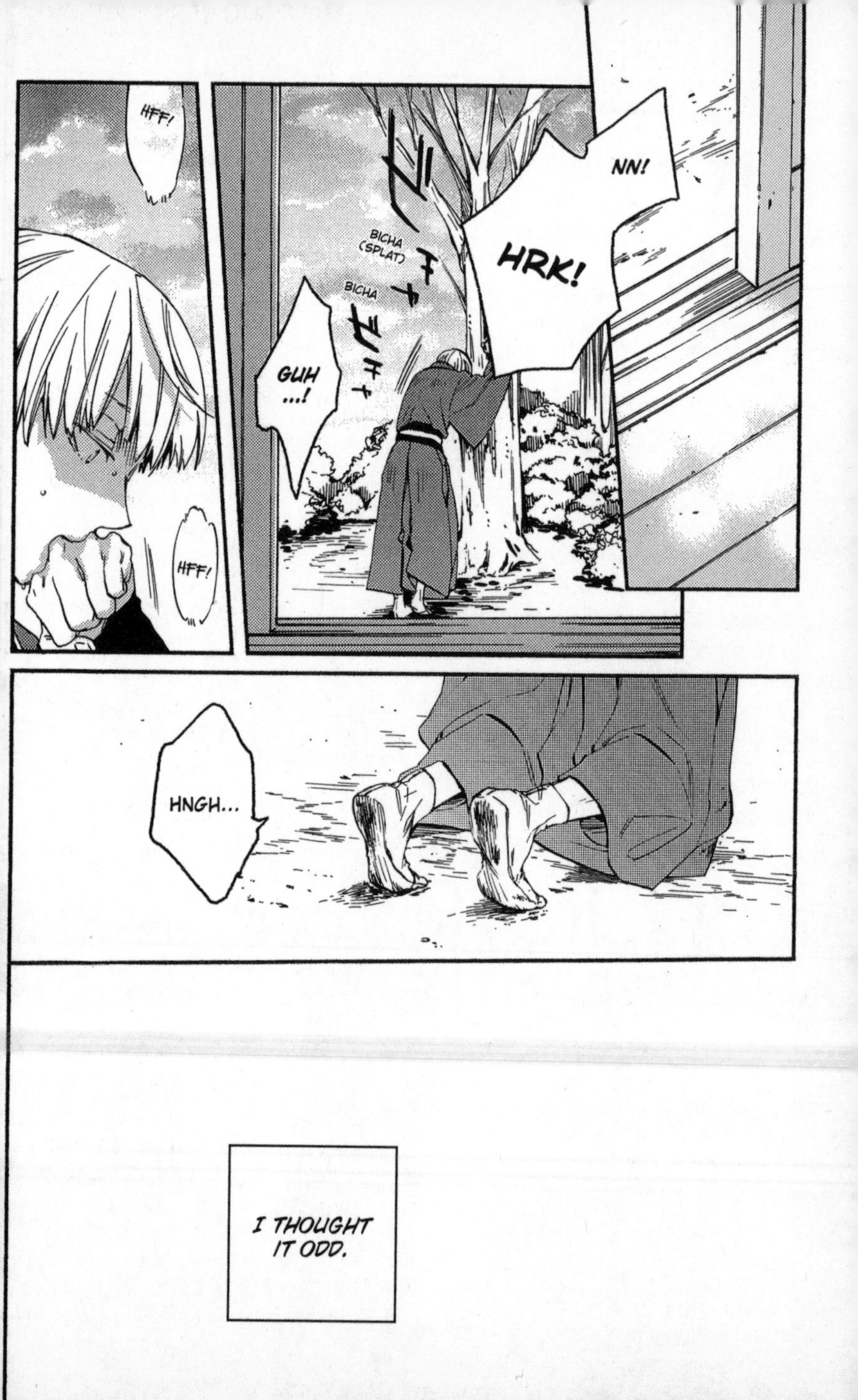
NN!
HRK!
BICHA (SPLAT)
BICHA
GUH ...!
HFF!
HFF!
HNGH...
I THOUGHT IT ODD.

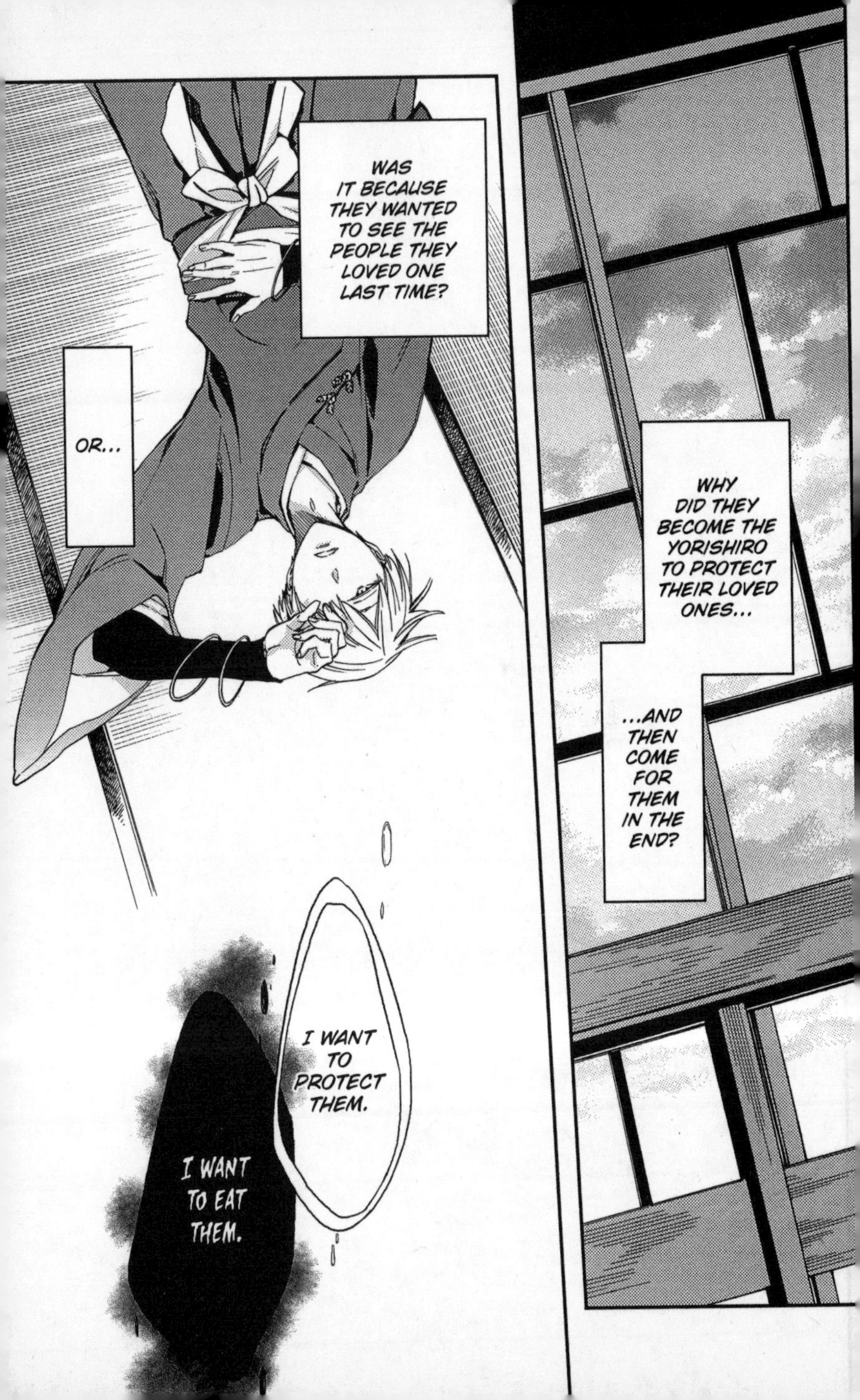
WHY DID THEY BECOME THE YORISHIRO TO PROTECT THEIR LOVED ONES...
...AND THEN COME FOR THEM IN THE END?
WAS IT BECAUSE THEY WANTED TO SEE THE PEOPLE THEY LOVED ONE LAST TIME?
OR...
I WANT TO PROTECT THEM.
I WANT TO EAT THEM.

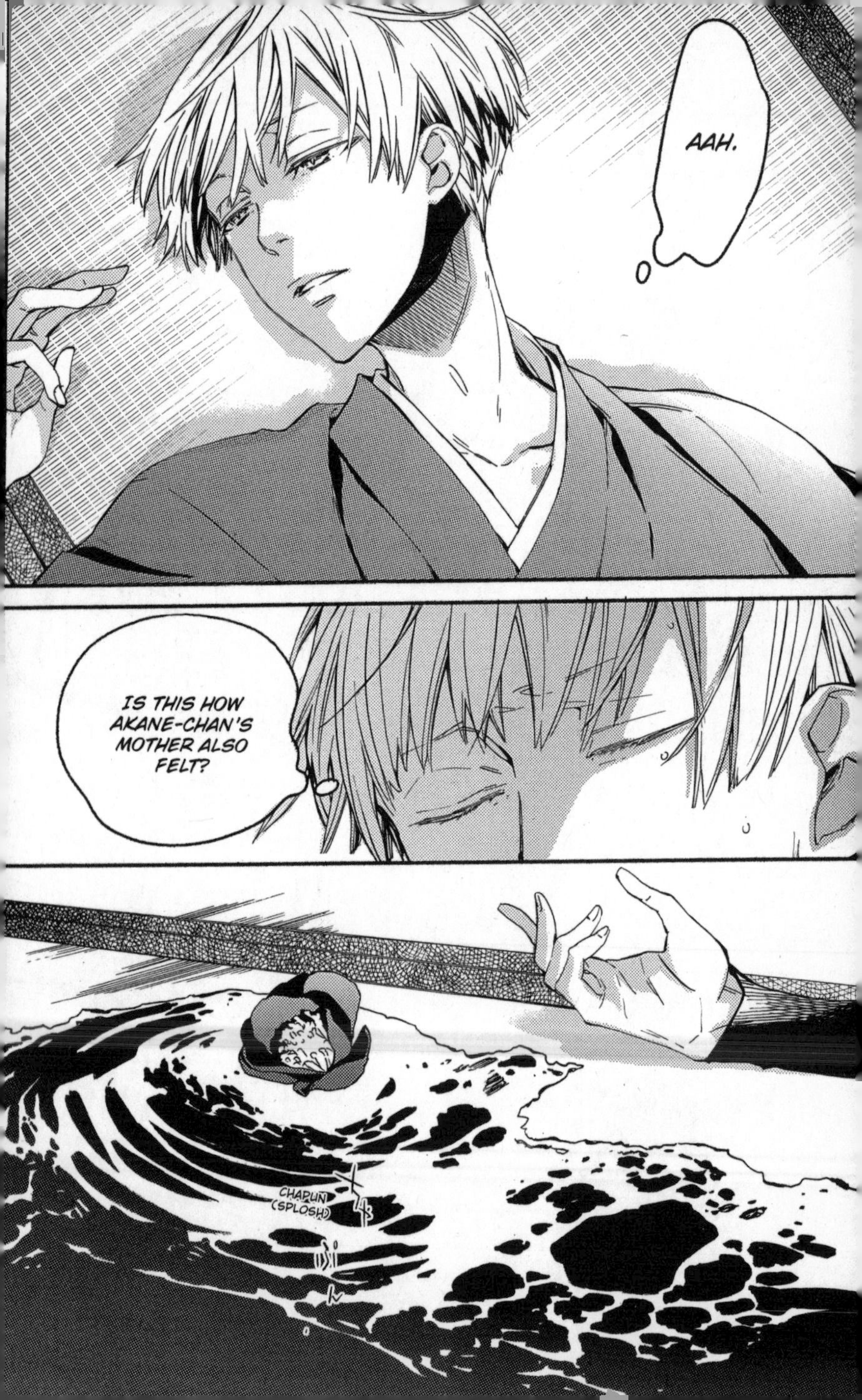
AAH.
IS THIS HOW AKANE-CHAN'S MOTHER ALSO FELT?
CHAPUN (SPLOSH)

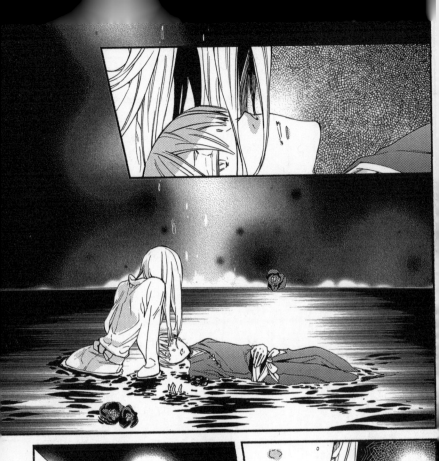

LISTEN...

...YOSHIKI.

AKANE...

PROMISE ME
YOU'LL PROTECT
HER, OKAY?

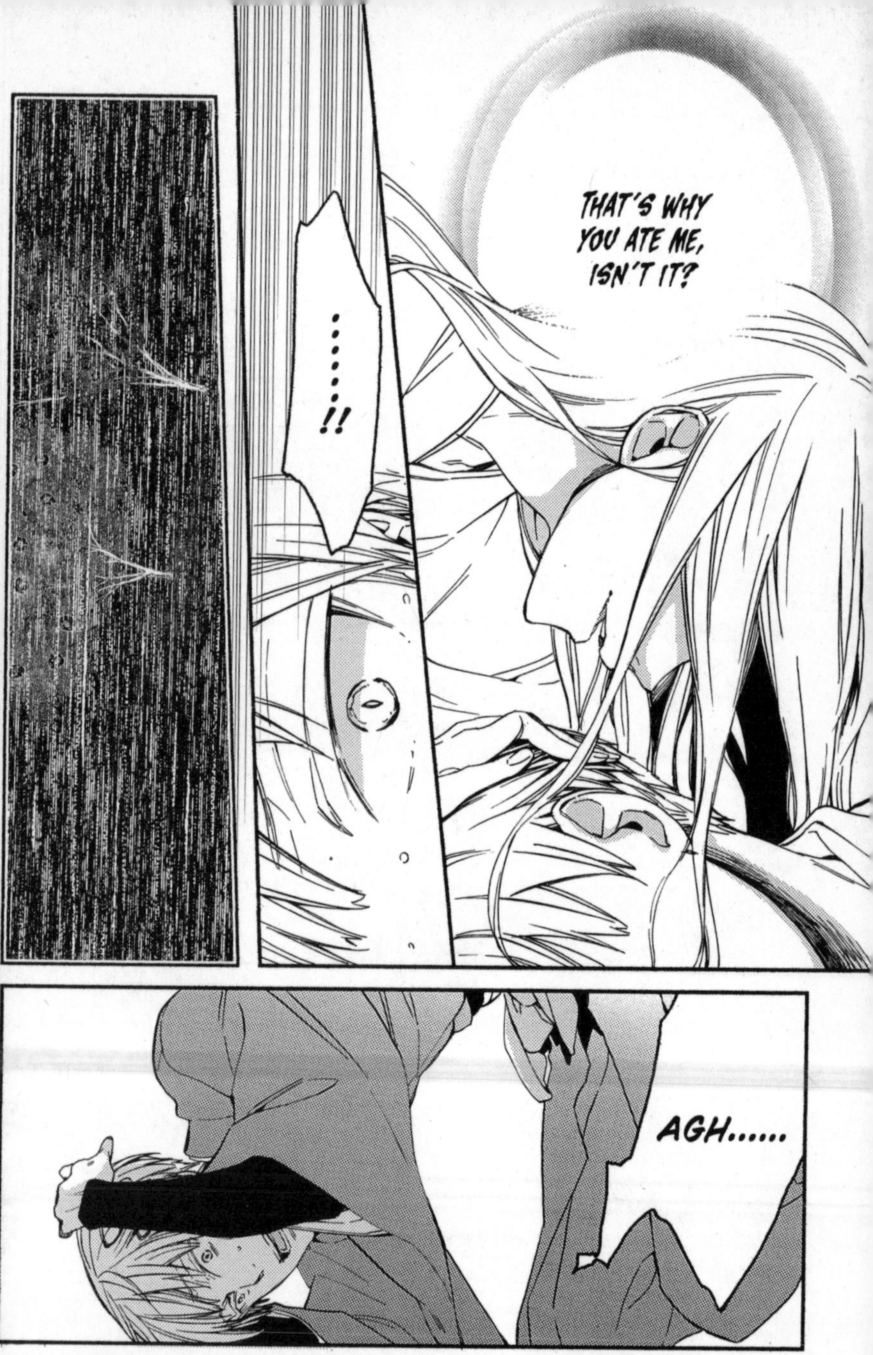
THAT'S WHY YOU ATE ME, ISN'T IT?
......!!
AGH......

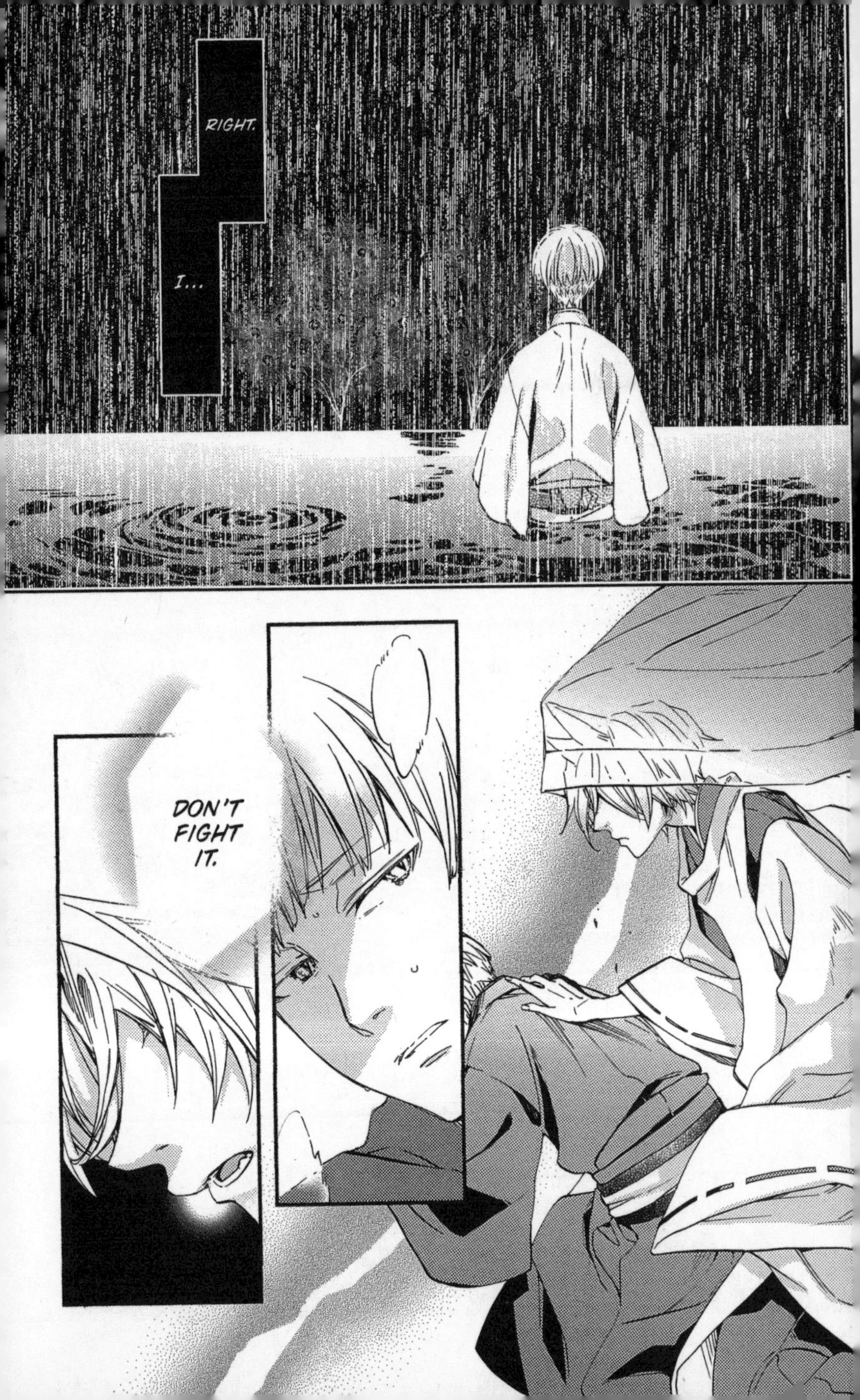
RIGHT.
I...
DON'T FIGHT IT.

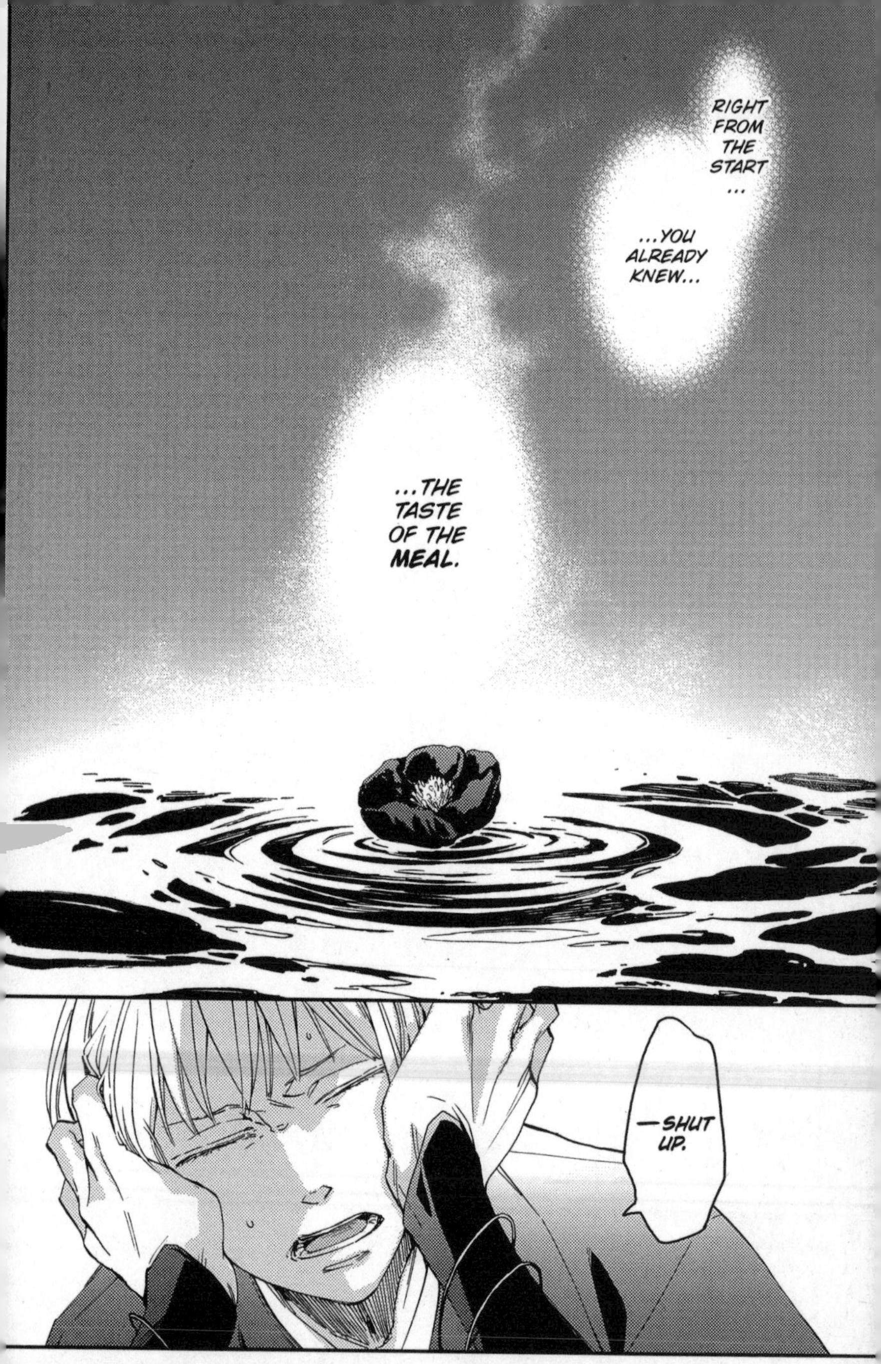
RIGHT FROM THE START ...
...YOU ALREADY KNEW...
...THE TASTE OF THE MEAL.
—SHUT UP.

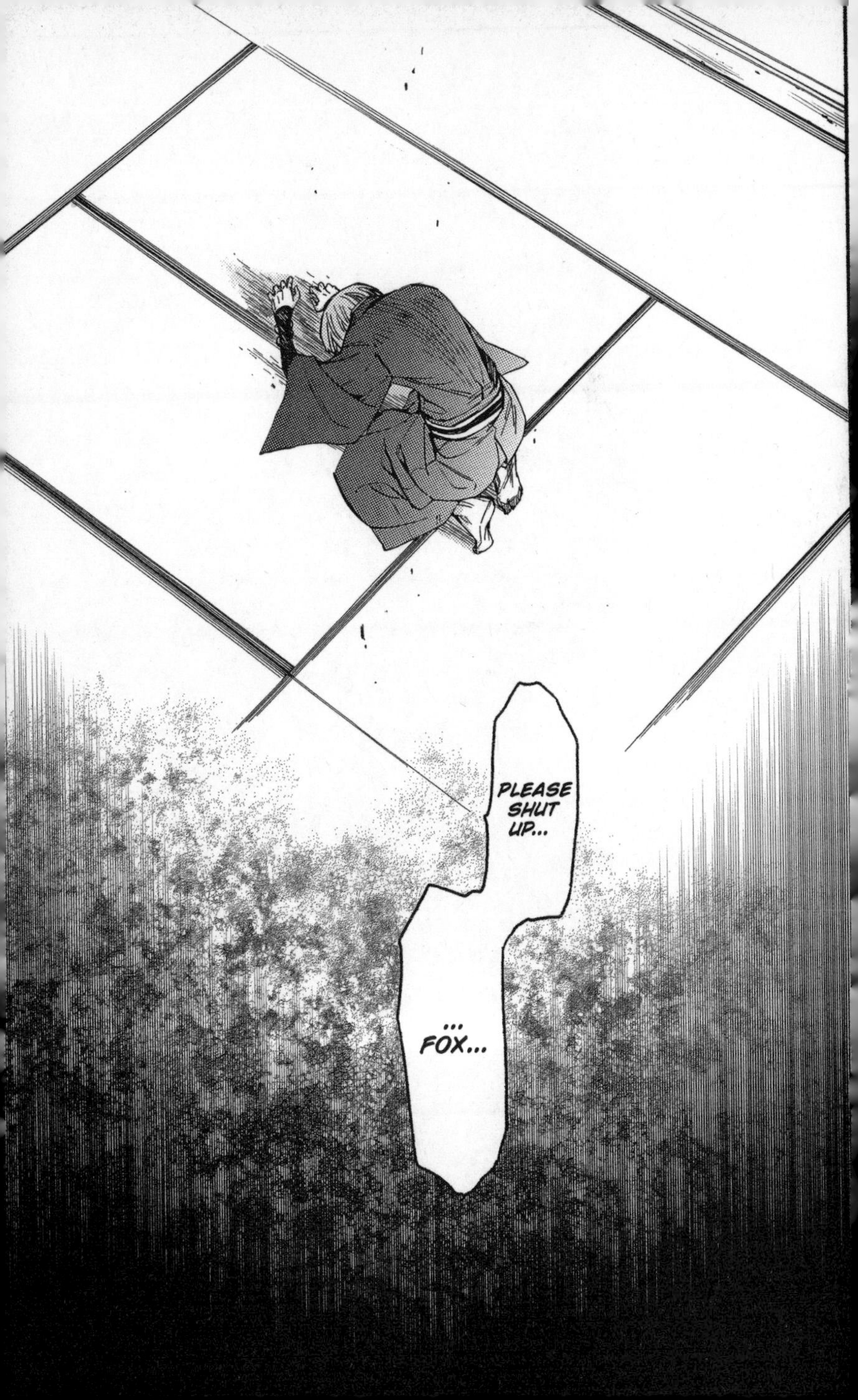
PLEASE SHUT UP...
... FOX...

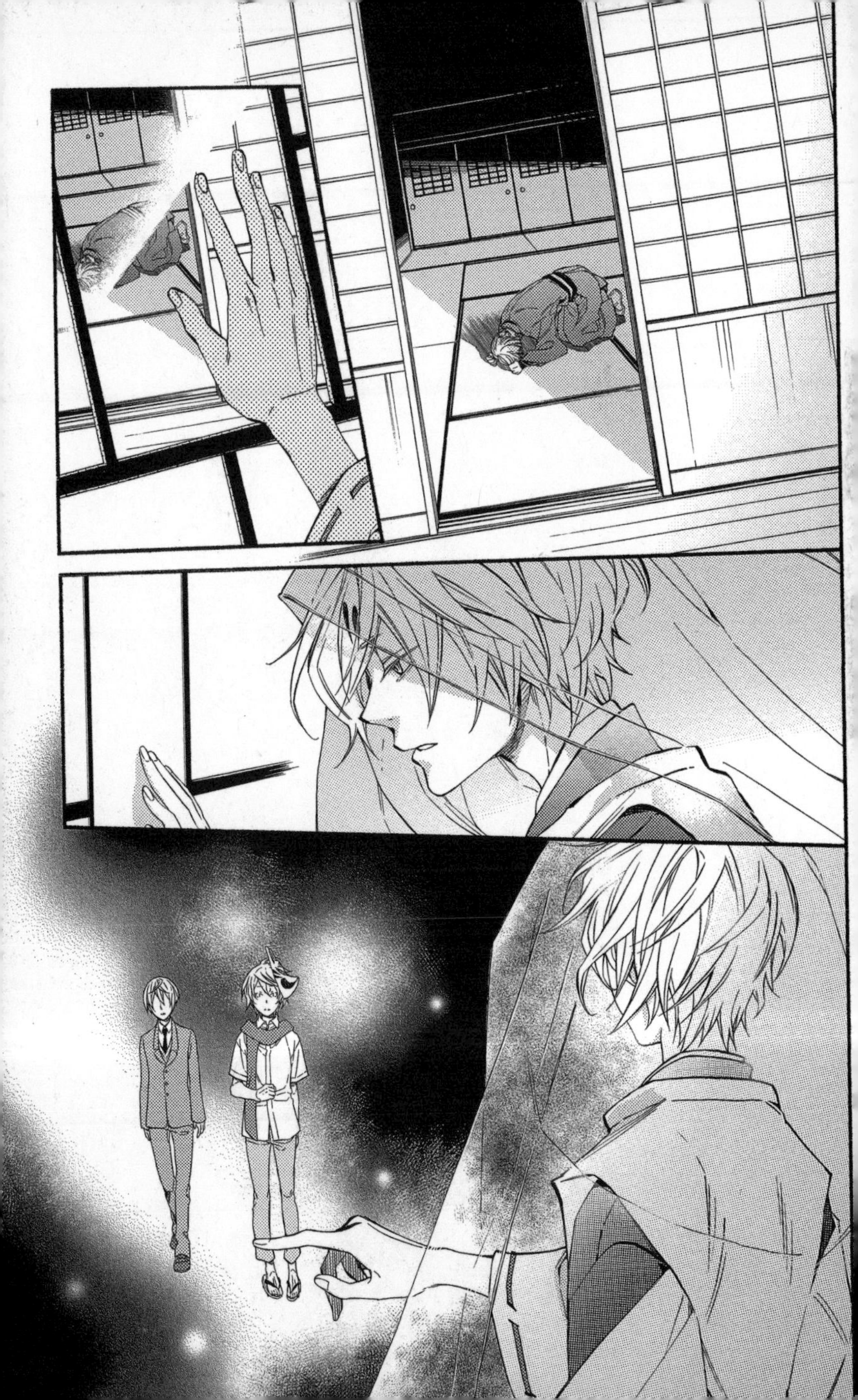

THE **42**ND TALE
PRAYER

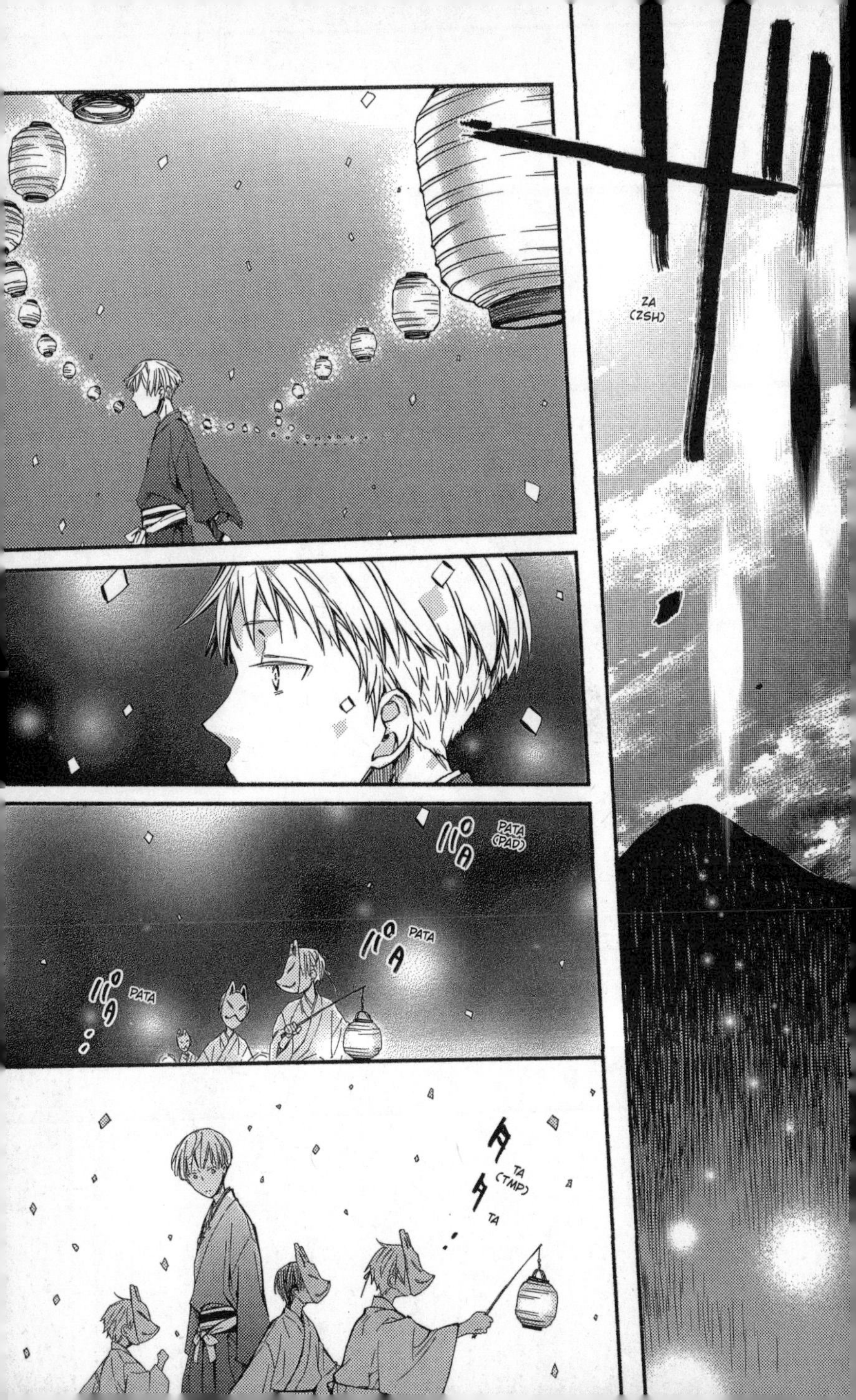
ZA
(ZSH)
PATA
(PAD)
PATA
PATA
TA
(TMP)
TA

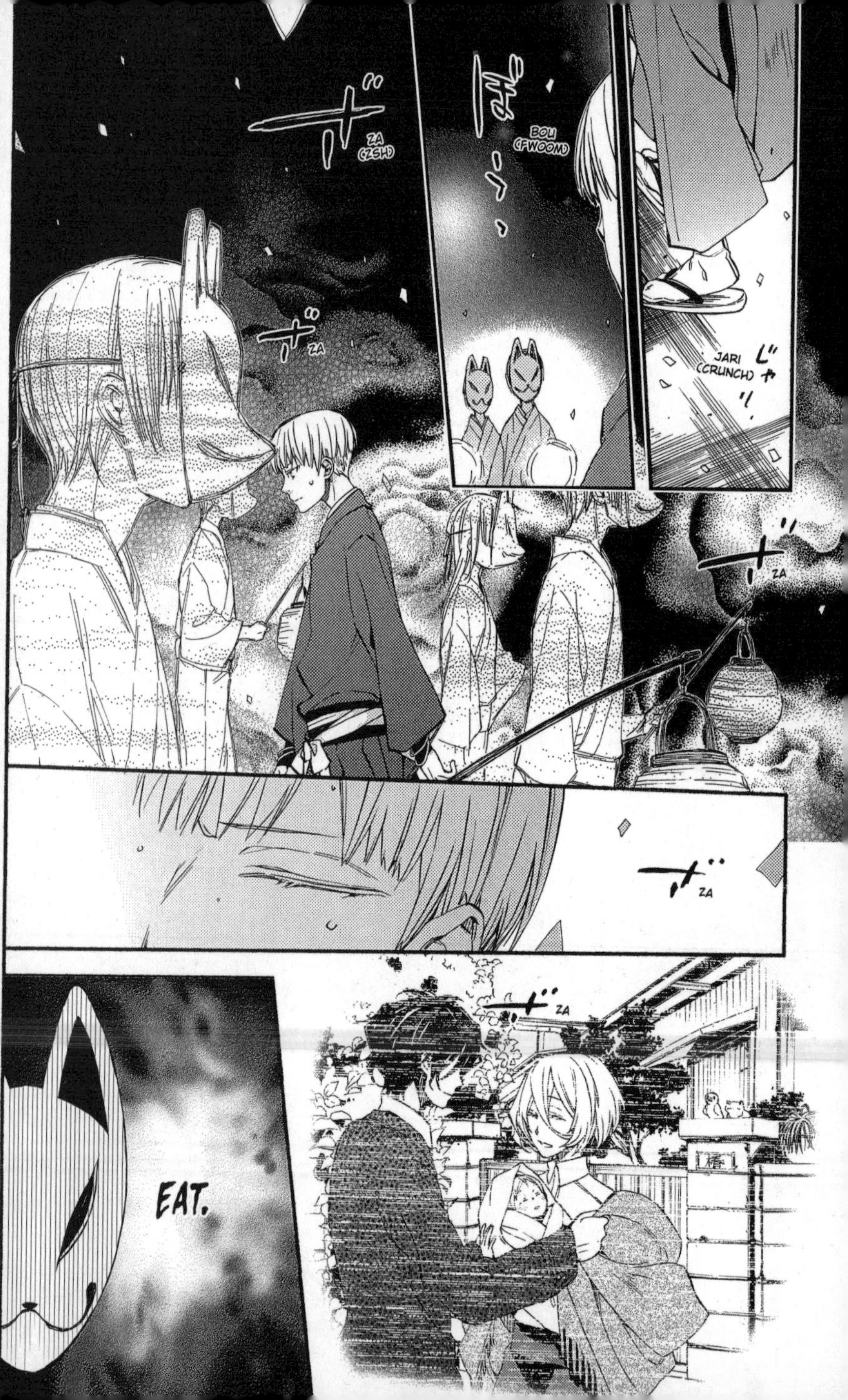
JARI (CRUNCH)
BOU (FWOOM)
ZA (ZSH)
ZA
ZA
ZA
ZA
EAT.

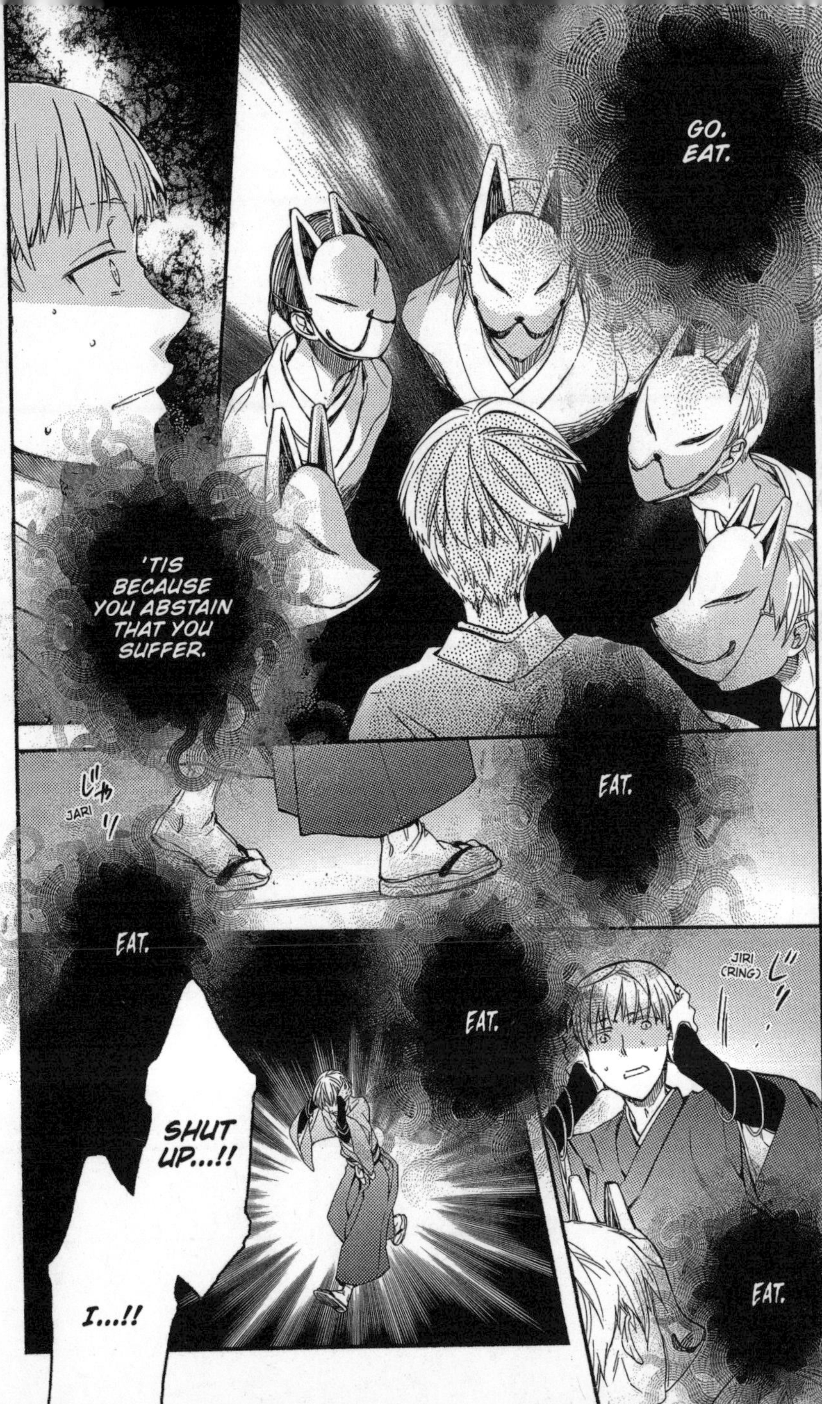
GO. EAT.
'TIS BECAUSE YOU ABSTAIN THAT YOU SUFFER.
EAT.
JARI
JIRI (RING)
EAT.
EAT.
EAT.
SHUT UP...!!
I...!!

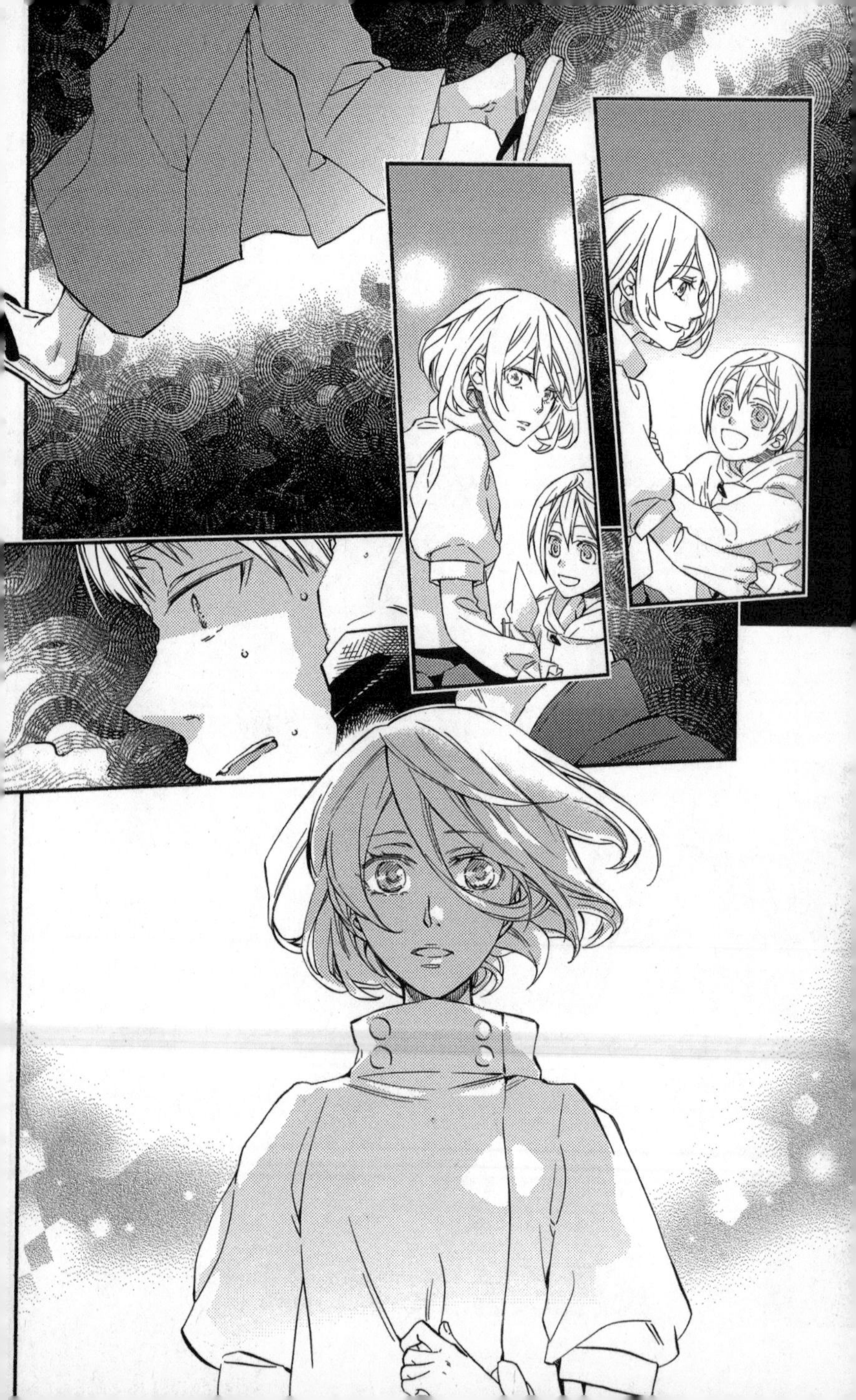

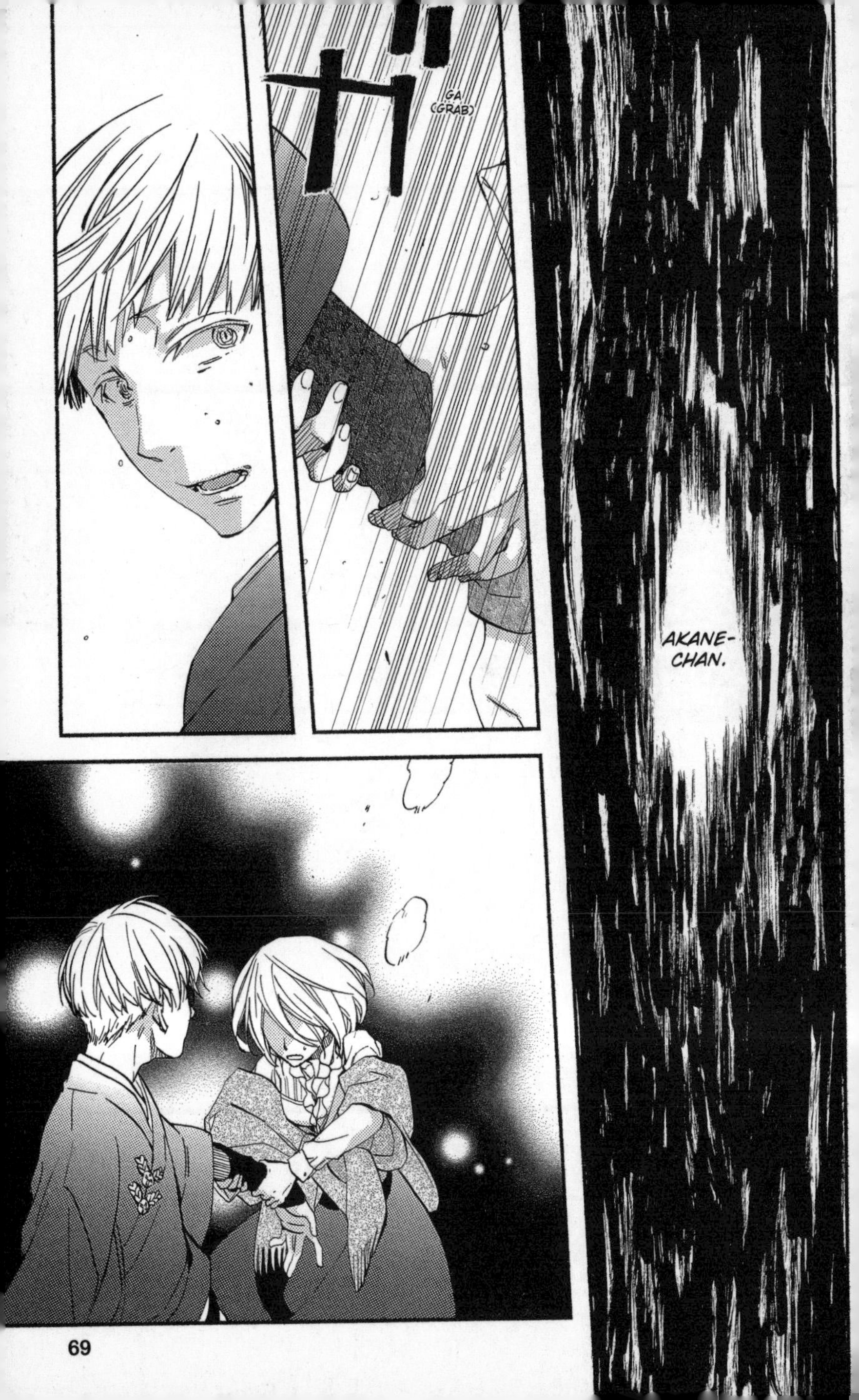
AKANE-CHAN.
GA (GRAB)

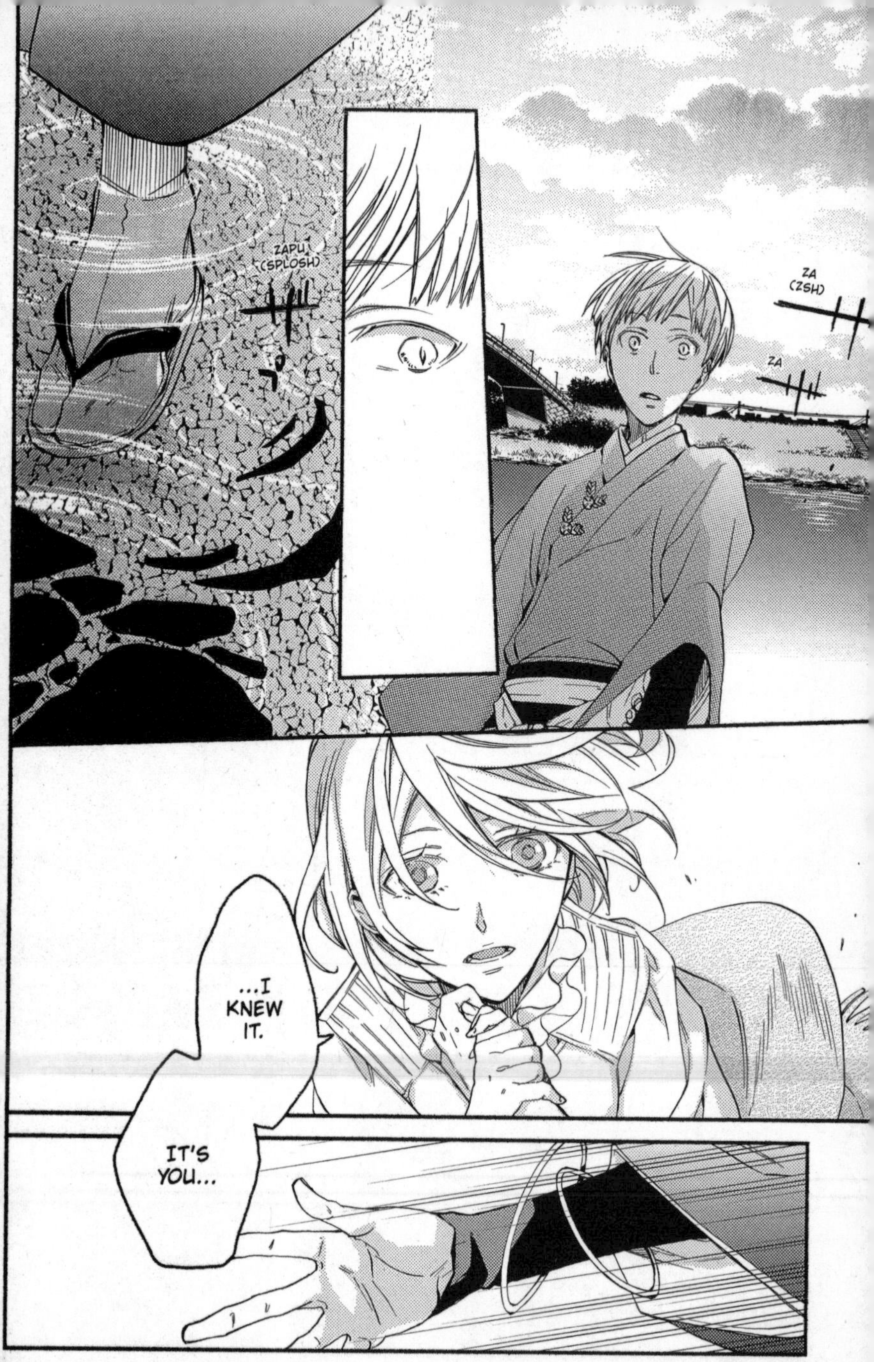
ZA (ZSH)
ZA
ZAPU (SPLOSH)
...I KNEW IT.
IT'S YOU...

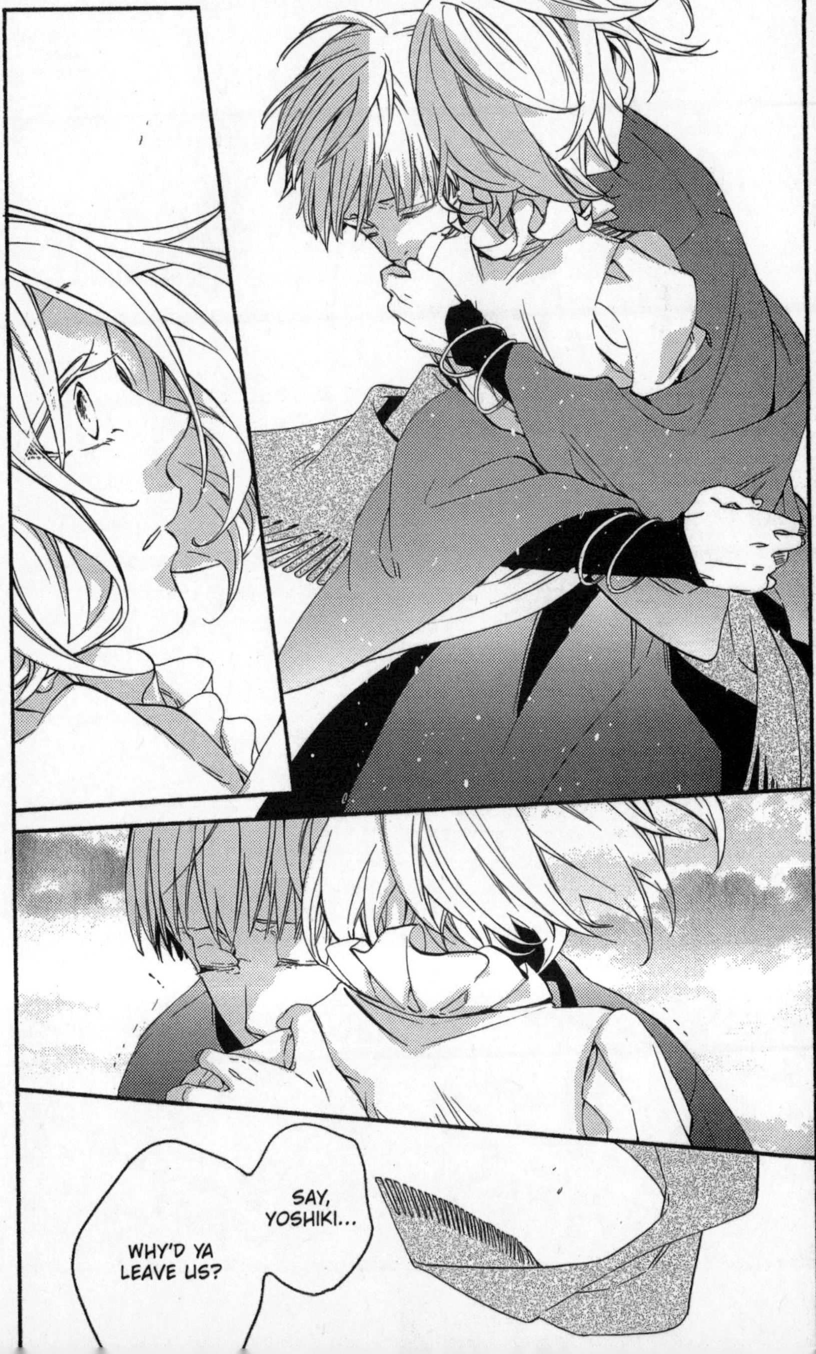
SAY, YOSHIKI...
WHY'D YA LEAVE US?

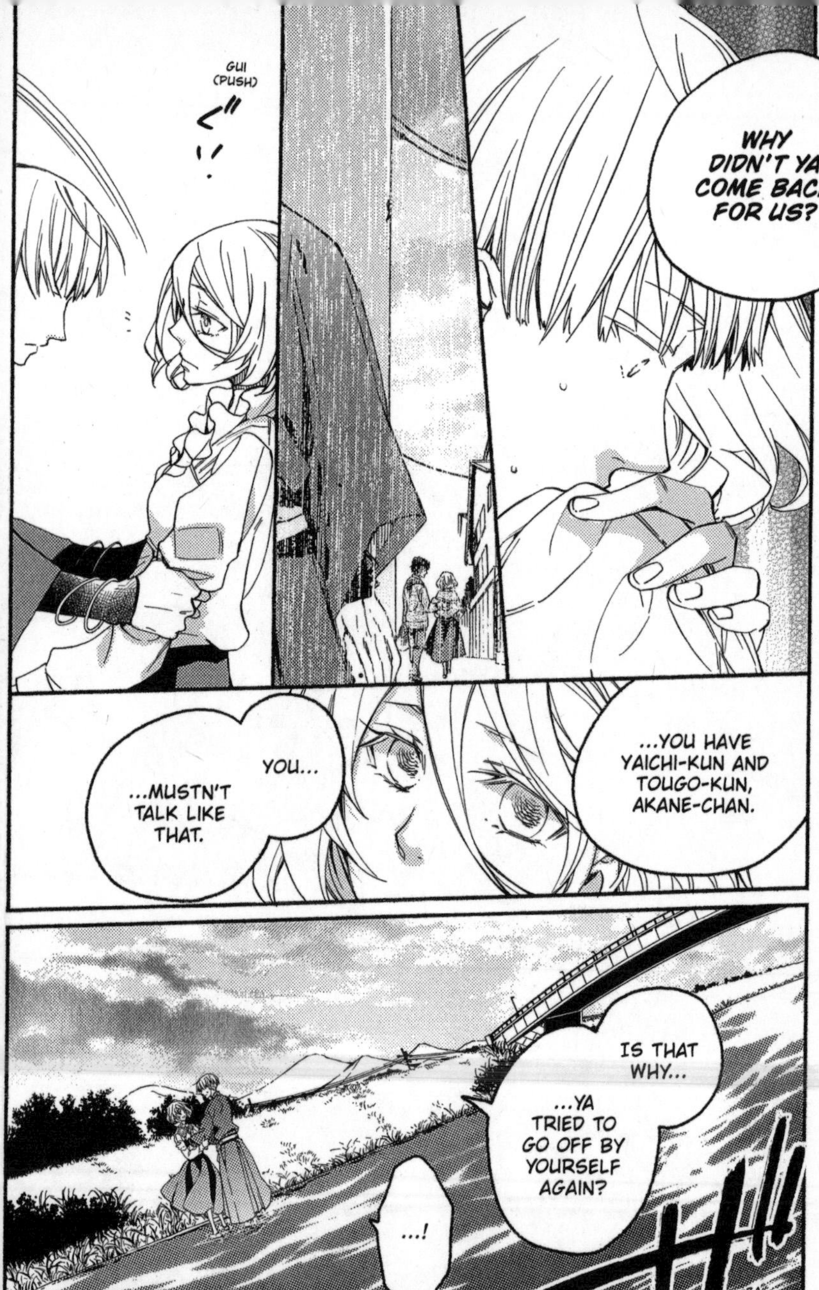
WHY DIDN'T YA COME BACK FOR US?
GUI (PUSH)
...YOU HAVE YAICHI-KUN AND TOUGO-KUN, AKANE-CHAN.
YOU...
...MUSTN'T TALK LIKE THAT.
IS THAT WHY...
...YA TRIED TO GO OFF BY YOURSELF AGAIN?
ZA (ZSH)
...!

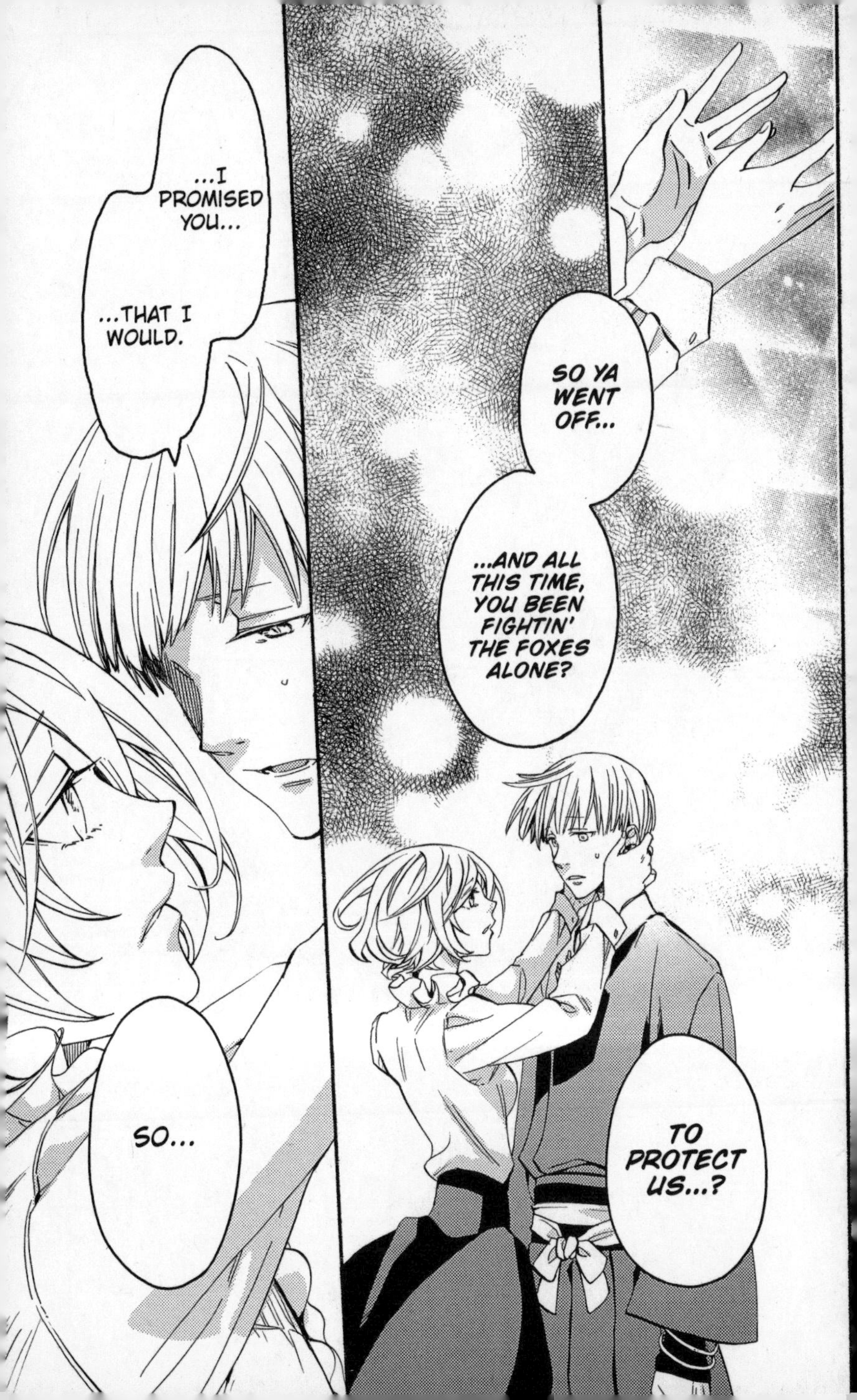
SO YA WENT OFF...
...AND ALL THIS TIME, YOU BEEN FIGHTIN' THE FOXES ALONE?
TO PROTECT US...?
...I PROMISED YOU...
...THAT I WOULD.
SO...

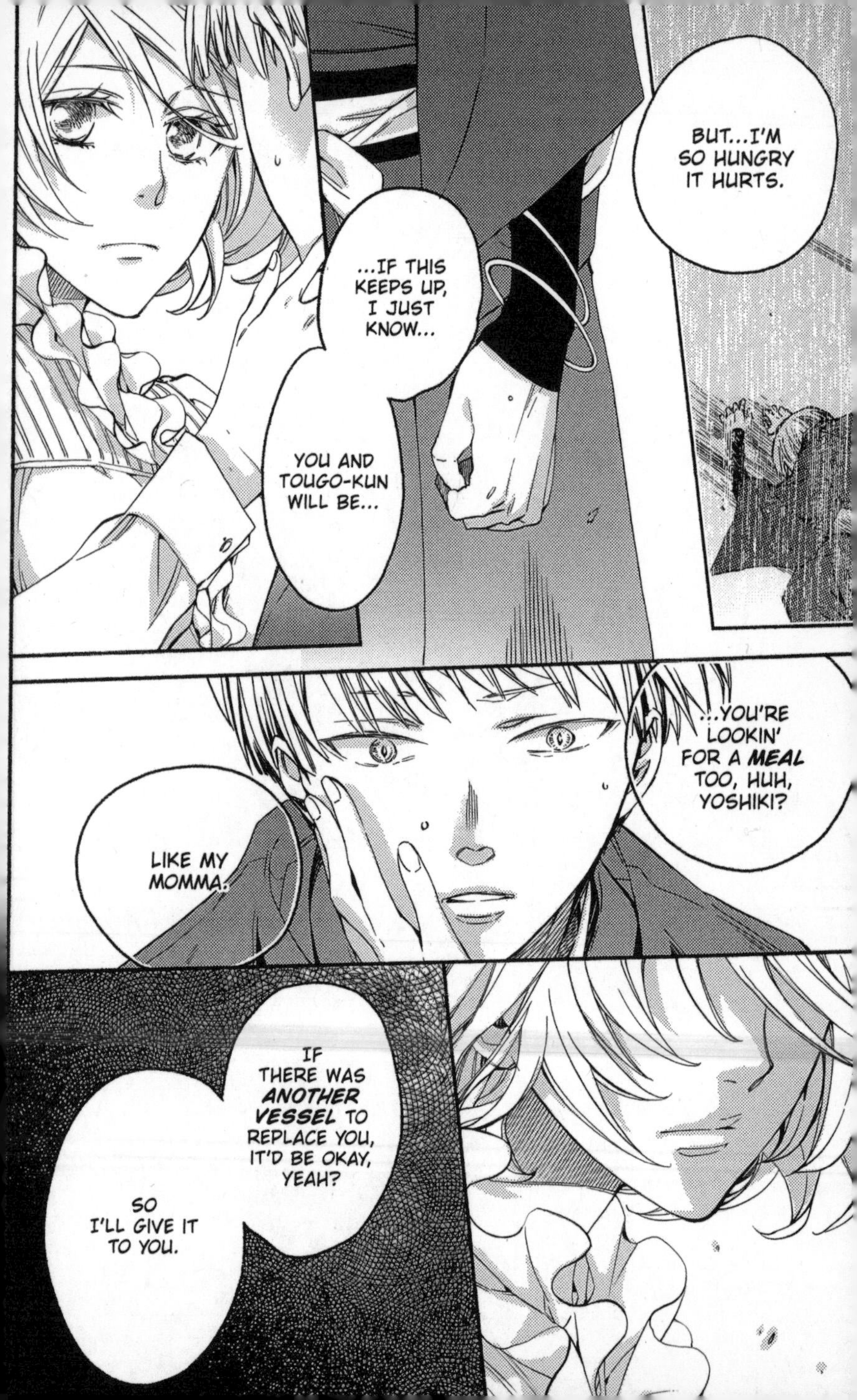
BUT...I'M SO HUNGRY IT HURTS.
...IF THIS KEEPS UP, I JUST KNOW...
YOU AND TOUGO-KUN WILL BE...
...YOU'RE LOOKIN' FOR A ***MEAL*** TOO, HUH, YOSHIKI?
LIKE MY MOMMA.
IF THERE WAS ***ANOTHER VESSEL*** TO REPLACE YOU, IT'D BE OKAY, YEAH?
SO I'LL GIVE IT TO YOU.

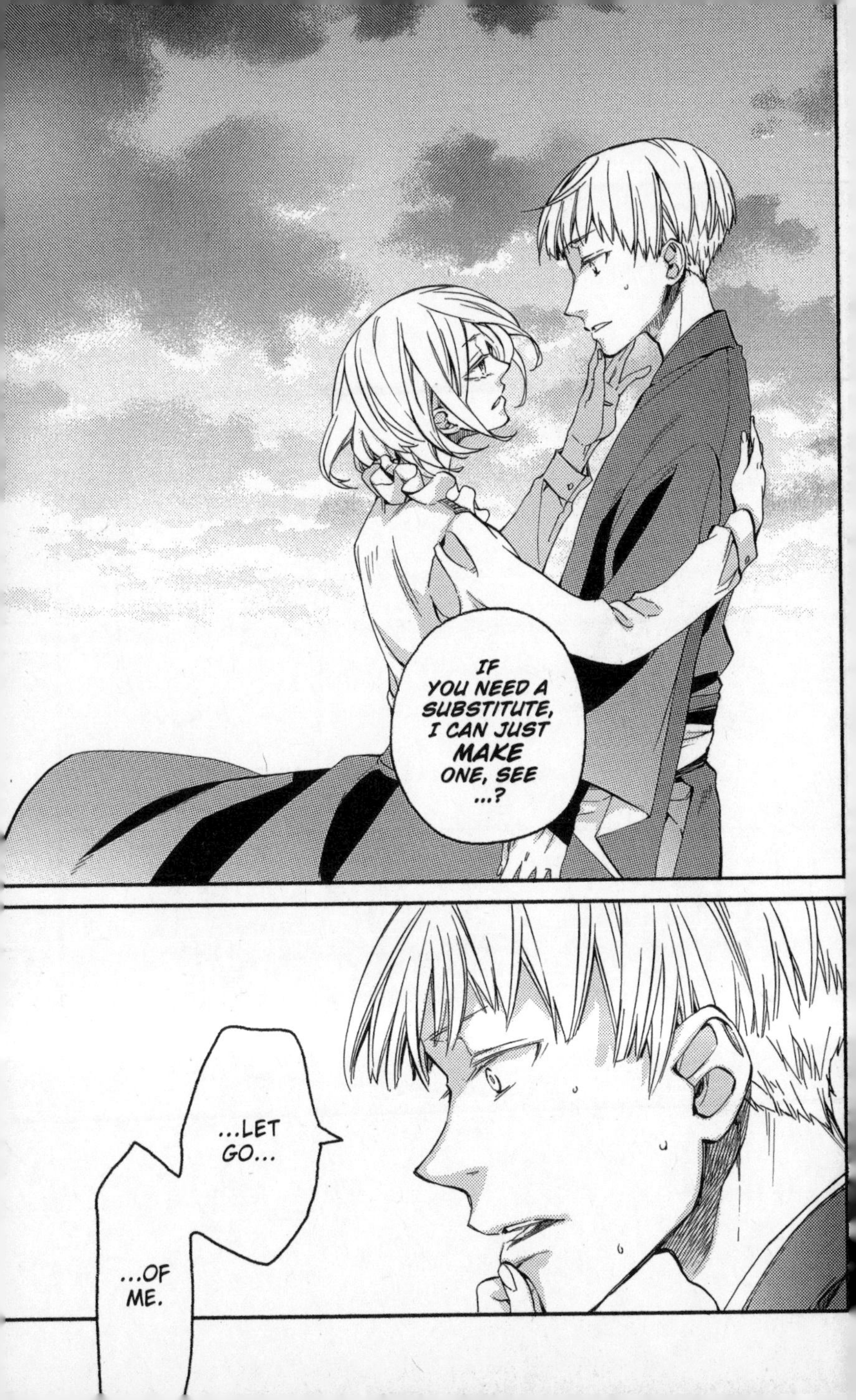
IF YOU NEED A SUBSTITUTE, I CAN JUST MAKE ONE, SEE ...?
...LET GO...
...OF ME.

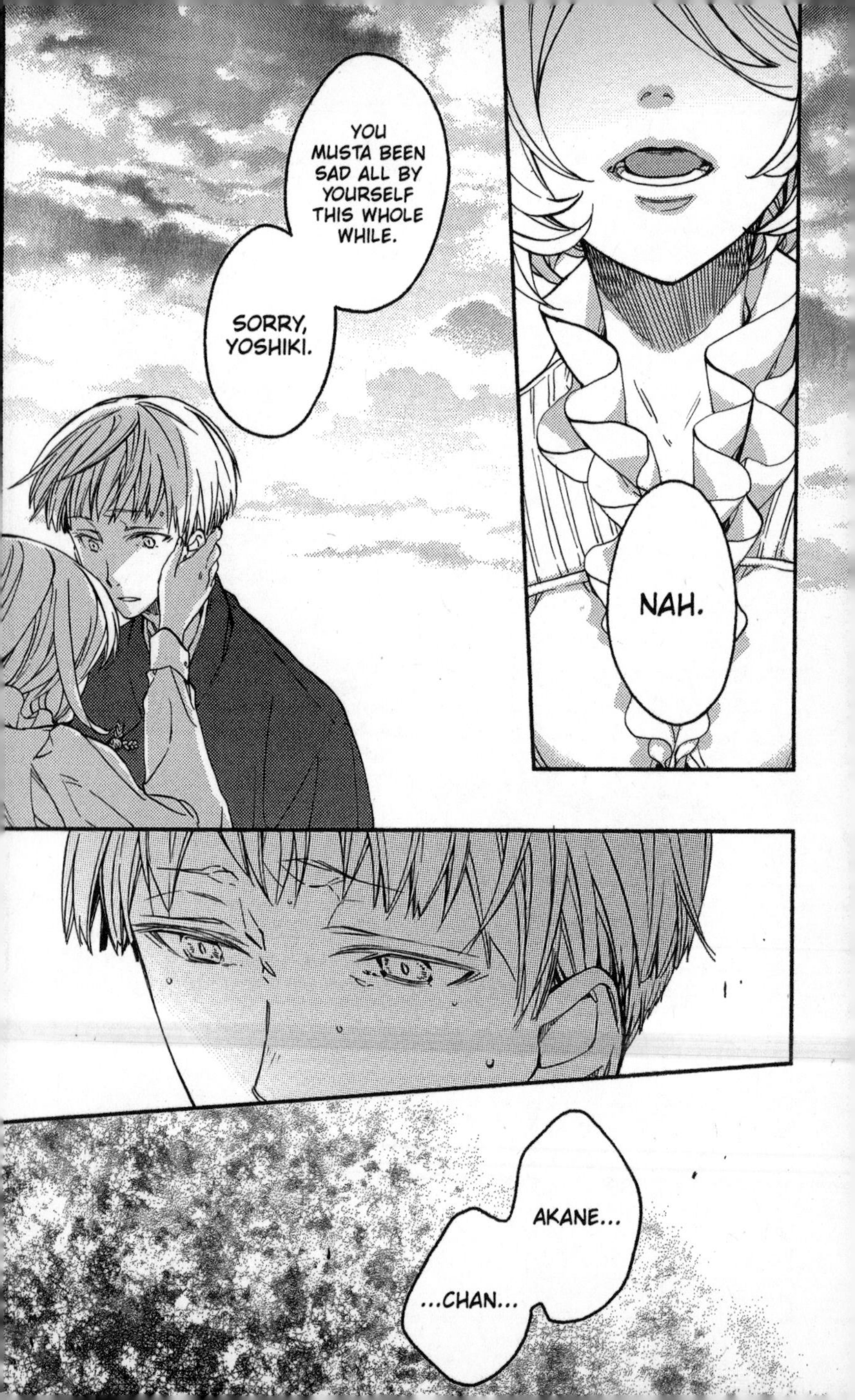
NAH.
YOU MUSTA BEEN SAD ALL BY YOURSELF THIS WHOLE WHILE.
SORRY, YOSHIKI.
AKANE...
...CHAN...

SIGN: TSUBAKI
椿

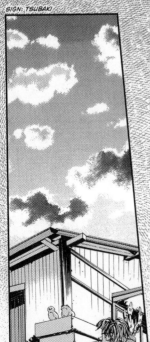

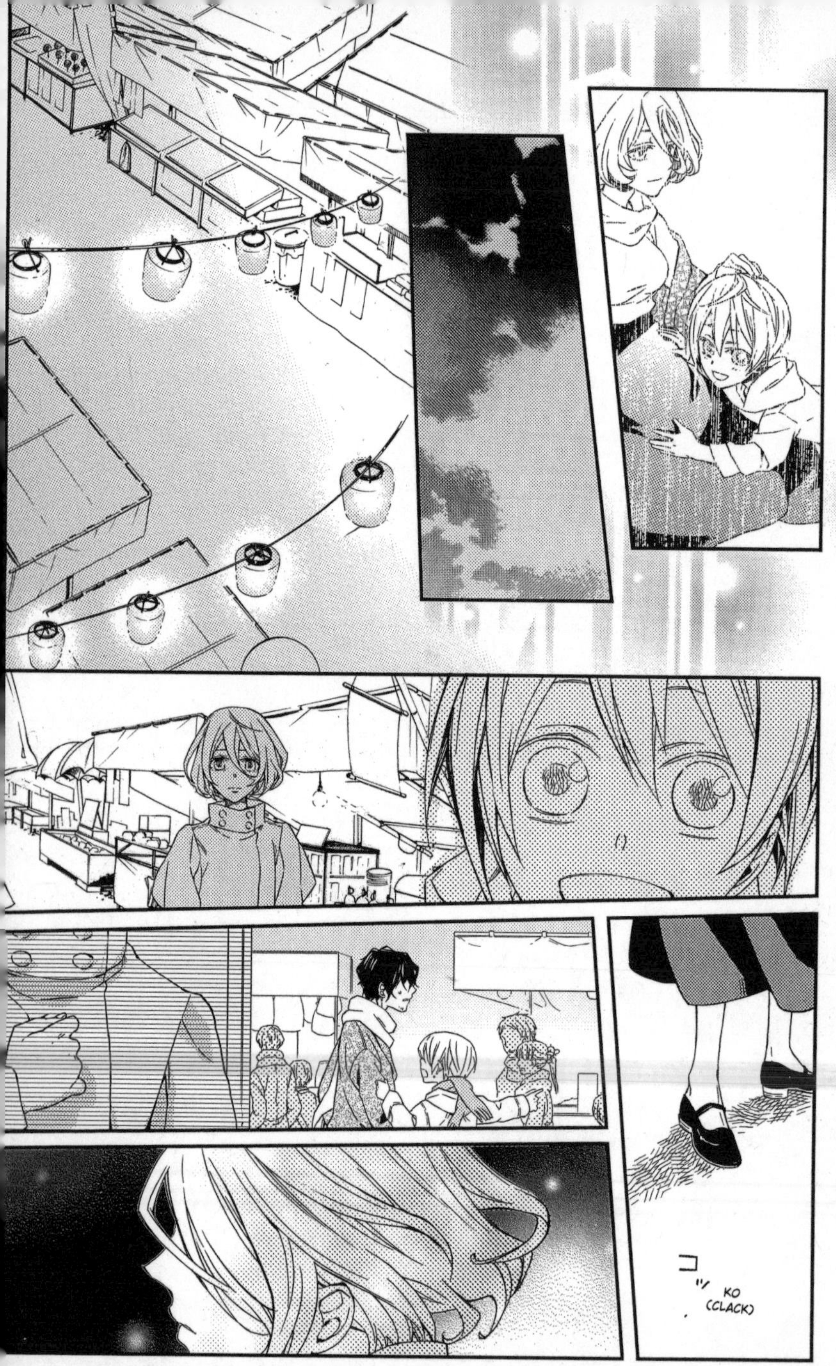
コッ
KO
(CLACK)

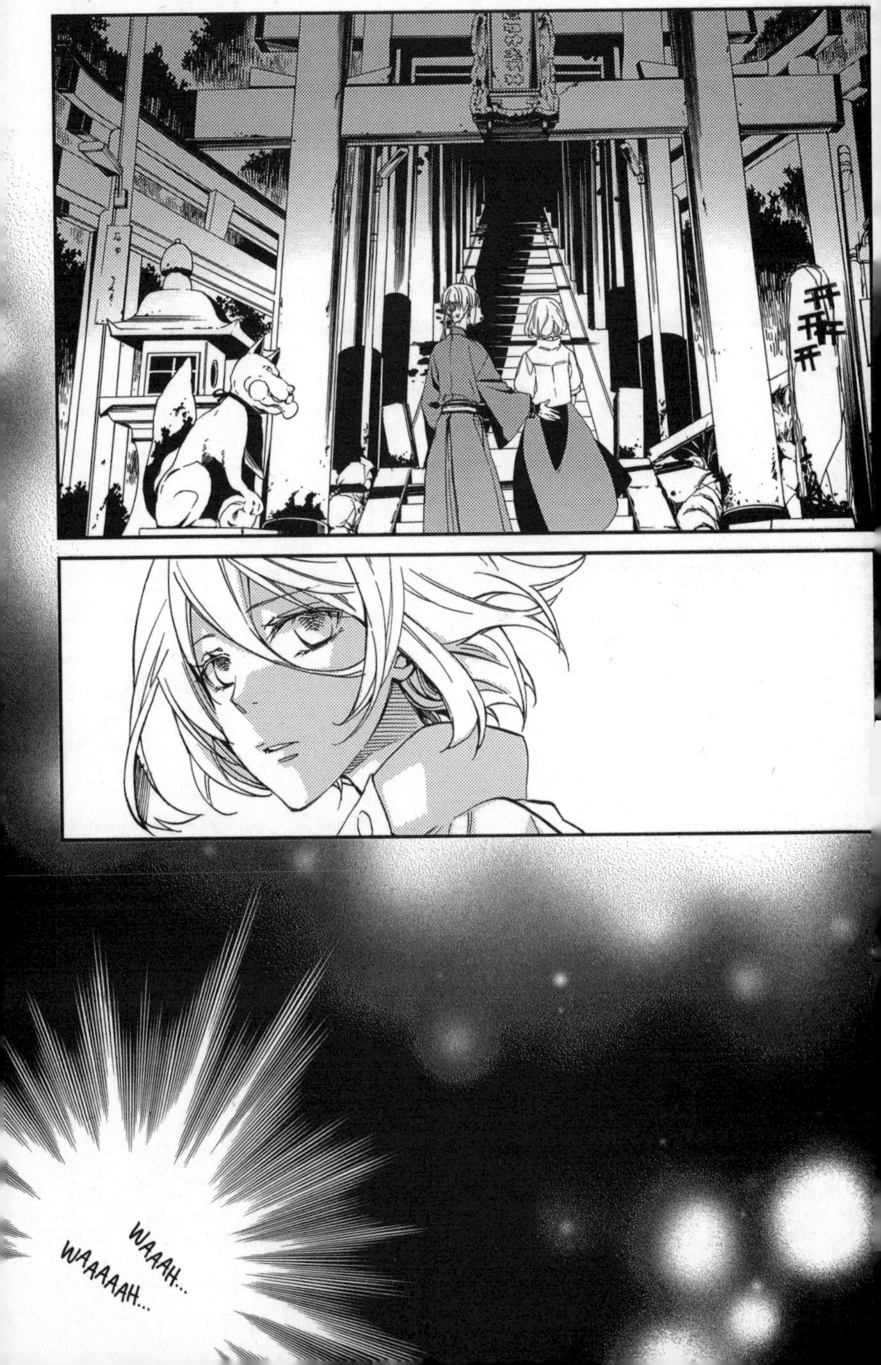
WAAAH...
WAAAAAH...

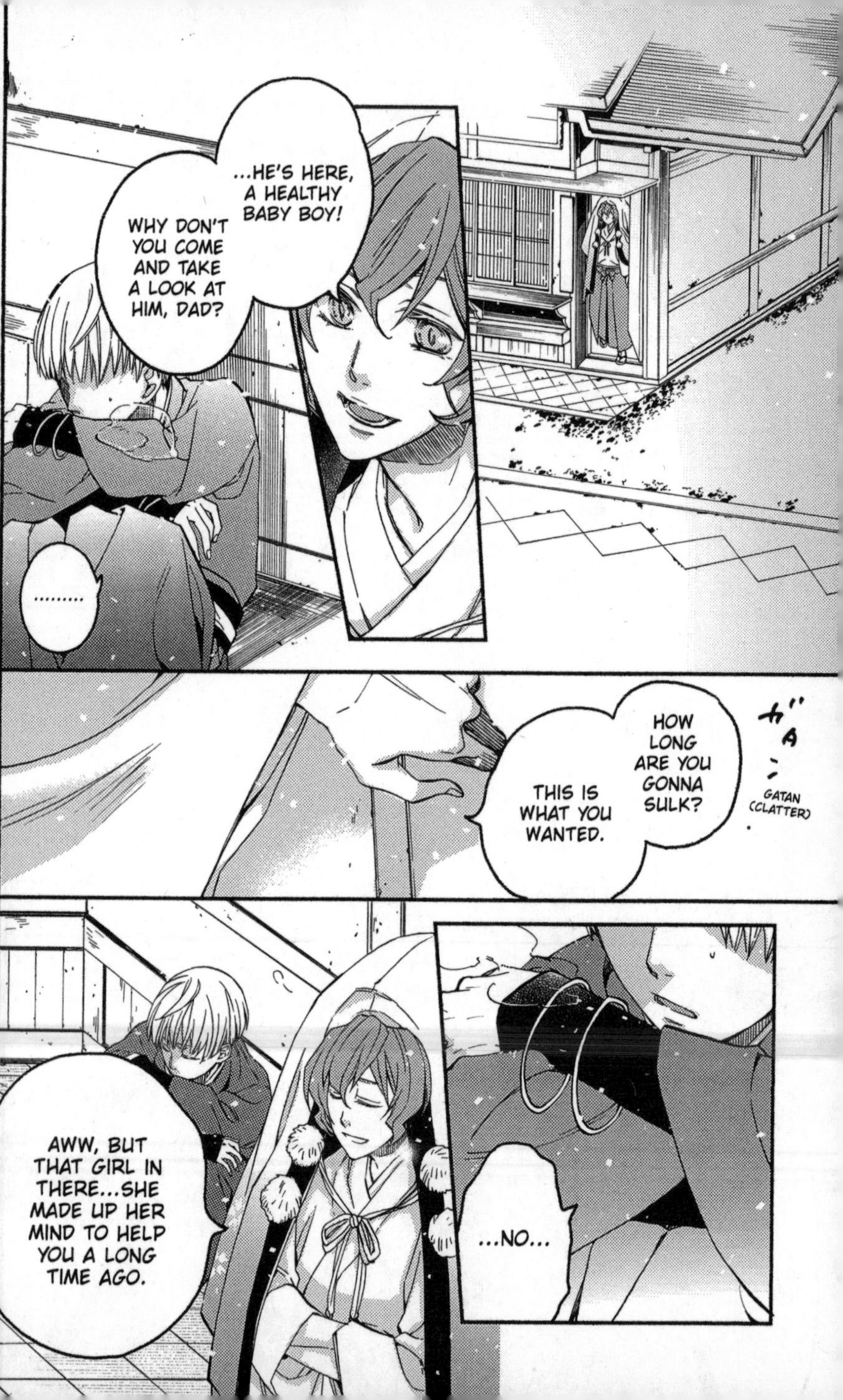

...HE'S HERE, A HEALTHY BABY BOY!
WHY DON'T YOU COME AND TAKE A LOOK AT HIM, DAD?
....
GATAN (CLATTER)
HOW LONG ARE YOU GONNA SULK?
THIS IS WHAT YOU WANTED.
...NO...
AWW, BUT THAT GIRL IN THERE...SHE MADE UP HER MIND TO HELP YOU A LONG TIME AGO.

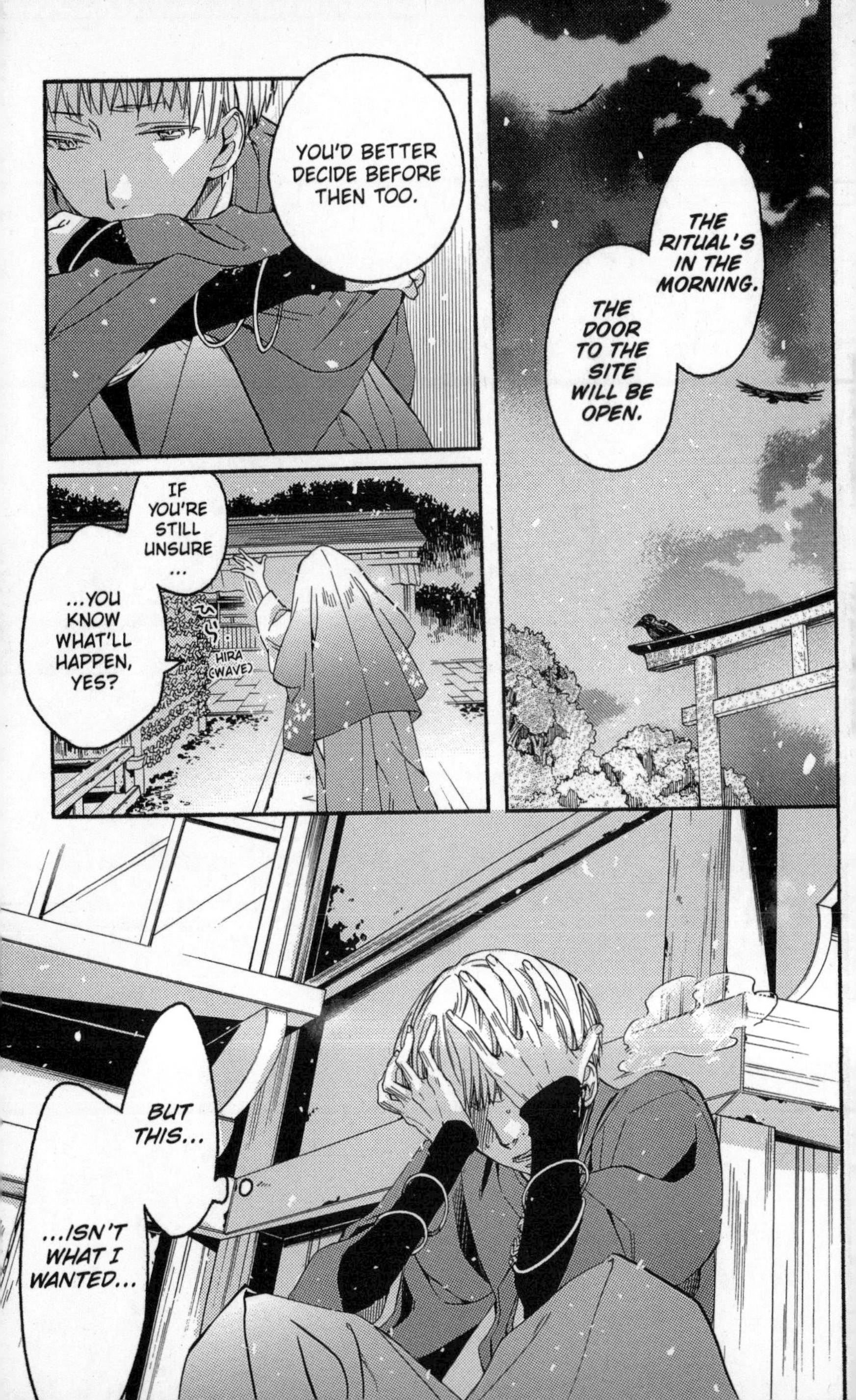
THE RITUAL'S IN THE MORNING.
THE DOOR TO THE SITE WILL BE OPEN.
YOU'D BETTER DECIDE BEFORE THEN TOO.
IF YOU'RE STILL UNSURE...
...YOU KNOW WHAT'LL HAPPEN, YES?
HIRA (WAVE)
BUT THIS...
...ISN'T WHAT I WANTED...

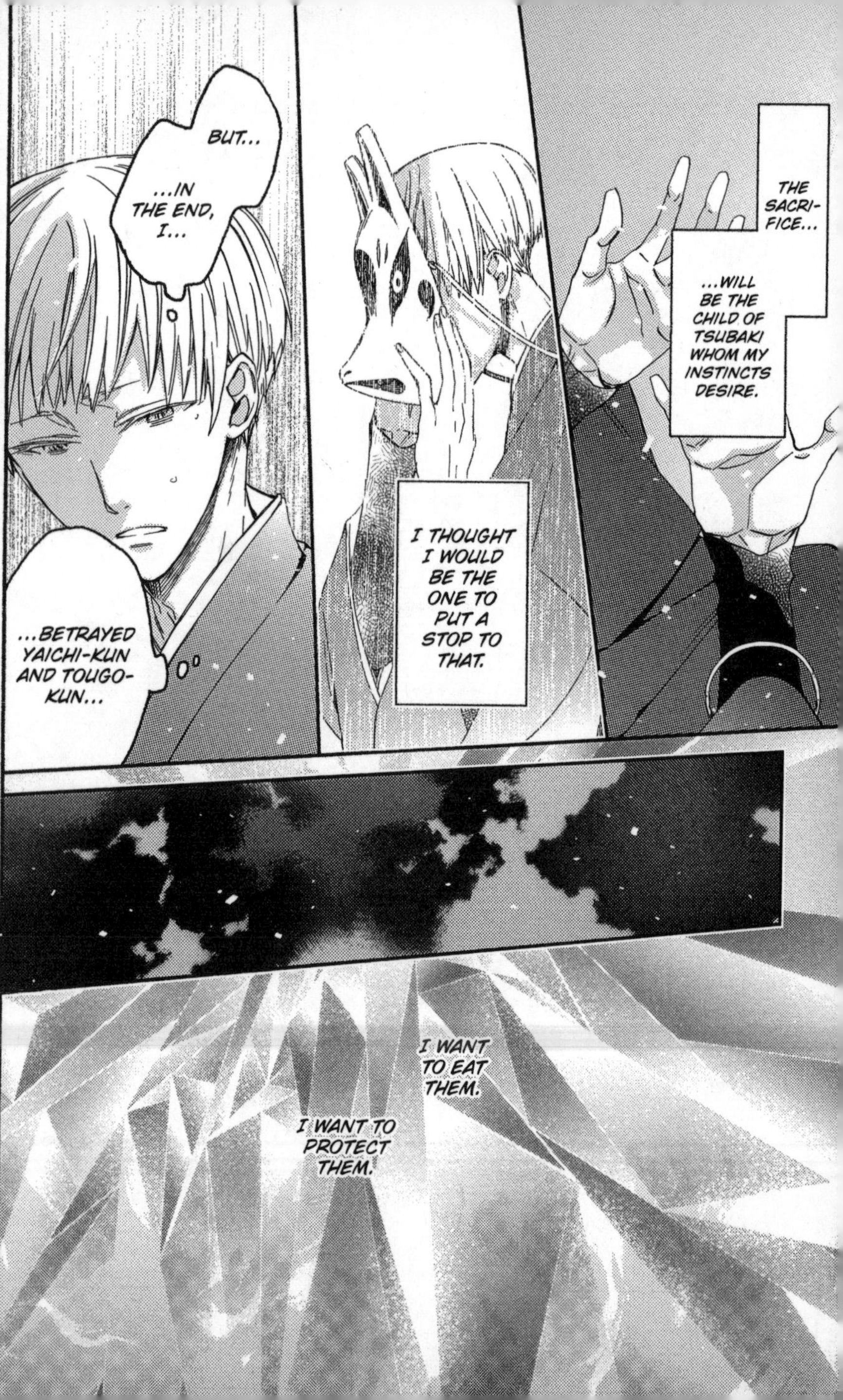
THE SACRIFICE...
...WILL BE THE CHILD OF TSUBAKI WHOM MY INSTINCTS DESIRE.
I THOUGHT I WOULD BE THE ONE TO PUT A STOP TO THAT.
BUT...
...IN THE END, I...
...BETRAYED YAICHI-KUN AND TOUGO-KUN...
I WANT TO EAT THEM.
I WANT TO PROTECT THEM.

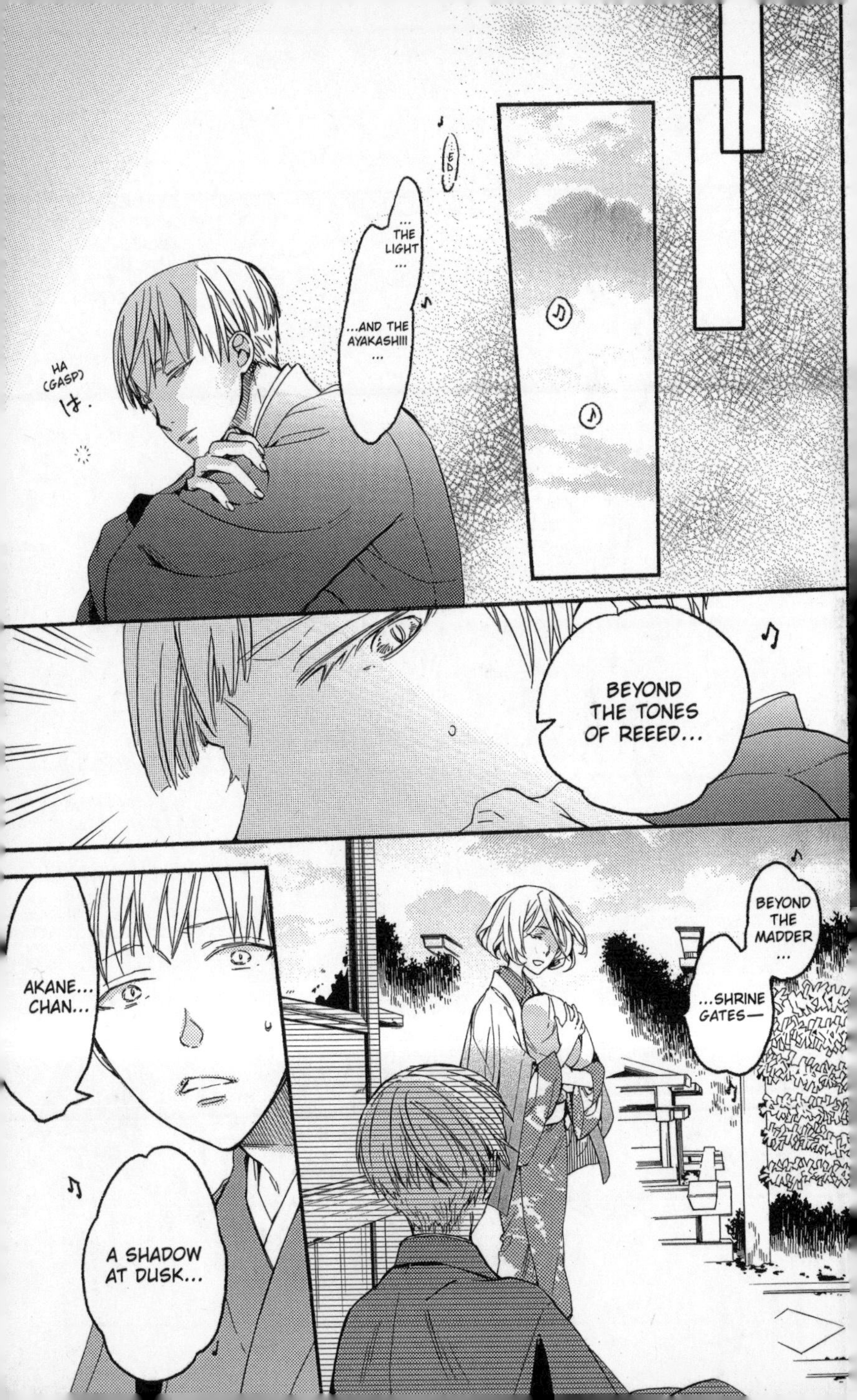
...ED...
... THE LIGHT ...
...AND THE AYAKASHIII ...
HA (GASP) は.
BEYOND THE TONES OF REEED...
BEYOND THE MADDER ...
...SHRINE GATES—
AKANE... CHAN...
A SHADOW AT DUSK...

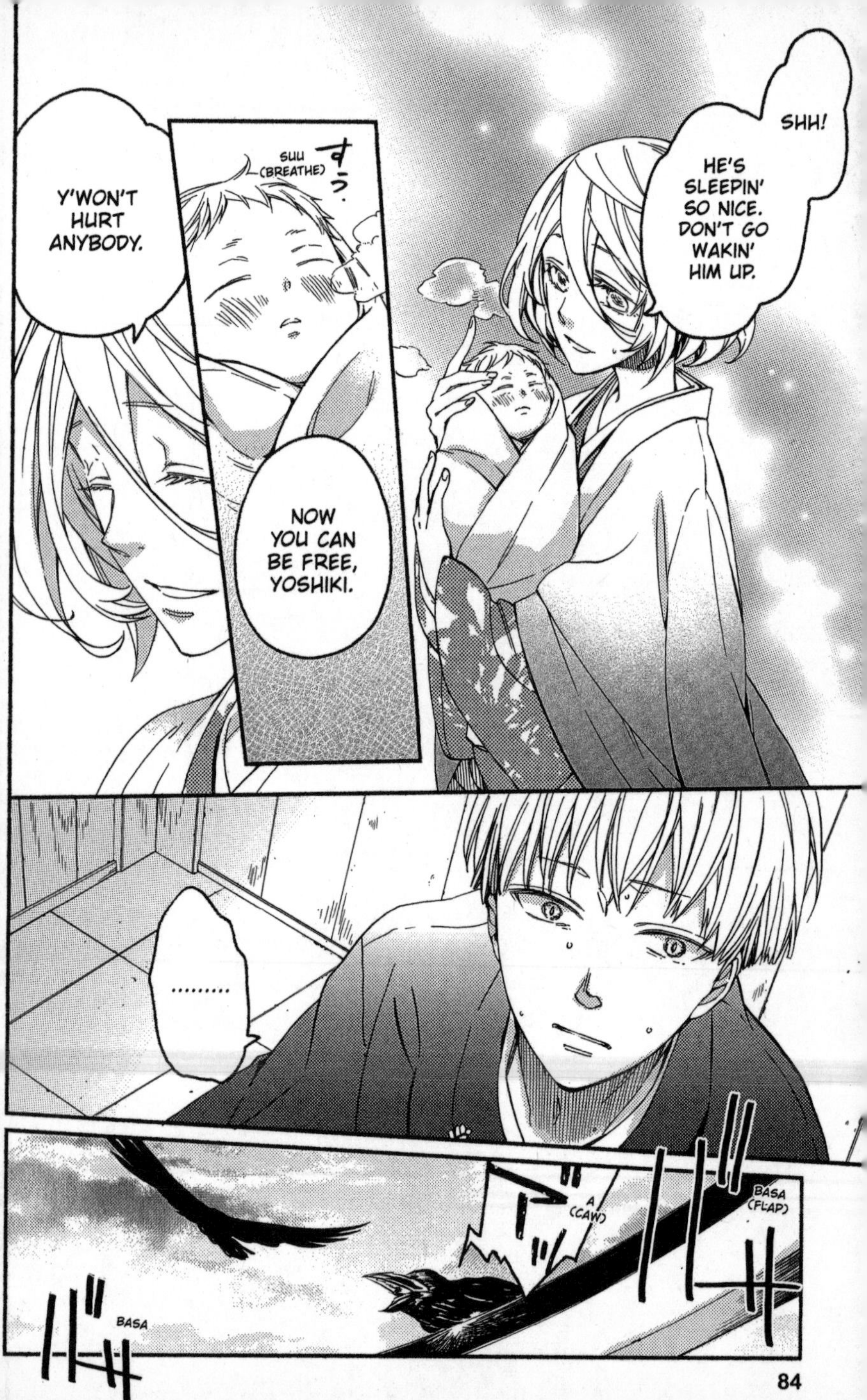
SHH!
HE'S SLEEPIN' SO NICE. DON'T GO WAKIN' HIM UP.
すぅ
SUU (BREATHE)
NOW YOU CAN BE FREE, YOSHIKI.
Y'WON'T HURT ANYBODY.
....
BASA (FLAP)
A (CAW)
BASA

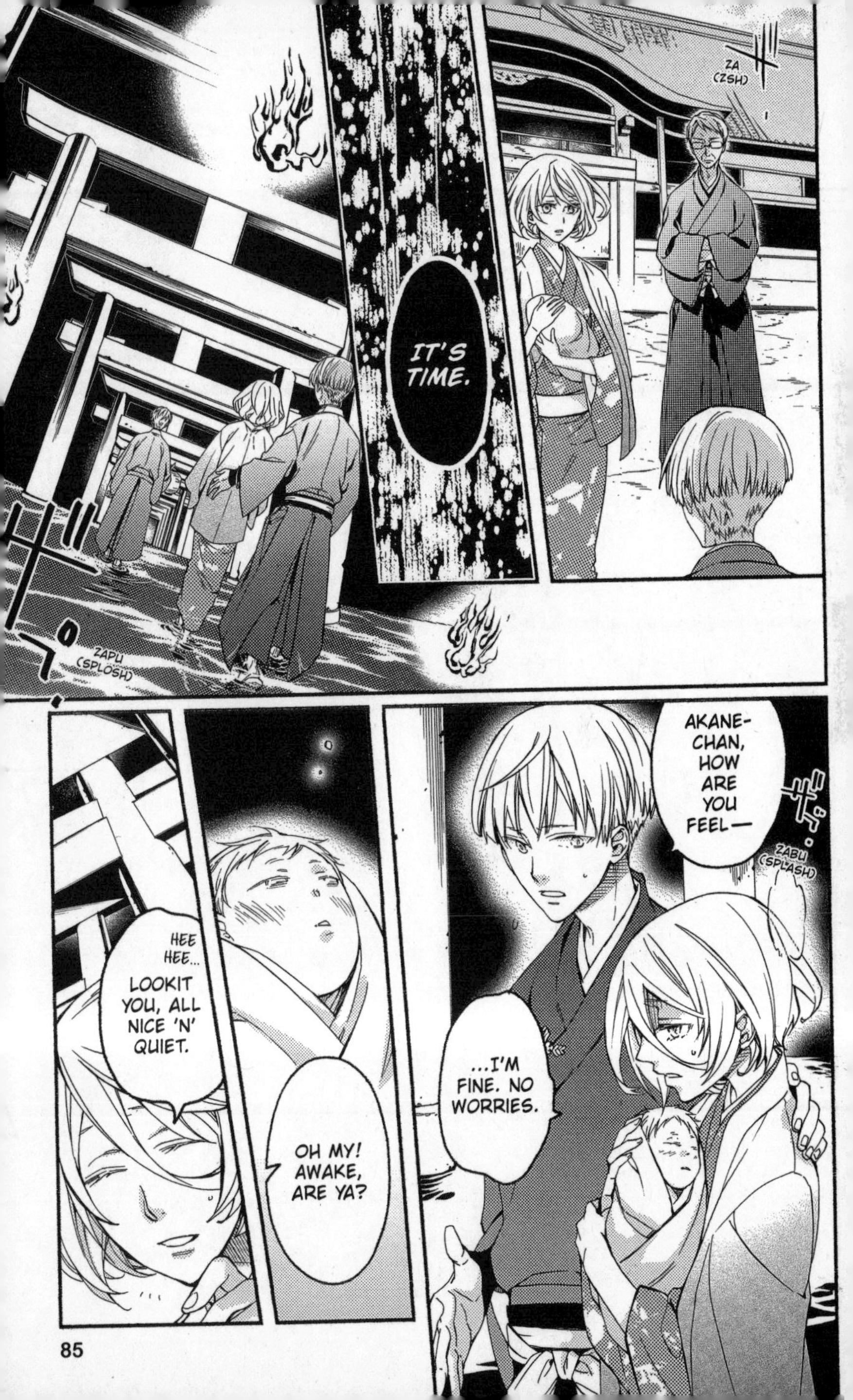
ZA (ZSH)
IT'S TIME.
ZAPU (SPLOSH)
AKANE-CHAN, HOW ARE YOU FEEL—
ZABU (SPLASH)
...I'M FINE. NO WORRIES.
OH MY! AWAKE, ARE YA?
HEE HEE...
LOOKIT YOU, ALL NICE 'N' QUIET.

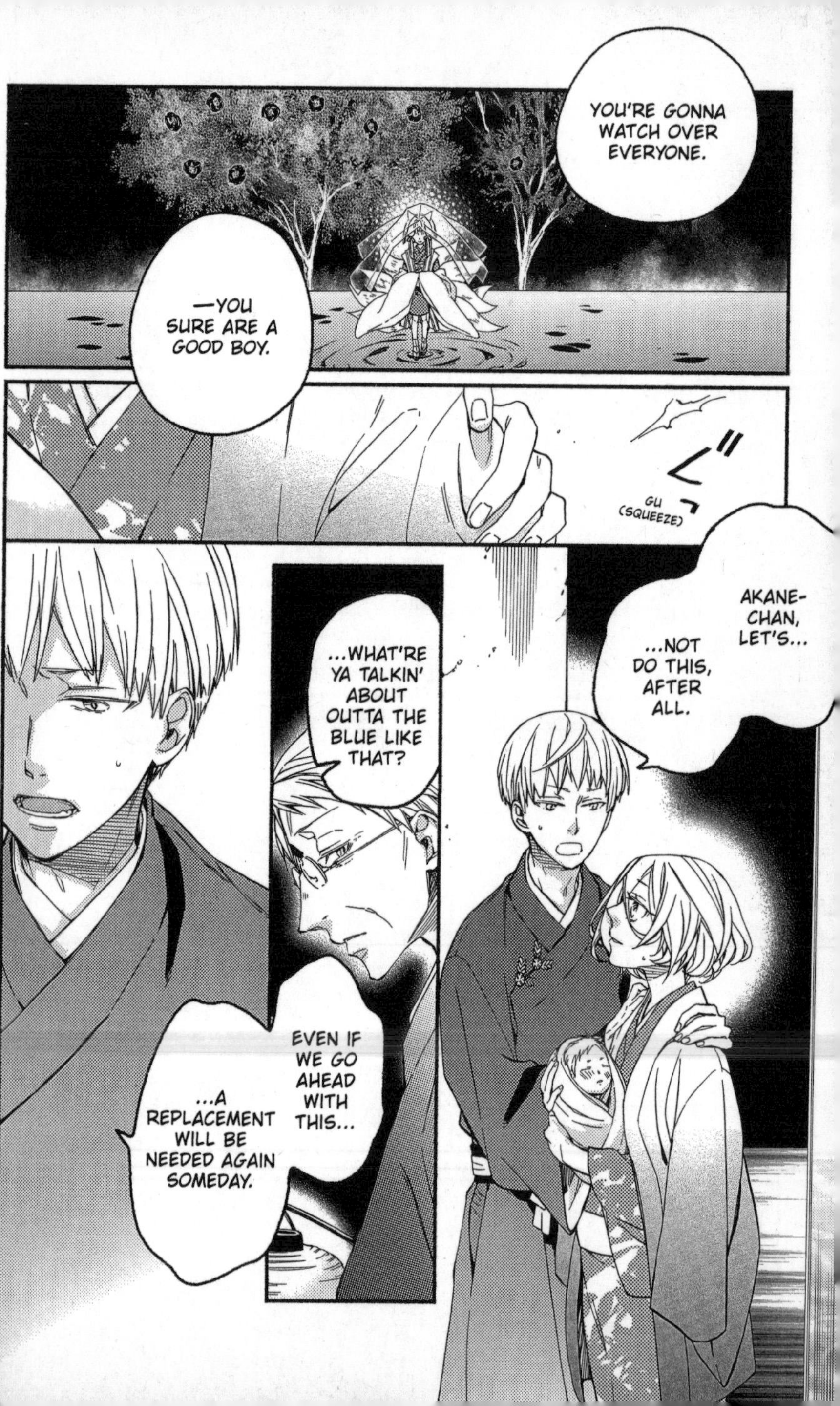
YOU'RE GONNA WATCH OVER EVERYONE.
—YOU SURE ARE A GOOD BOY.
GU (SQUEEZE)
AKANE-CHAN, LET'S...
...NOT DO THIS, AFTER ALL.
...WHAT'RE YA TALKIN' ABOUT OUTTA THE BLUE LIKE THAT?
EVEN IF WE GO AHEAD WITH THIS...
...A REPLACEMENT WILL BE NEEDED AGAIN SOMEDAY.

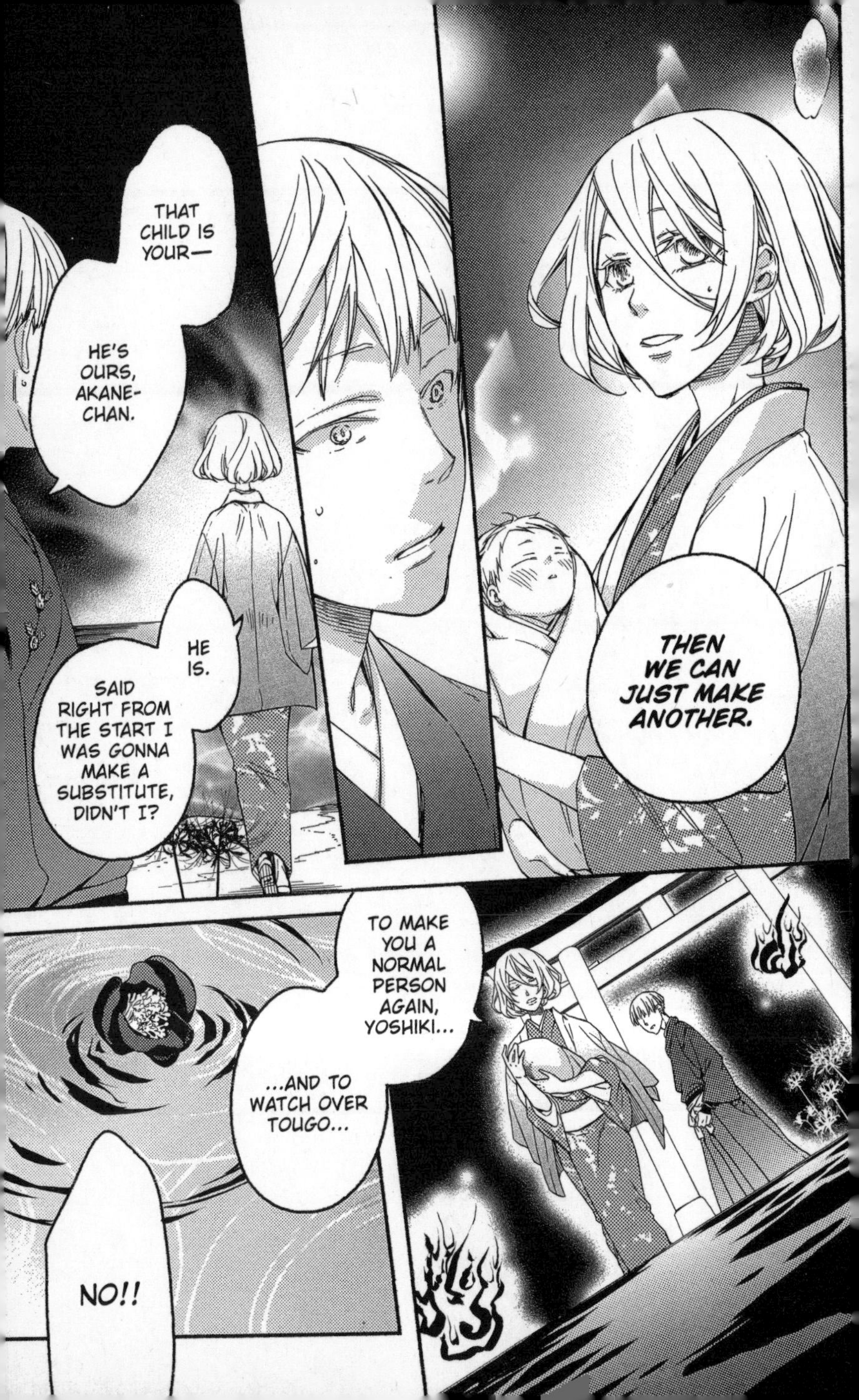
THEN WE CAN JUST MAKE ANOTHER.
THAT CHILD IS YOUR—
HE'S OURS, AKANE-CHAN.
HE IS.
SAID RIGHT FROM THE START I WAS GONNA MAKE A SUBSTITUTE, DIDN'T I?
TO MAKE YOU A NORMAL PERSON AGAIN, YOSHIKI...
...AND TO WATCH OVER TOUGO...
NO!!

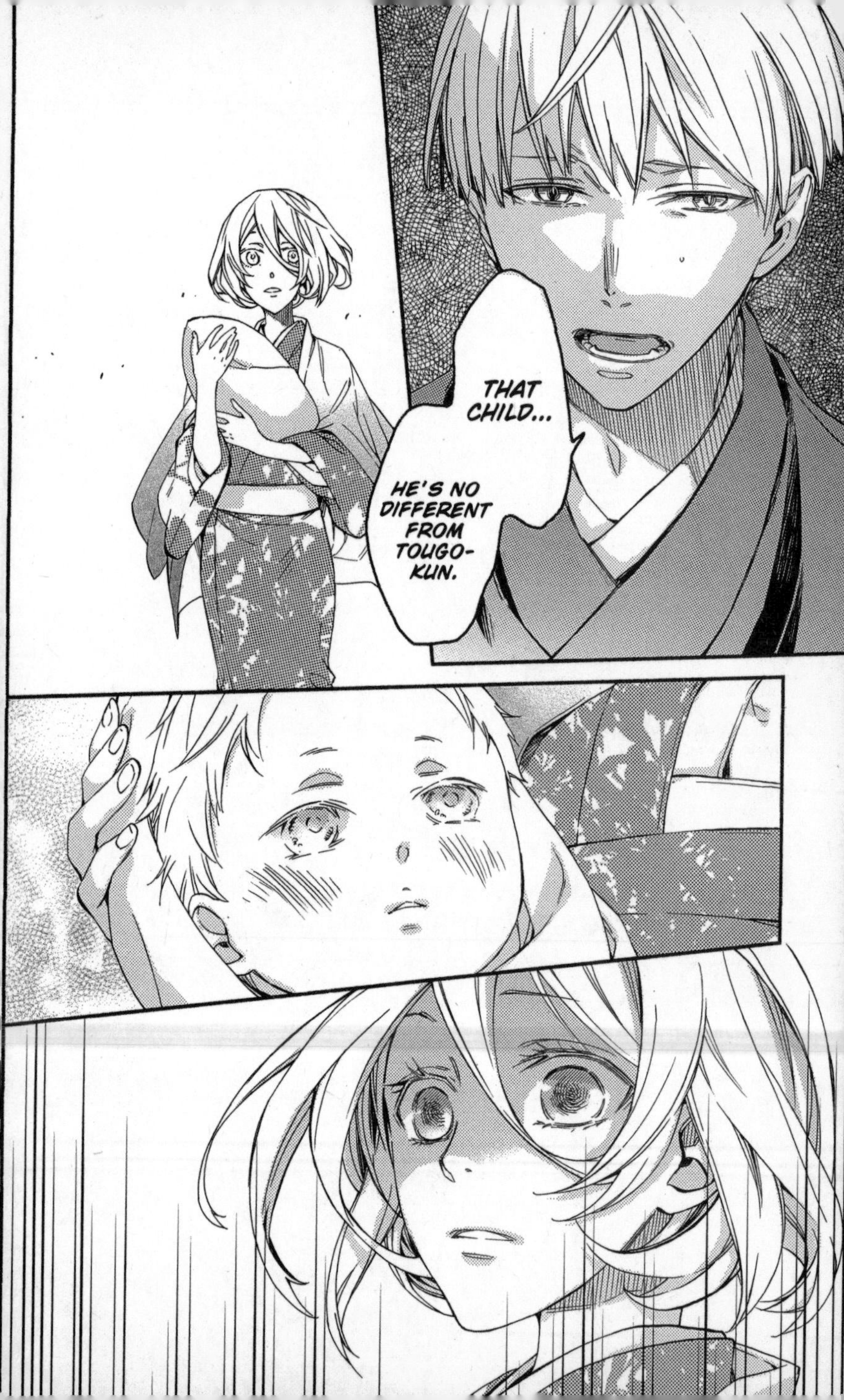
THAT CHILD...
HE'S NO DIFFERENT FROM TOUGO-KUN.

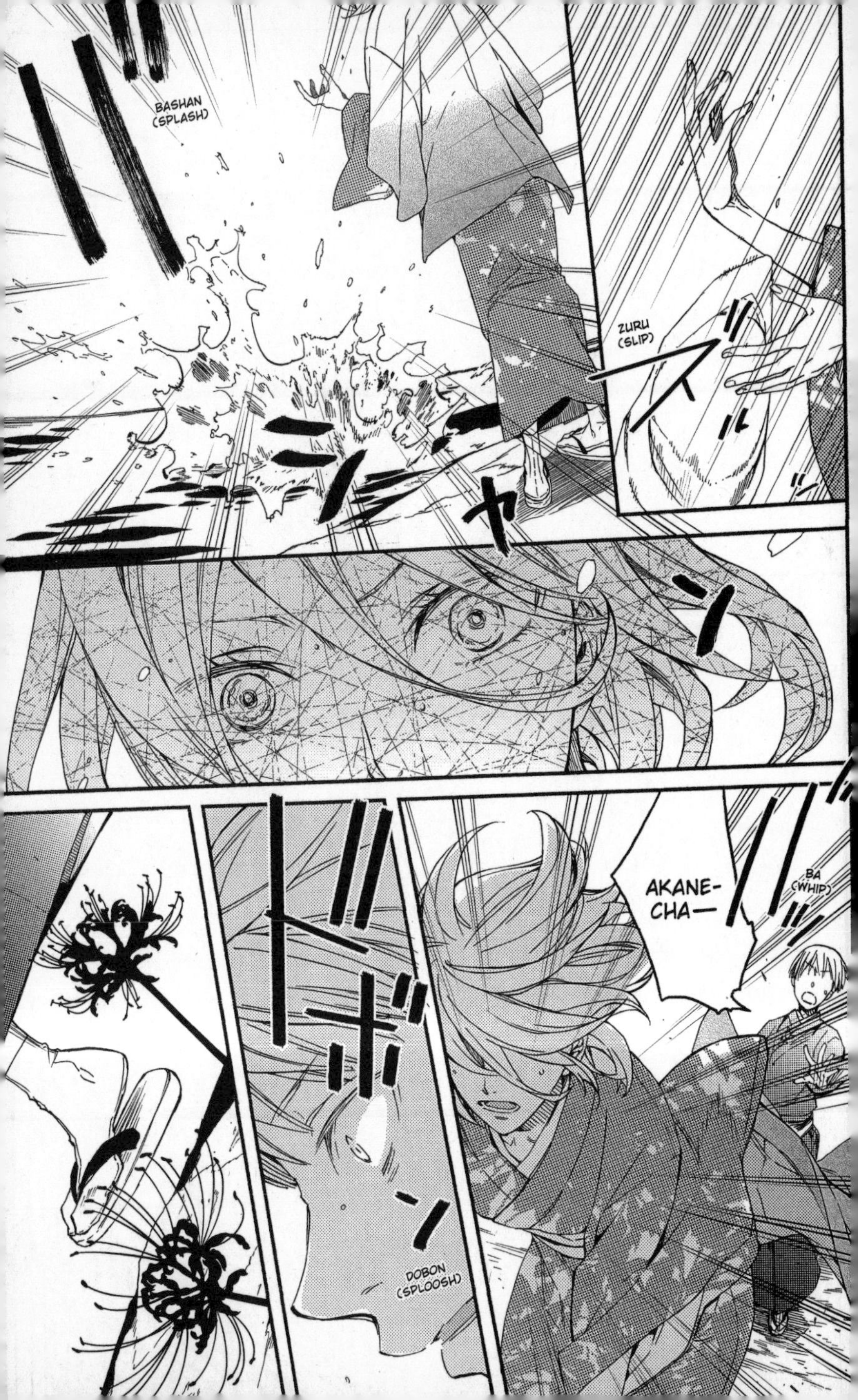
ZURU (SLIP)
BASHAN (SPLASH)
BA (WHIP)
AKANE-CHA—
DOBON (SPLOOSH)

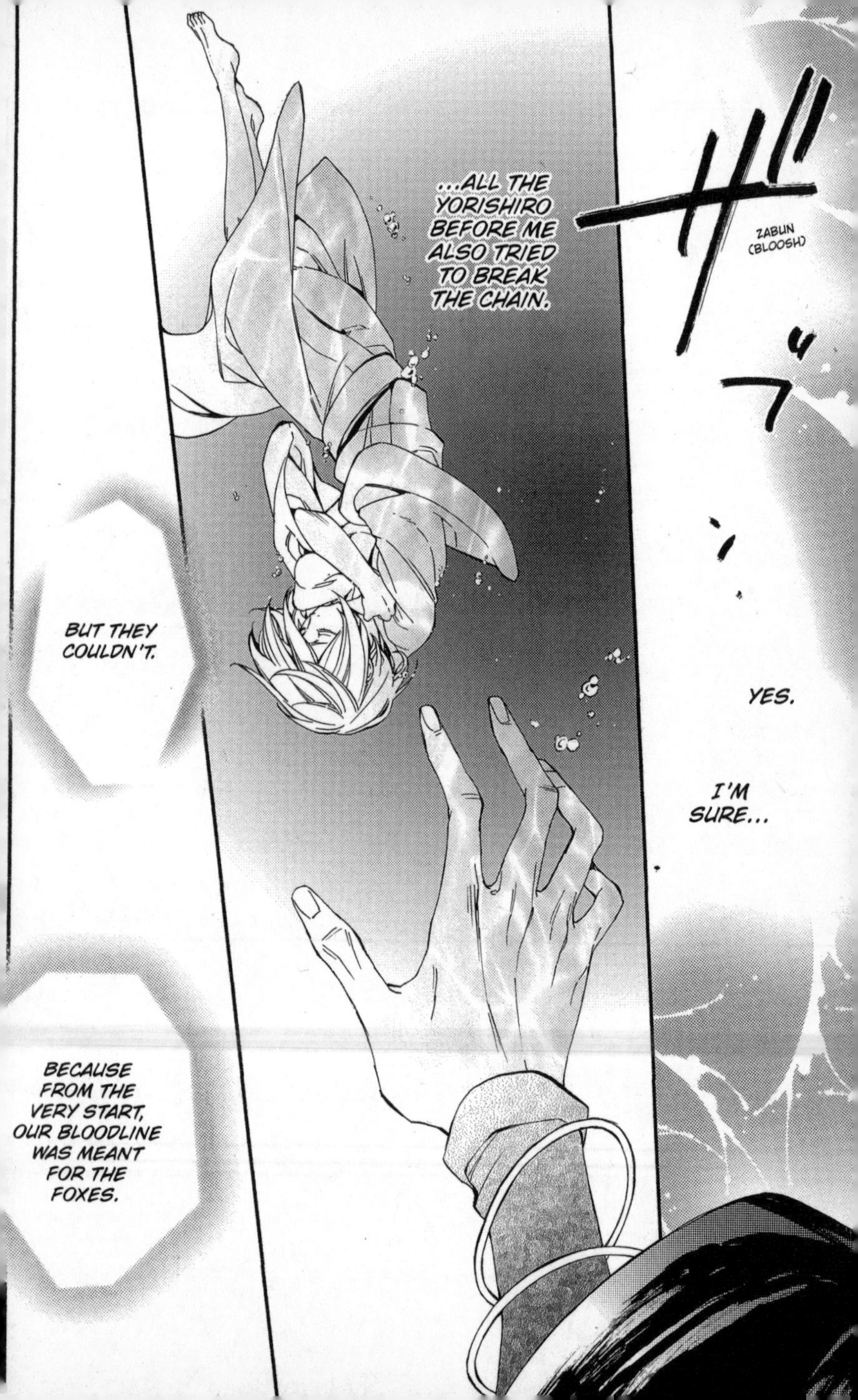
ZABUN (BLOOSH)
YES.
I'M SURE...
...ALL THE YORISHIRO BEFORE ME ALSO TRIED TO BREAK THE CHAIN.
BUT THEY COULDN'T.
BECAUSE FROM THE VERY START, OUR BLOODLINE WAS MEANT FOR THE FOXES.

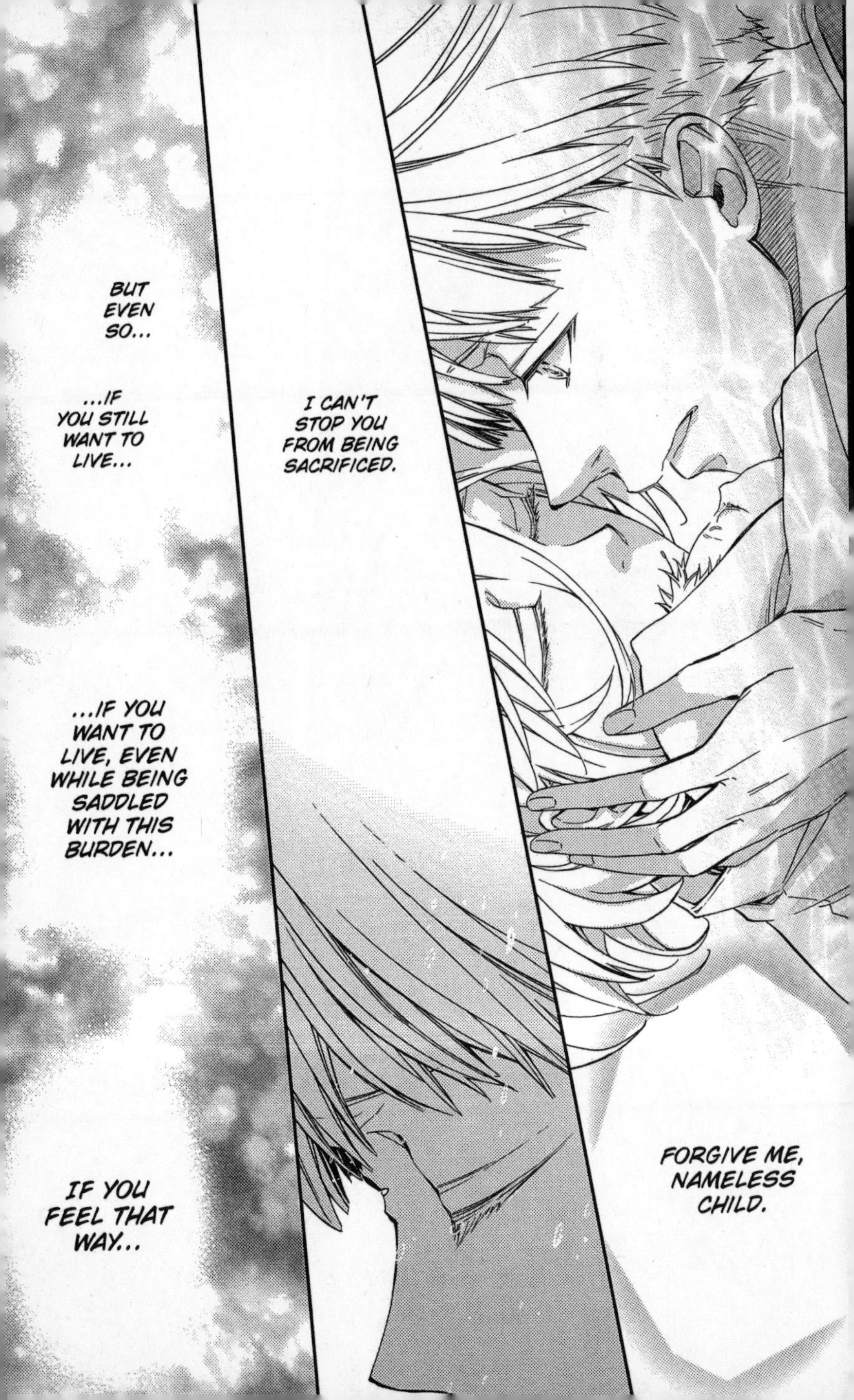
FORGIVE ME, NAMELESS CHILD.
I CAN'T STOP YOU FROM BEING SACRIFICED.
BUT EVEN SO...
...IF YOU STILL WANT TO LIVE...
...IF YOU WANT TO LIVE, EVEN WHILE BEING SADDLED WITH THIS BURDEN...
IF YOU FEEL THAT WAY...

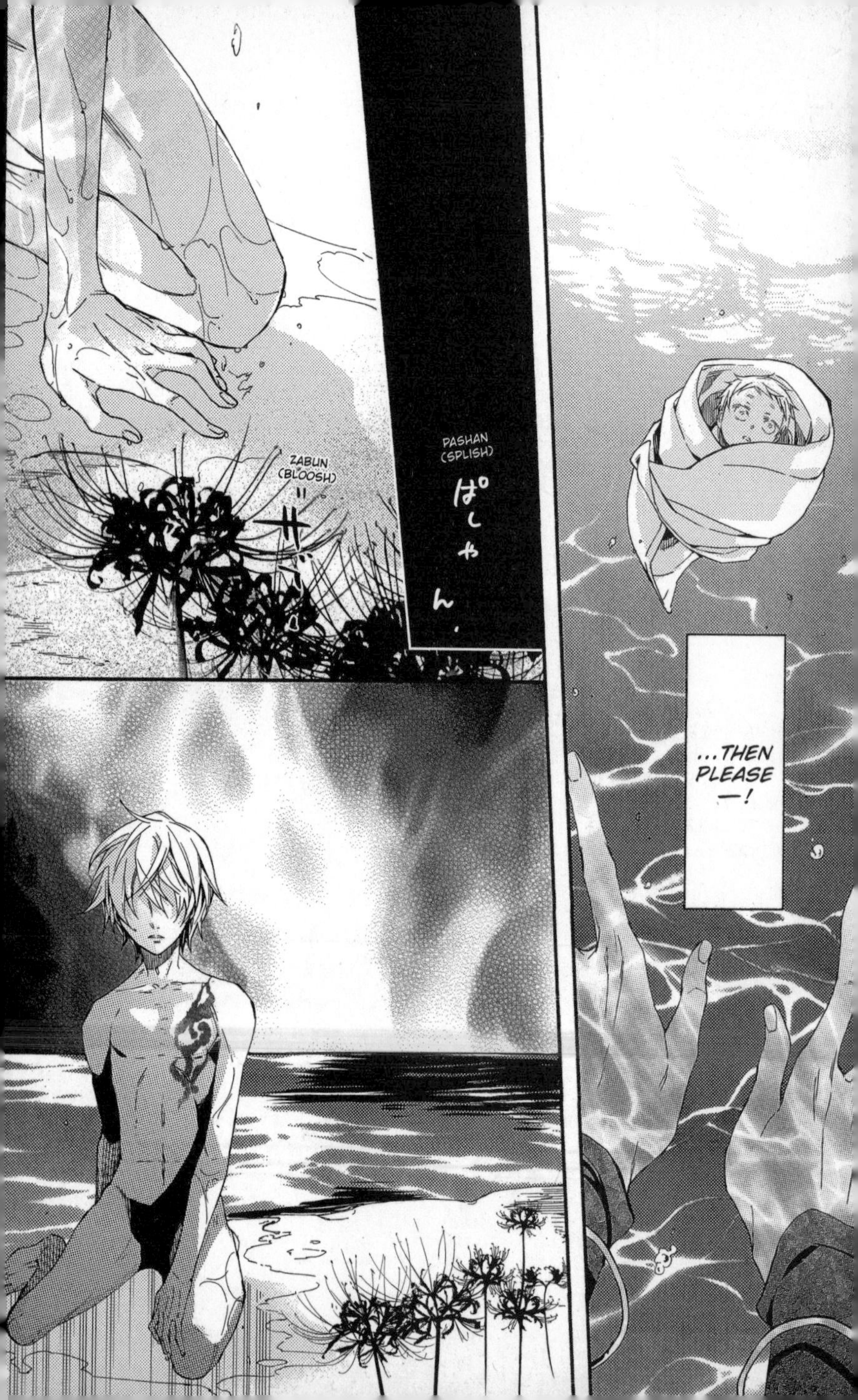
...THEN PLEASE—!
PASHAN (SPLISH)
ぱしゃん.
ZABUN (BLOOSH)

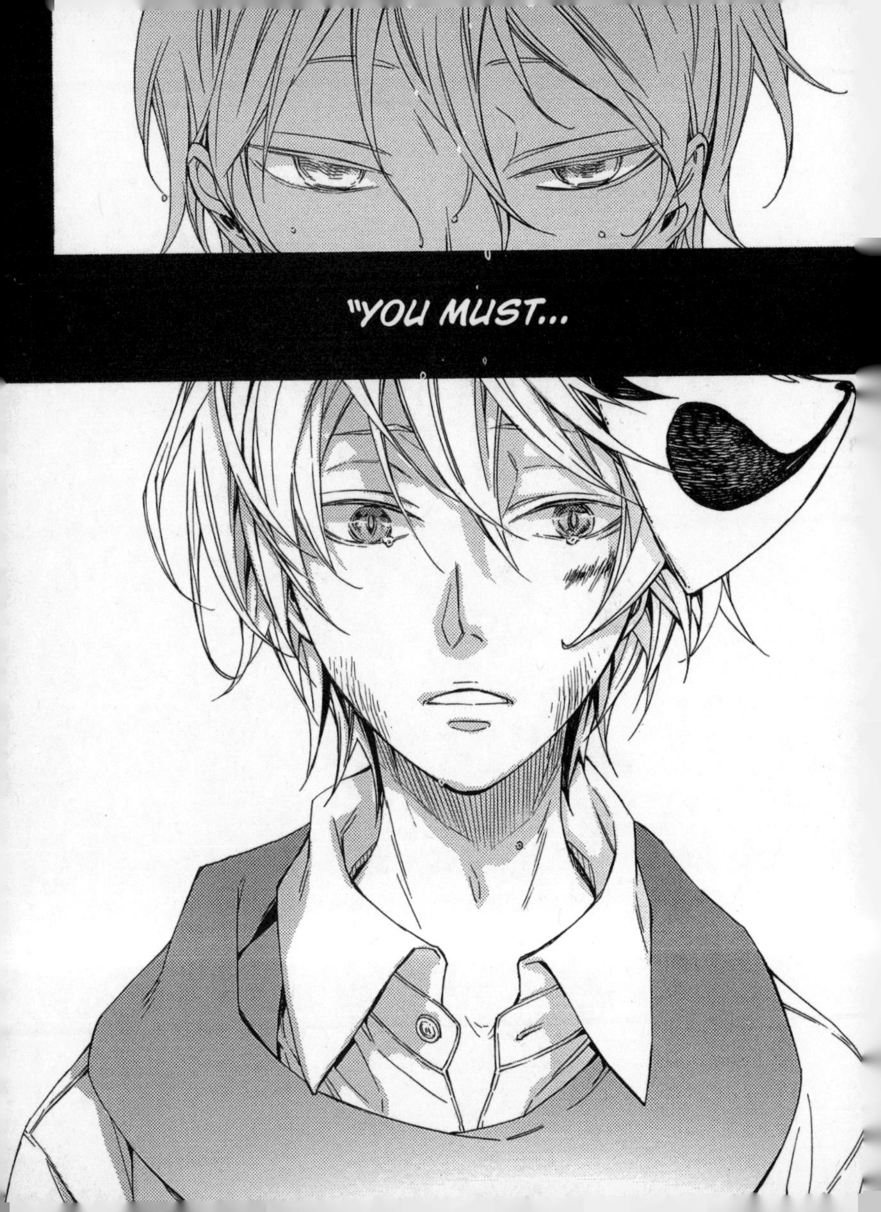
"YOU MUST...

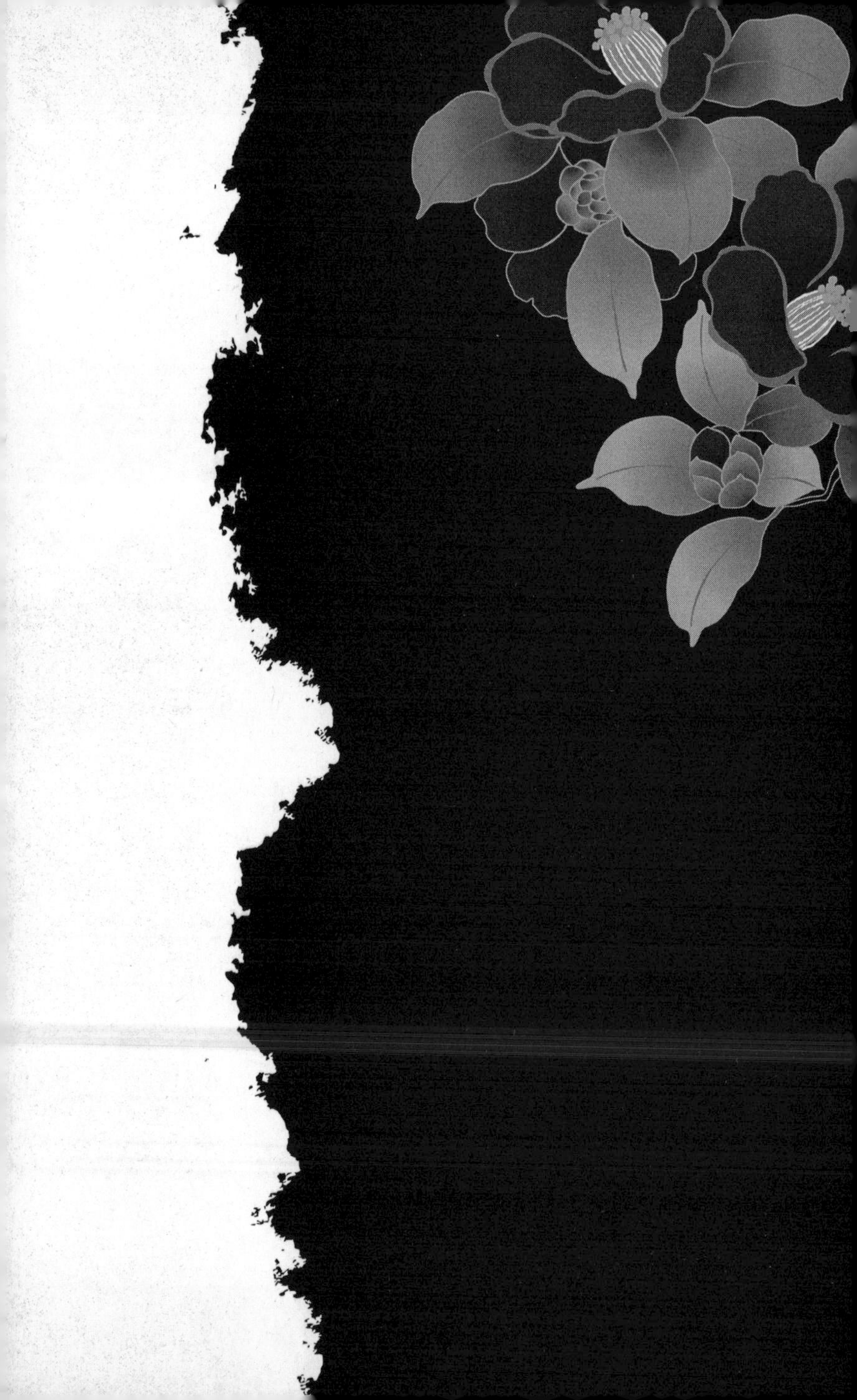

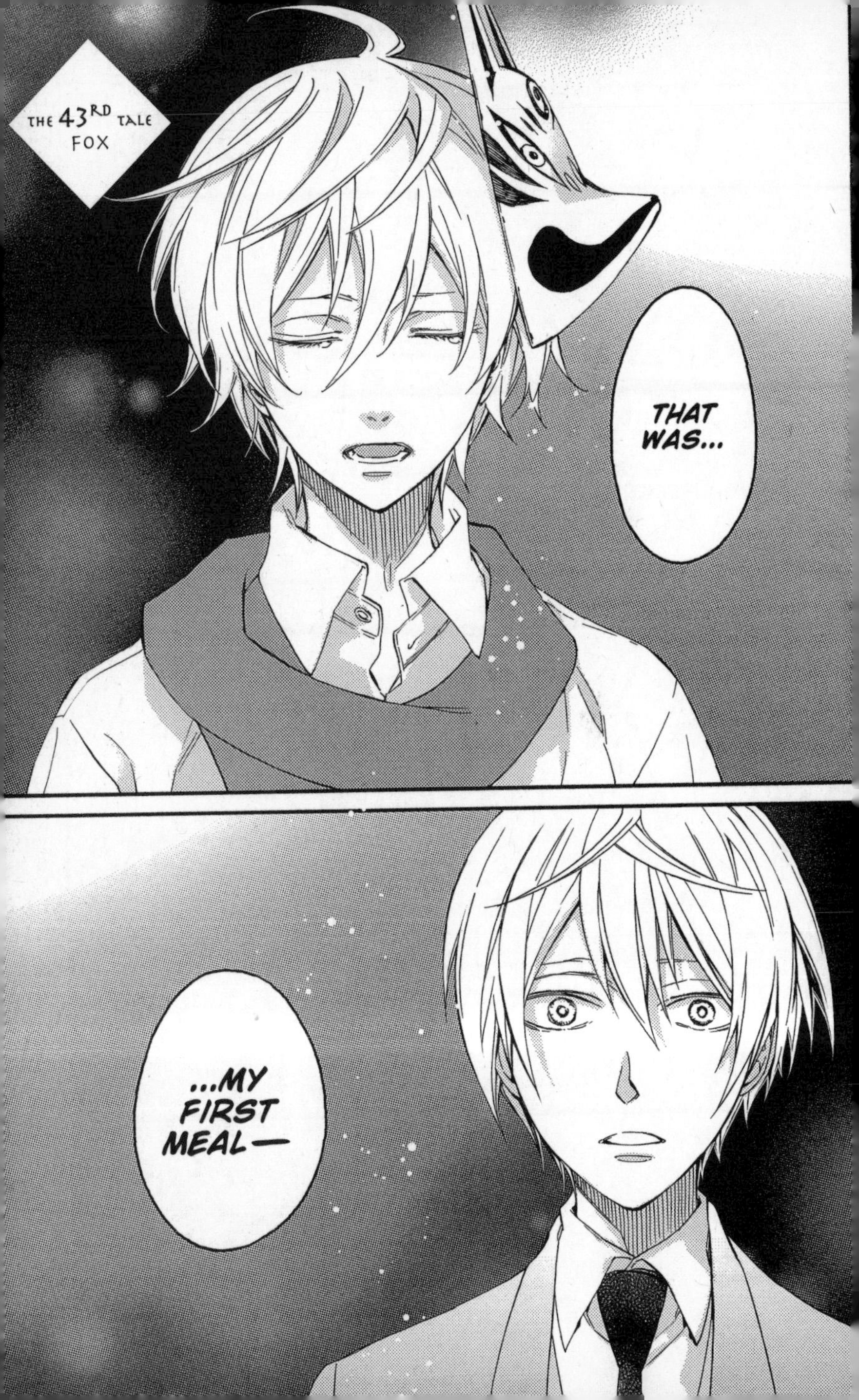
THE 43RD TALE
FOX
THAT WAS...
...MY FIRST MEAL—

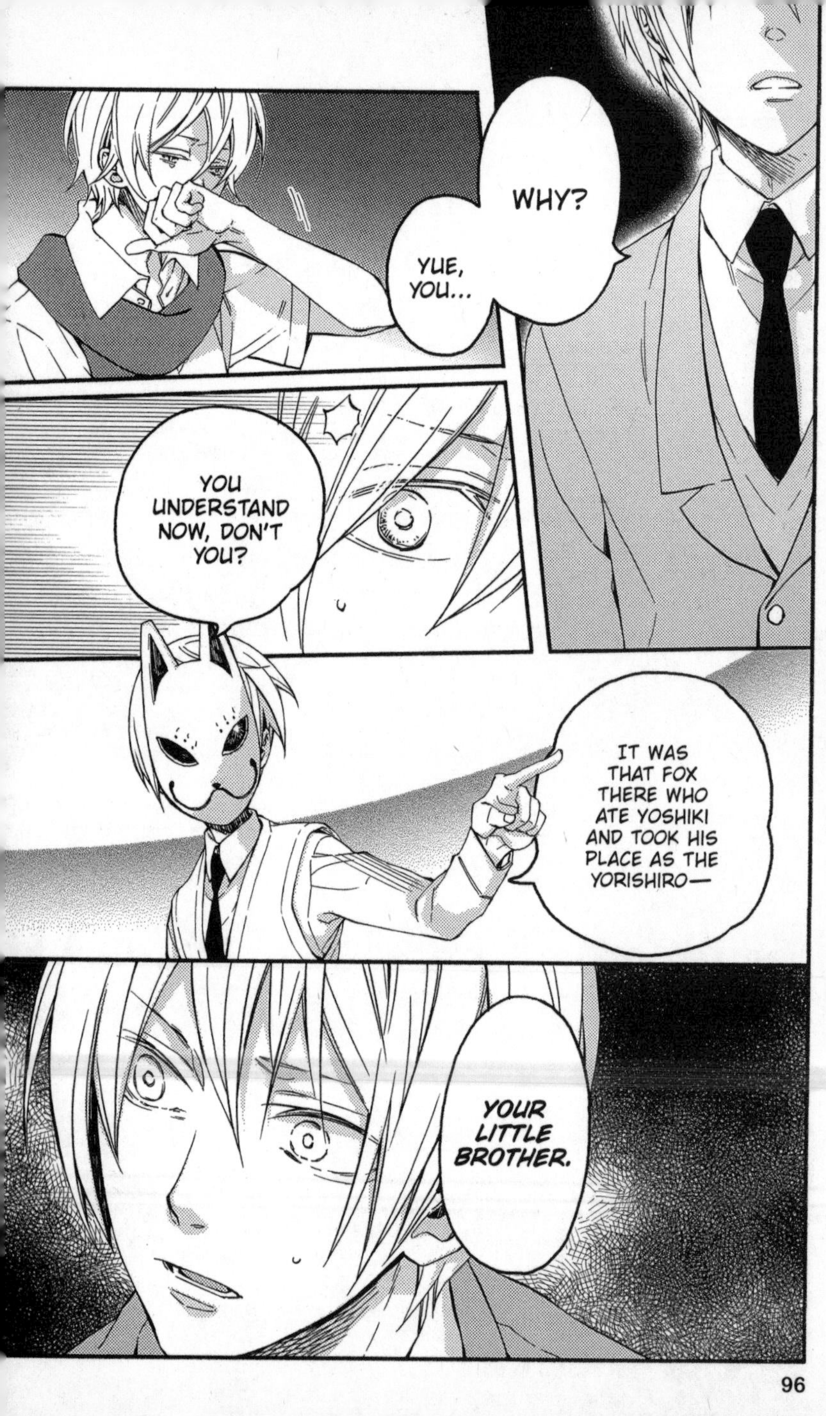
WHY?
YUE, YOU...
YOU UNDERSTAND NOW, DON'T YOU?
IT WAS THAT FOX THERE WHO ATE YOSHIKI AND TOOK HIS PLACE AS THE YORISHIRO—
YOUR LITTLE BROTHER.

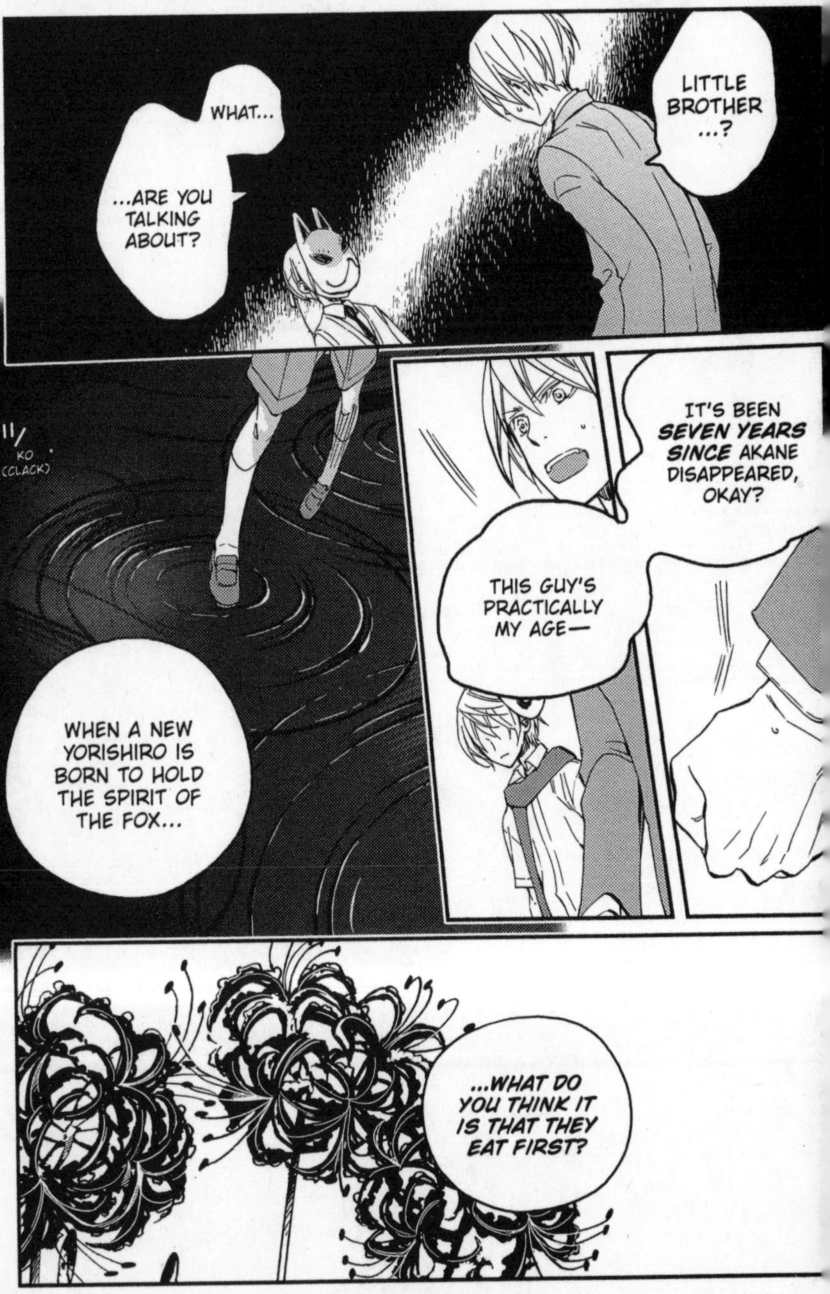
LITTLE BROTHER ...?
WHAT...
...ARE YOU TALKING ABOUT?
IT'S BEEN SEVEN YEARS SINCE AKANE DISAPPEARED, OKAY?
THIS GUY'S PRACTICALLY MY AGE—
KO (CLACK)
WHEN A NEW YORISHIRO IS BORN TO HOLD THE SPIRIT OF THE FOX...
...WHAT DO YOU THINK IT IS THAT THEY EAT FIRST?

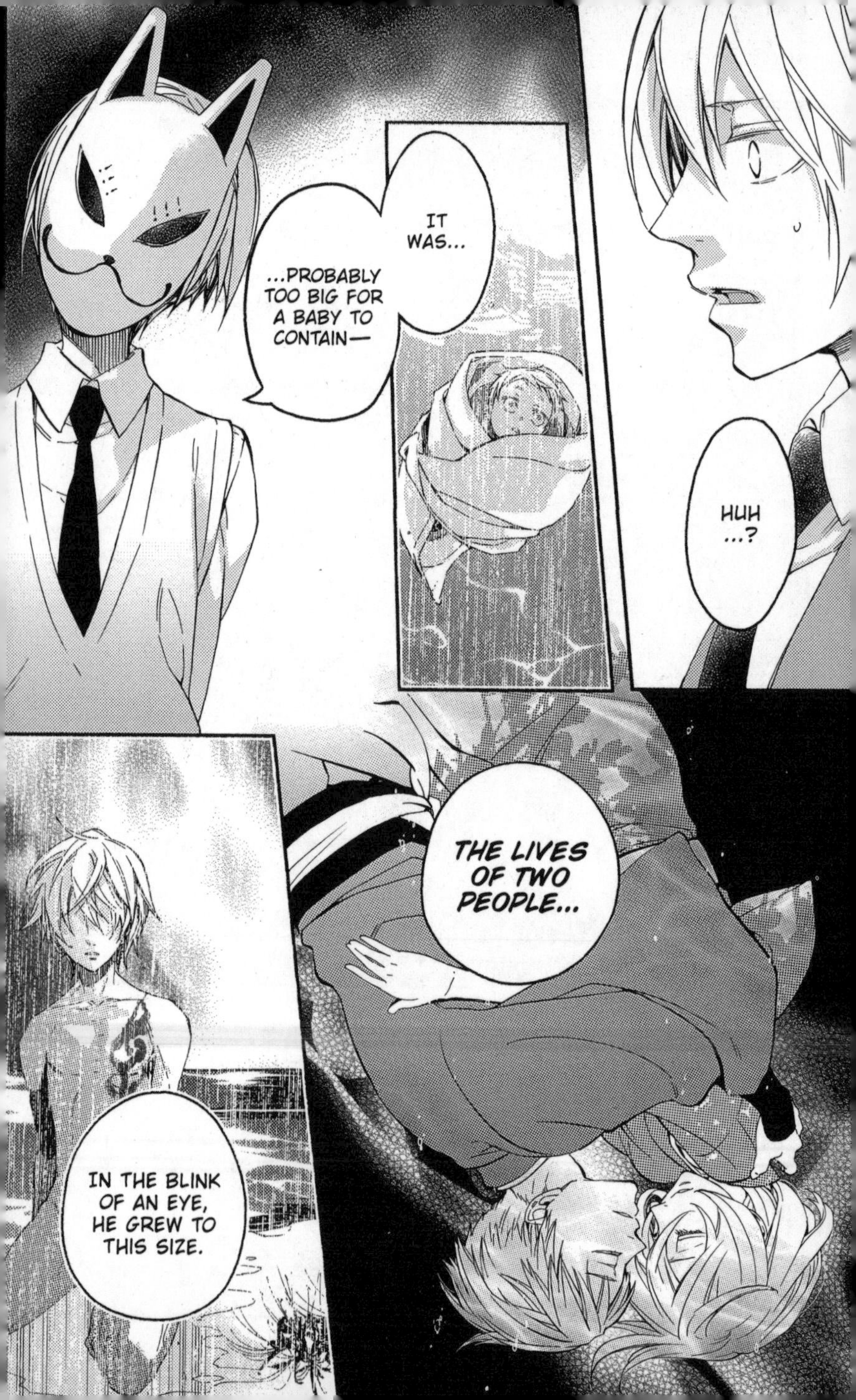
IT WAS...
...PROBABLY TOO BIG FOR A BABY TO CONTAIN—
HUH ...?
THE LIVES OF TWO PEOPLE...
IN THE BLINK OF AN EYE, HE GREW TO THIS SIZE.

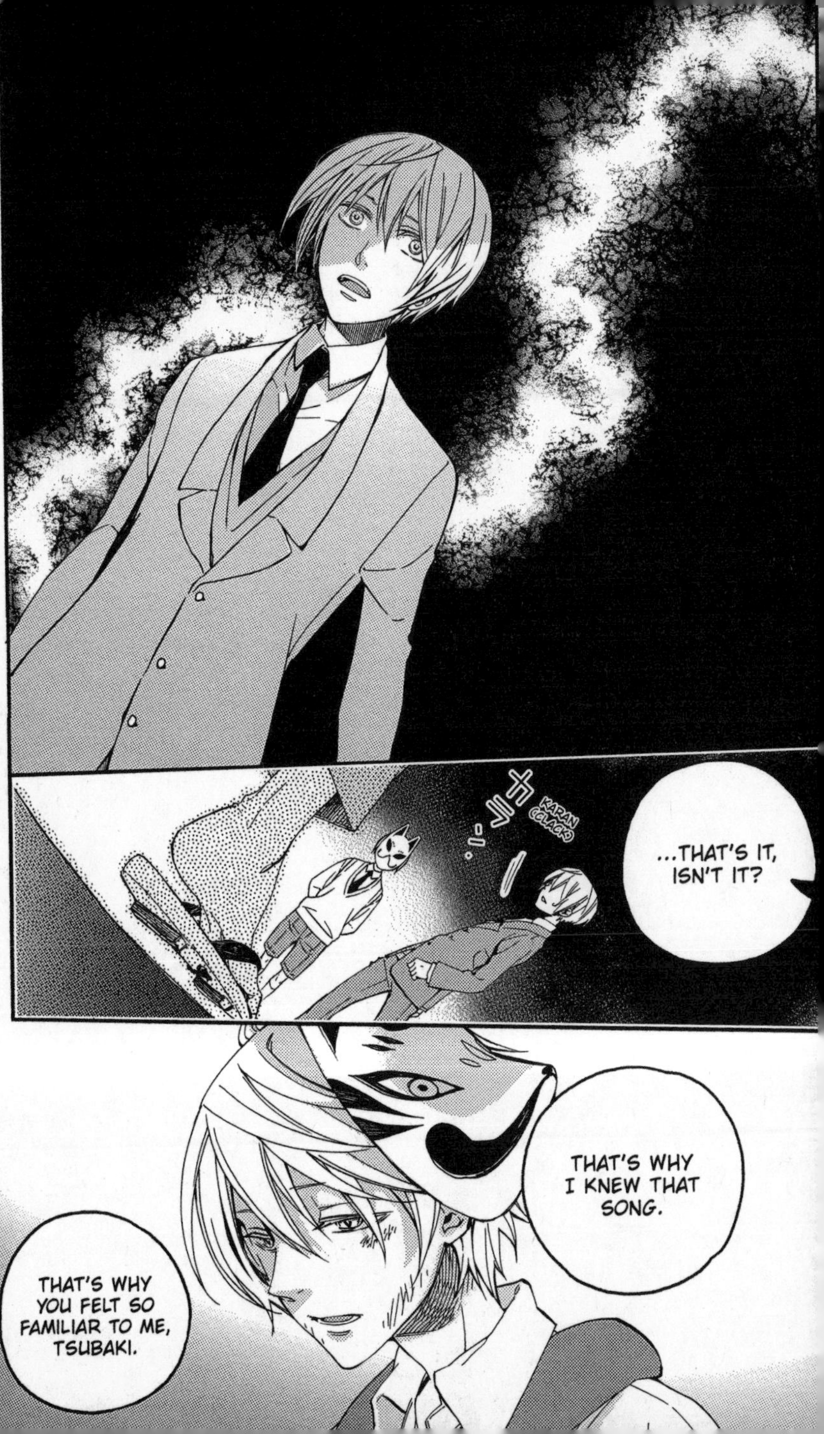
...THAT'S IT, ISN'T IT?
KARAN (CLACK)
THAT'S WHY I KNEW THAT SONG.
THAT'S WHY YOU FELT SO FAMILIAR TO ME, TSUBAKI.

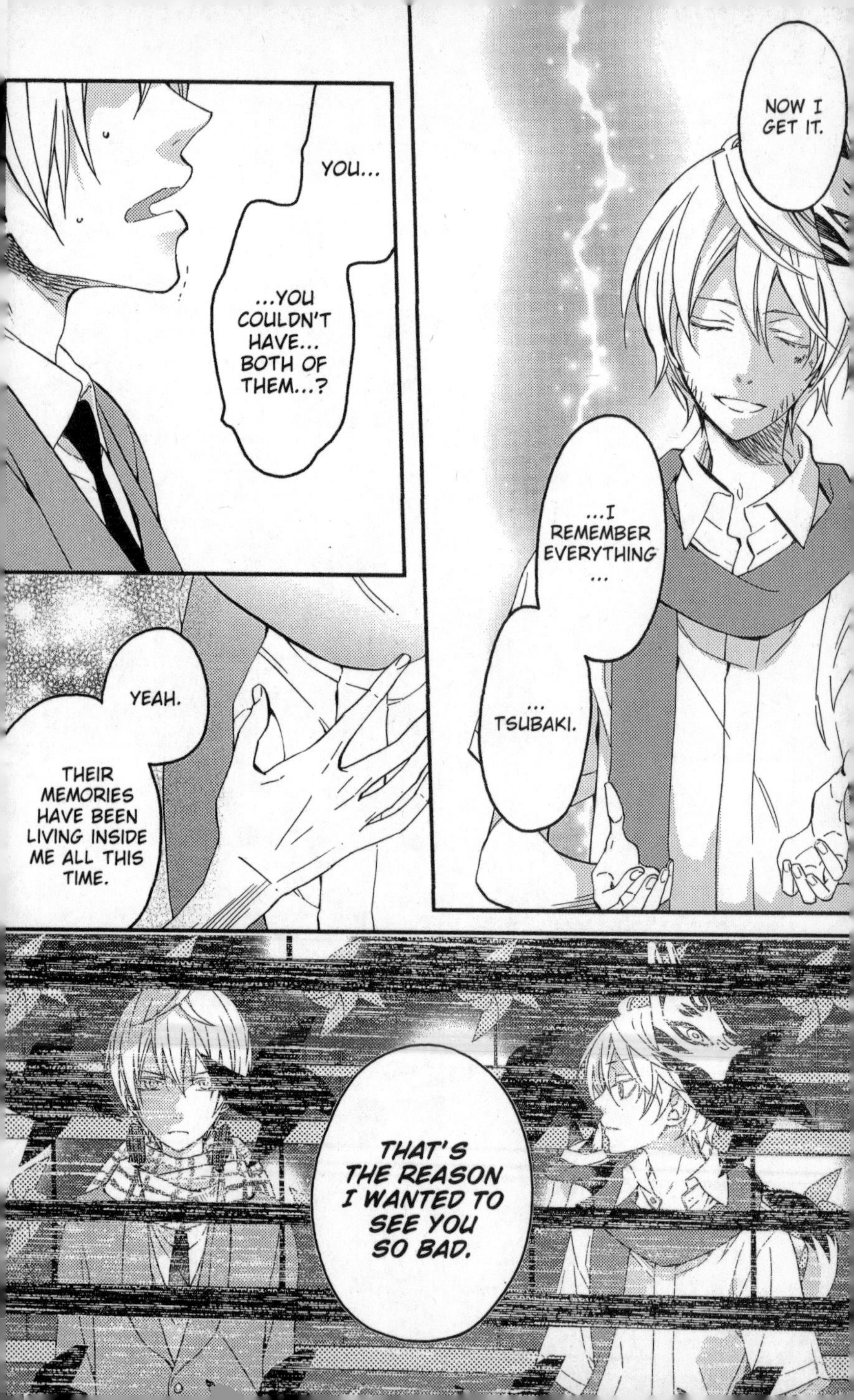
NOW I GET IT.
...I REMEMBER EVERYTHING...
...TSUBAKI.
YOU...
...YOU COULDN'T HAVE... BOTH OF THEM...?
YEAH.
THEIR MEMORIES HAVE BEEN LIVING INSIDE ME ALL THIS TIME.
THAT'S THE REASON I WANTED TO SEE YOU SO BAD.

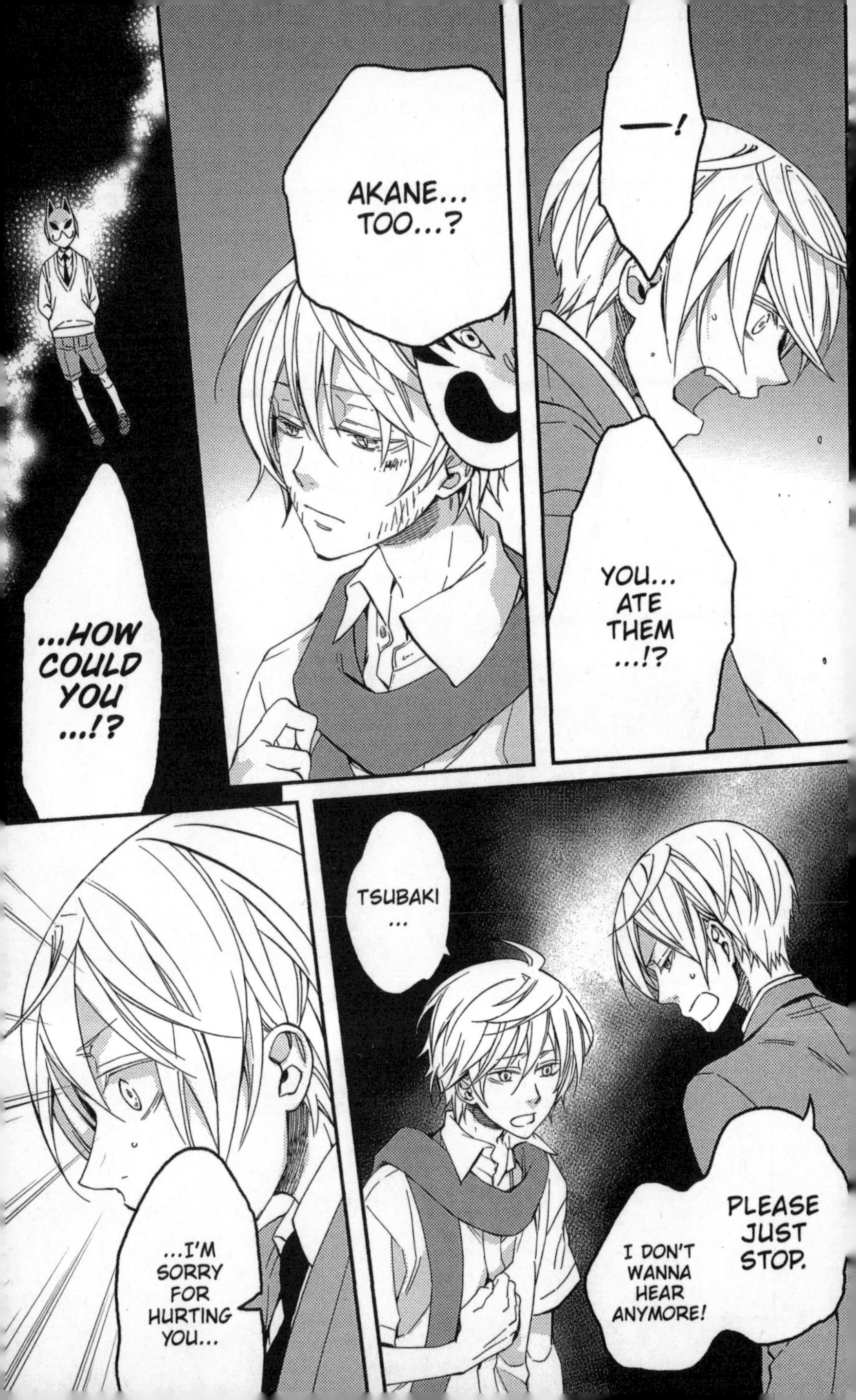
——!
YOU... ATE THEM ...!?
AKANE... TOO...?
...HOW COULD YOU ...!?
TSUBAKI ...
PLEASE JUST STOP.
I DON'T WANNA HEAR ANYMORE!
...I'M SORRY FOR HURTING YOU...

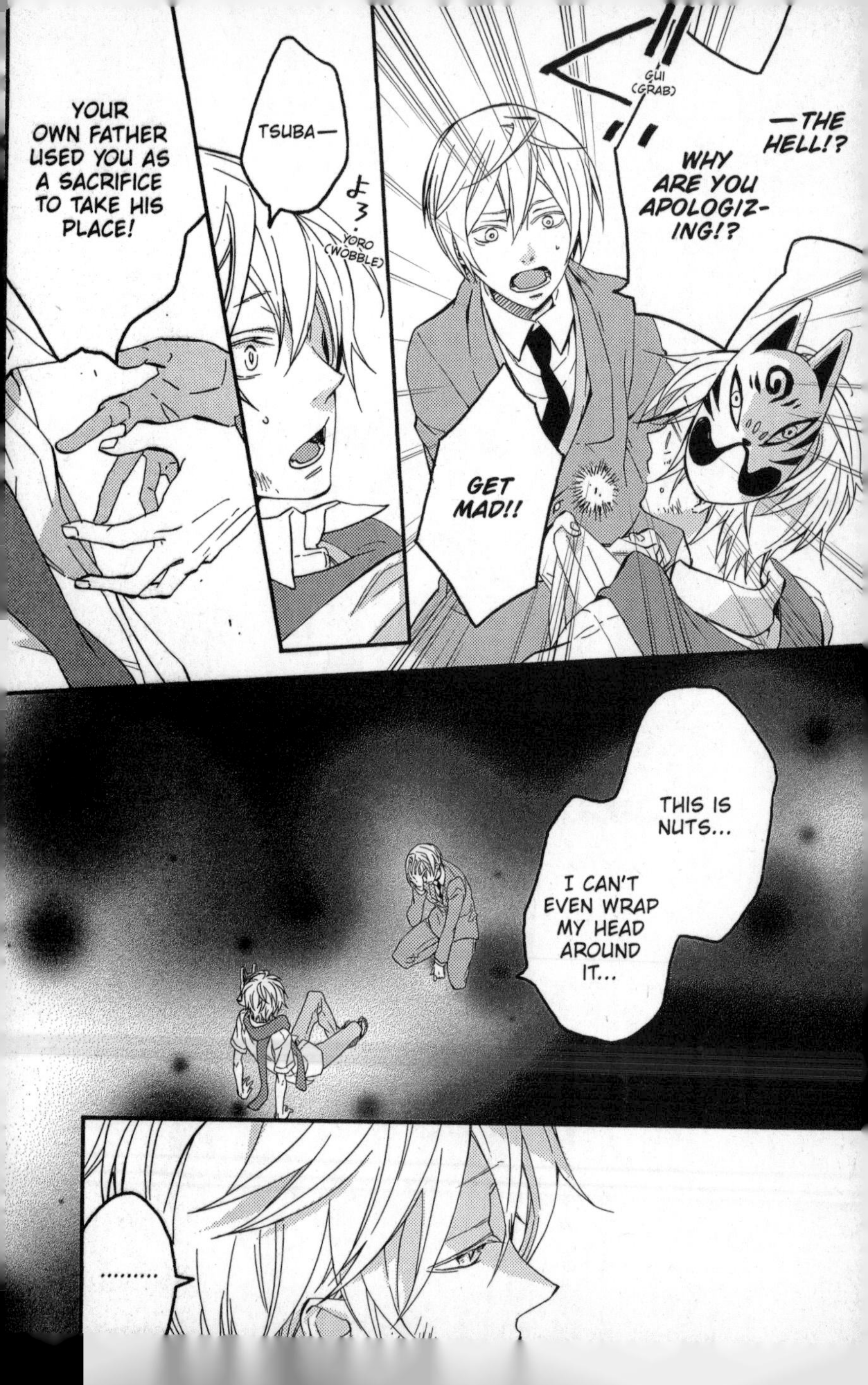

GUI (GRAB)
WHY ARE YOU APOLOGIZING!?
—THE HELL!?
GET MAD!!
TSUBA—
よろ
YORO (WOBBLE)
YOUR OWN FATHER USED YOU AS A SACRIFICE TO TAKE HIS PLACE!
THIS IS NUTS...
I CAN'T EVEN WRAP MY HEAD AROUND IT...
....

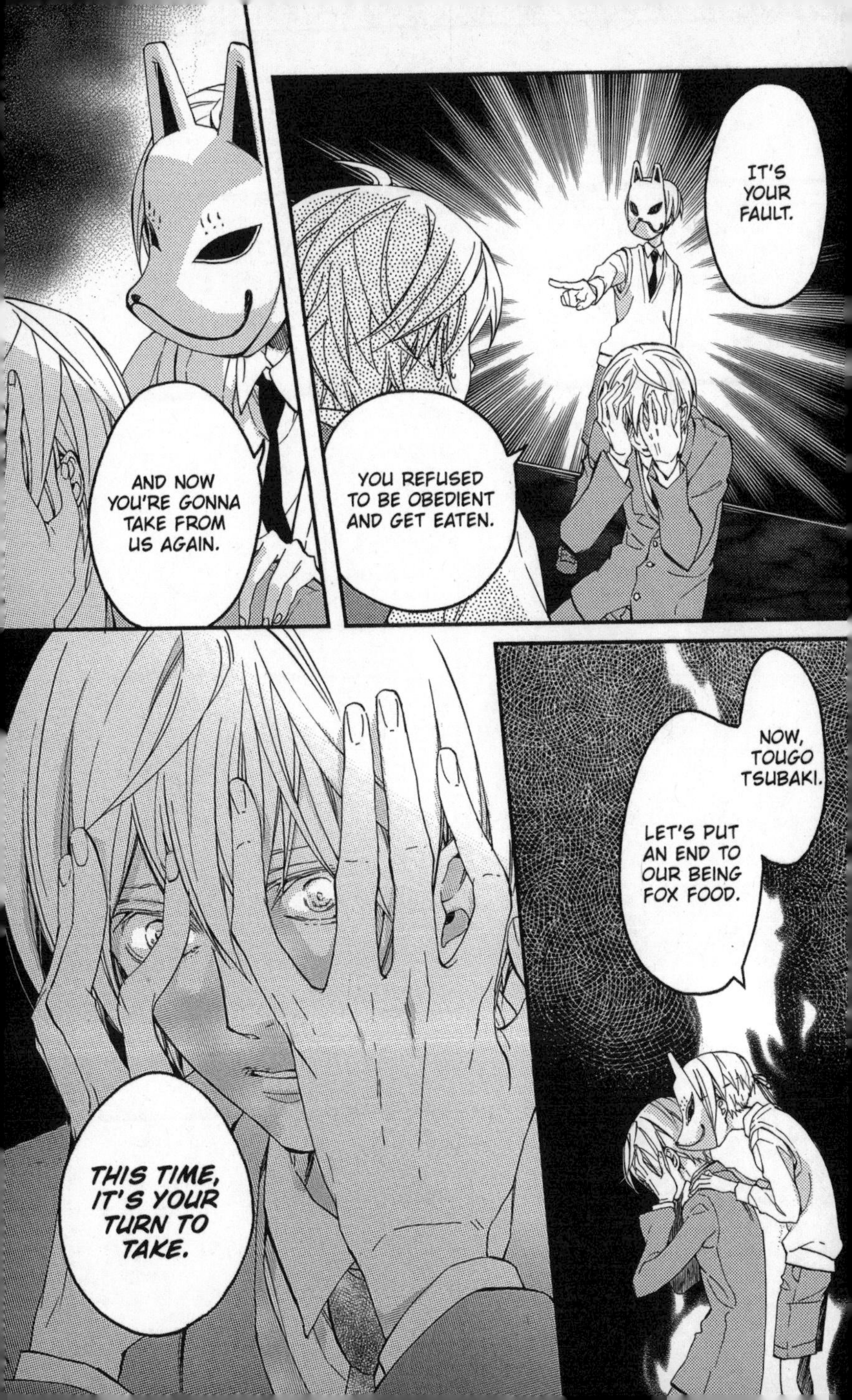
IT'S YOUR FAULT.
YOU REFUSED TO BE OBEDIENT AND GET EATEN.
AND NOW YOU'RE GONNA TAKE FROM US AGAIN.
NOW, TOUGO TSUBAKI.
LET'S PUT AN END TO OUR BEING FOX FOOD.
THIS TIME, IT'S YOUR TURN TO TAKE.

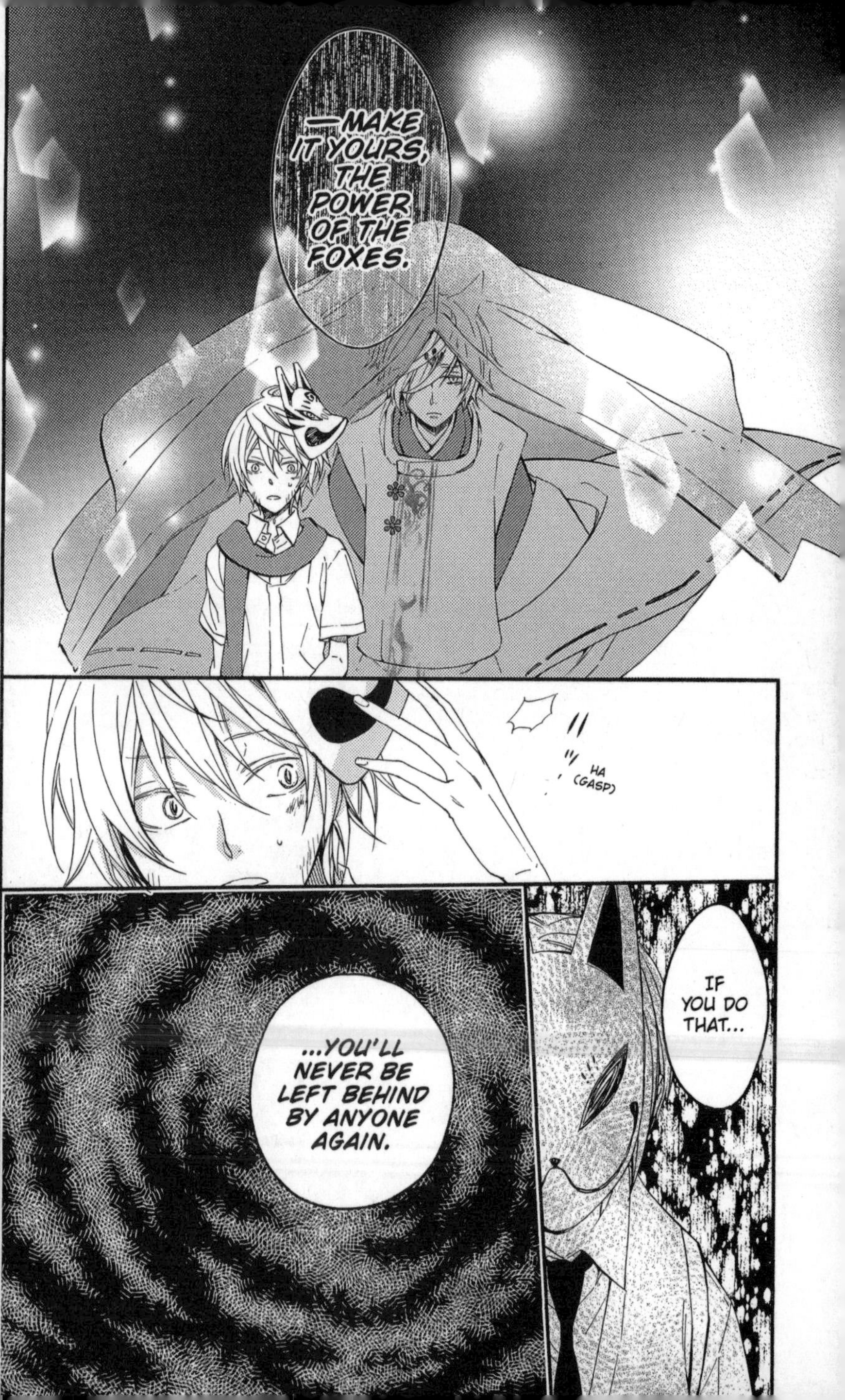
—MAKE IT YOURS, THE POWER OF THE FOXES.
HA (GASP)
IF YOU DO THAT...
...YOU'LL NEVER BE LEFT BEHIND BY ANYONE AGAIN.

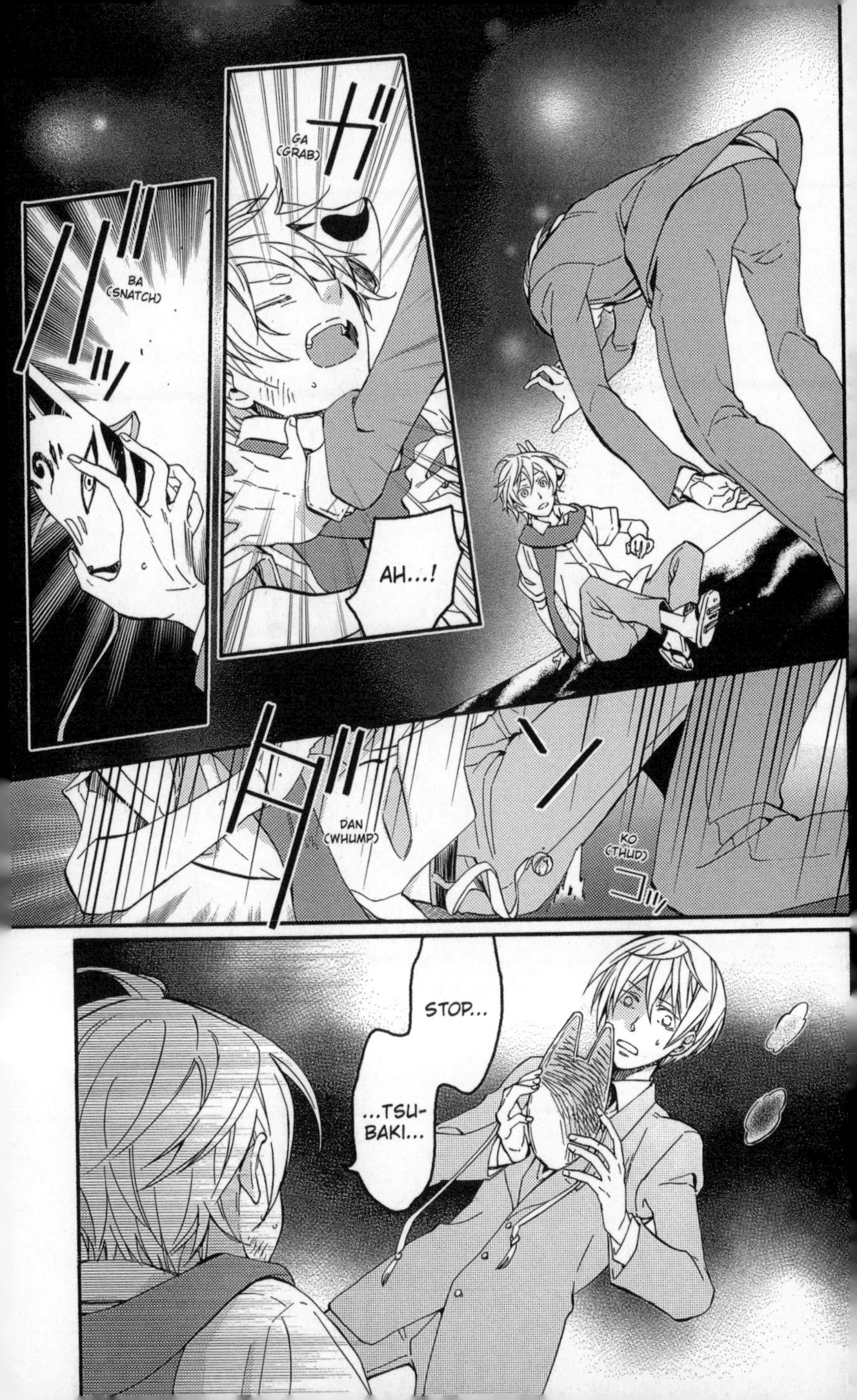
GA (GRAB)
AH...!
BA (SNATCH)
KO (THUD)
DAN (WHUMP)
STOP...
...TSU-BAKI...

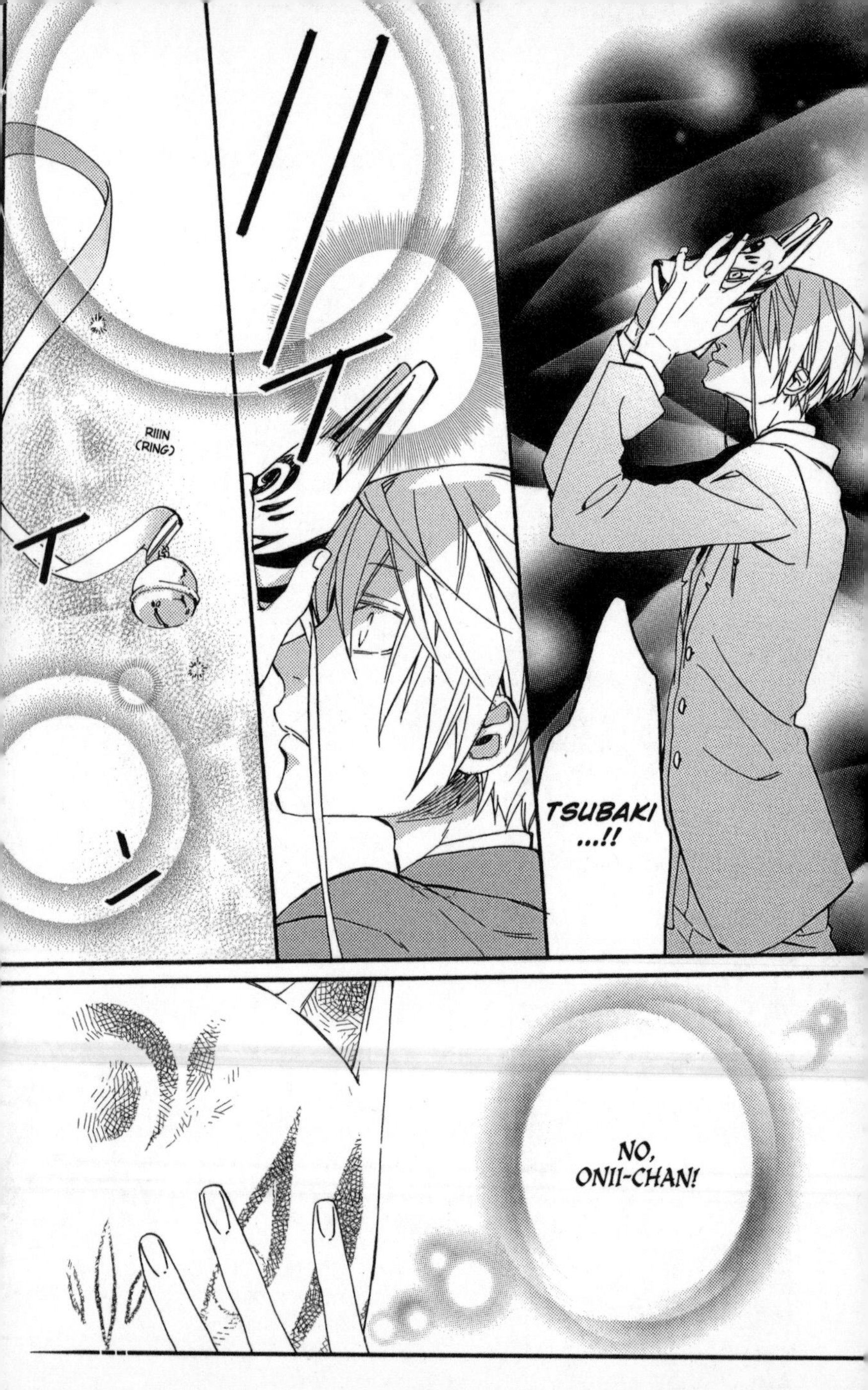
TSUBAKI ...!!
RIIIN (RING)
NO, ONII-CHAN!

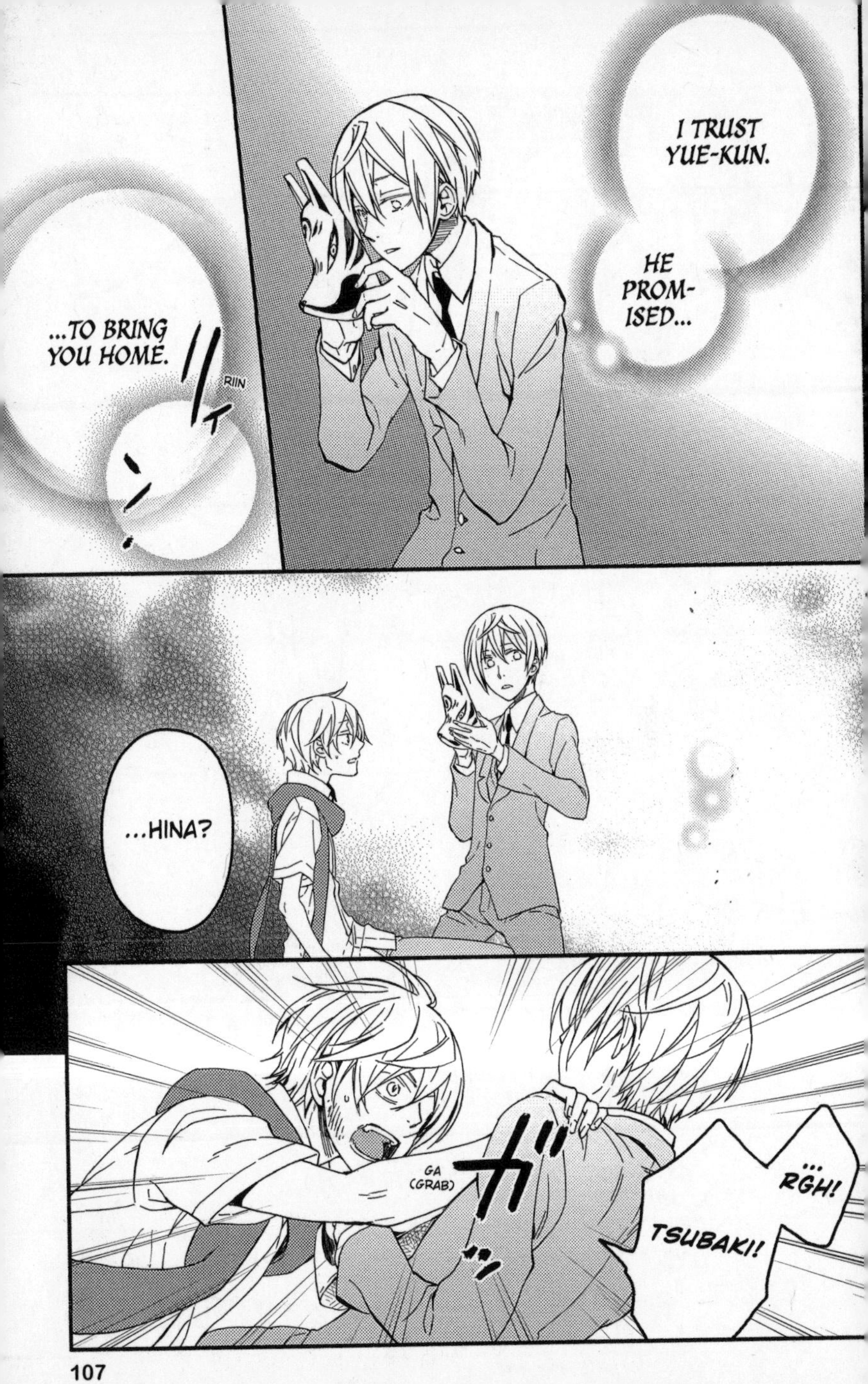
I TRUST YUE-KUN.
HE PROMISED...
...TO BRING YOU HOME.
RIIN
...HINA?
...RGH!
TSUBAKI!
GA (GRAB)

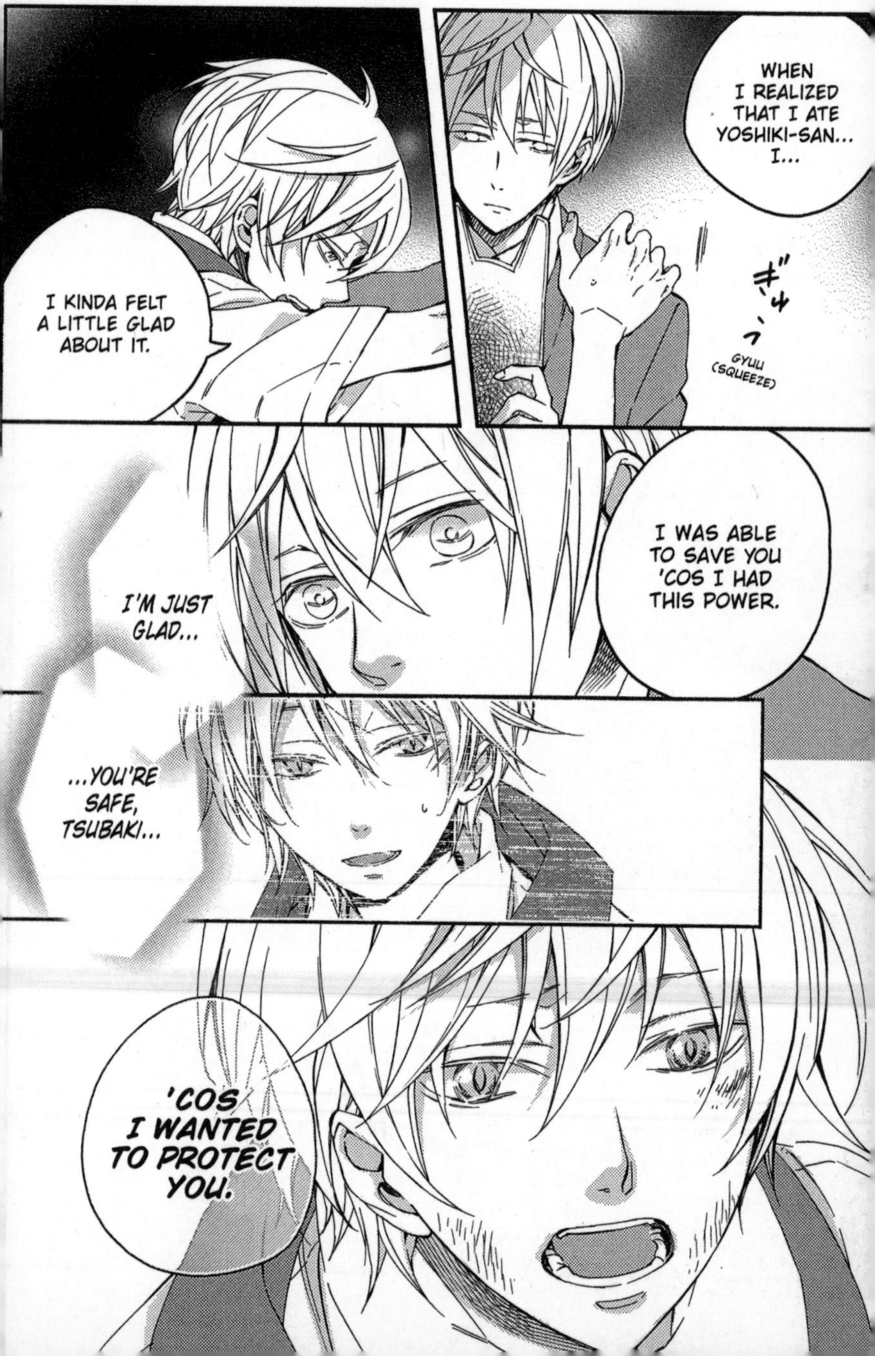
WHEN I REALIZED THAT I ATE YOSHIKI-SAN... I...
ギュッ
GYUU (SQUEEZE)
I KINDA FELT A LITTLE GLAD ABOUT IT.
I WAS ABLE TO SAVE YOU 'COS I HAD THIS POWER.
I'M JUST GLAD...
...YOU'RE SAFE, TSUBAKI...
'COS I WANTED TO PROTECT YOU.

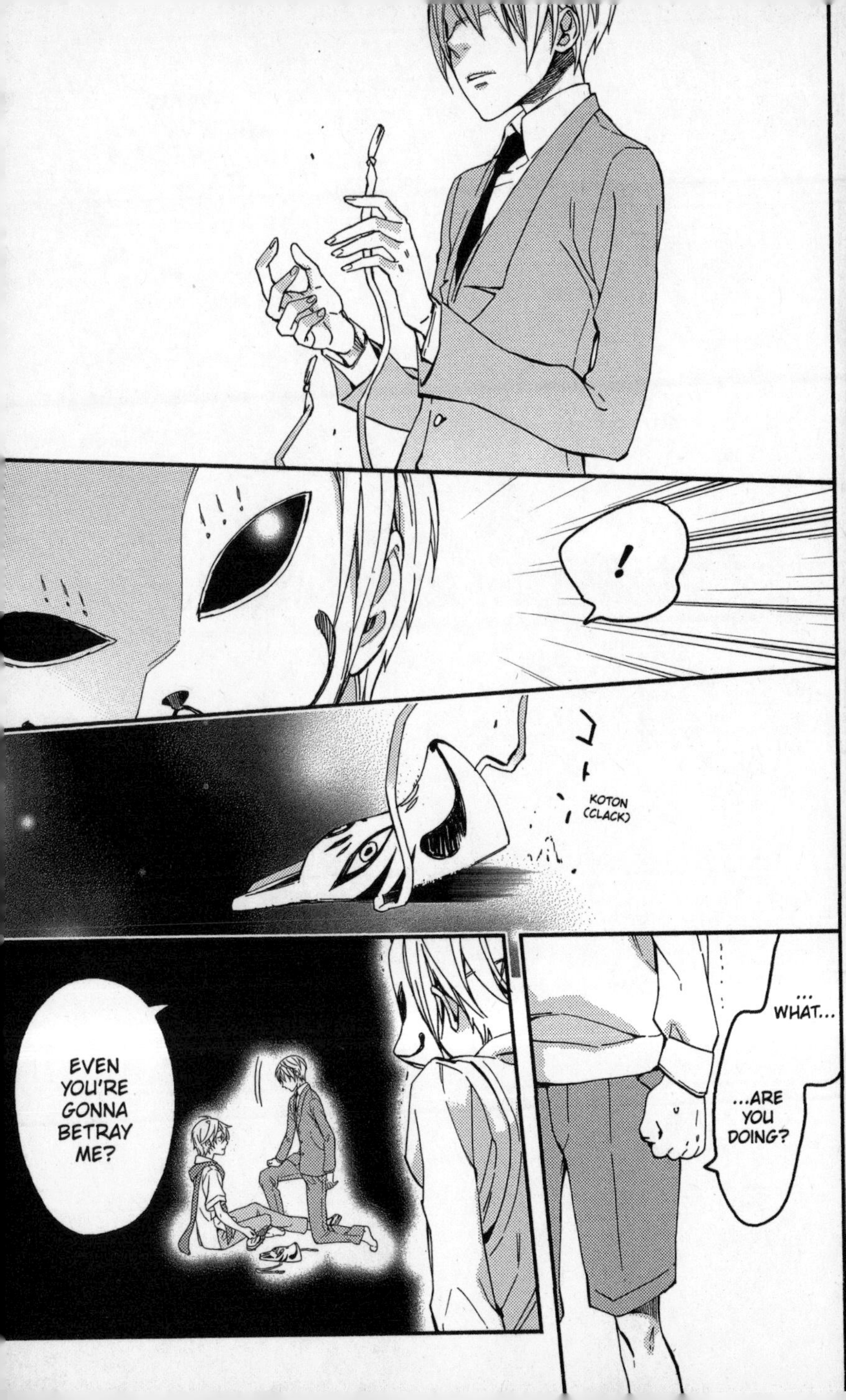
!
KOTON (CLACK)
...WHAT...
...ARE YOU DOING?
EVEN YOU'RE GONNA BETRAY ME?

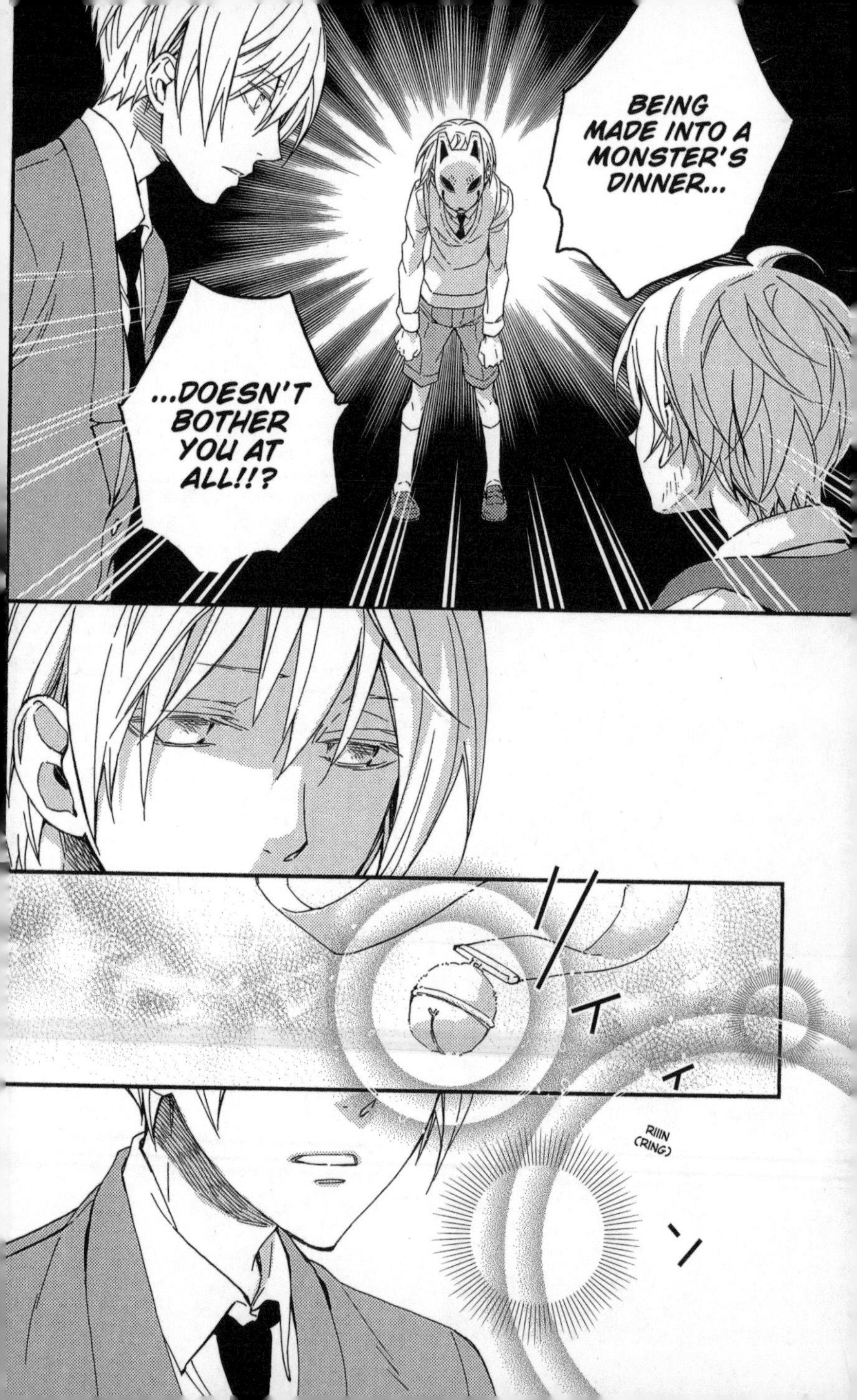
BEING MADE INTO A MONSTER'S DINNER...
...DOESN'T BOTHER YOU AT ALL!!?
RIIN (RING)

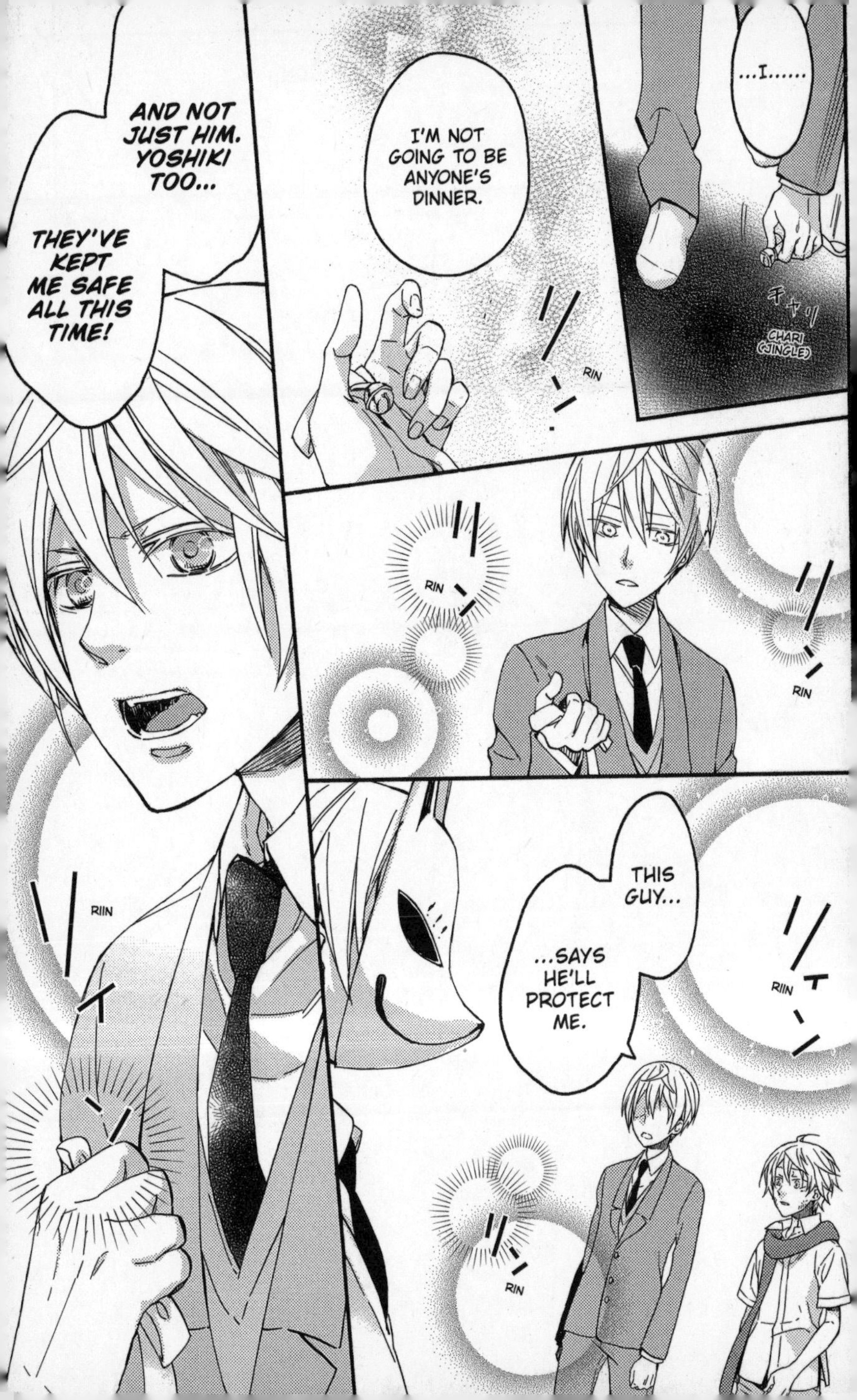
...I......
チャリ
CHARI (JINGLE)
I'M NOT GOING TO BE ANYONE'S DINNER.
RIN
RIN
RIN
THIS GUY...
...SAYS HE'LL PROTECT ME.
RIIN
RIN
AND NOT JUST HIM. YOSHIKI TOO...
THEY'VE KEPT ME SAFE ALL THIS TIME!
RIIN

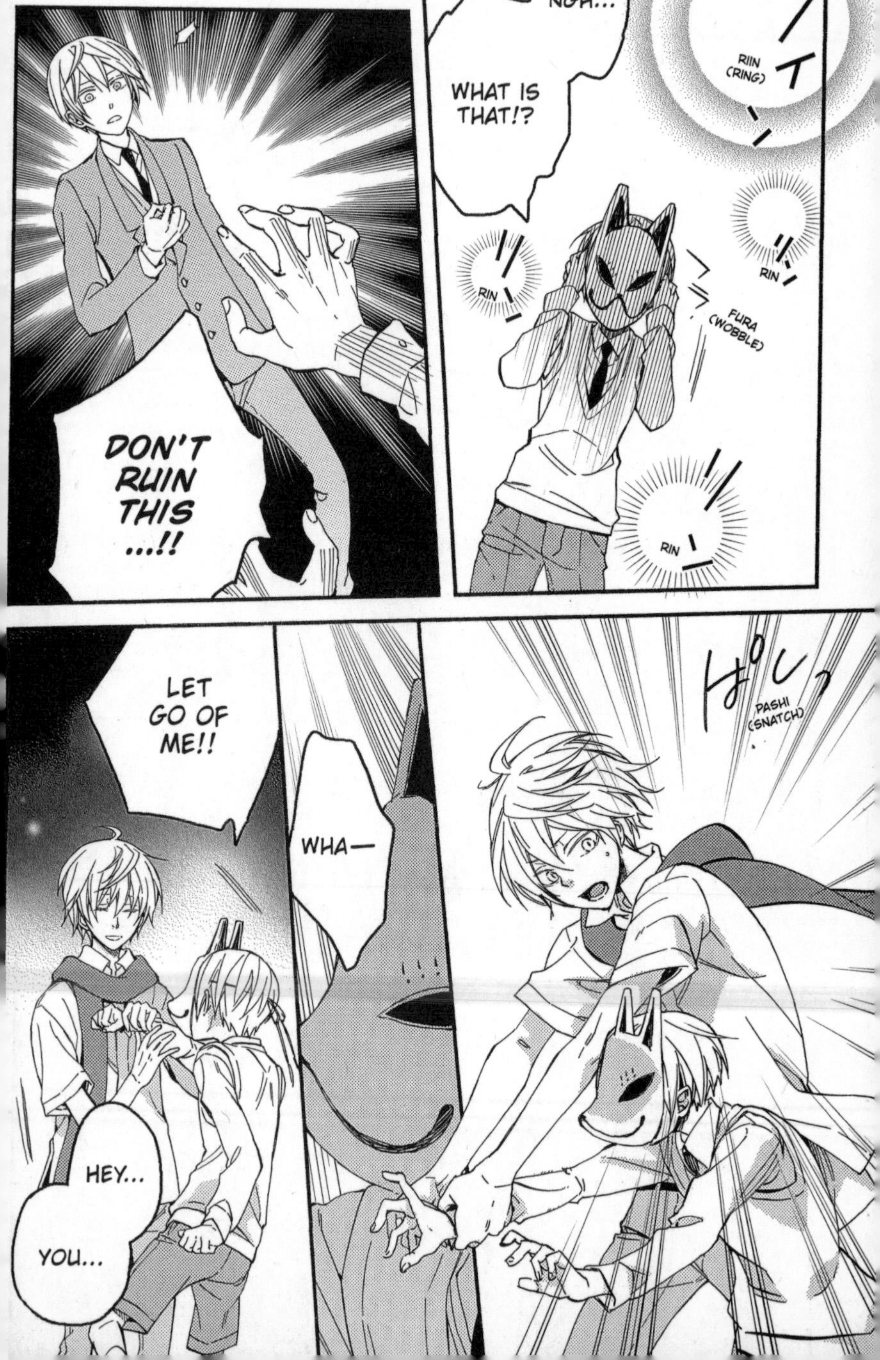
RIIN (RING)
NGH...
WHAT IS THAT!?
RIN
FURA (WOBBLE)
RIN
RIN
DON'T RUIN THIS ...!!
ぱしっ
PASHI (SNATCH)
WHA—
LET GO OF ME!!
HEY...
YOU...

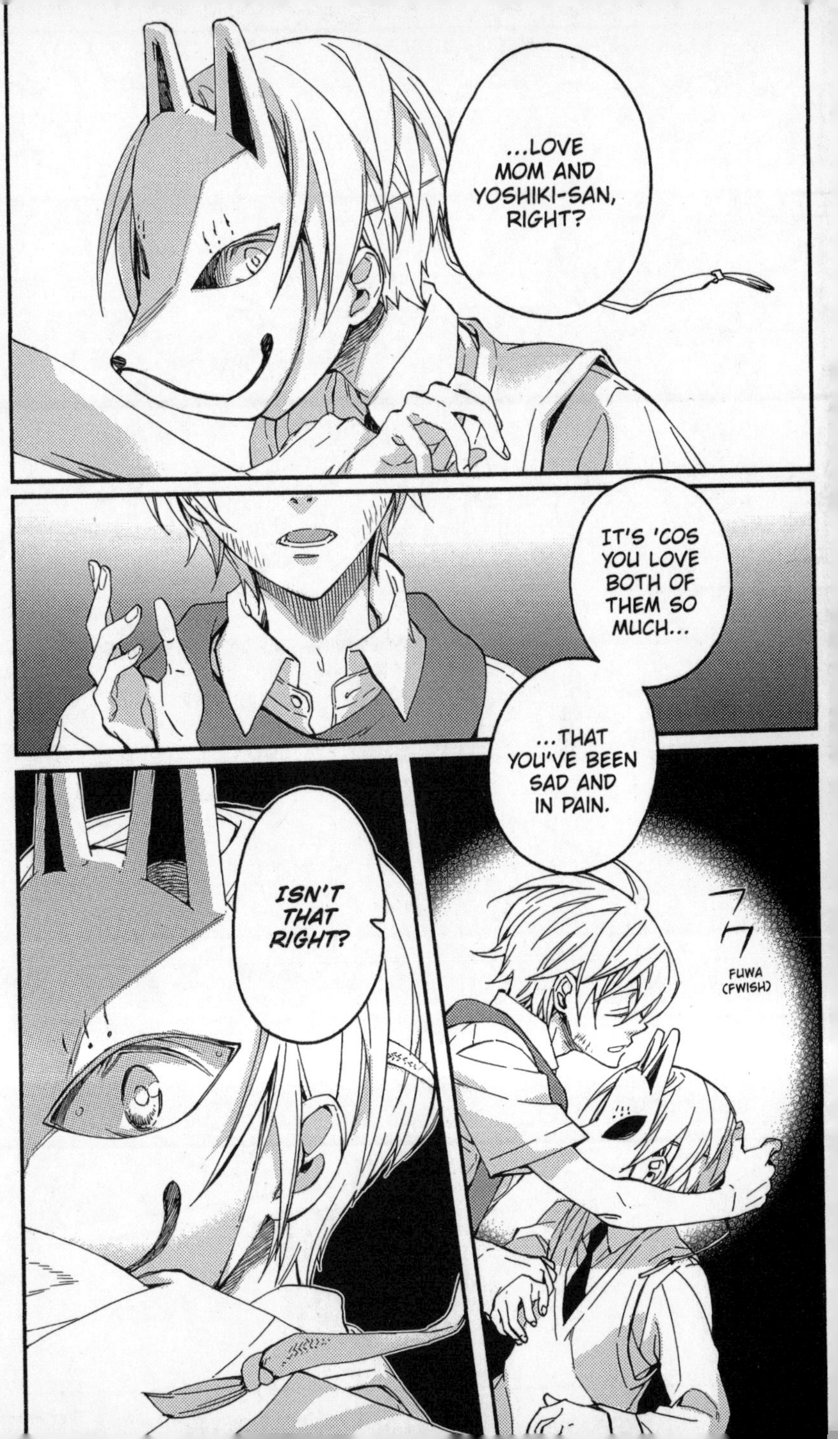
...LOVE MOM AND YOSHIKI-SAN, RIGHT?
IT'S 'COS YOU LOVE BOTH OF THEM SO MUCH...
...THAT YOU'VE BEEN SAD AND IN PAIN.
FUWA (FWISH)
ISN'T THAT RIGHT?

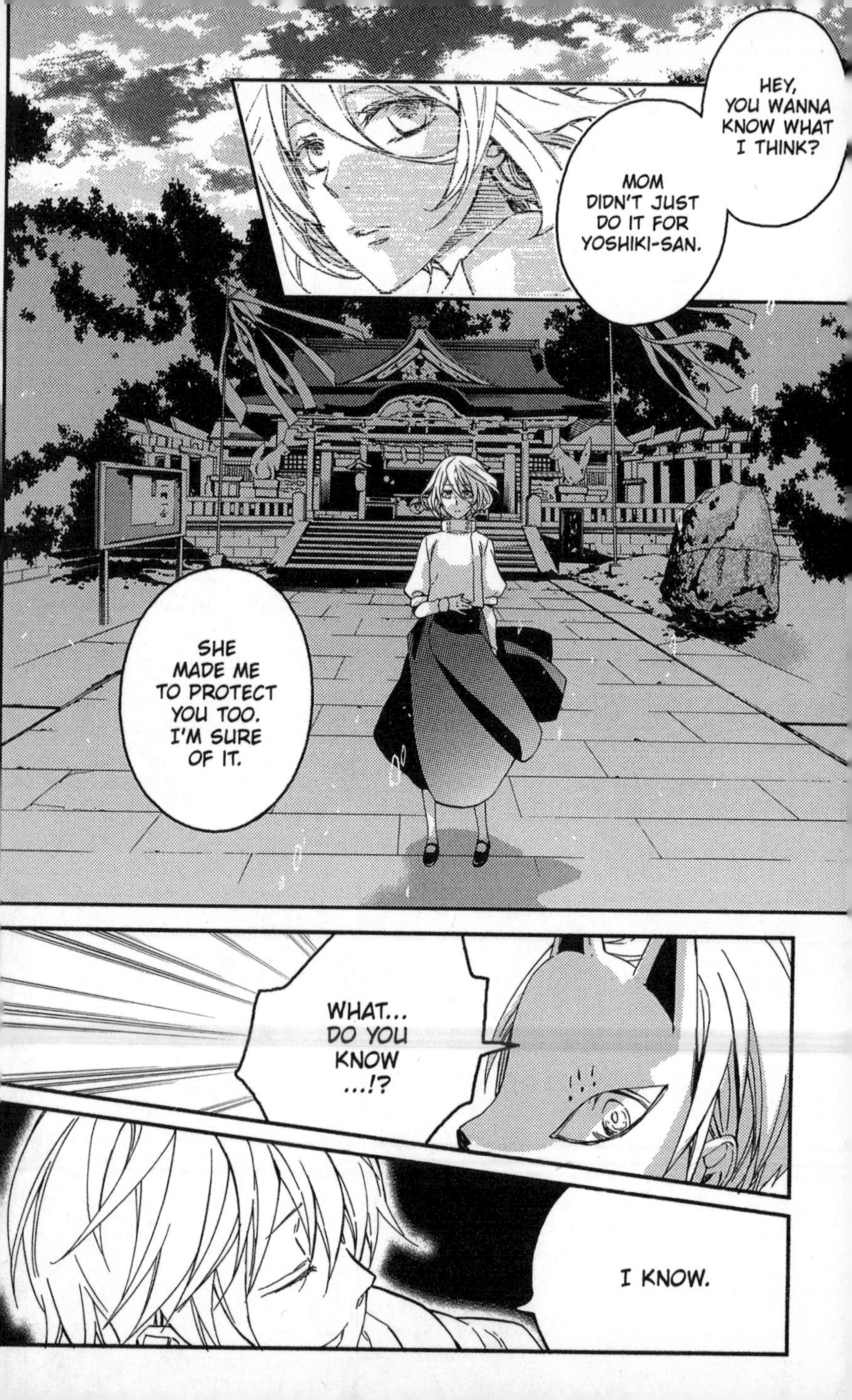
HEY, YOU WANNA KNOW WHAT I THINK?
MOM DIDN'T JUST DO IT FOR YOSHIKI-SAN.
SHE MADE ME TO PROTECT YOU TOO. I'M SURE OF IT.
WHAT... DO YOU KNOW ...!?
I KNOW.

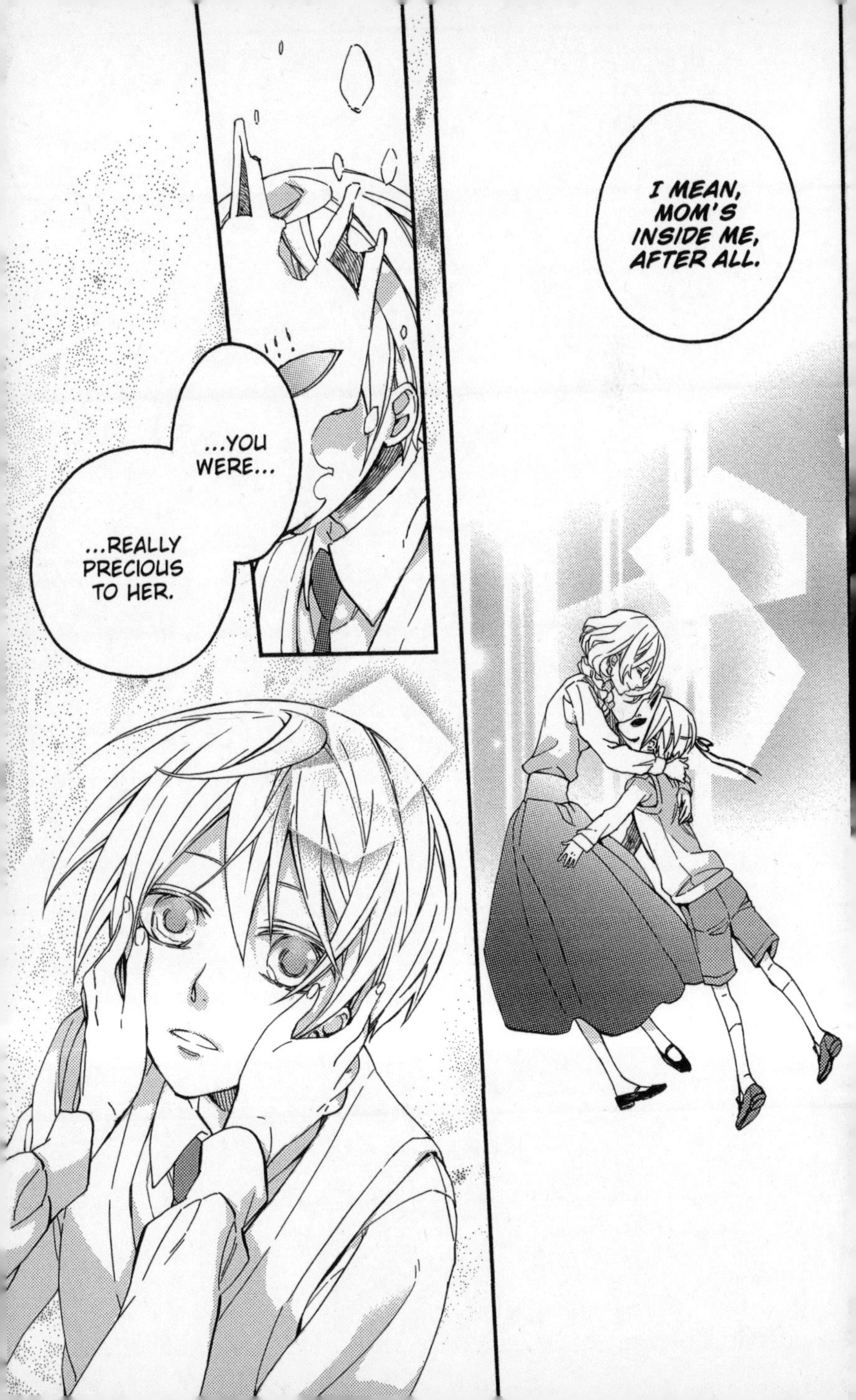
I MEAN, MOM'S INSIDE ME, AFTER ALL.
...YOU WERE...
...REALLY PRECIOUS TO HER.

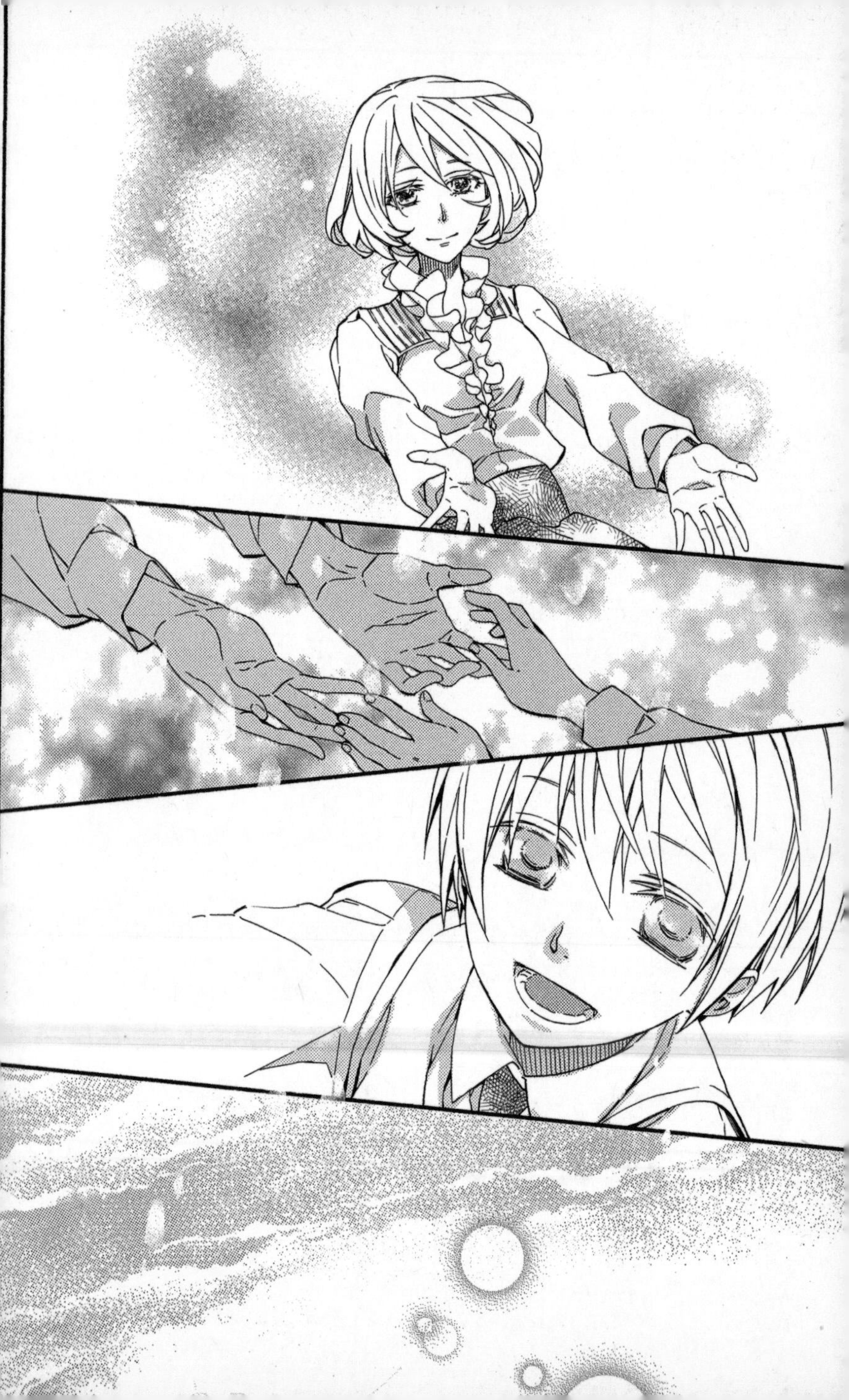

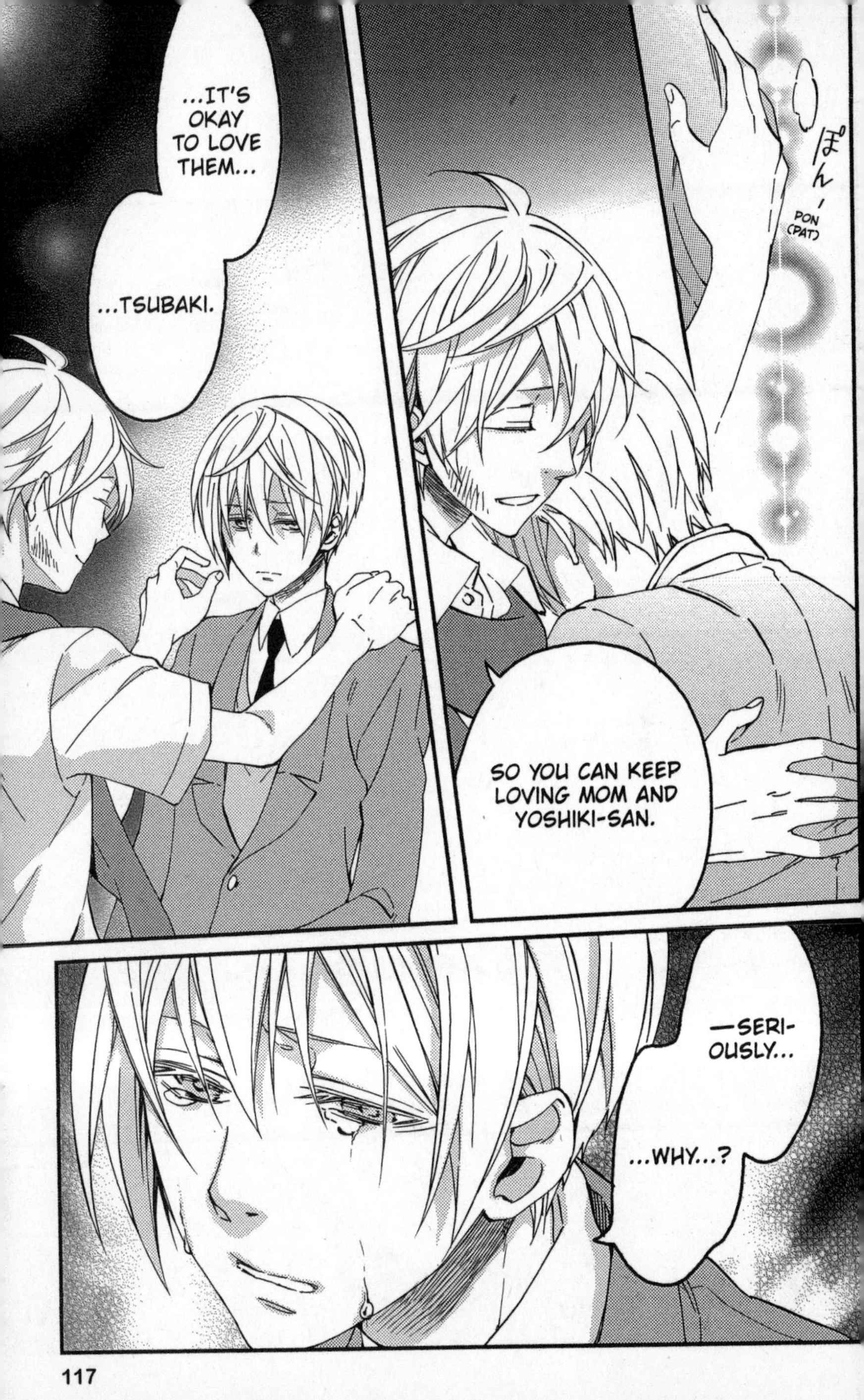
ぽん
PON (PAT)
SO YOU CAN KEEP LOVING MOM AND YOSHIKI-SAN.
...IT'S OKAY TO LOVE THEM...
...TSUBAKI.
—SERIOUSLY...
...WHY...?

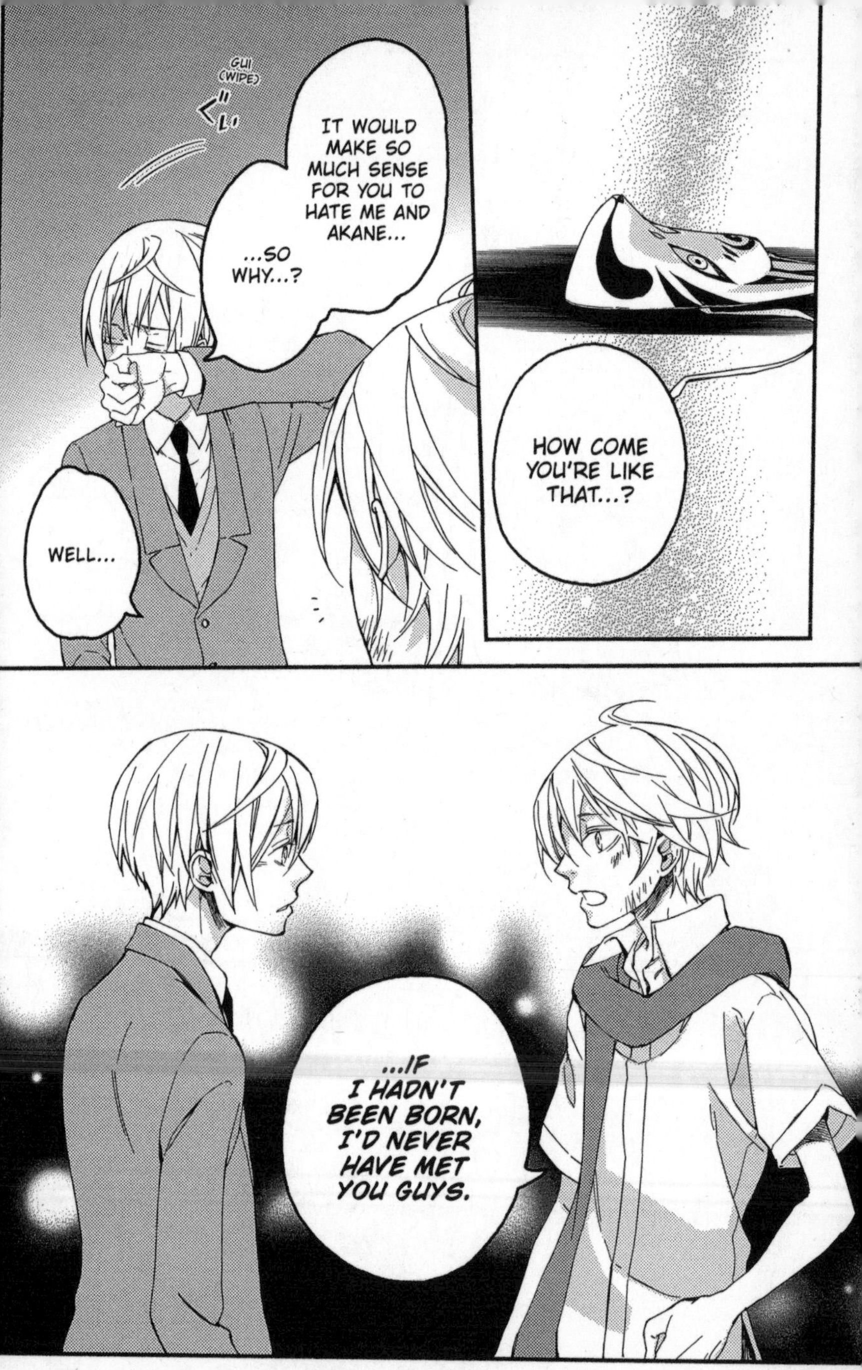
HOW COME YOU'RE LIKE THAT...?
IT WOULD MAKE SO MUCH SENSE FOR YOU TO HATE ME AND AKANE...
...SO WHY...?
GUI (WIPE)
WELL...
...IF I HADN'T BEEN BORN, I'D NEVER HAVE MET YOU GUYS.

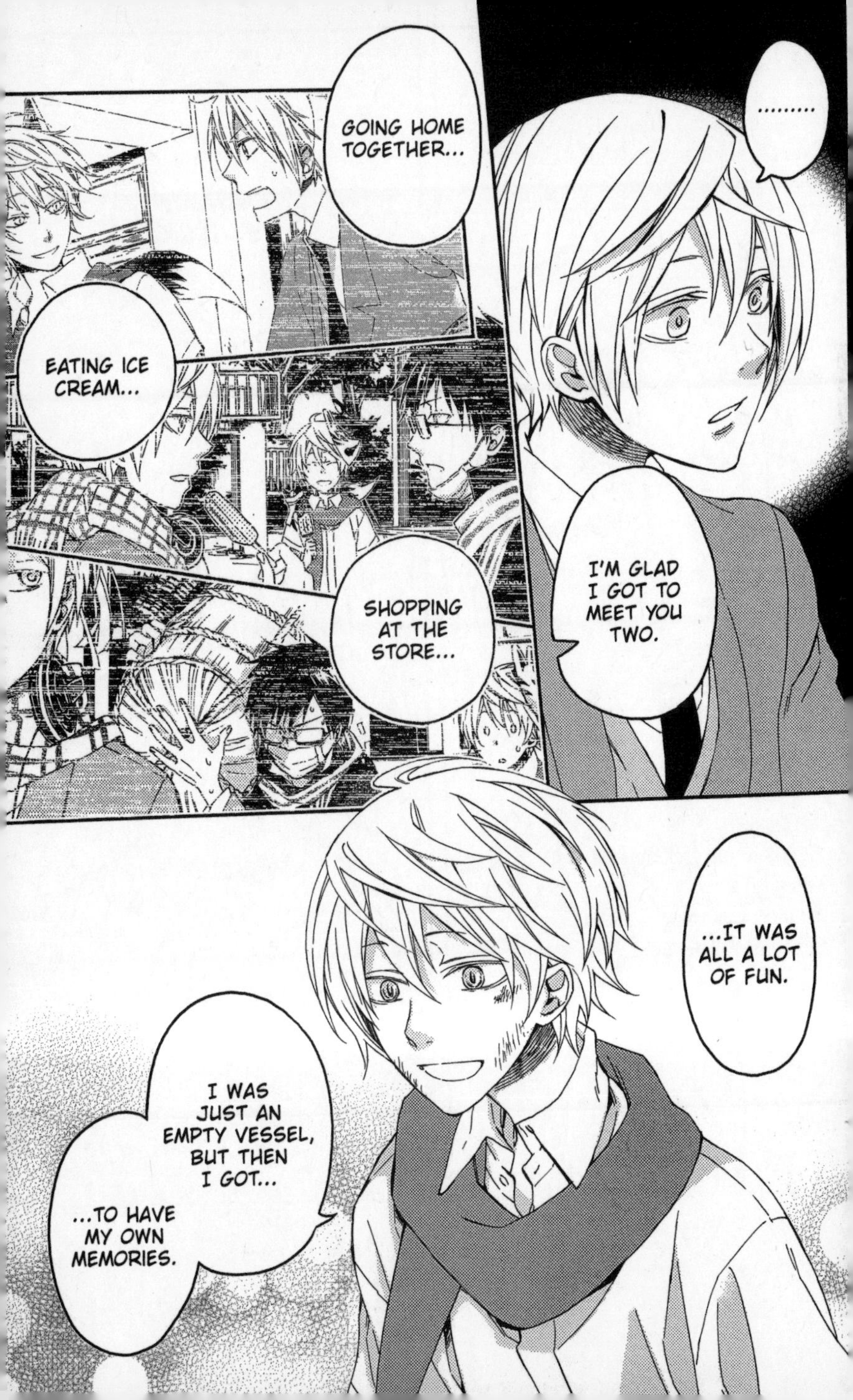
....
I'M GLAD I GOT TO MEET YOU TWO.
GOING HOME TOGETHER...
EATING ICE CREAM...
SHOPPING AT THE STORE...
...IT WAS ALL A LOT OF FUN.
I WAS JUST AN EMPTY VESSEL, BUT THEN I GOT...
...TO HAVE MY OWN MEMORIES.

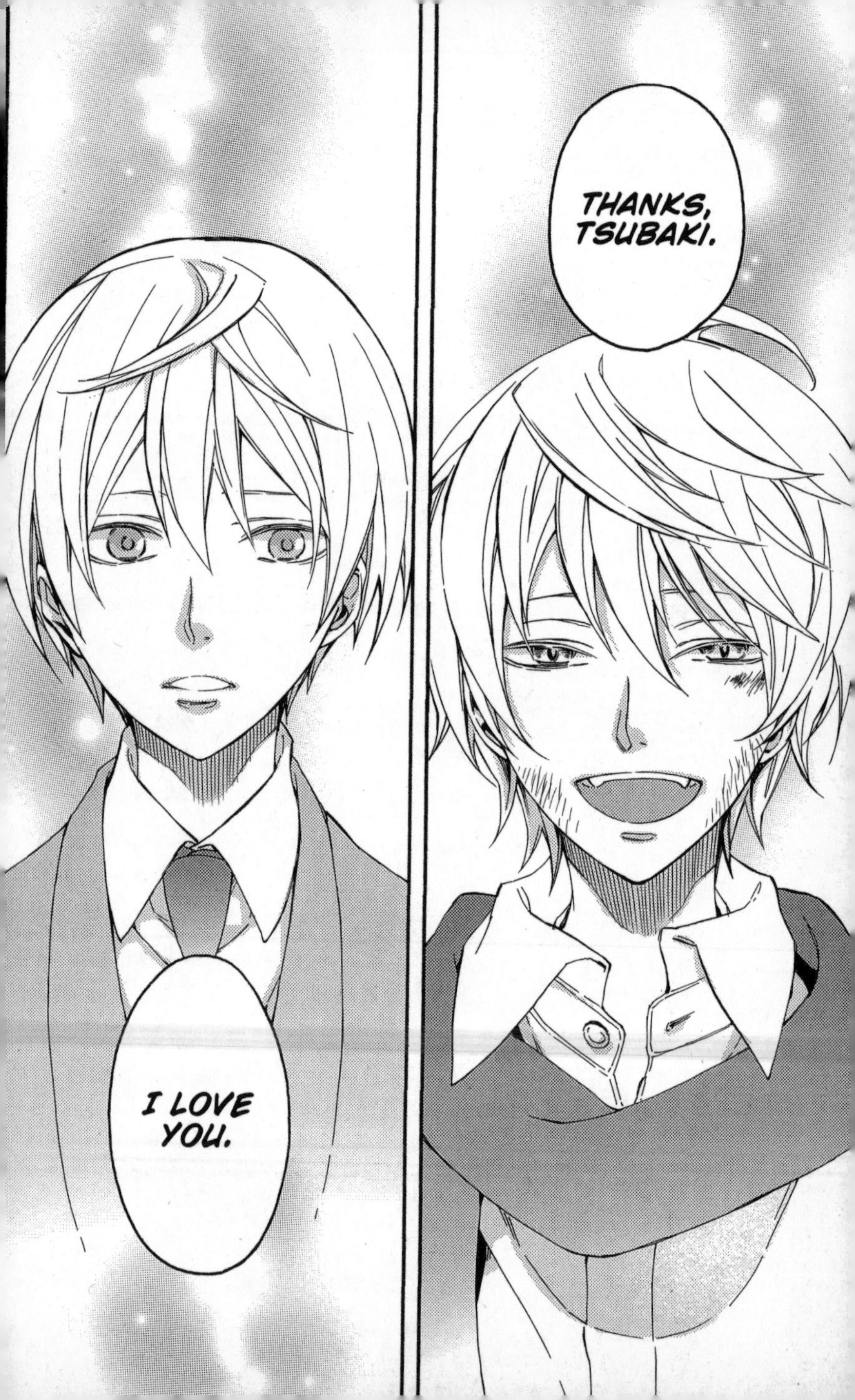
THANKS, TSUBAKI.
I LOVE YOU.

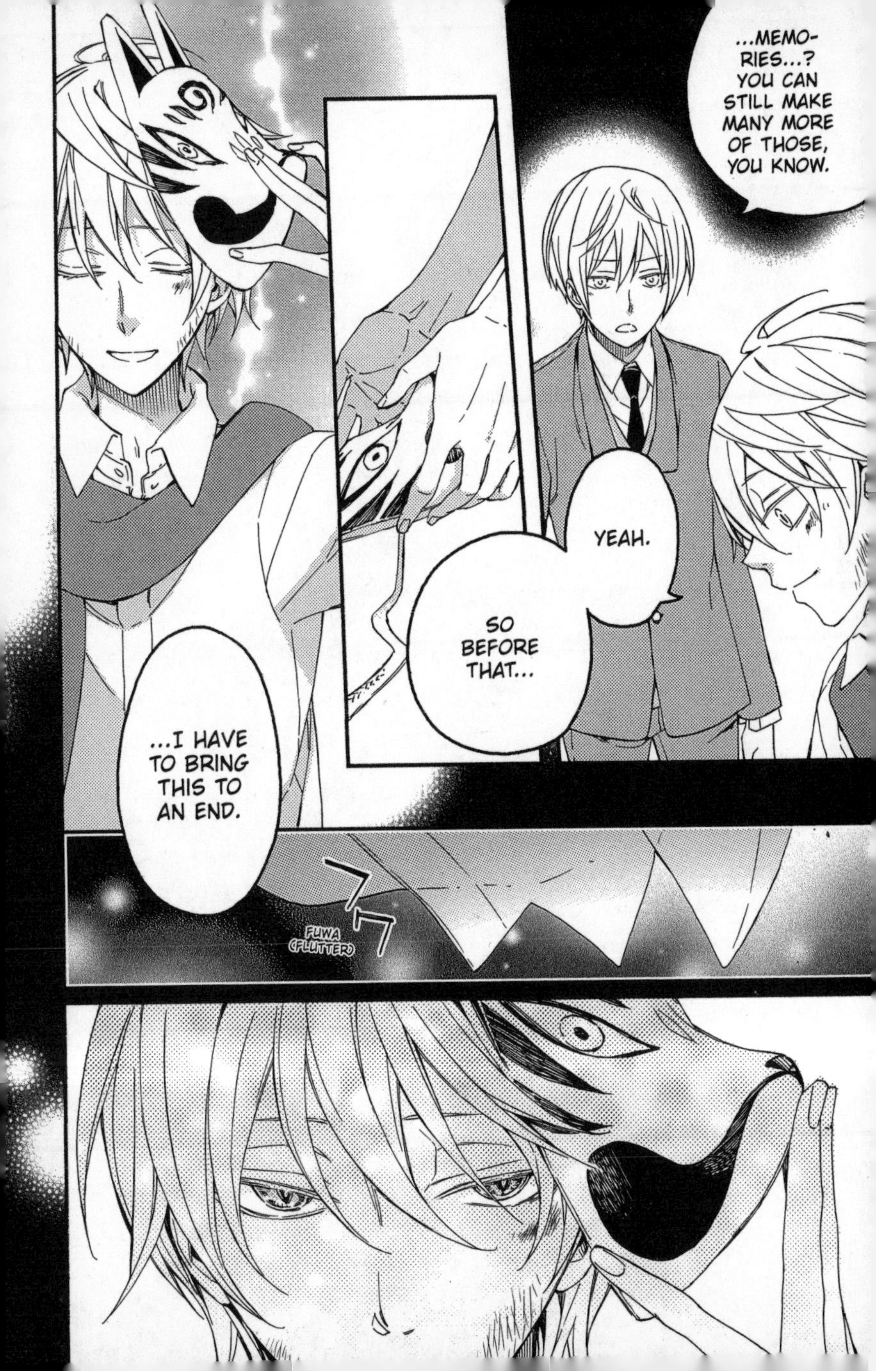
...MEMO-RIES...? YOU CAN STILL MAKE MANY MORE OF THOSE, YOU KNOW.
YEAH.
SO BEFORE THAT...
...I HAVE TO BRING THIS TO AN END.
FUWA (FLUTTER)

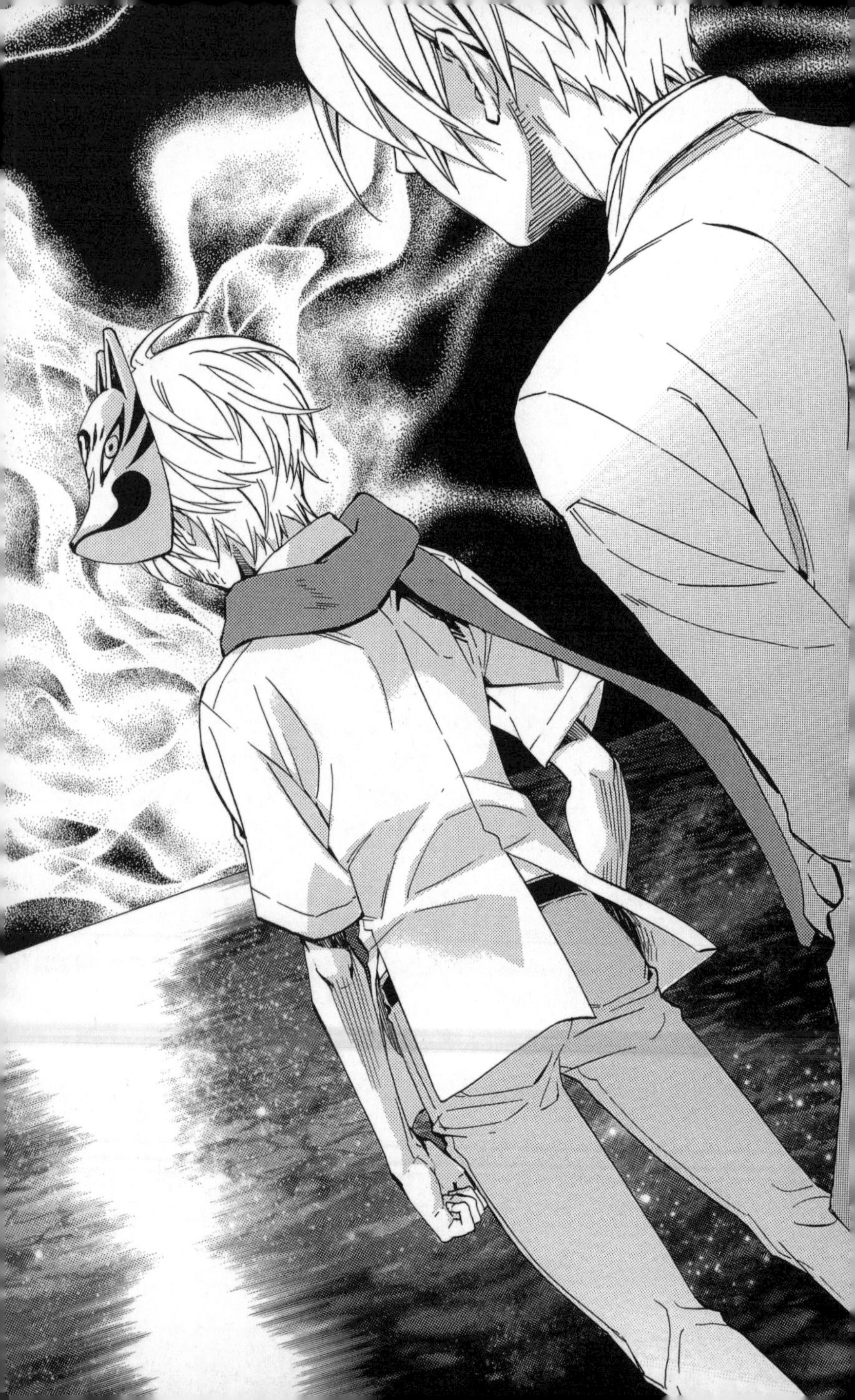

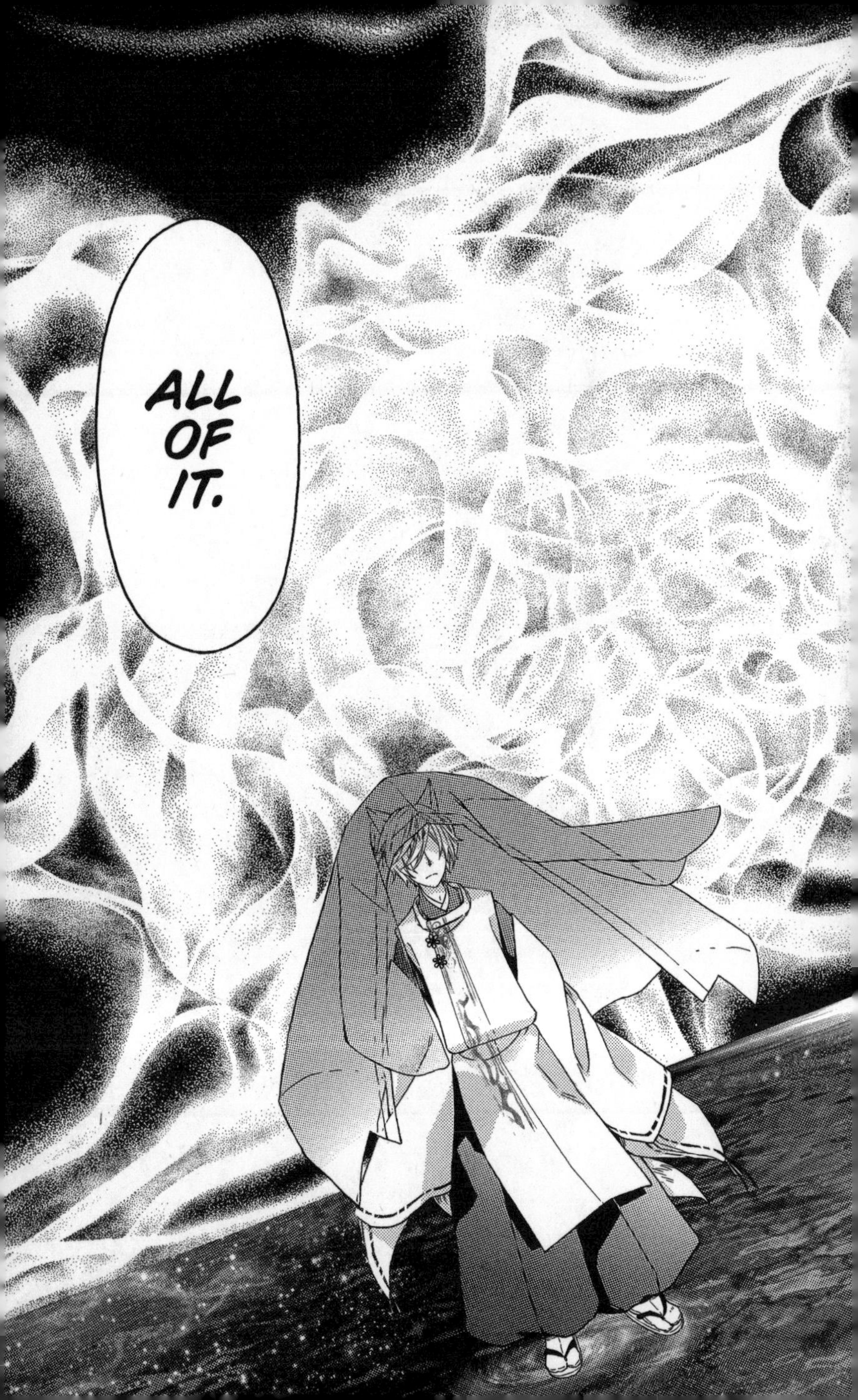
ALL OF IT.

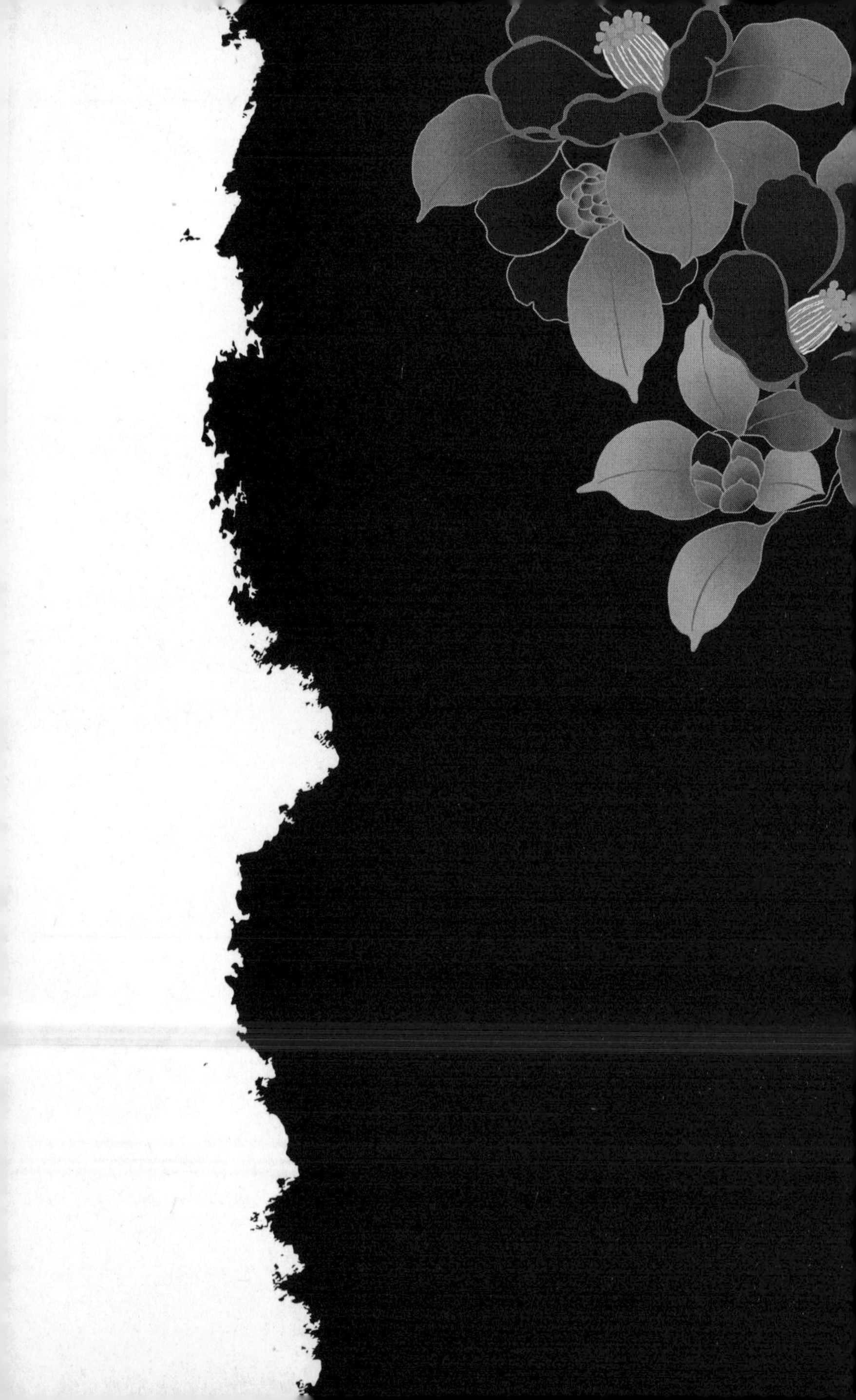

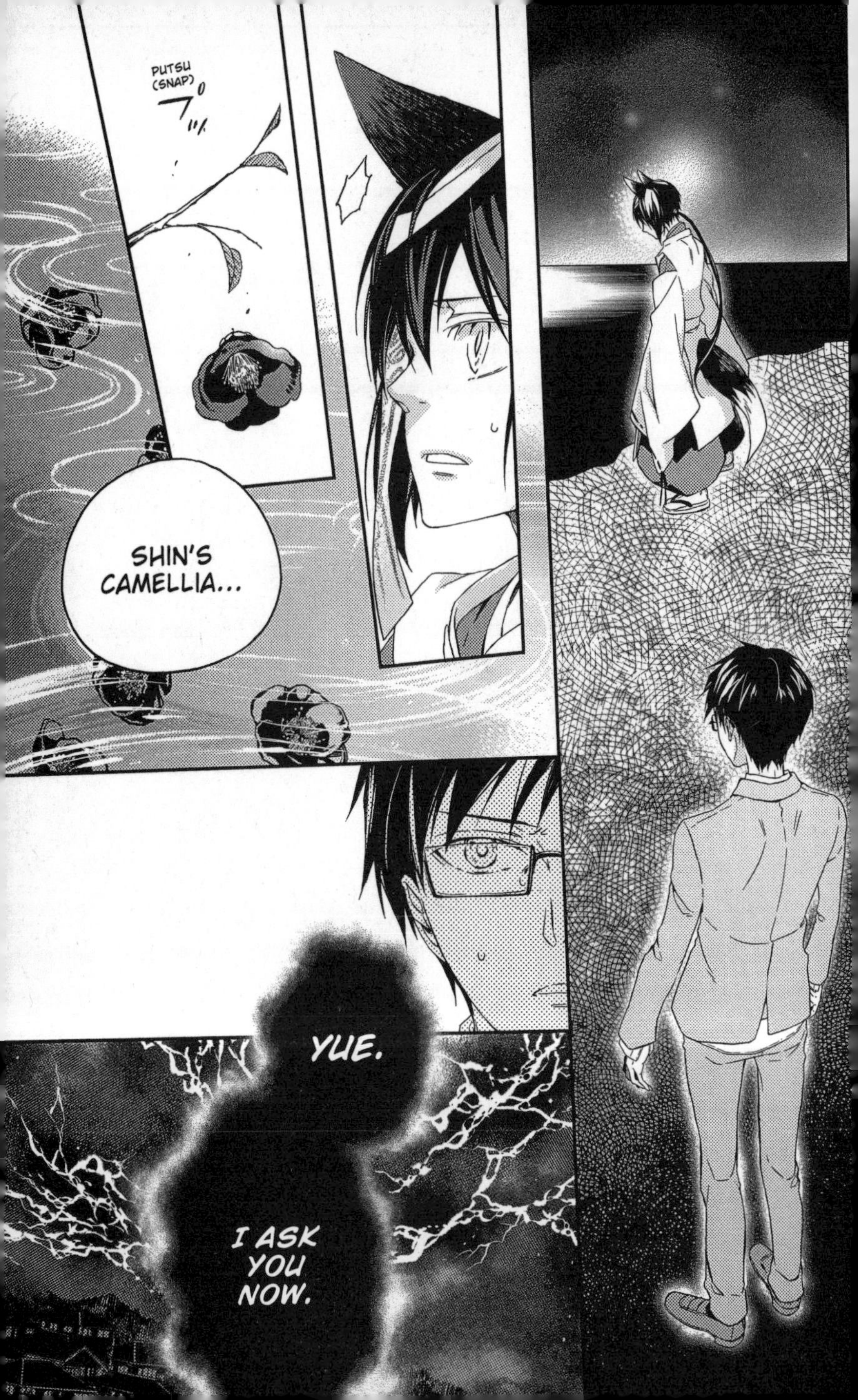
PUTSU (SNAP)
SHIN'S CAMELLIA...
YUE.
I ASK YOU NOW.

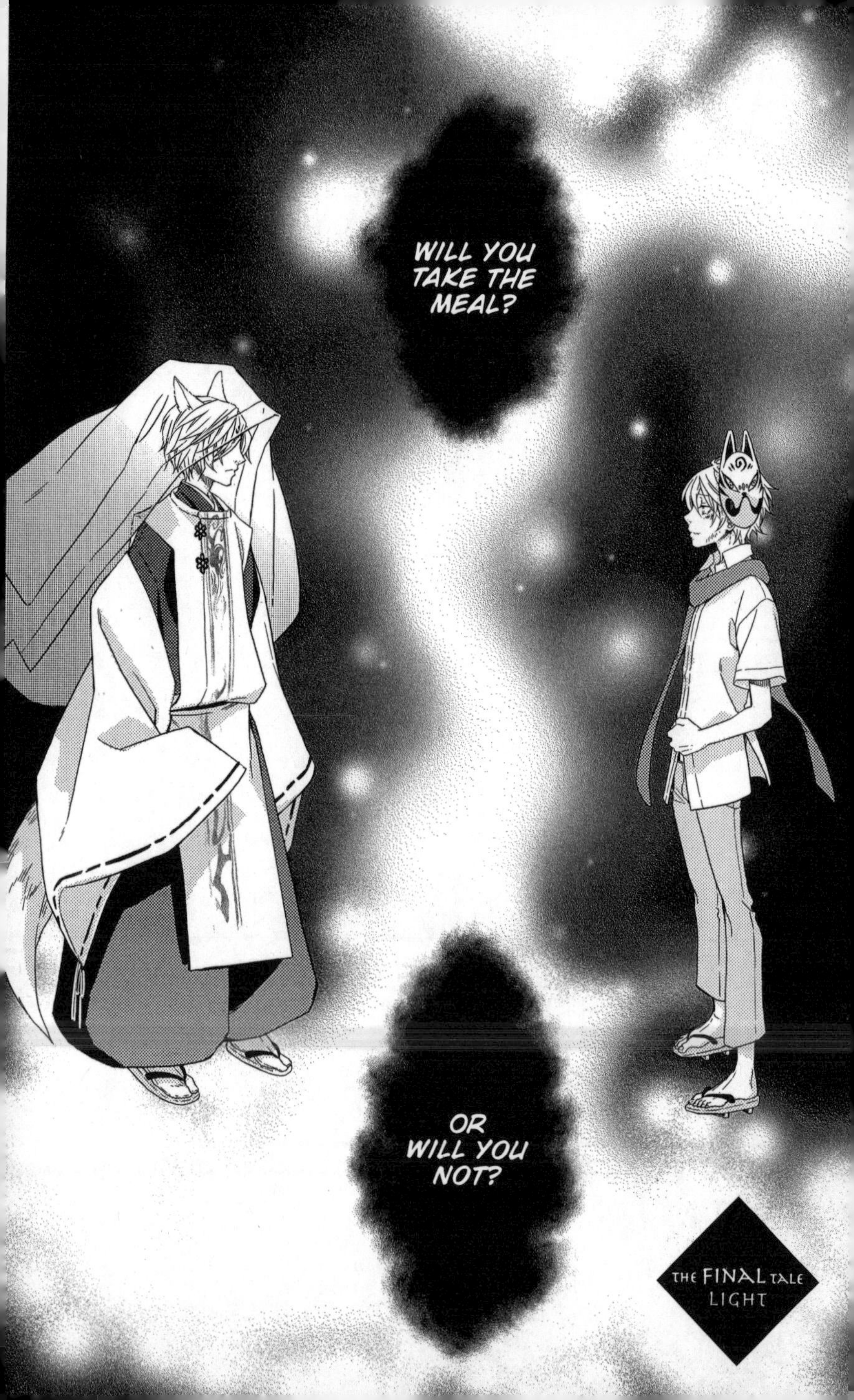
WILL YOU TAKE THE MEAL?
OR WILL YOU NOT?
THE FINAL TALE
LIGHT

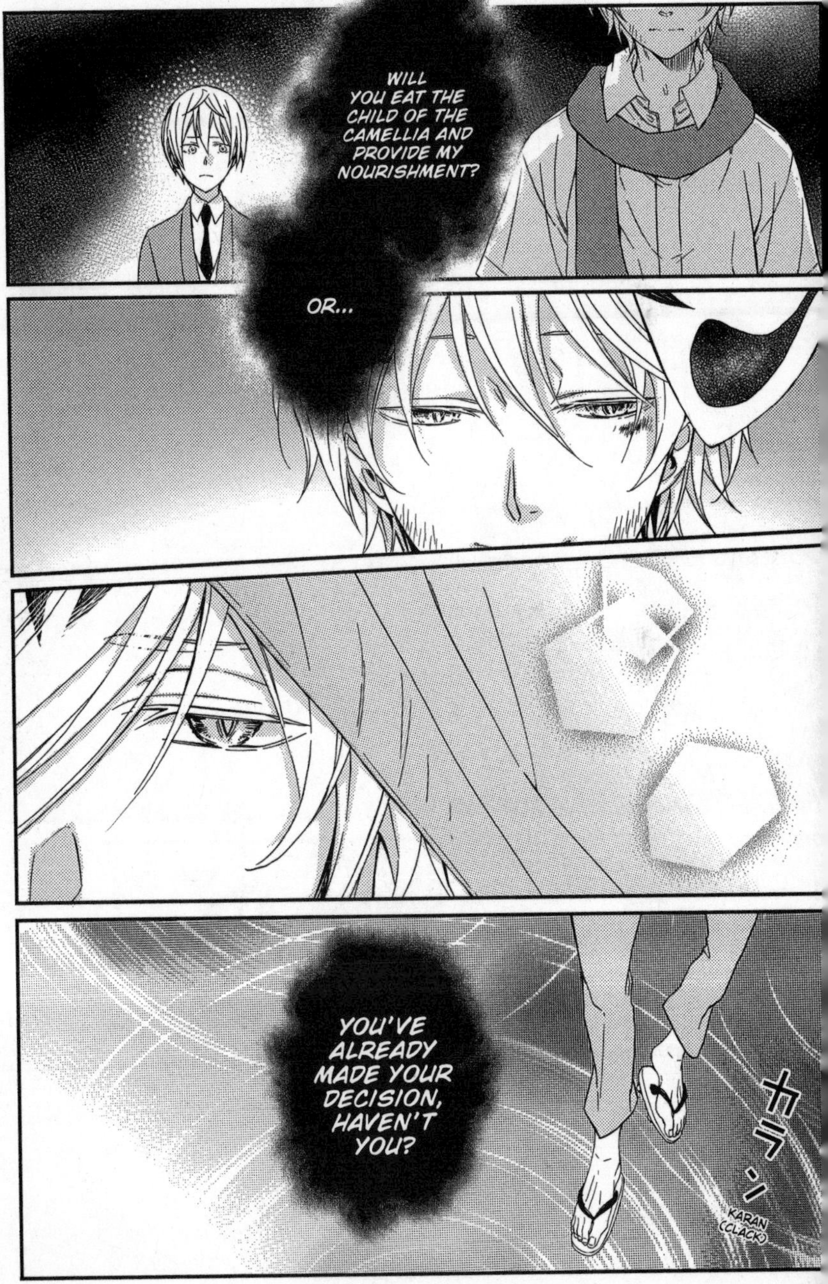
WILL YOU EAT THE CHILD OF THE CAMELLIA AND PROVIDE MY NOURISHMENT?
OR...
YOU'VE ALREADY MADE YOUR DECISION, HAVEN'T YOU?
KARAN (CLACK)

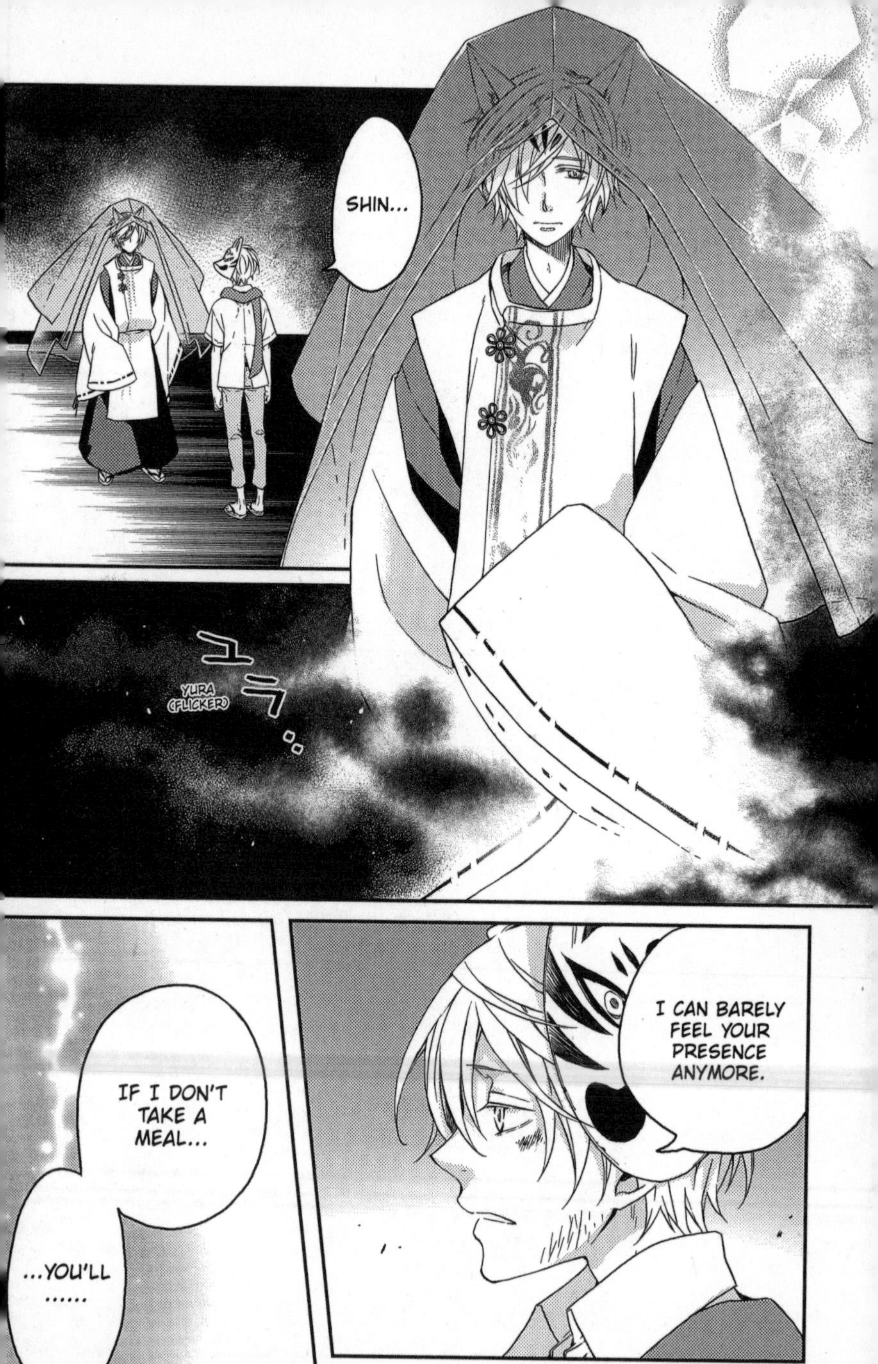
SHIN...
ユラ
YURA (FLICKER)
I CAN BARELY FEEL YOUR PRESENCE ANYMORE.
IF I DON'T TAKE A MEAL...
...YOU'LL ......

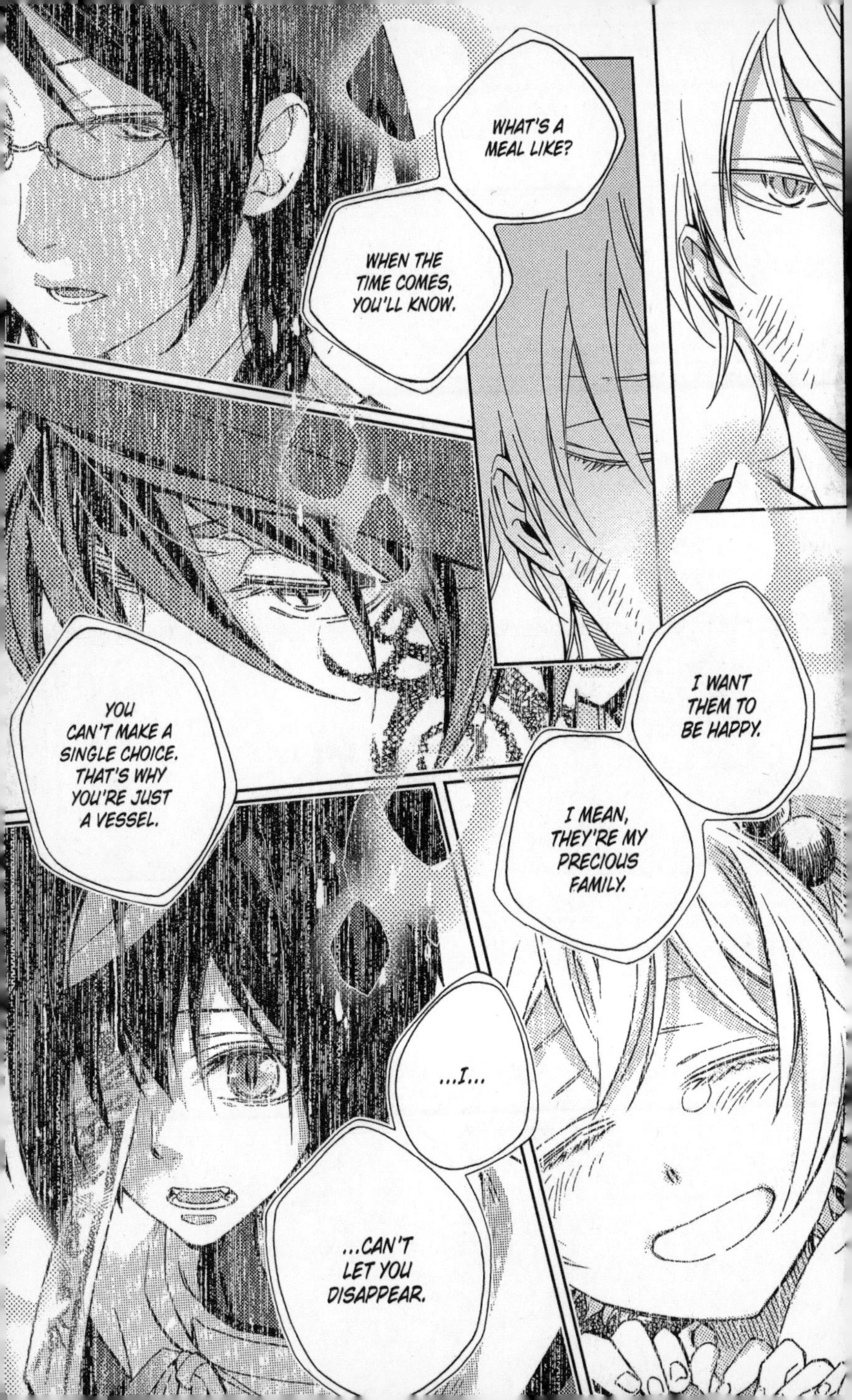
WHAT'S A MEAL LIKE?
WHEN THE TIME COMES, YOU'LL KNOW.
I WANT THEM TO BE HAPPY.
I MEAN, THEY'RE MY PRECIOUS FAMILY.
YOU CAN'T MAKE A SINGLE CHOICE. THAT'S WHY YOU'RE JUST A VESSEL.
...I...
...CAN'T LET YOU DISAPPEAR.

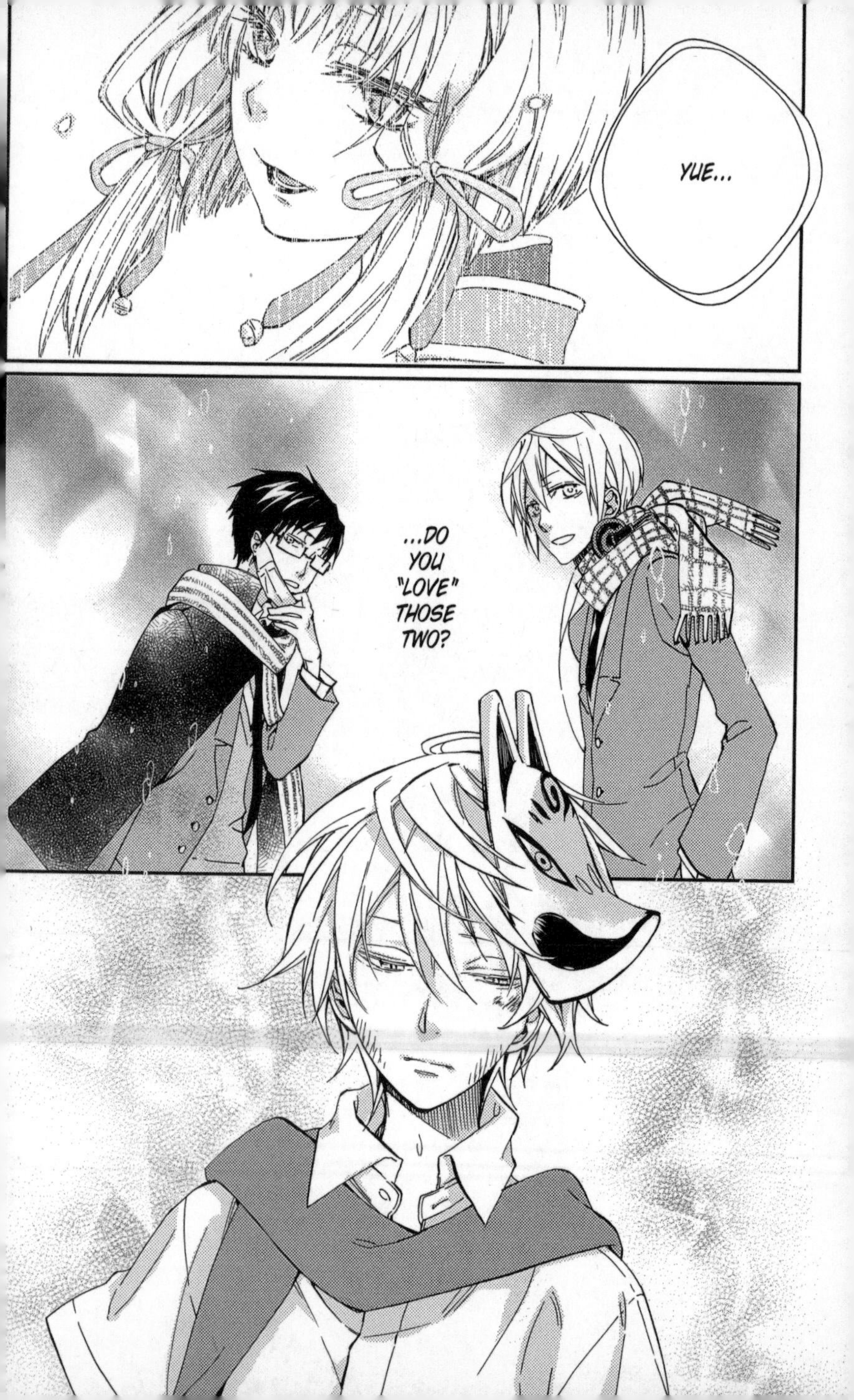
YUE...
...DO YOU "LOVE" THOSE TWO?

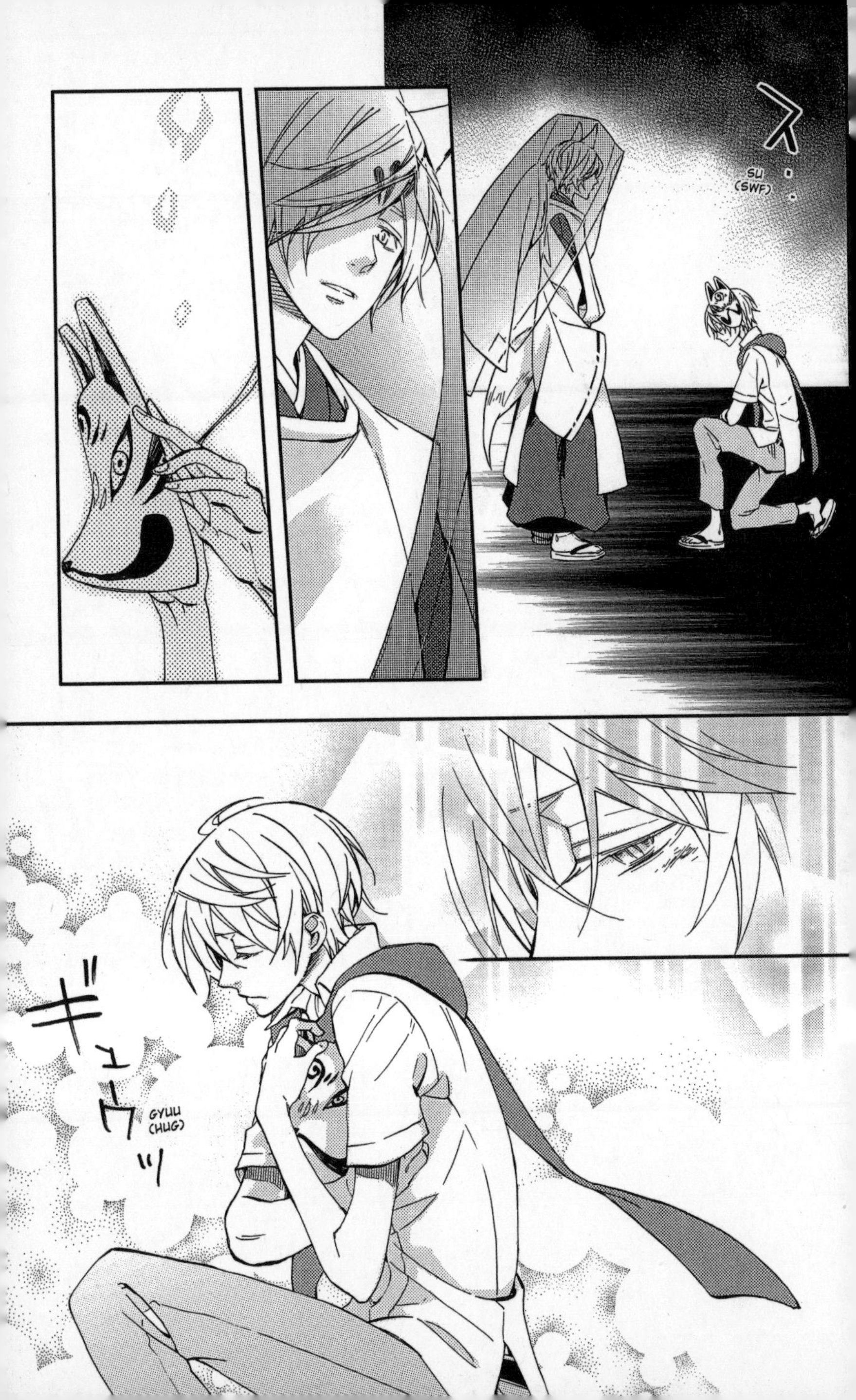
ス・・
SU (SWF)
ギューウッ
GYUU (HUG)

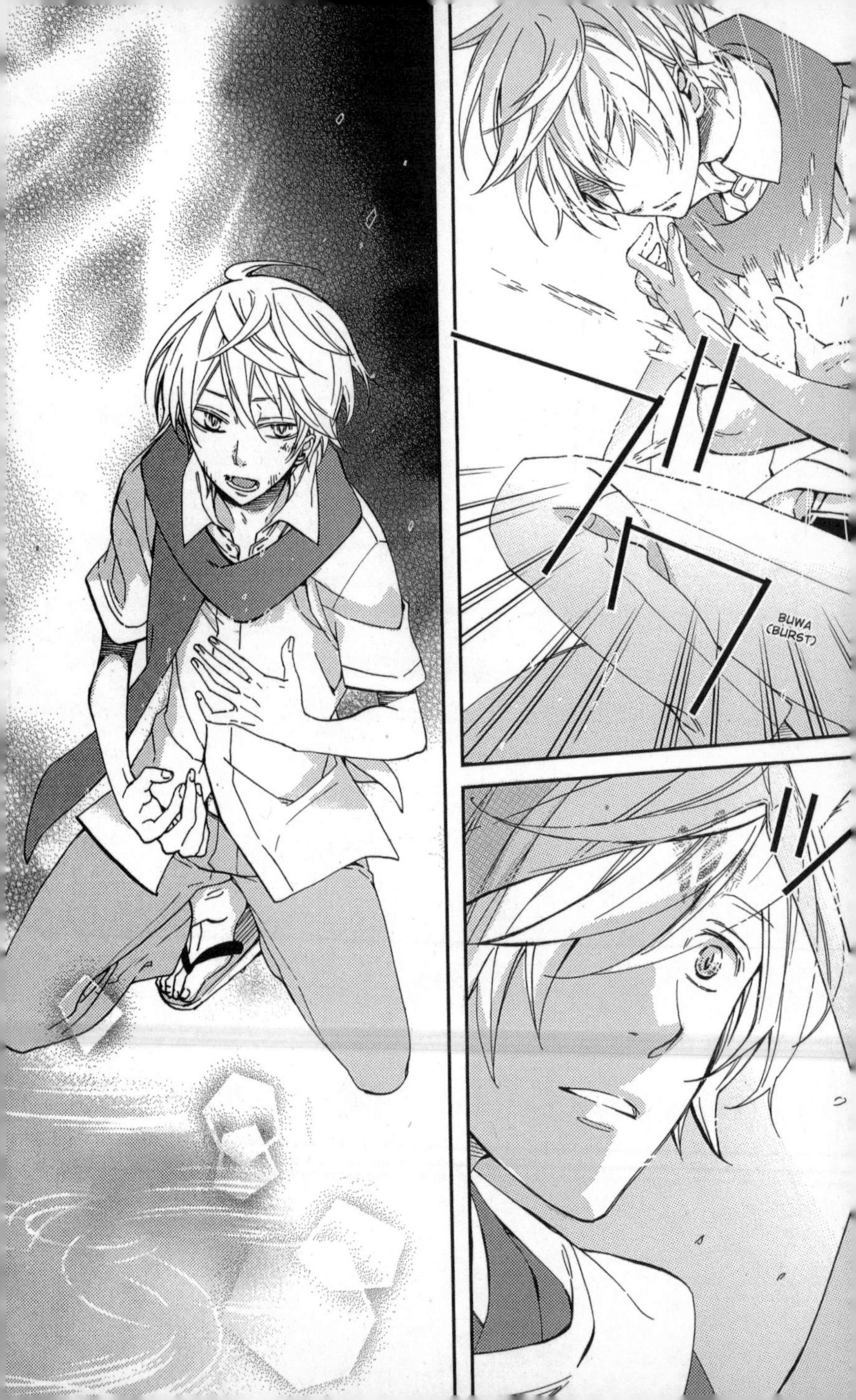
BUWA
(BURST)

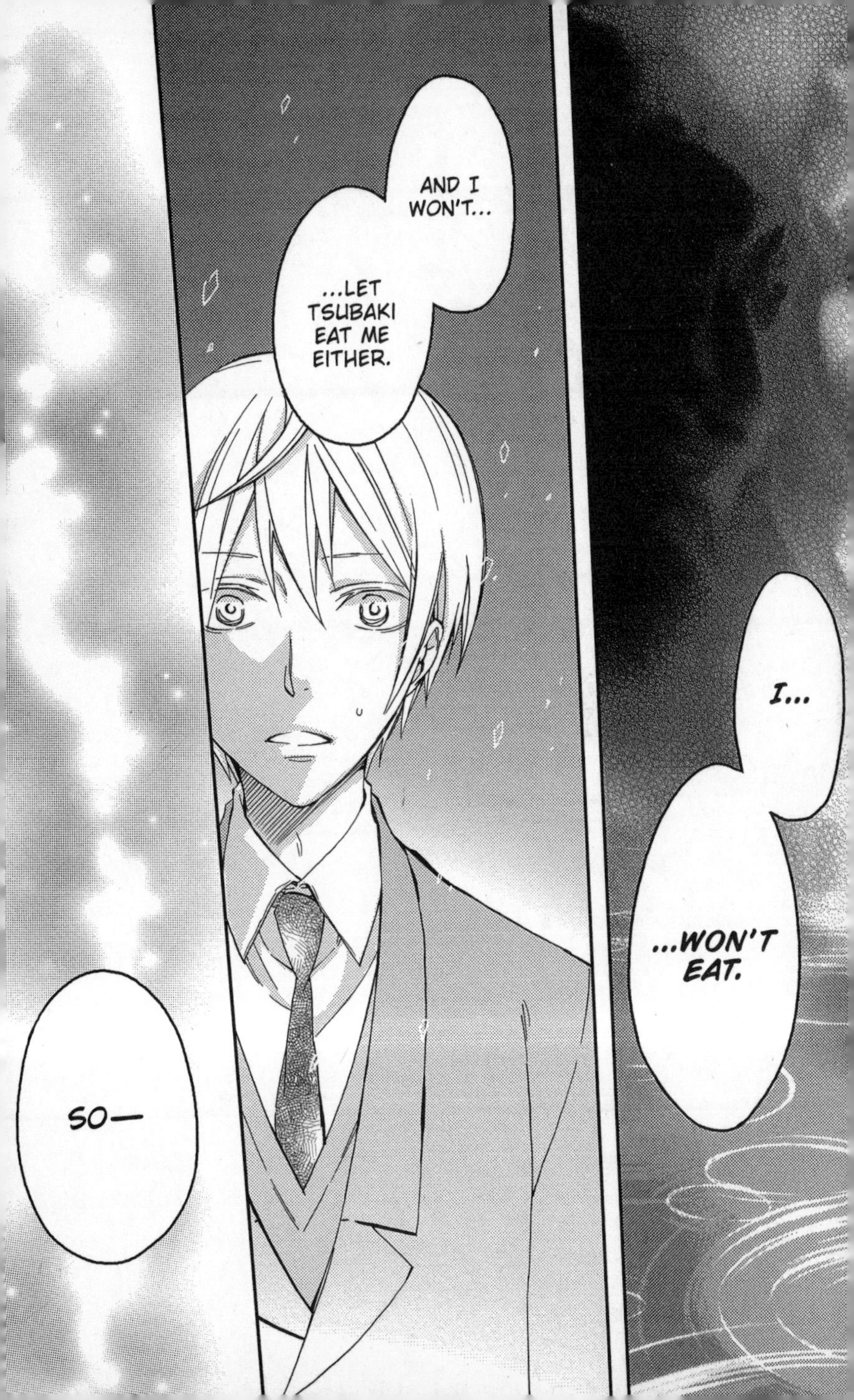
I...
...WON'T EAT.
AND I WON'T...
...LET TSUBAKI EAT ME EITHER.
SO—

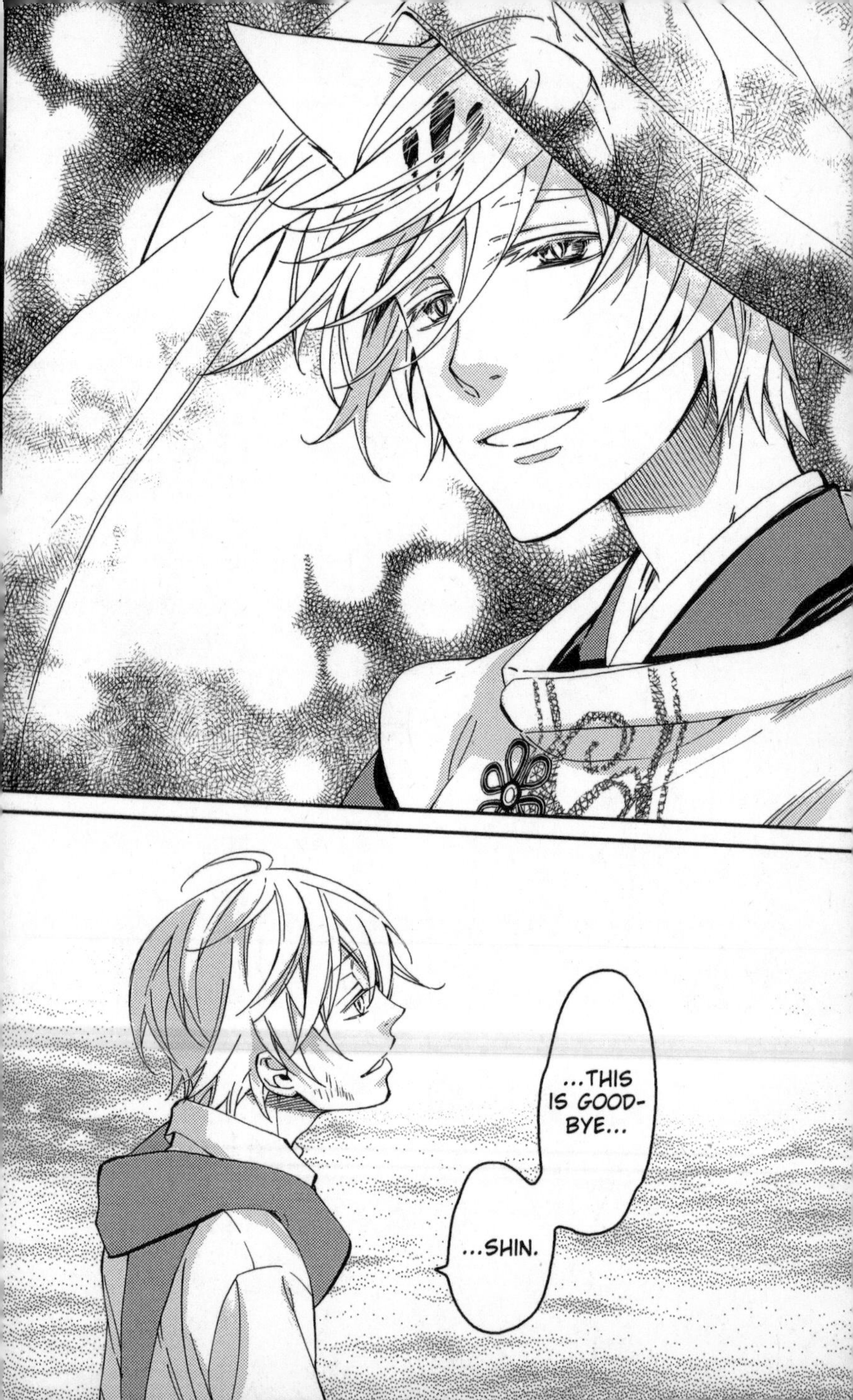
...THIS IS GOOD-BYE...
...SHIN.

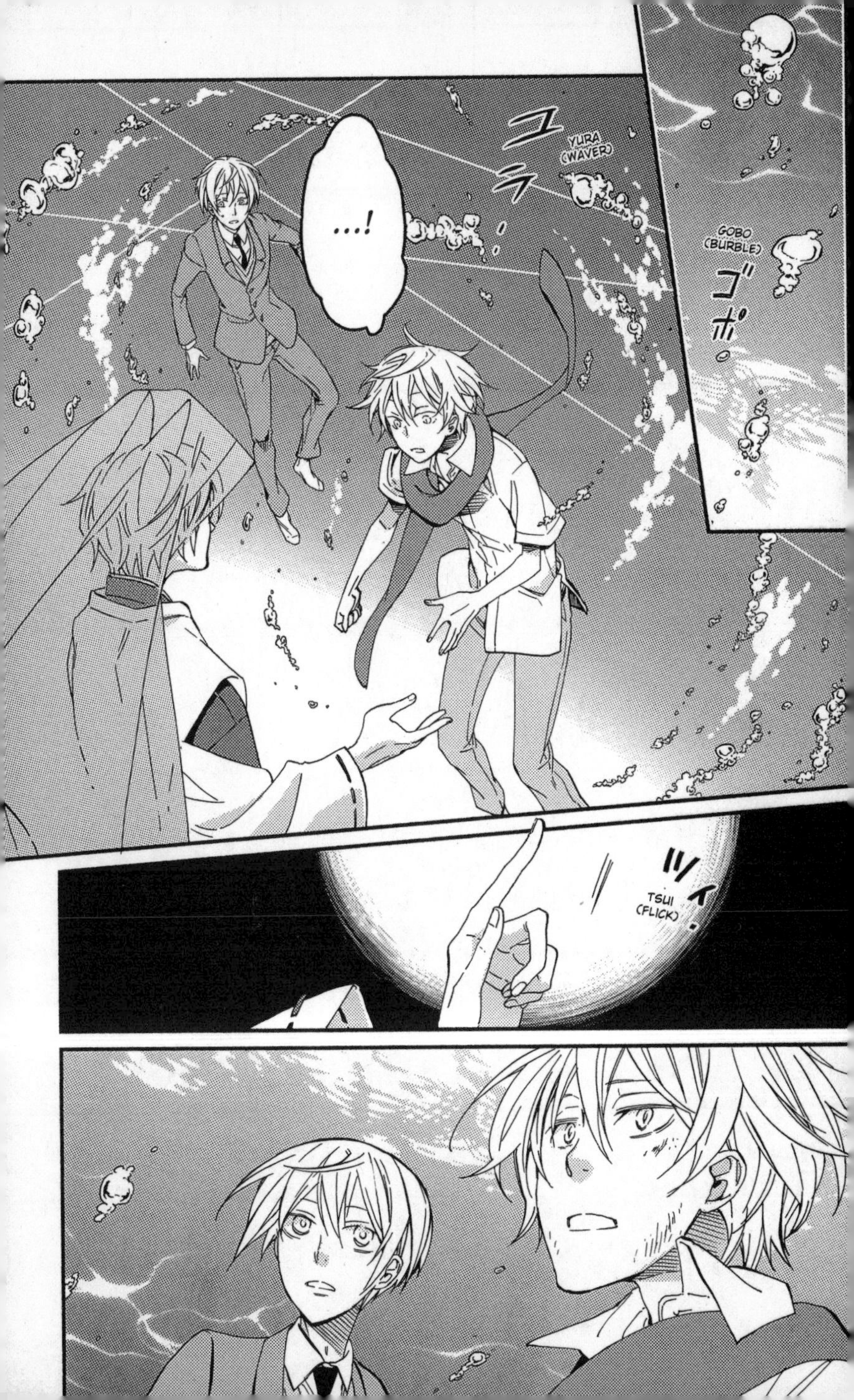
ゴポ
GOBO (BURBLE)
ユラ
YURA (WAVER)
...!
ツイ
TSUI (FLICK)

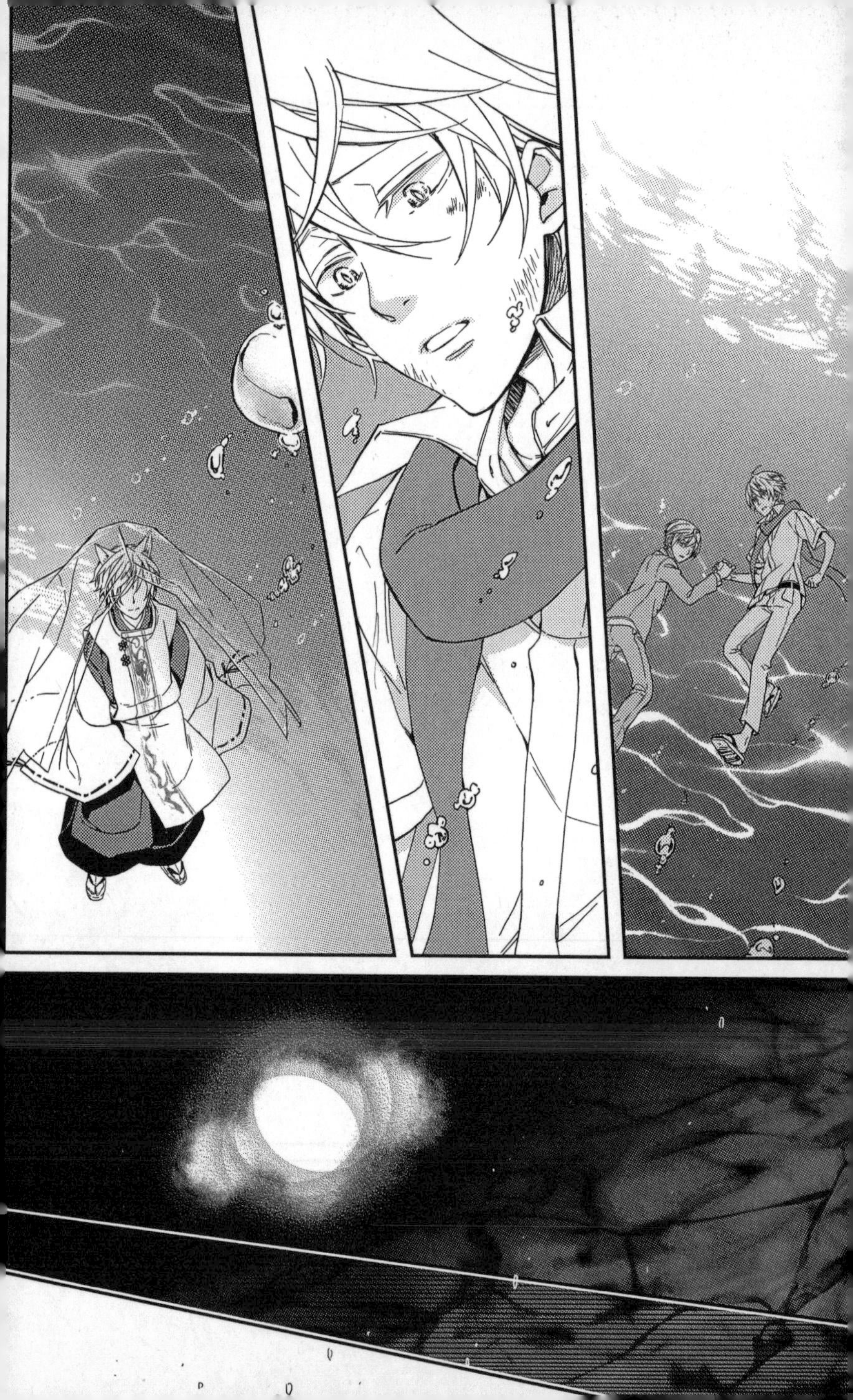

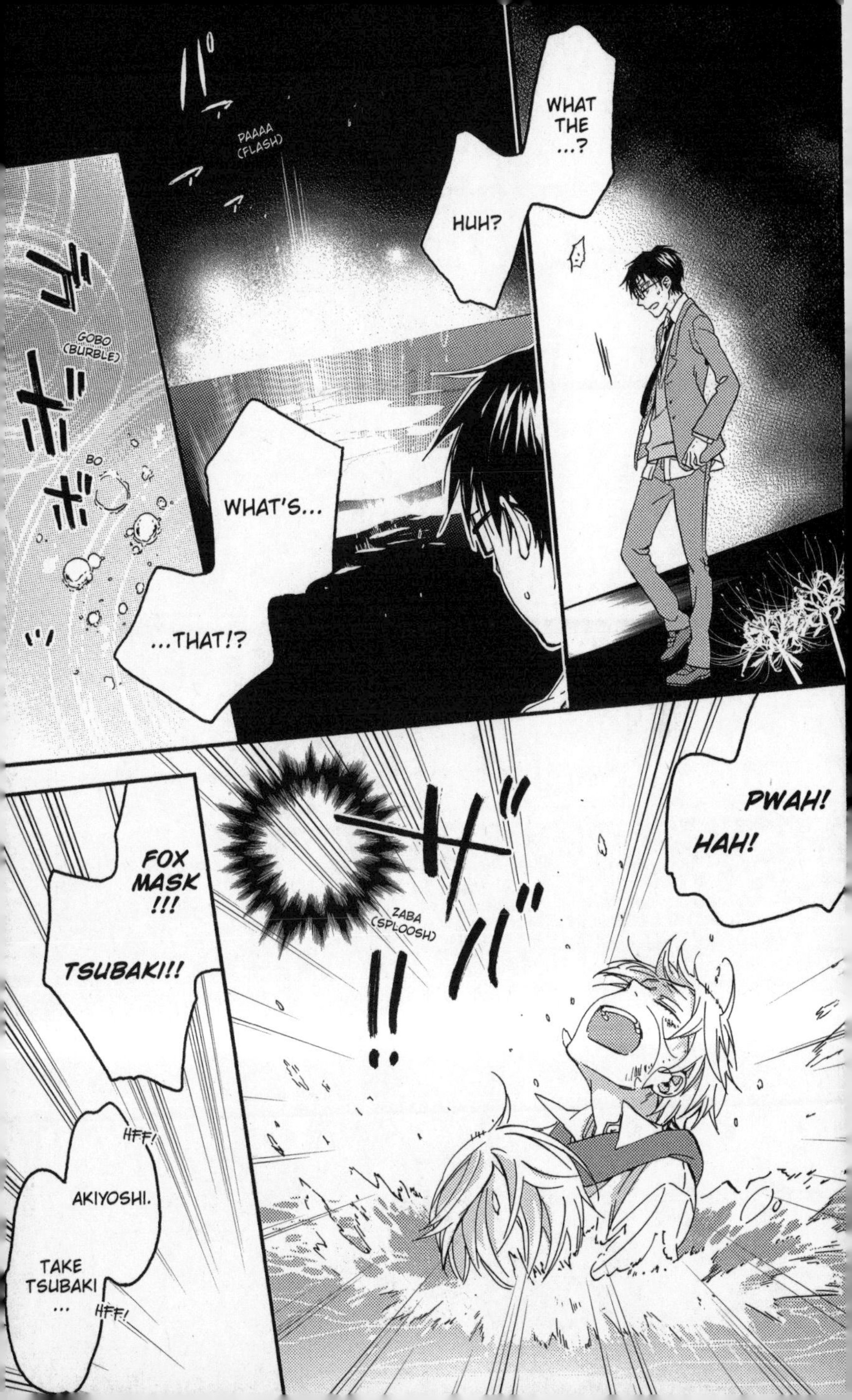
WHAT THE ...?
HUH?
PAAAA (FLASH)
WHAT'S...
...THAT!?
GOBO (BURBLE)
BO
PWAH!
HAH!
ZABA (SPLOOSH)
FOX MASK!!!
TSUBAKI!!!
HFF!
AKIYOSHI.
TAKE TSUBAKI ...
HFF!

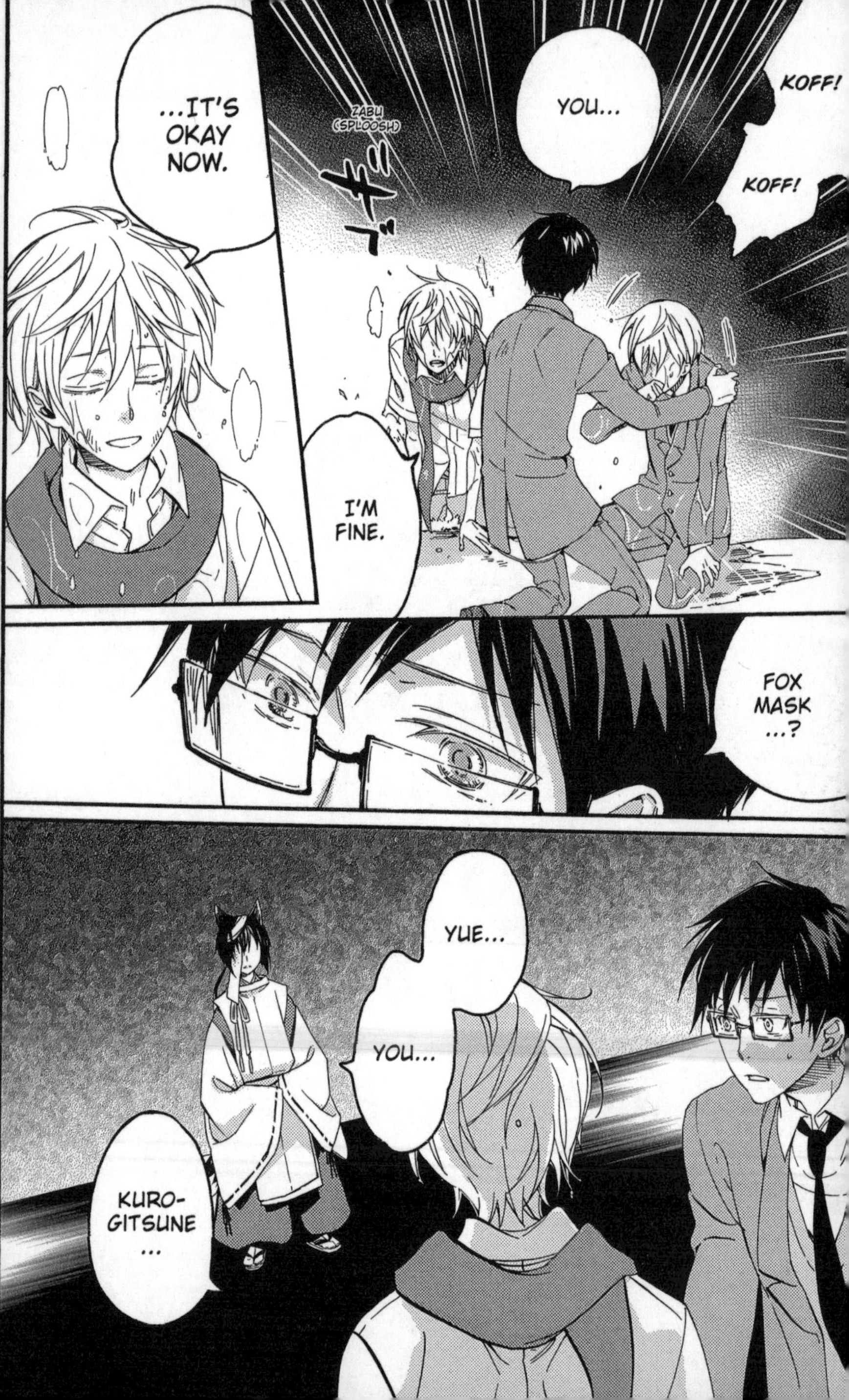
KOFF!
KOFF!
YOU...
ZABU (SPLOOSH)
I'M FINE.
...IT'S OKAY NOW.
FOX MASK ...?
YUE...
YOU...
KURO-GITSUNE ...

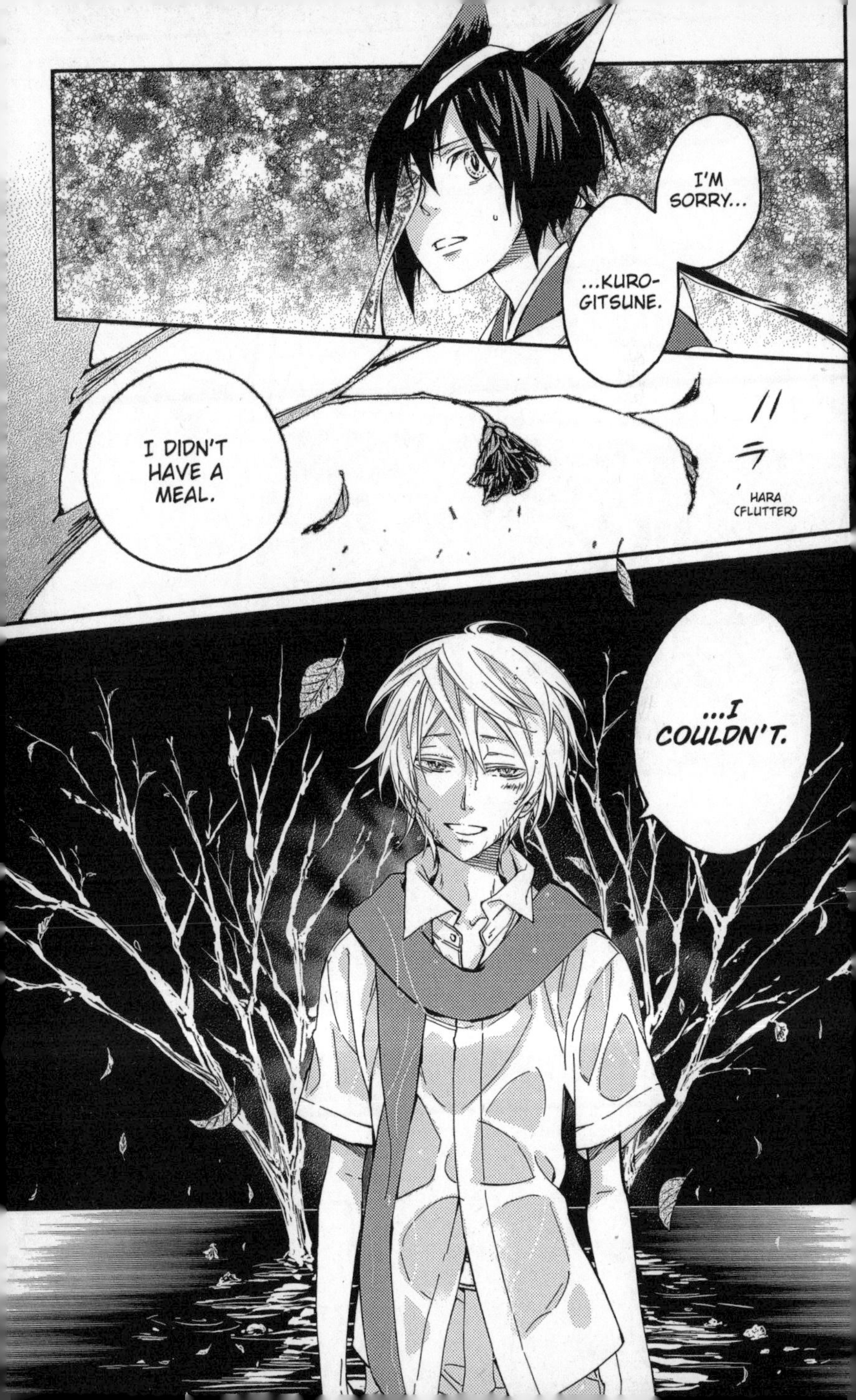
I'M SORRY...
...KURO-GITSUNE.
ハラ
HARA (FLUTTER)
I DIDN'T HAVE A MEAL.
...I COULDN'T.

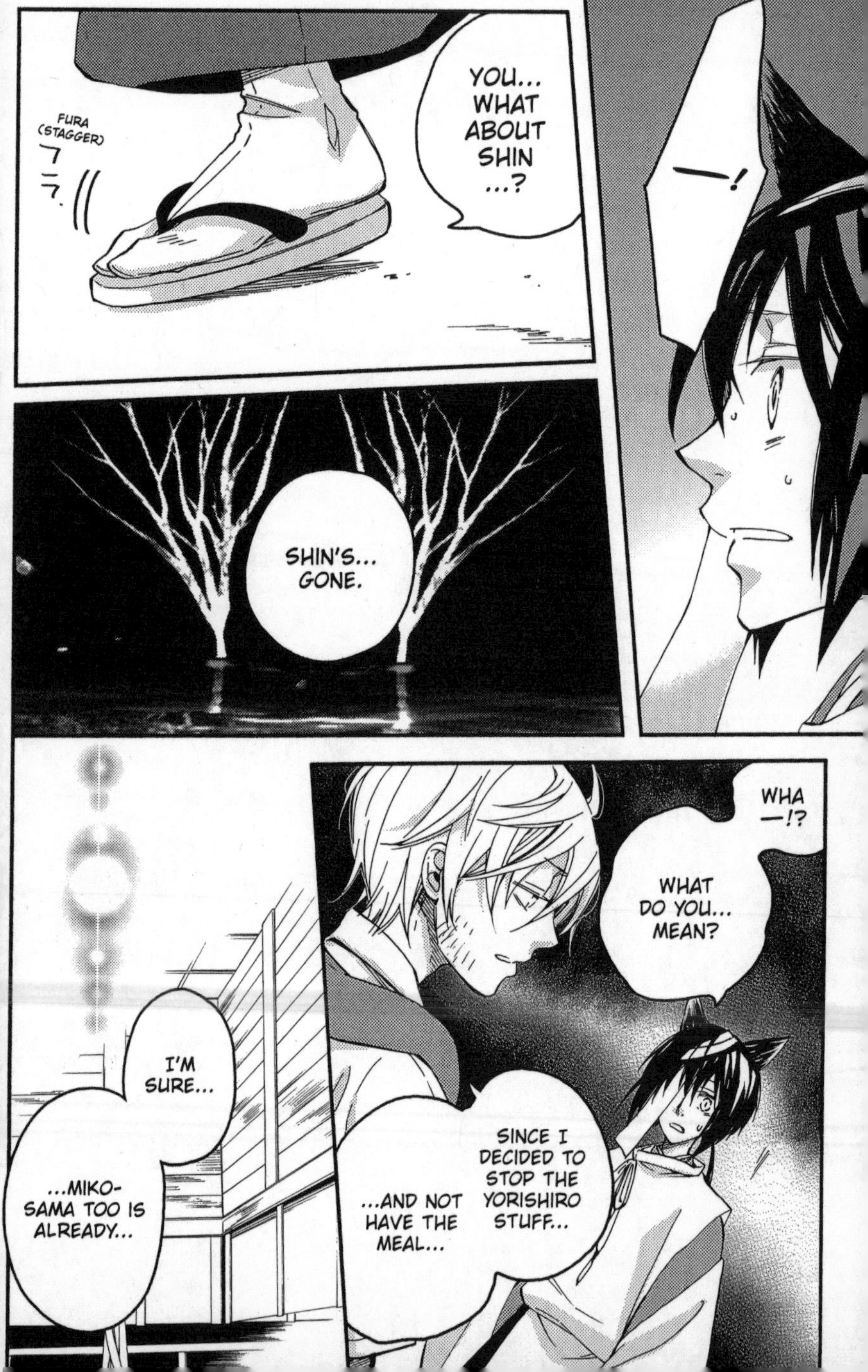
—!
YOU... WHAT ABOUT SHIN ...?
FURA (STAGGER)
SHIN'S... GONE.
WHA —!?
WHAT DO YOU... MEAN?
SINCE I DECIDED TO STOP THE YORISHIRO STUFF...
...AND NOT HAVE THE MEAL...
I'M SURE...
...MIKO-SAMA TOO IS ALREADY...

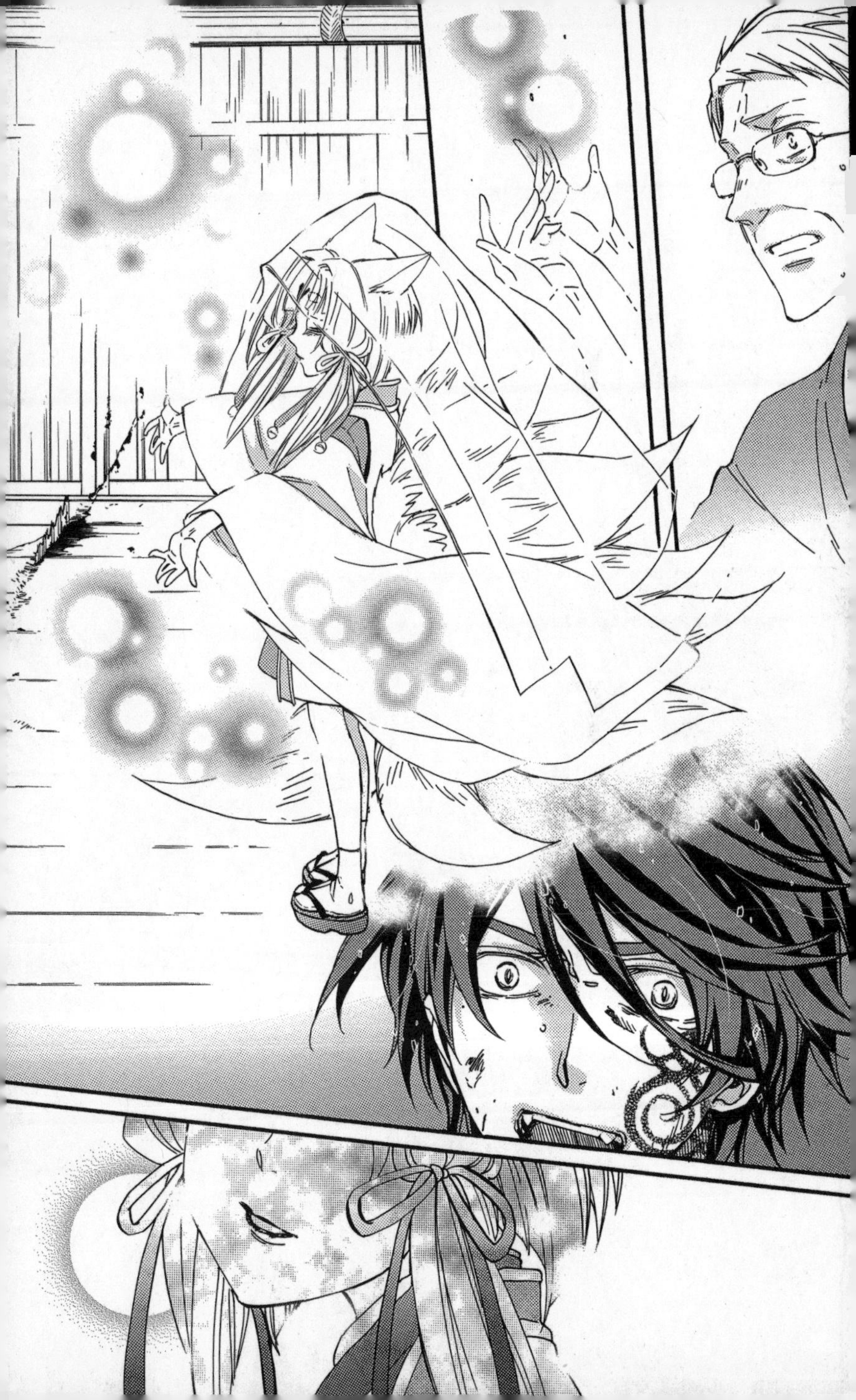

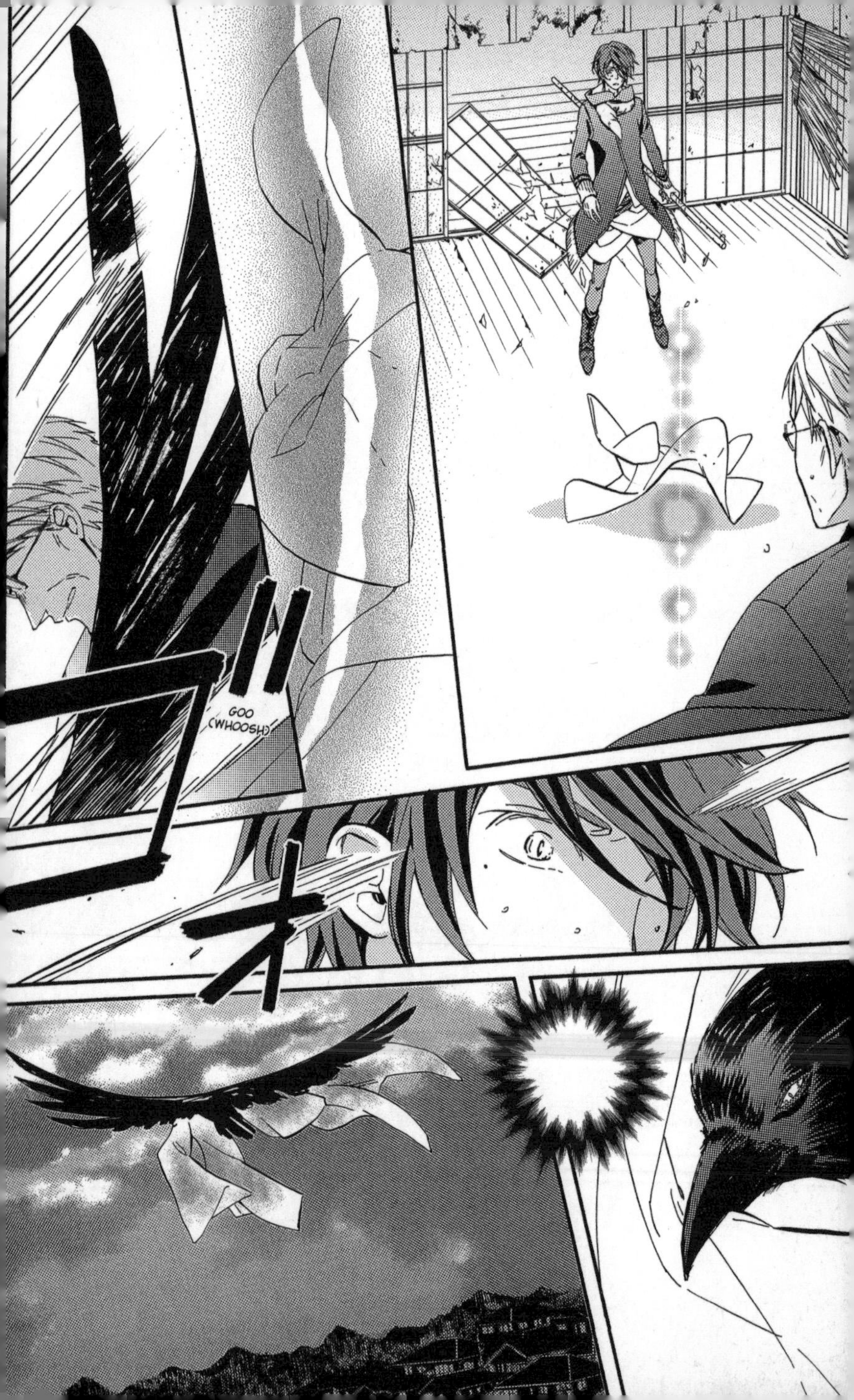
GOO (WHOOSH)

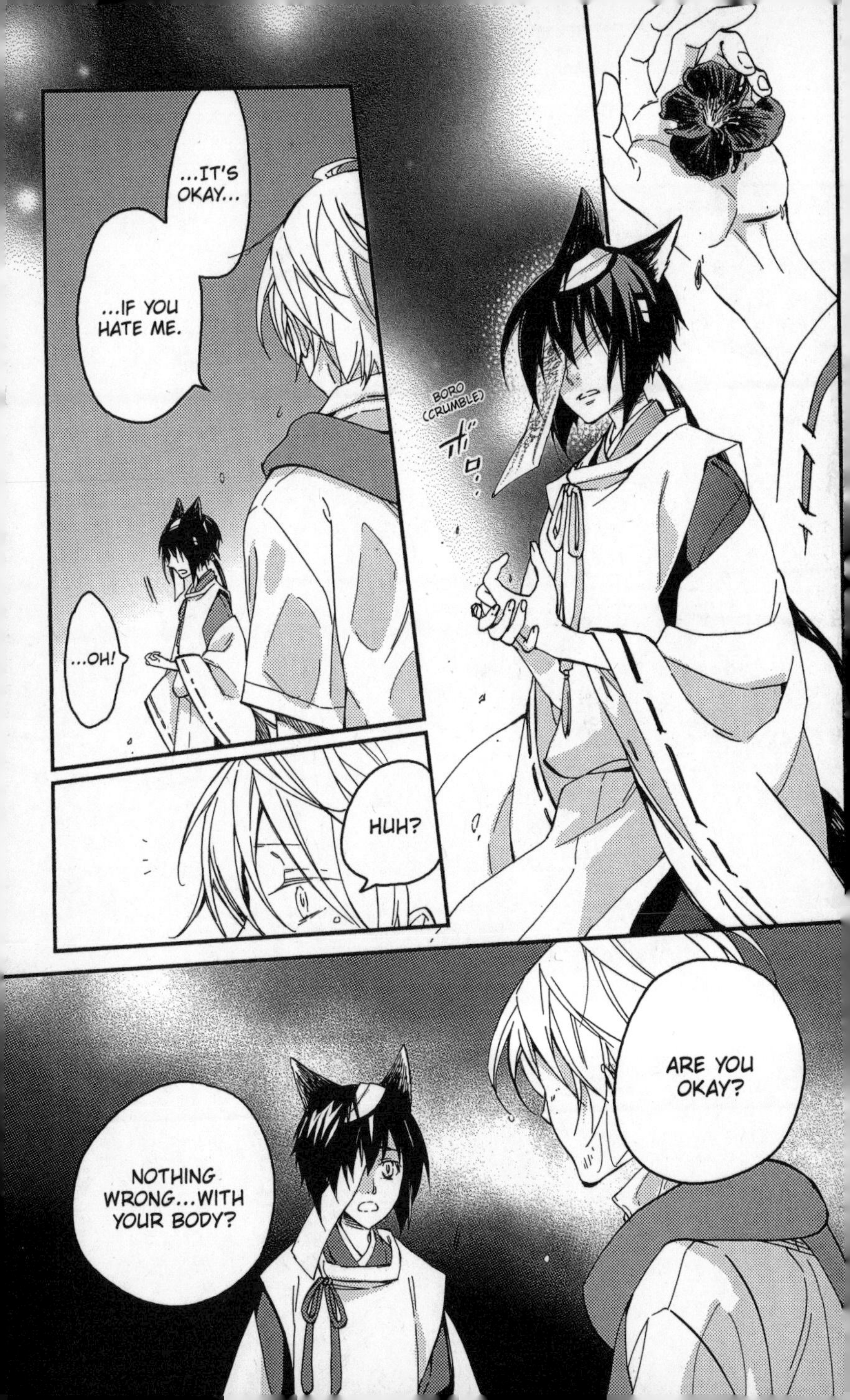
BORO (CRUMBLE)
...IT'S OKAY...
...IF YOU HATE ME.
...OH!
HUH?
ARE YOU OKAY?
NOTHING WRONG...WITH YOUR BODY?

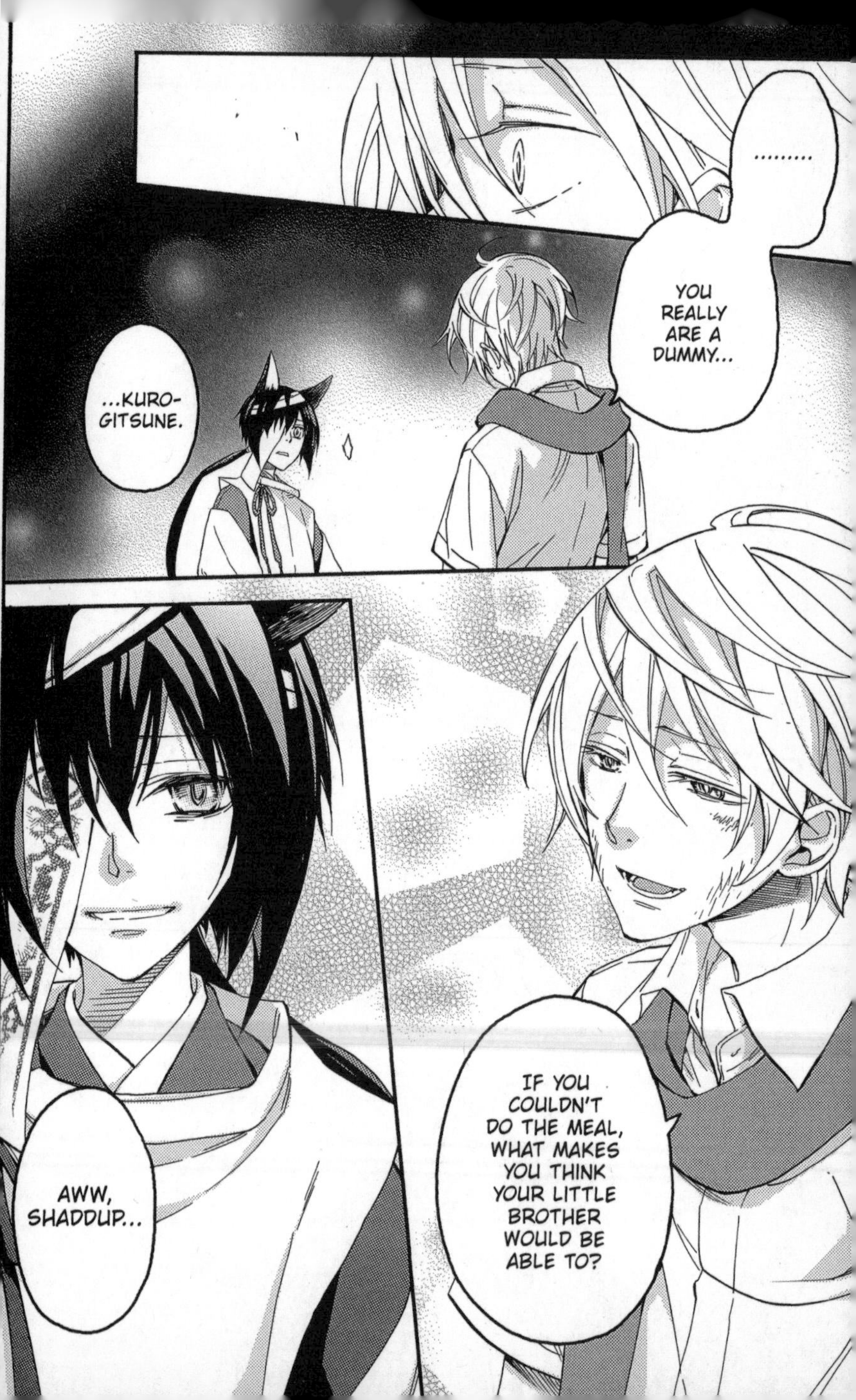
....
YOU REALLY ARE A DUMMY...
...KURO-GITSUNE.
IF YOU COULDN'T DO THE MEAL, WHAT MAKES YOU THINK YOUR LITTLE BROTHER WOULD BE ABLE TO?
AWW, SHADDUP...

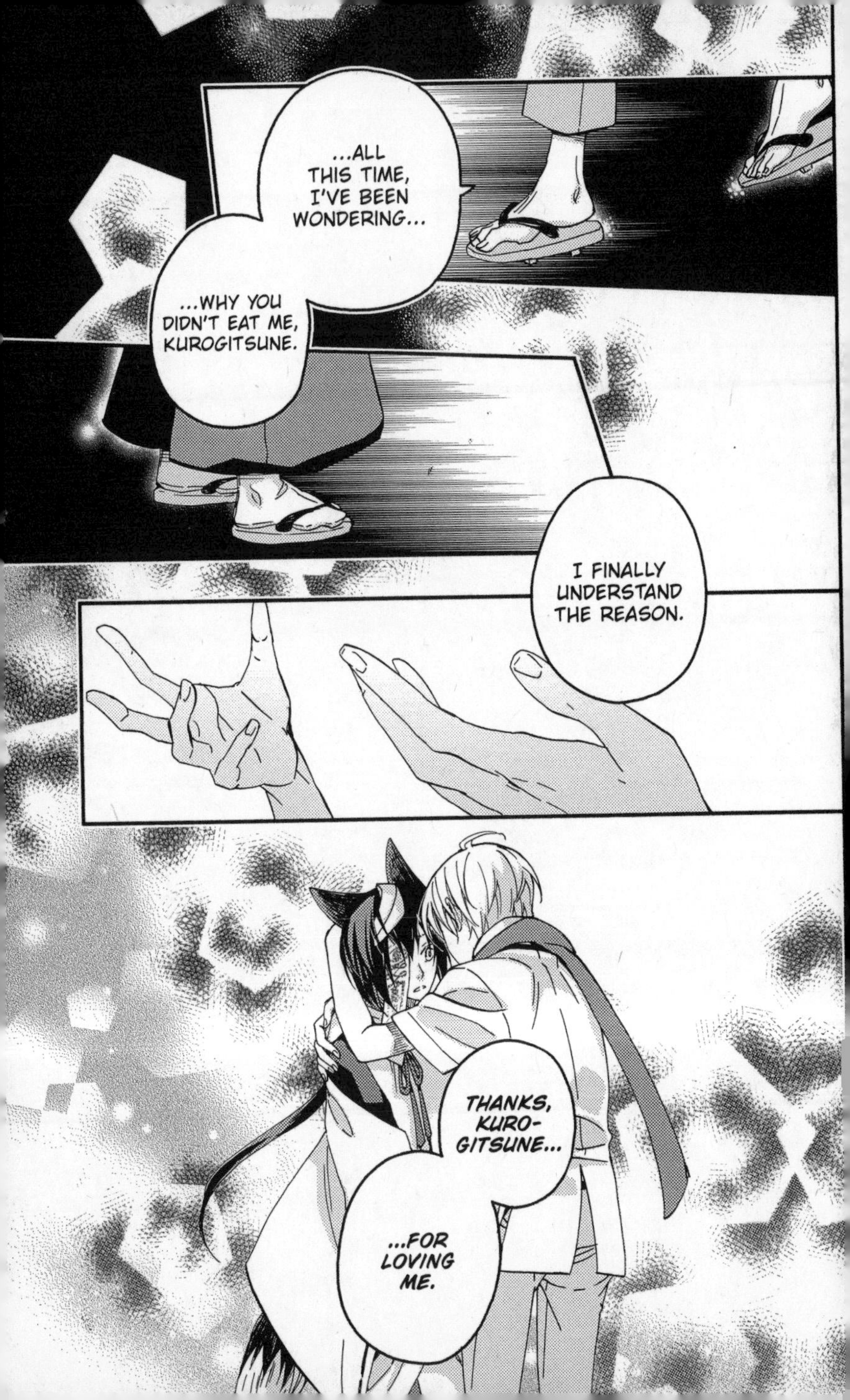
...ALL THIS TIME, I'VE BEEN WONDERING...
...WHY YOU DIDN'T EAT ME, KUROGITSUNE.
I FINALLY UNDERSTAND THE REASON.
THANKS, KURO-GITSUNE...
...FOR LOVING ME.

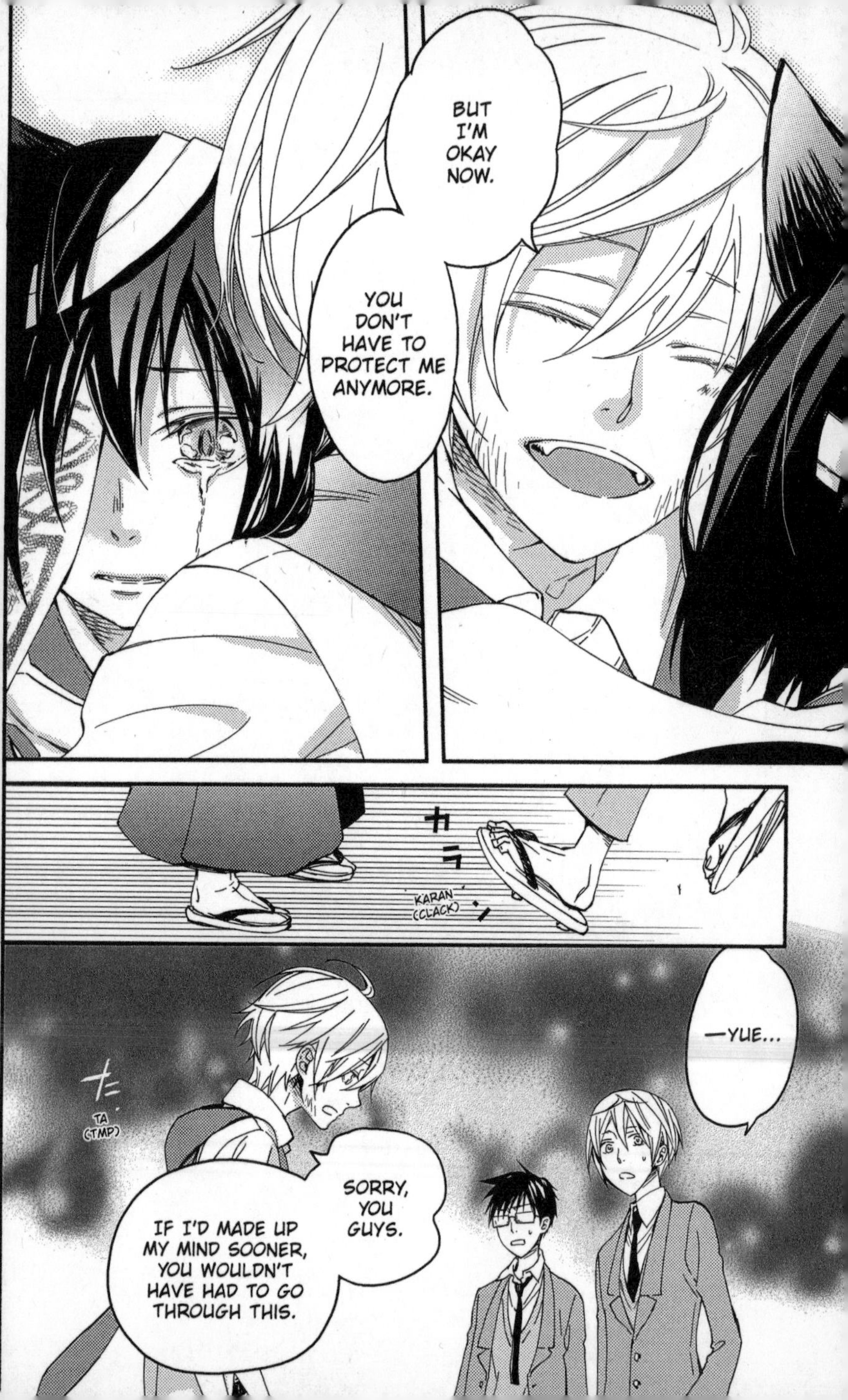
BUT I'M OKAY NOW.
YOU DON'T HAVE TO PROTECT ME ANYMORE.
KARAN (CLACK)
—YUE...
TA (TMP)
SORRY, YOU GUYS.
IF I'D MADE UP MY MIND SOONER, YOU WOULDN'T HAVE HAD TO GO THROUGH THIS.

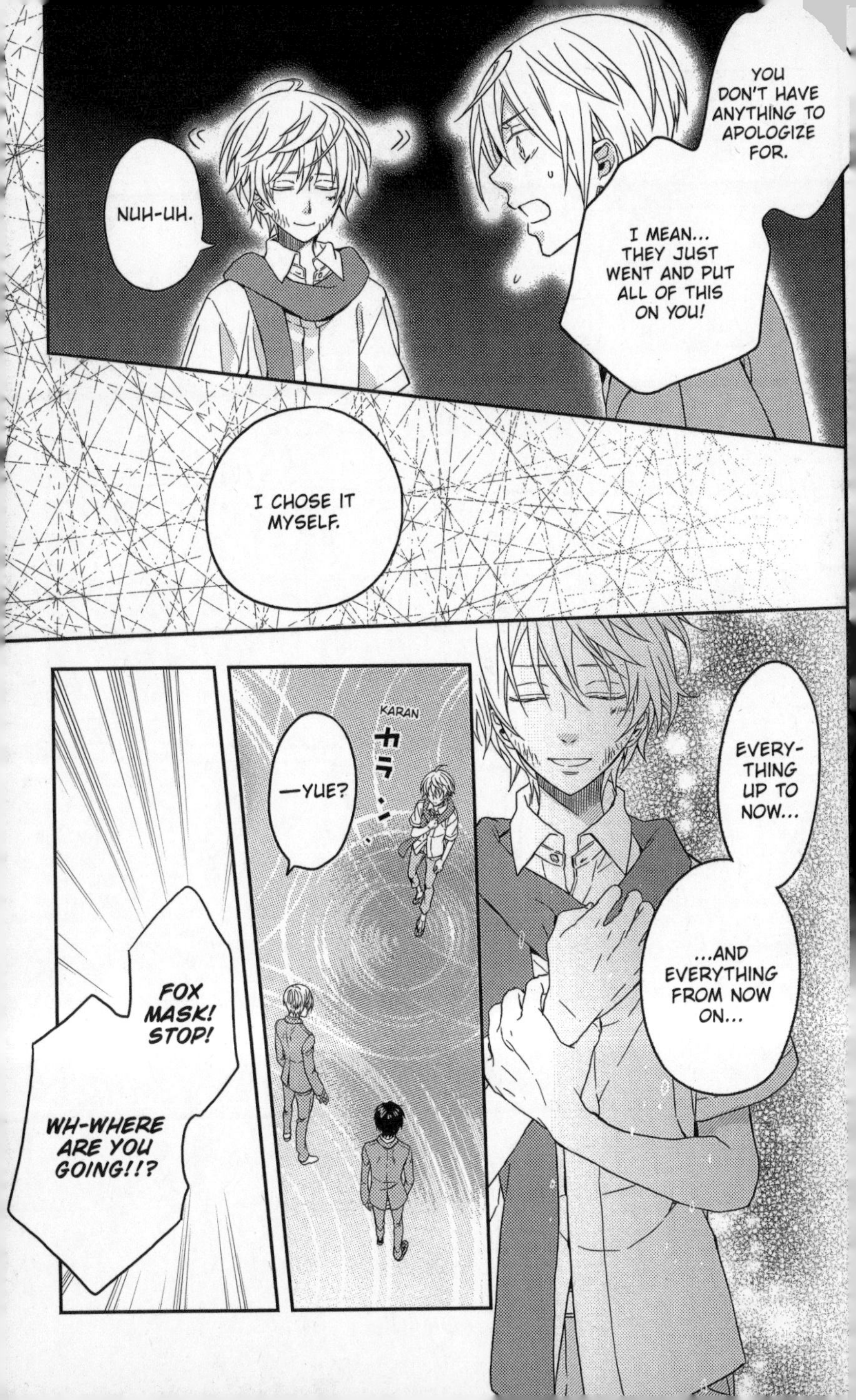
YOU DON'T HAVE ANYTHING TO APOLOGIZE FOR.
I MEAN... THEY JUST WENT AND PUT ALL OF THIS ON YOU!
NUH-UH.
I CHOSE IT MYSELF.
EVERY-THING UP TO NOW...
...AND EVERYTHING FROM NOW ON...
KARAN
—YUE?
FOX MASK! STOP!
WH-WHERE ARE YOU GOING!!?

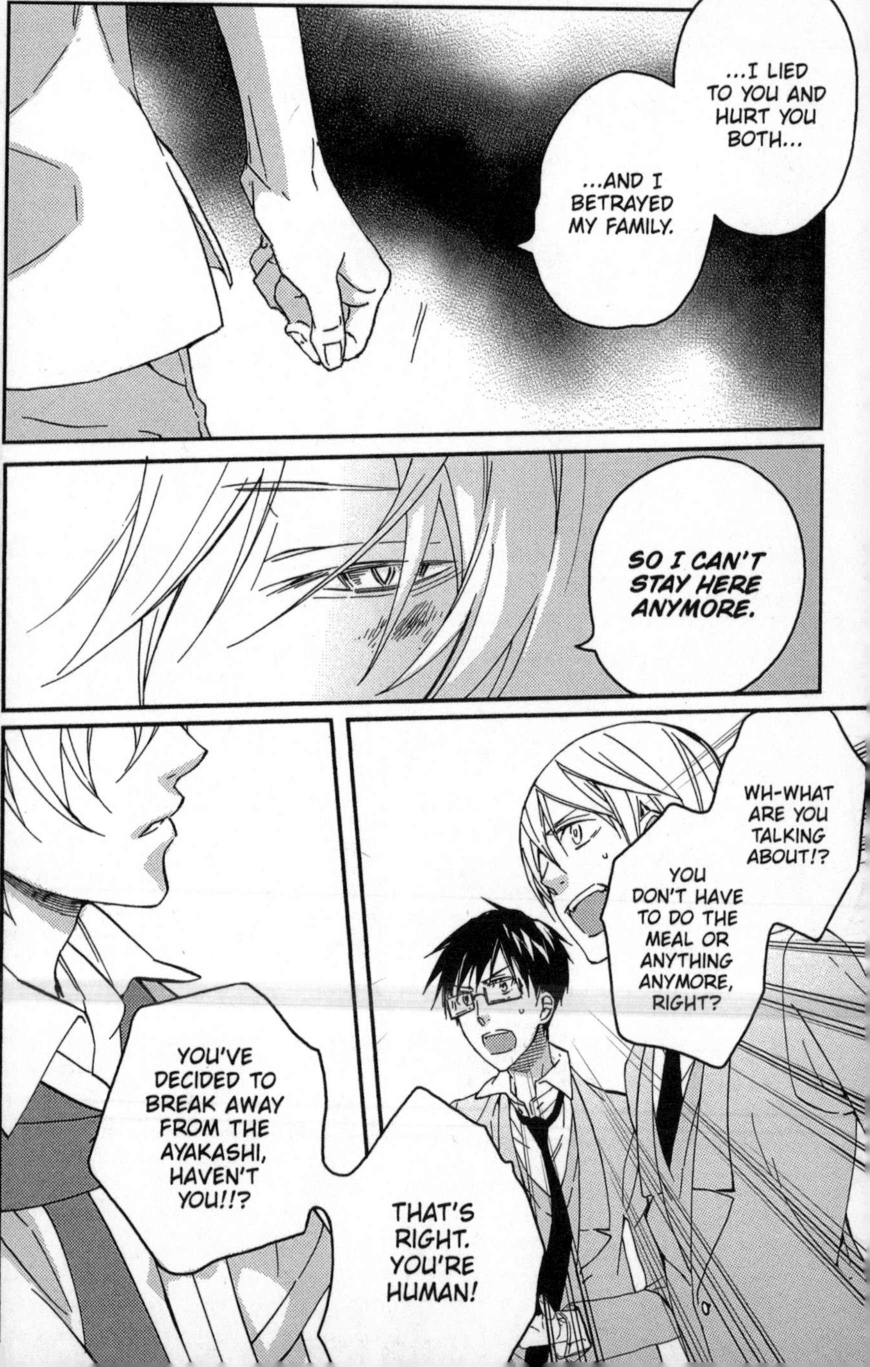
...I LIED TO YOU AND HURT YOU BOTH...
...AND I BETRAYED MY FAMILY.
SO I CAN'T STAY HERE ANYMORE.
WH-WHAT ARE YOU TALKING ABOUT!?
YOU DON'T HAVE TO DO THE MEAL OR ANYTHING ANYMORE, RIGHT?
YOU'VE DECIDED TO BREAK AWAY FROM THE AYAKASHI, HAVEN'T YOU!!?
THAT'S RIGHT. YOU'RE HUMAN!

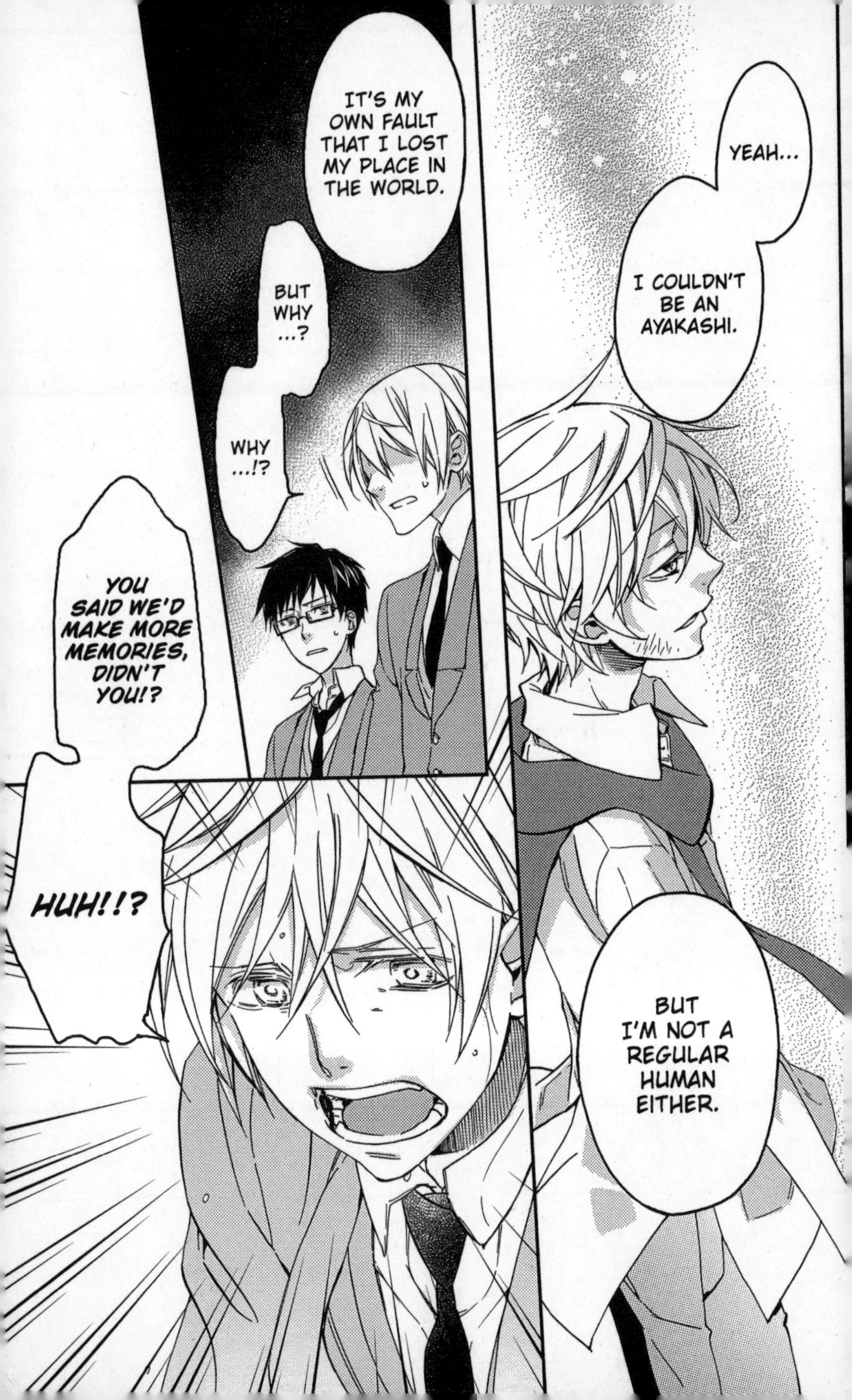
YEAH...
I COULDN'T BE AN AYAKASHI.
BUT I'M NOT A REGULAR HUMAN EITHER.
IT'S MY OWN FAULT THAT I LOST MY PLACE IN THE WORLD.
BUT WHY ...?
WHY ...!?
YOU SAID WE'D MAKE MORE MEMORIES, DIDN'T YOU!?
HUH!!?

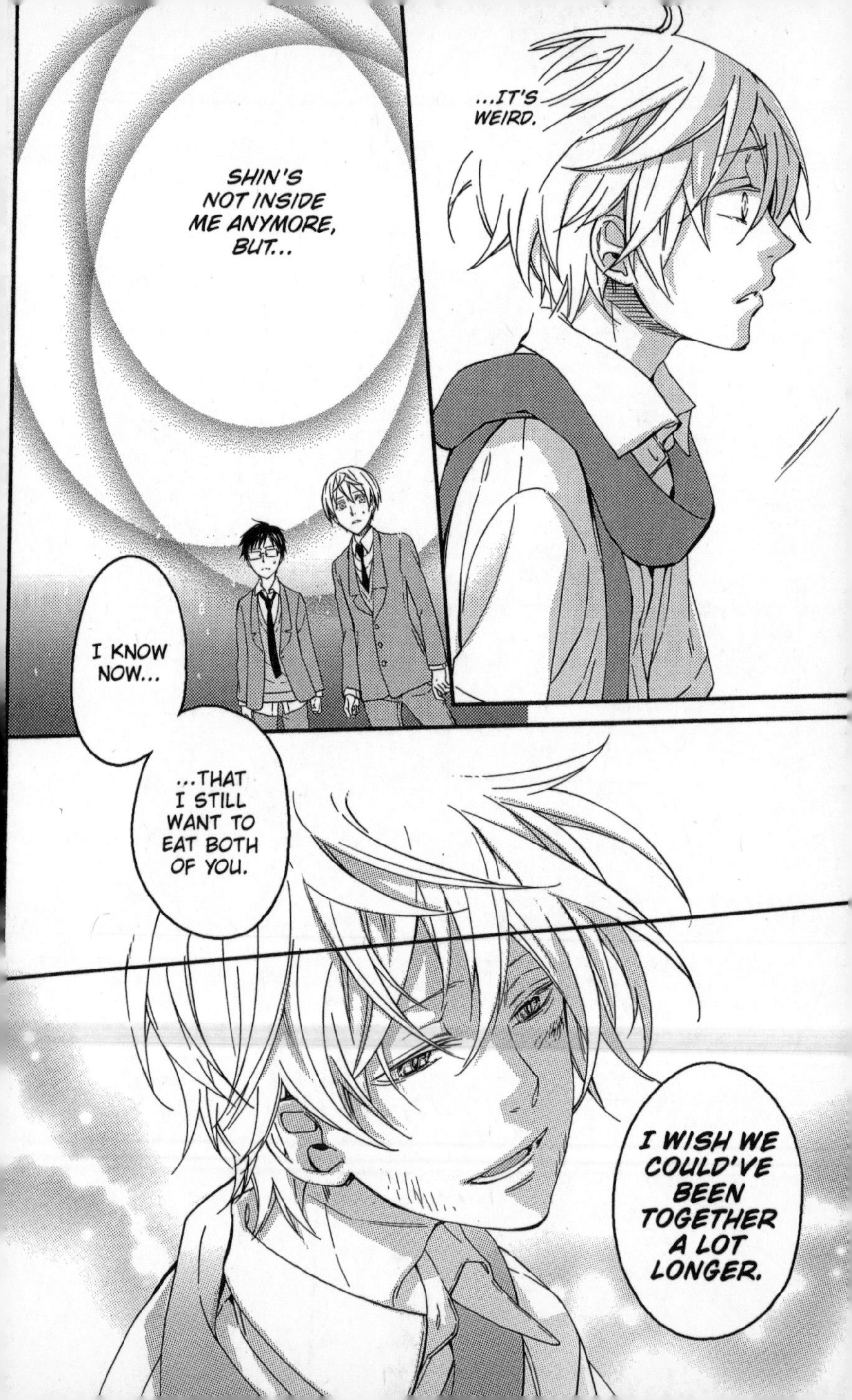
...IT'S WEIRD.
SHIN'S NOT INSIDE ME ANYMORE, BUT...
I KNOW NOW...
...THAT I STILL WANT TO EAT BOTH OF YOU.
I WISH WE COULD'VE BEEN TOGETHER A LOT LONGER.

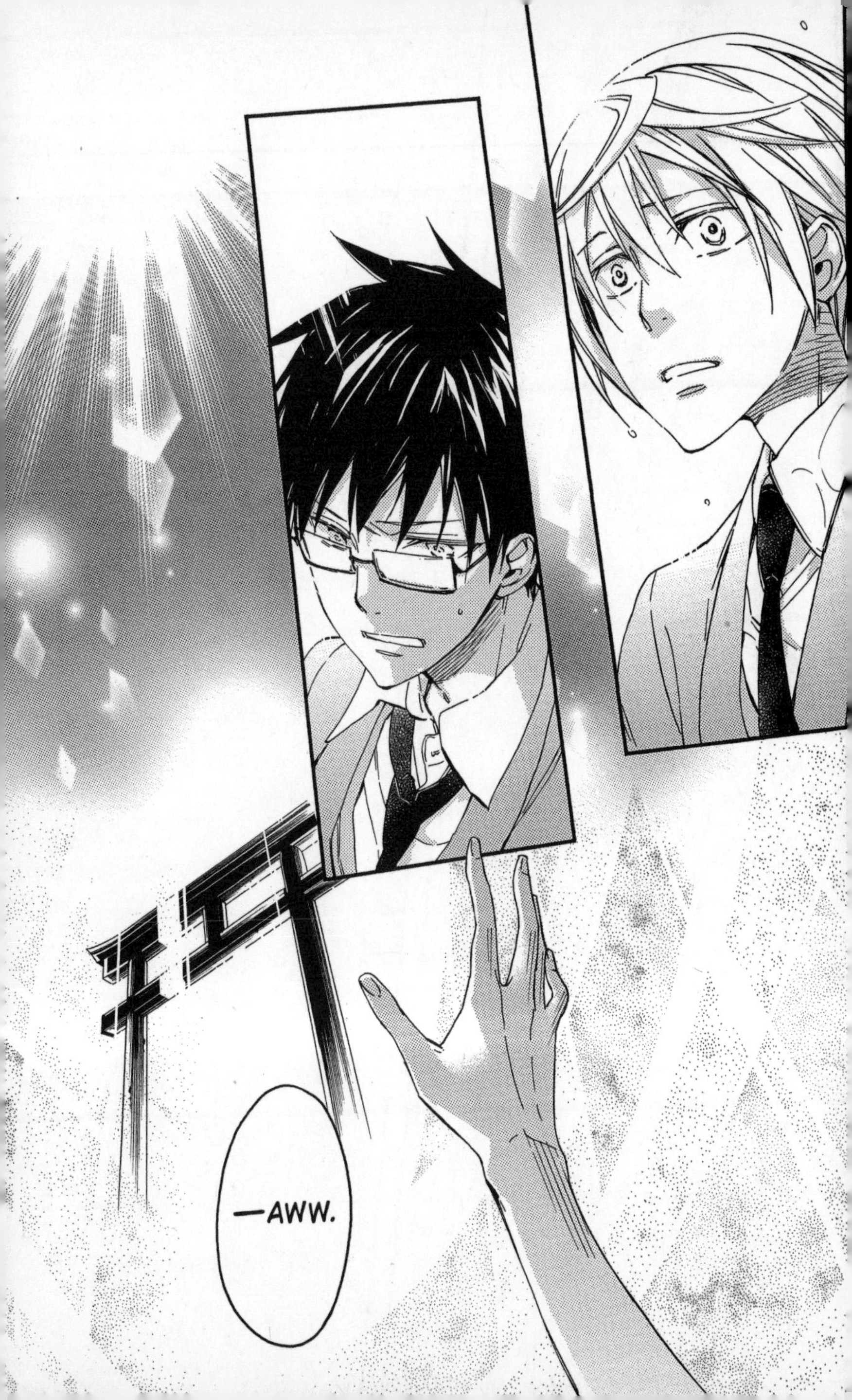
—AWW.

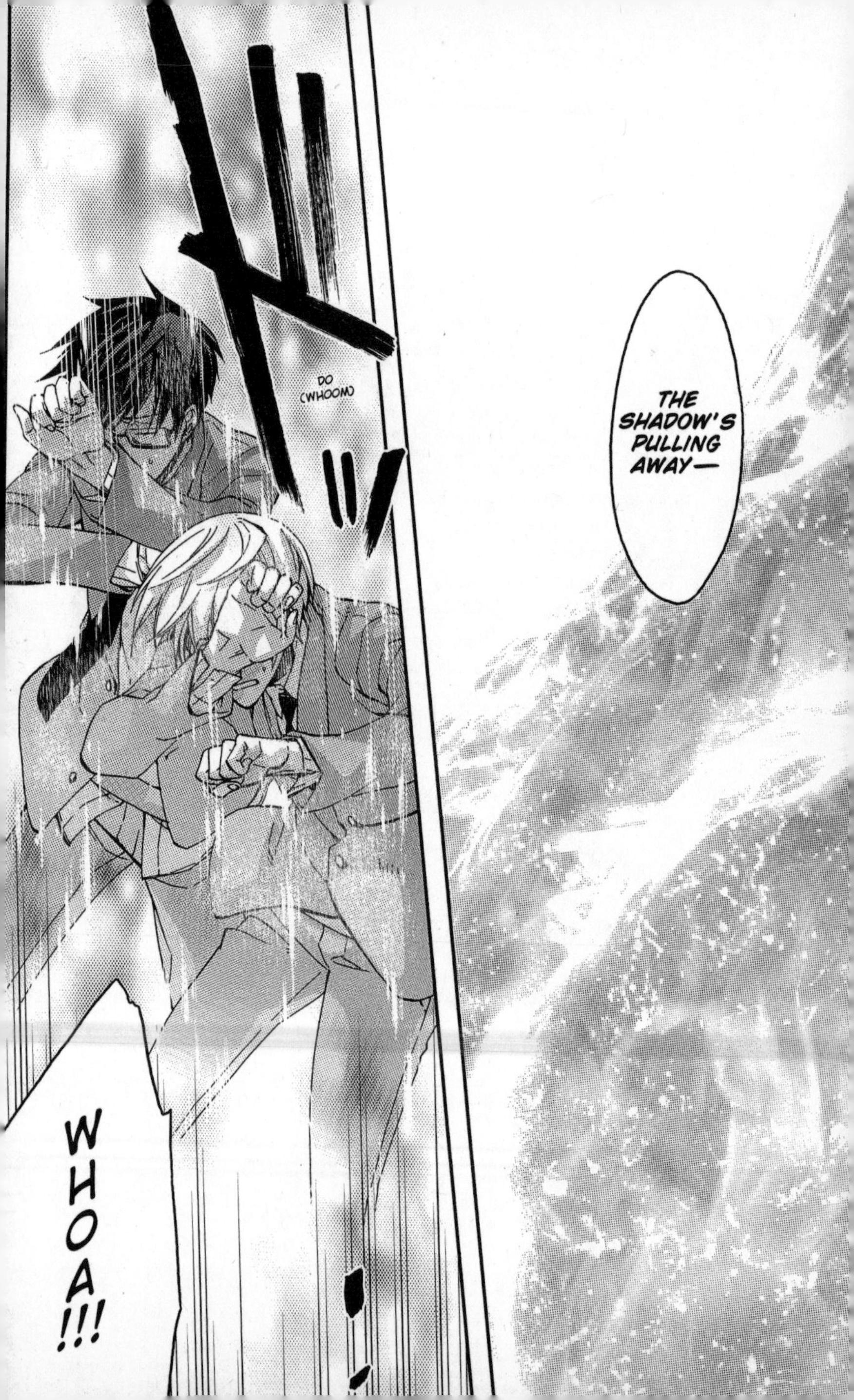
THE SHADOW'S PULLING AWAY—
DO (WHOOM)
WHOA!!!

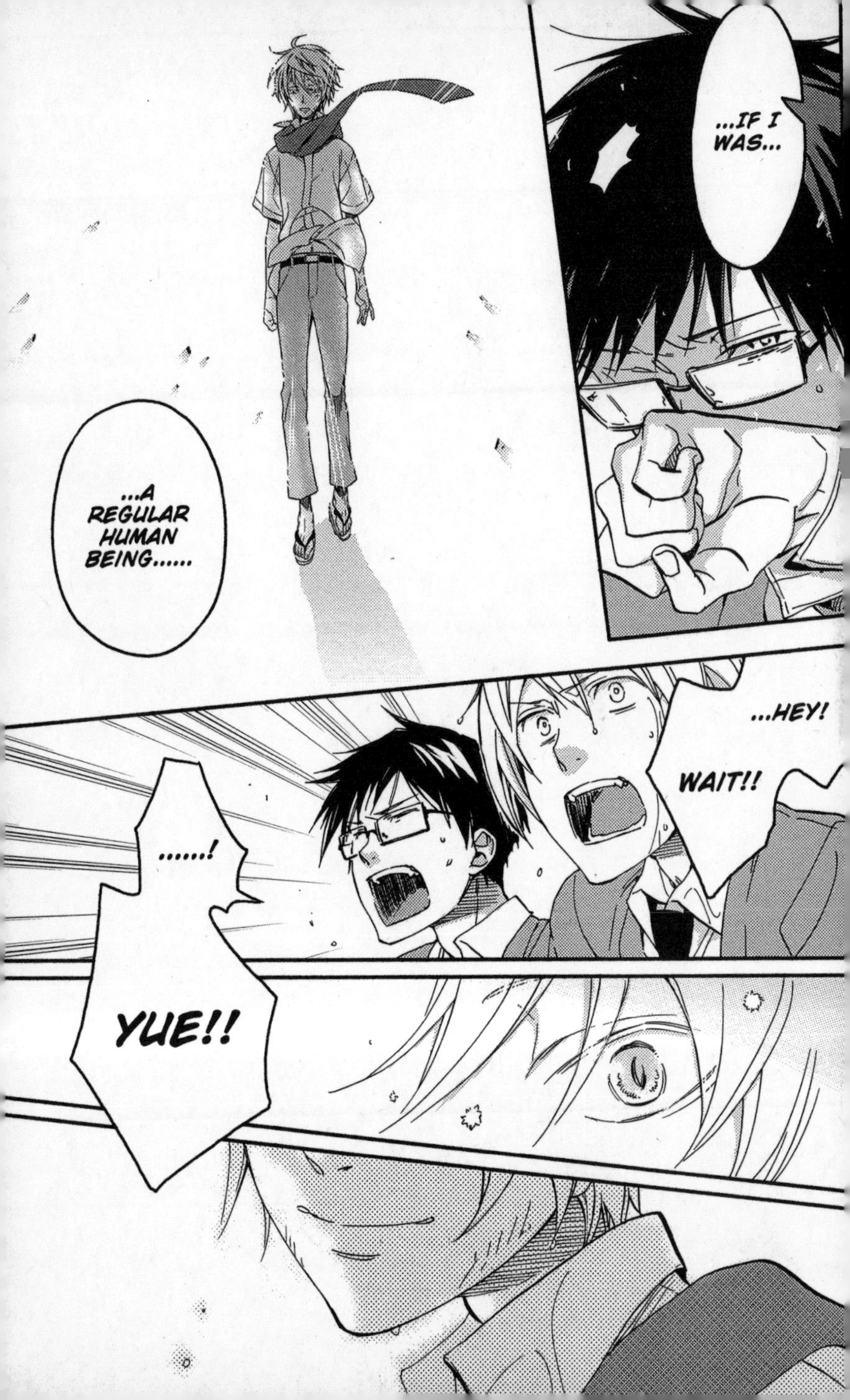
...IF I WAS...
...A REGULAR HUMAN BEING......
...HEY!
WAIT!!
......!
YUE!!

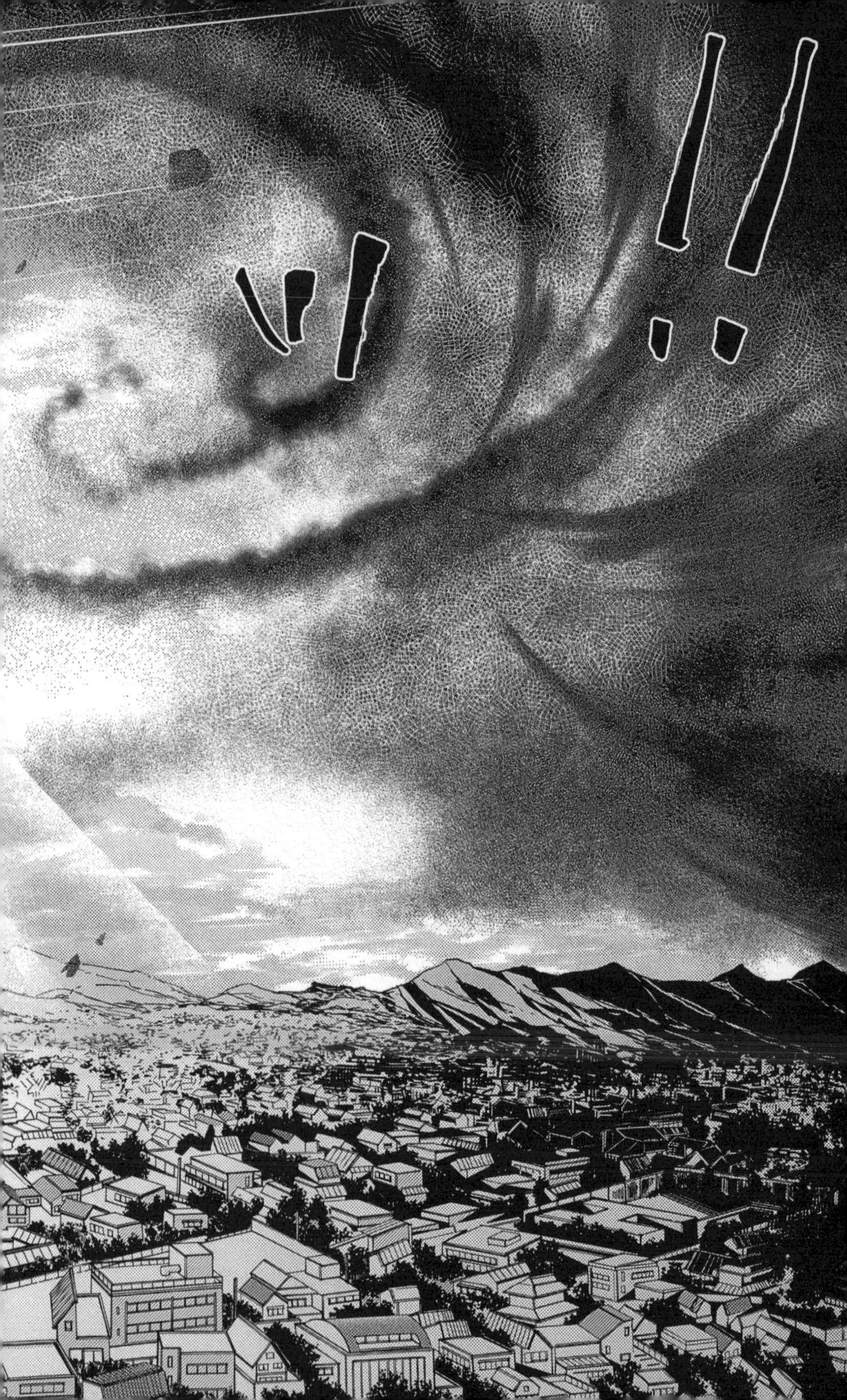
!!

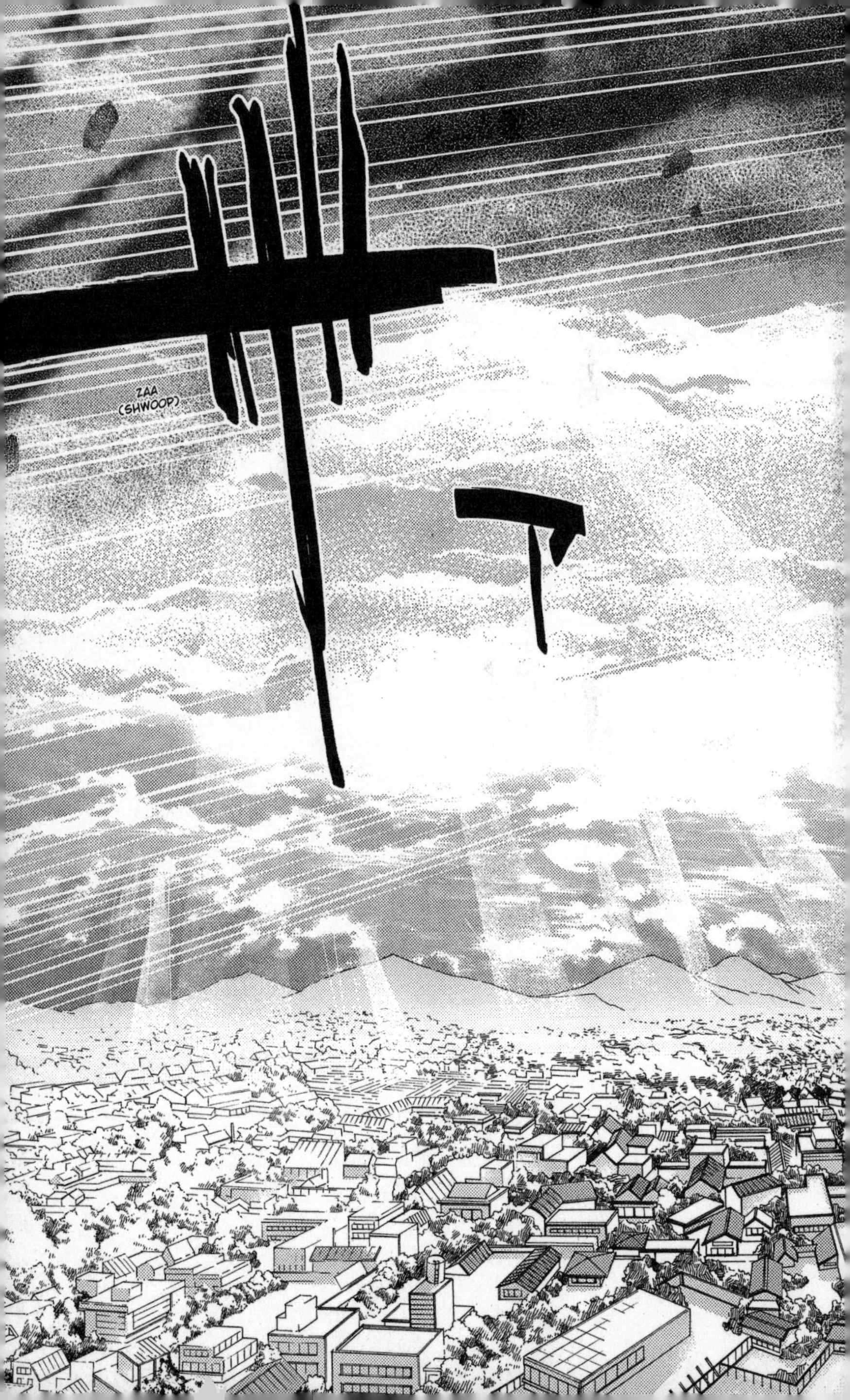
ZAA
(SHWOOP)

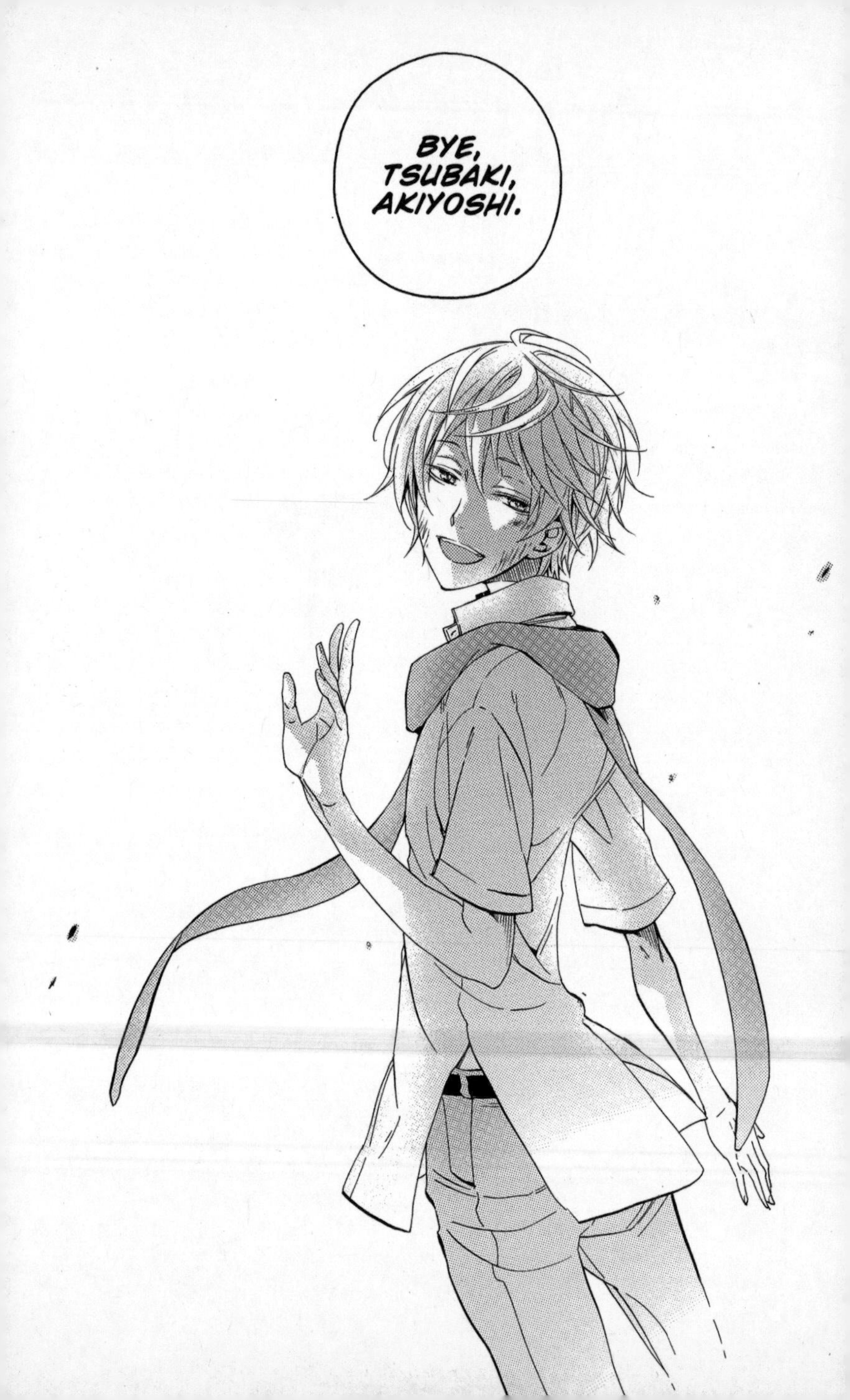
BYE, TSUBAKI, AKIYOSHI.

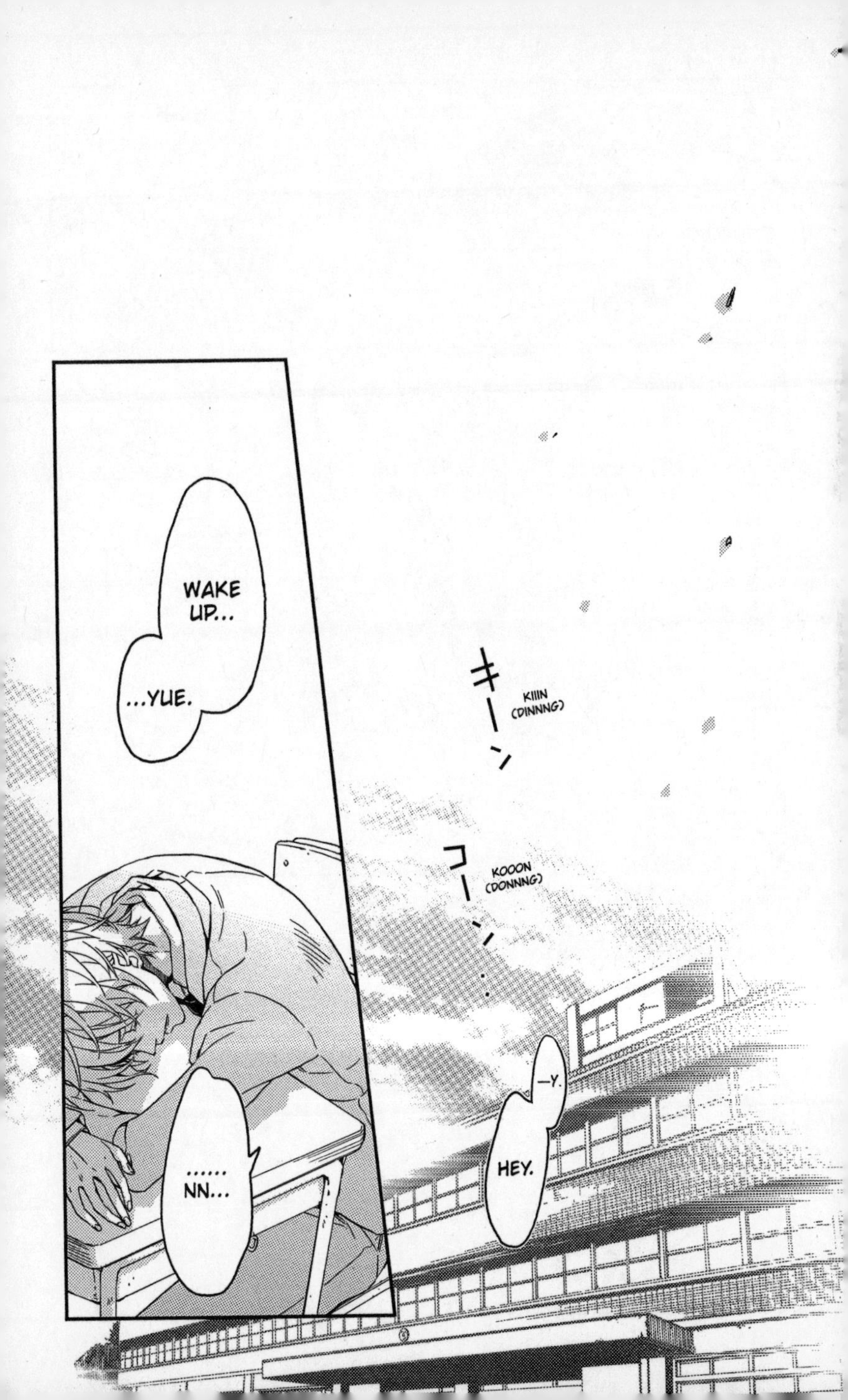
キーン
KIIIN (DINNNG)
コーン..
KOOON (DONNNG)
—Y.
HEY.
WAKE UP...
...YUE.
......
NN...

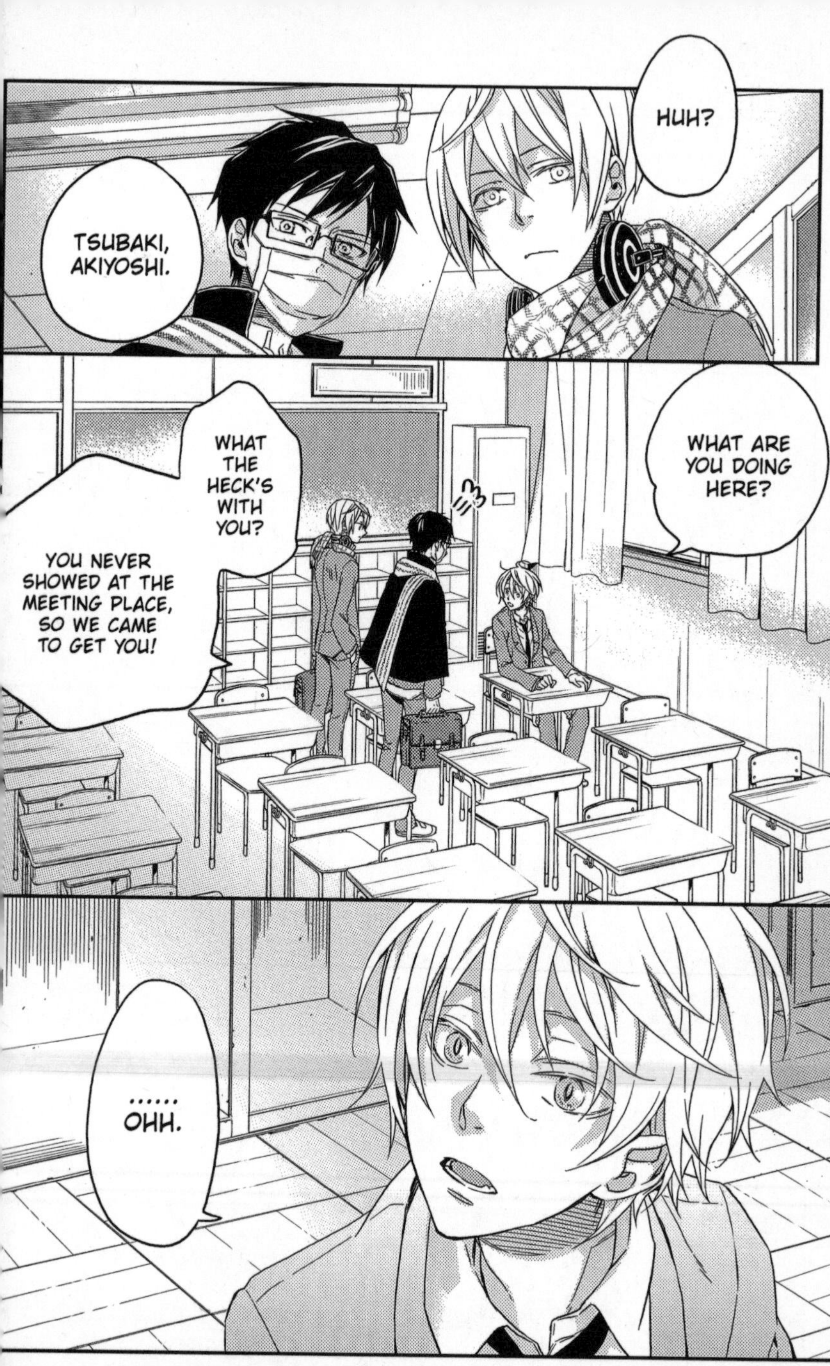
HUH?
TSUBAKI, AKIYOSHI.
WHAT ARE YOU DOING HERE?
WHAT THE HECK'S WITH YOU?
YOU NEVER SHOWED AT THE MEETING PLACE, SO WE CAME TO GET YOU!
...... OHH.

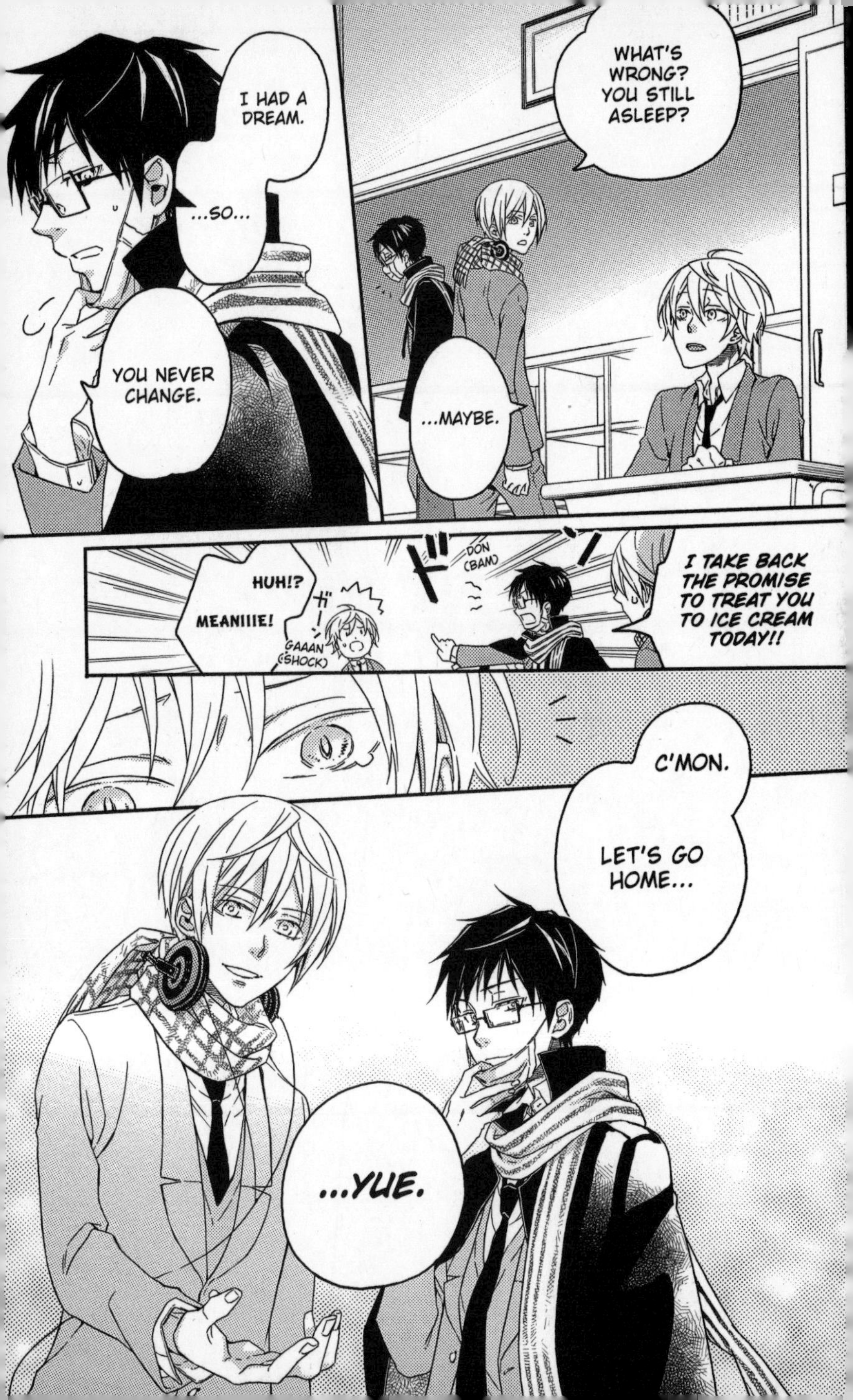
WHAT'S WRONG? YOU STILL ASLEEP?
...MAYBE.
I HAD A DREAM.
...SO...
YOU NEVER CHANGE.
I TAKE BACK THE PROMISE TO TREAT YOU TO ICE CREAM TODAY!!
DON (BAM)
GAAAN (SHOCK)
HUH!?
MEANIIIE!
C'MON.
LET'S GO HOME...
...YUE.

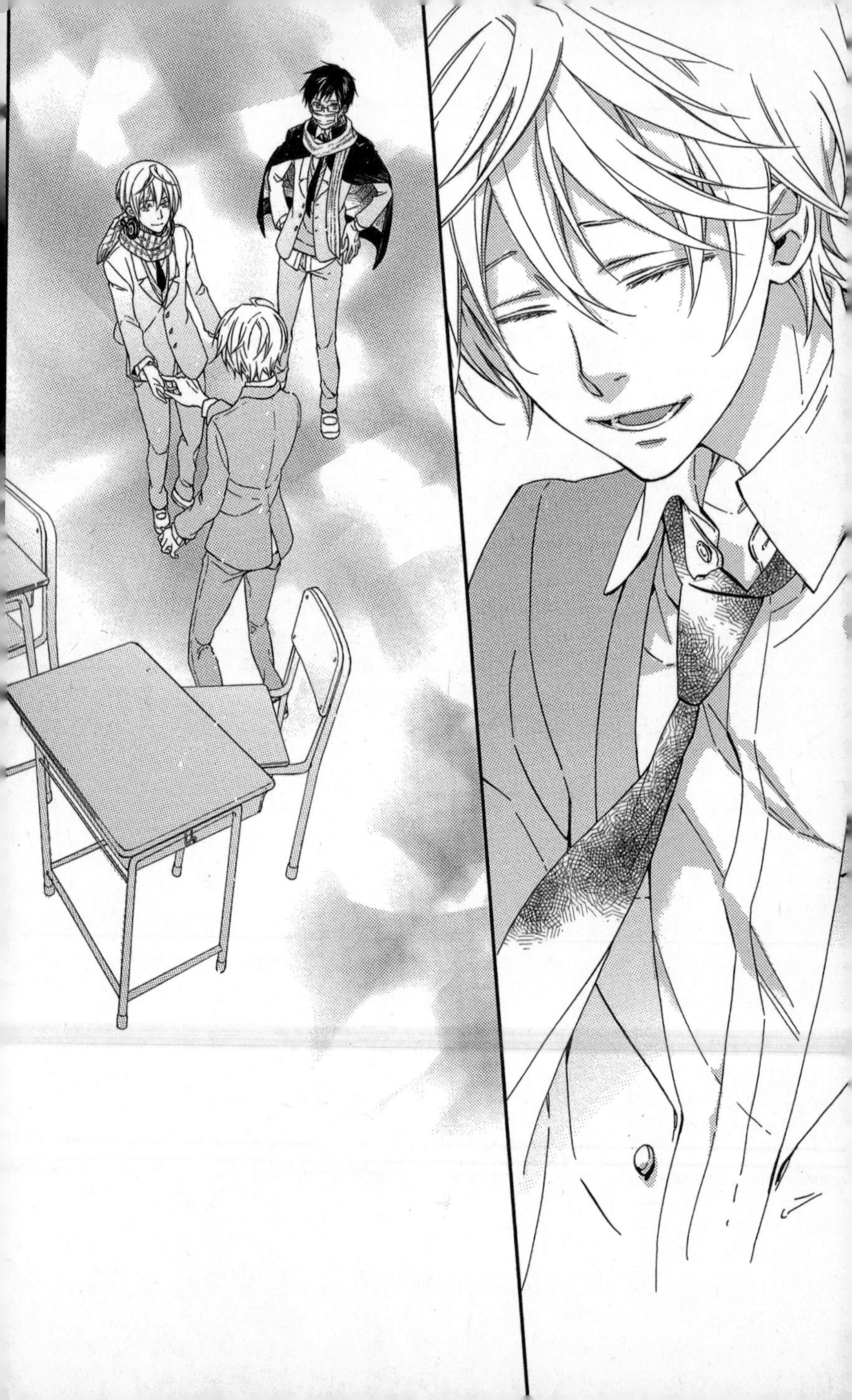

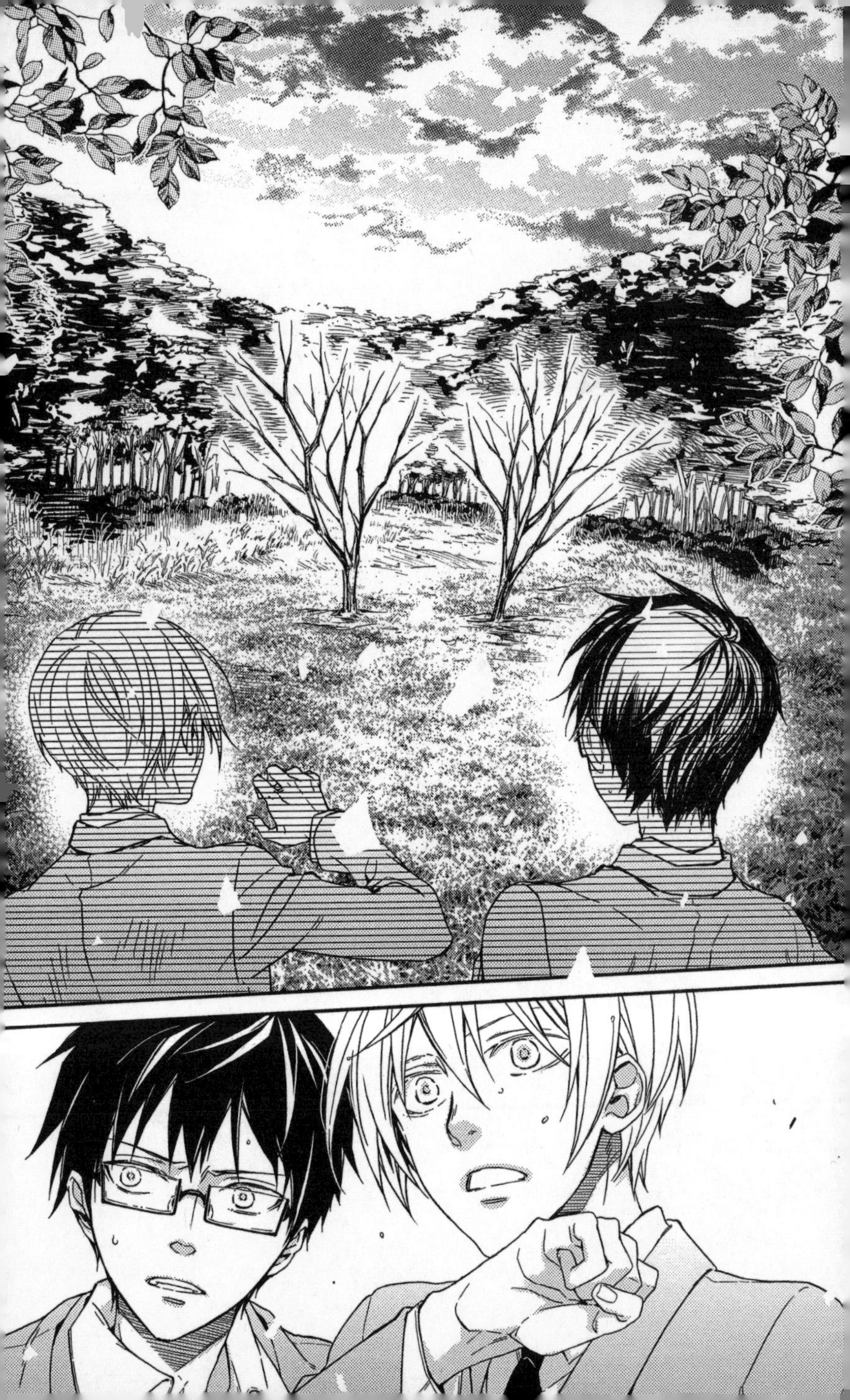

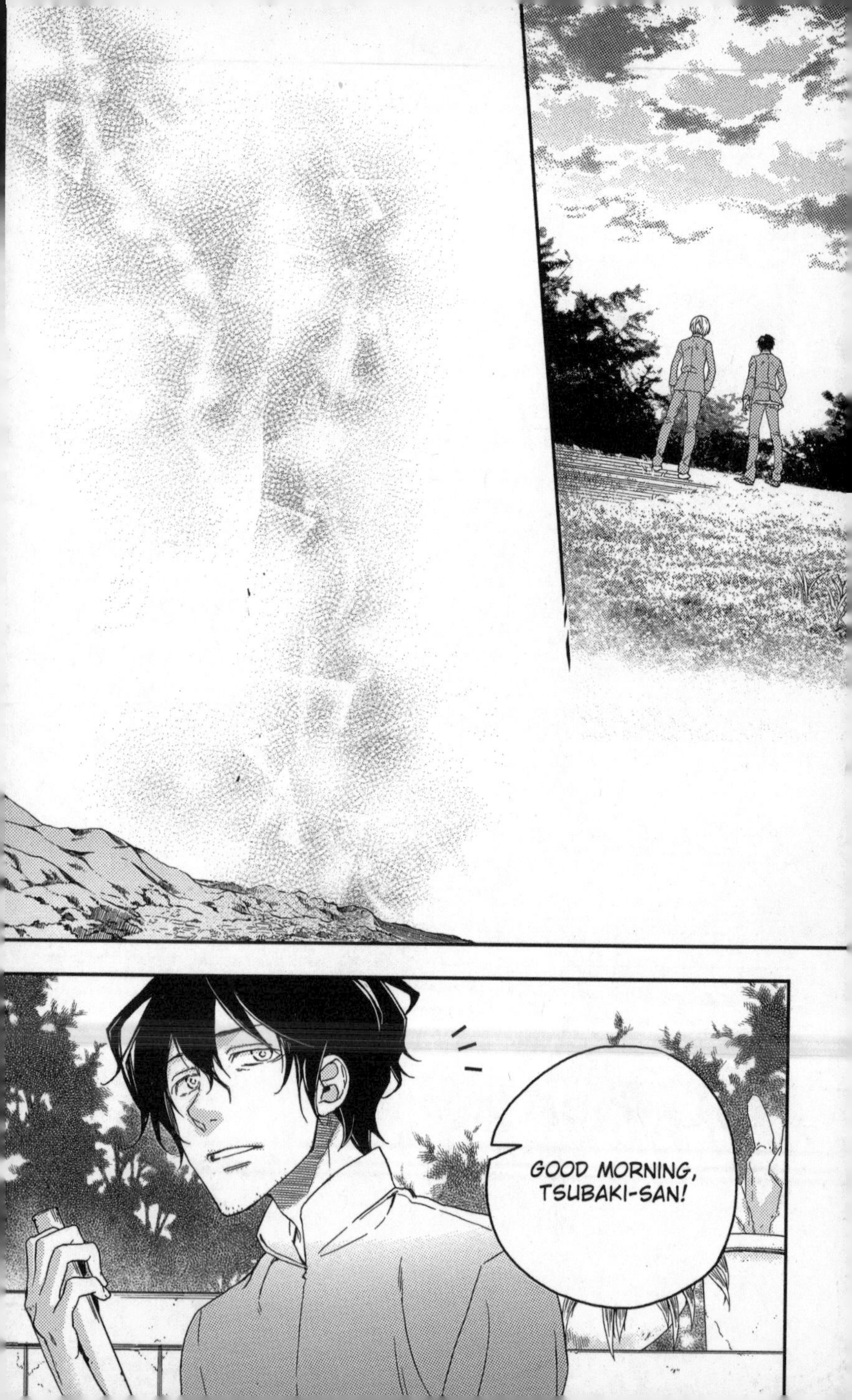
GOOD MORNING, TSUBAKI-SAN!

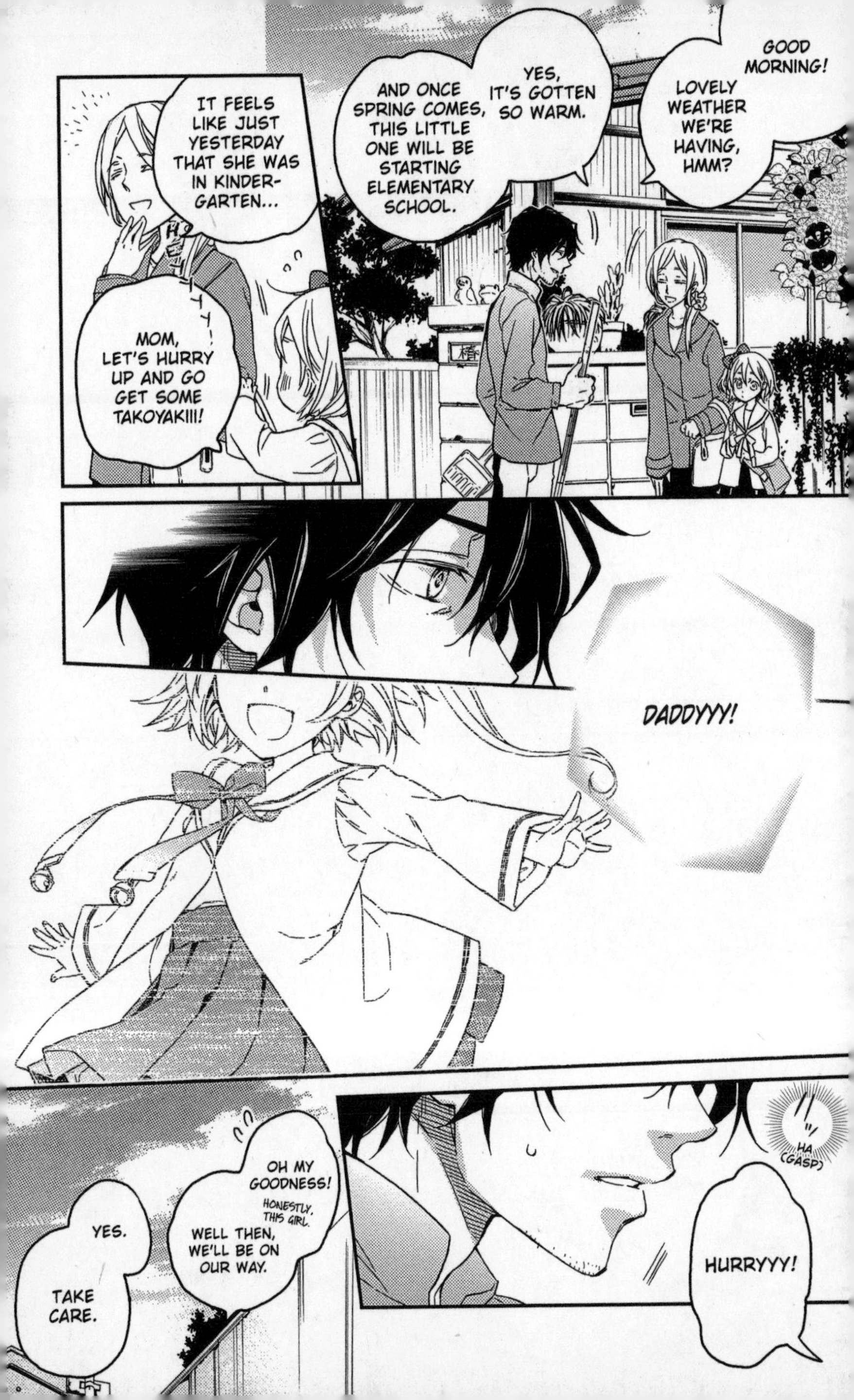
GOOD MORNING!
LOVELY WEATHER WE'RE HAVING, HMM?
YES, IT'S GOTTEN SO WARM.
AND ONCE SPRING COMES, THIS LITTLE ONE WILL BE STARTING ELEMENTARY SCHOOL.
IT FEELS LIKE JUST YESTERDAY THAT SHE WAS IN KINDER-GARTEN...
MOM, LET'S HURRY UP AND GO GET SOME TAKOYAKIII!
DADDYYY!
HA (GASP)
HURRYYY!
OH MY GOODNESS!
HONESTLY, THIS GIRL.
WELL THEN, WE'LL BE ON OUR WAY.
YES.
TAKE CARE.

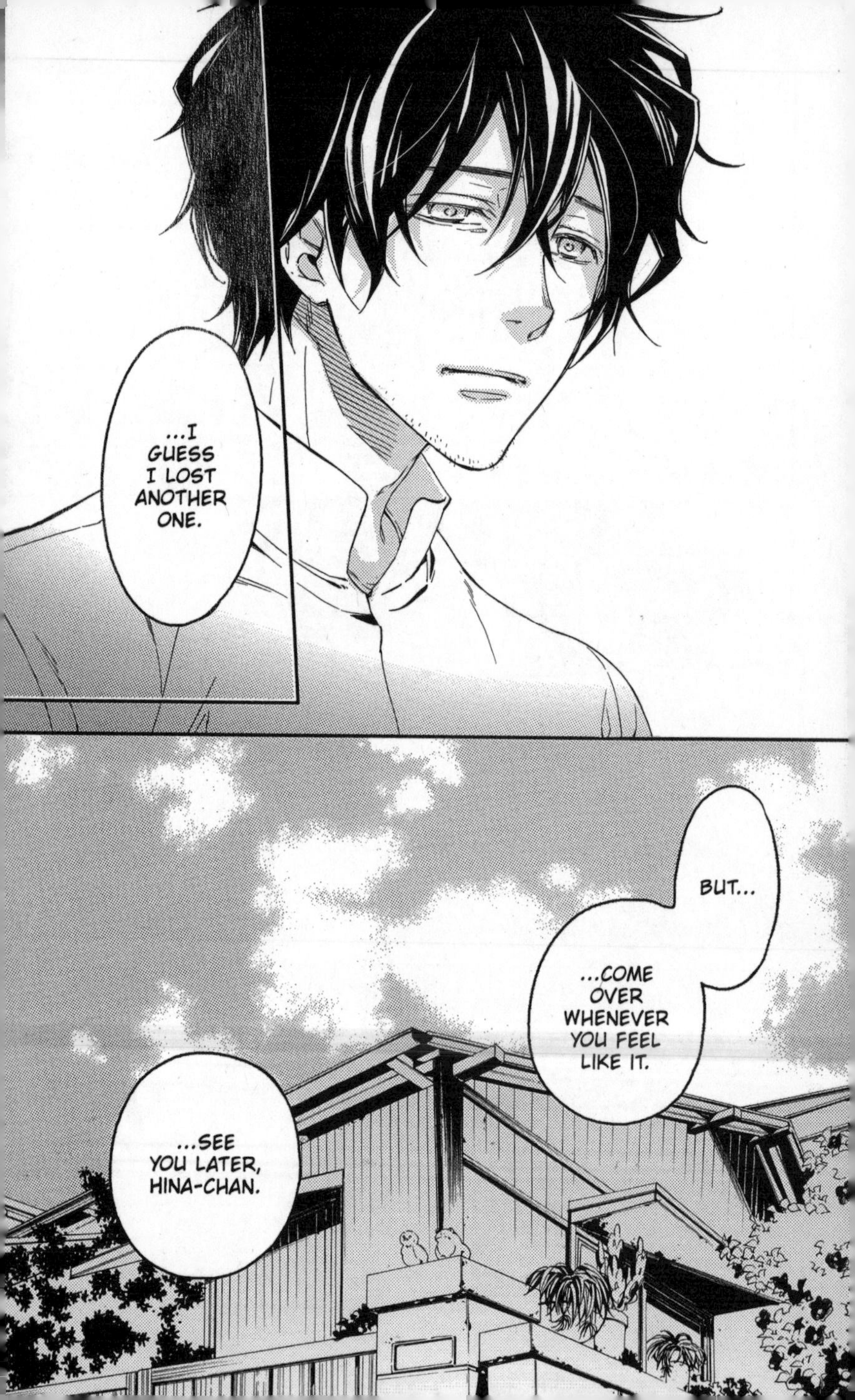
...I GUESS I LOST ANOTHER ONE.
BUT...
...COME OVER WHENEVER YOU FEEL LIKE IT.
...SEE YOU LATER, HINA-CHAN.

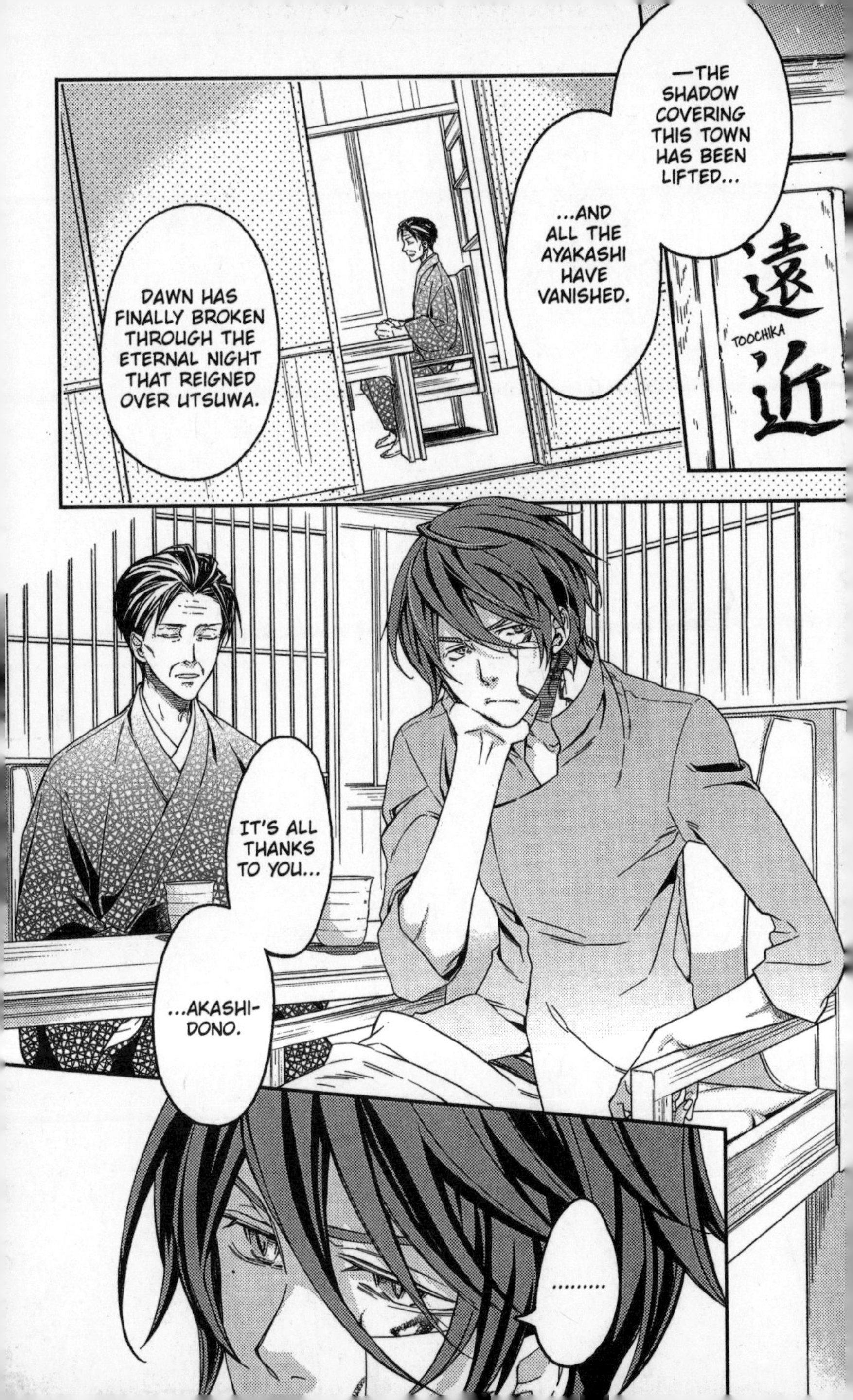
—THE SHADOW COVERING THIS TOWN HAS BEEN LIFTED...
...AND ALL THE AYAKASHI HAVE VANISHED.
遠近
TOOCHIKA
DAWN HAS FINALLY BROKEN THROUGH THE ETERNAL NIGHT THAT REIGNED OVER UTSUWA.
IT'S ALL THANKS TO YOU...
...AKASHI-DONO.
....

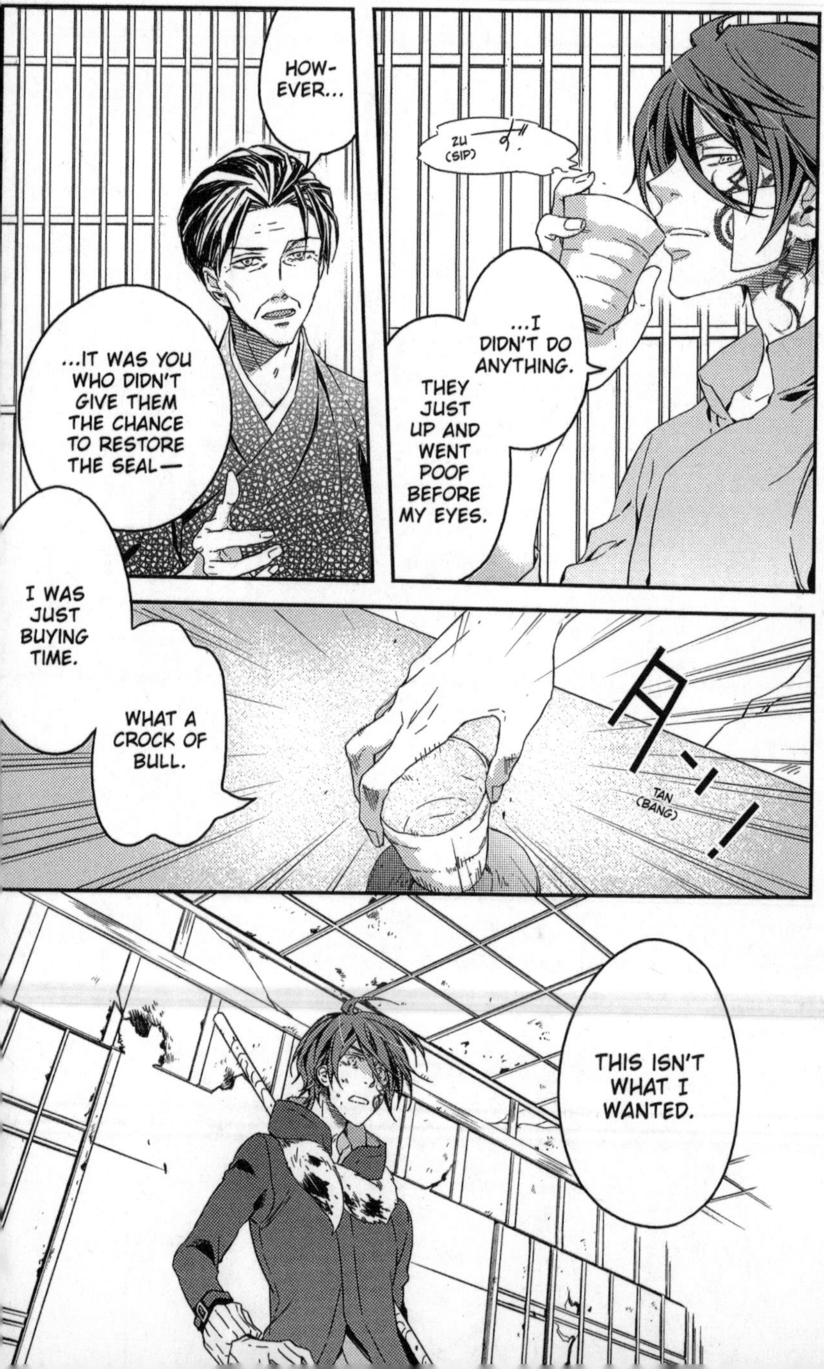
ZU (SIP)
...I DIDN'T DO ANYTHING.
THEY JUST UP AND WENT POOF BEFORE MY EYES.
HOW-EVER...
...IT WAS YOU WHO DIDN'T GIVE THEM THE CHANCE TO RESTORE THE SEAL—
TAN (BANG)
I WAS JUST BUYING TIME.
WHAT A CROCK OF BULL.
THIS ISN'T WHAT I WANTED.

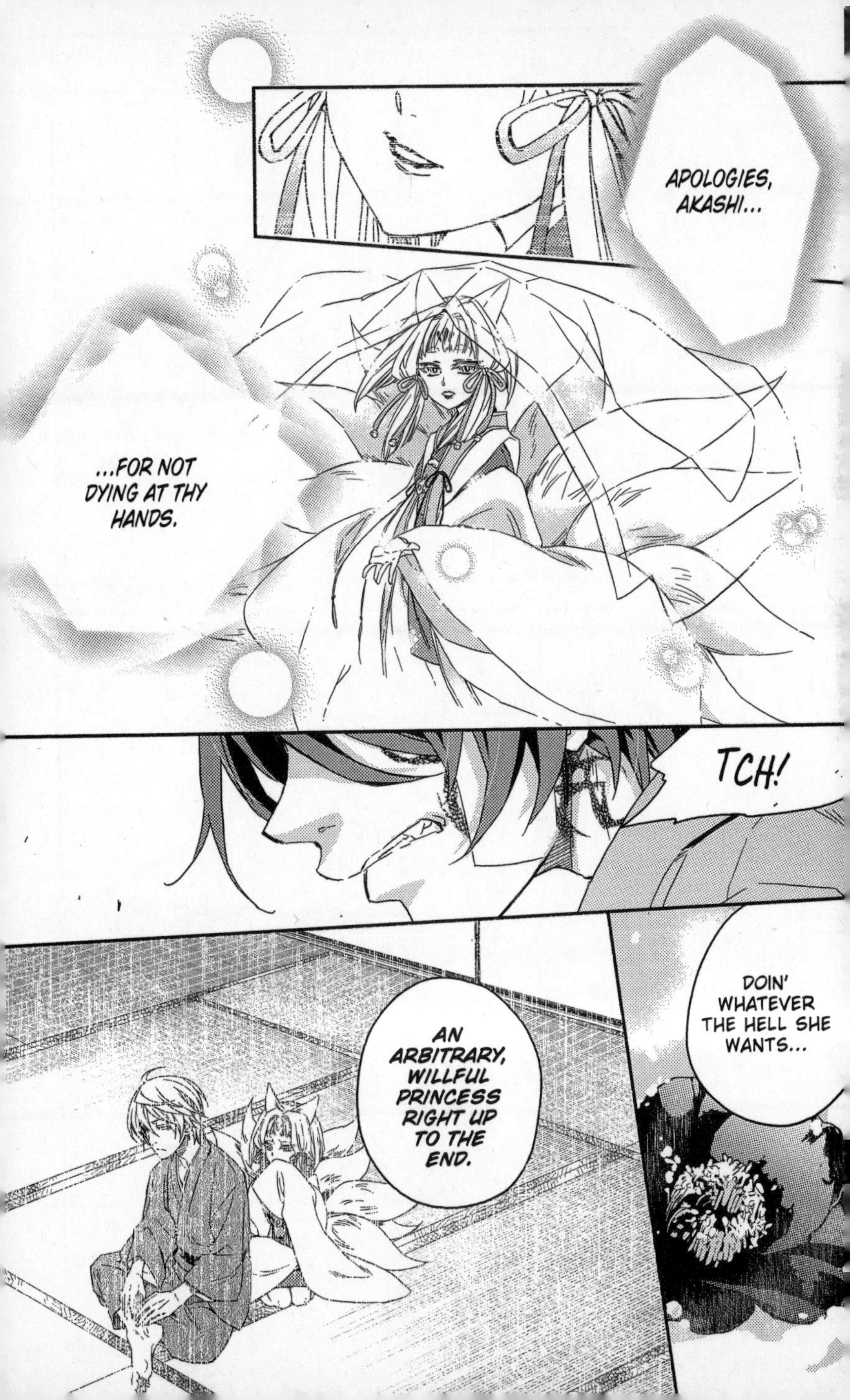
APOLOGIES, AKASHI...
...FOR NOT DYING AT THY HANDS.
TCH!
DOIN' WHATEVER THE HELL SHE WANTS...
AN ARBITRARY, WILLFUL PRINCESS RIGHT UP TO THE END.

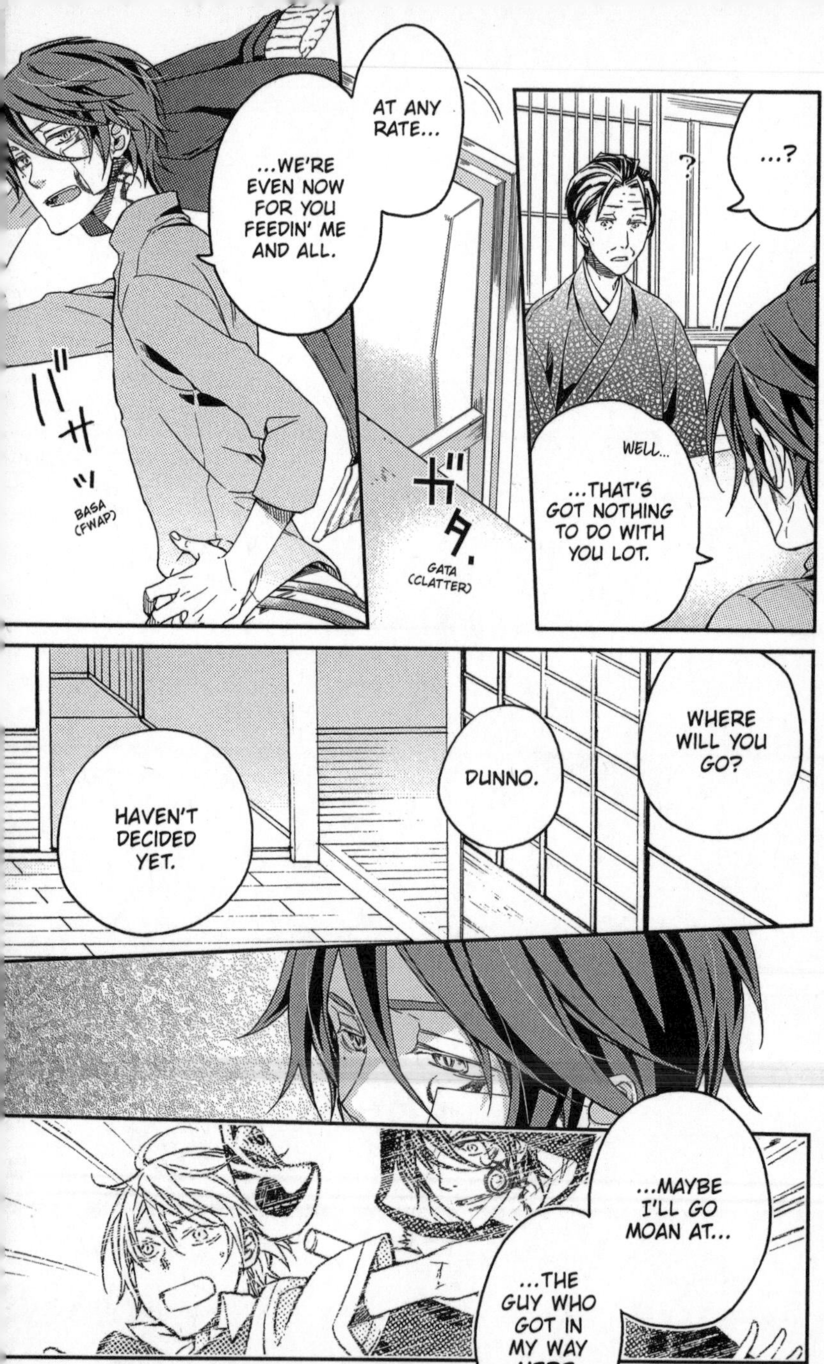
...?
?
WELL...
...THAT'S GOT NOTHING TO DO WITH YOU LOT.
ガタ.
GATA (CLATTER)
AT ANY RATE...
...WE'RE EVEN NOW FOR YOU FEEDIN' ME AND ALL.
バサッ
BASA (FWAP)
WHERE WILL YOU GO?
DUNNO.
HAVEN'T DECIDED YET.
...MAYBE I'LL GO MOAN AT...
...THE GUY WHO GOT IN MY WAY *HERE*.

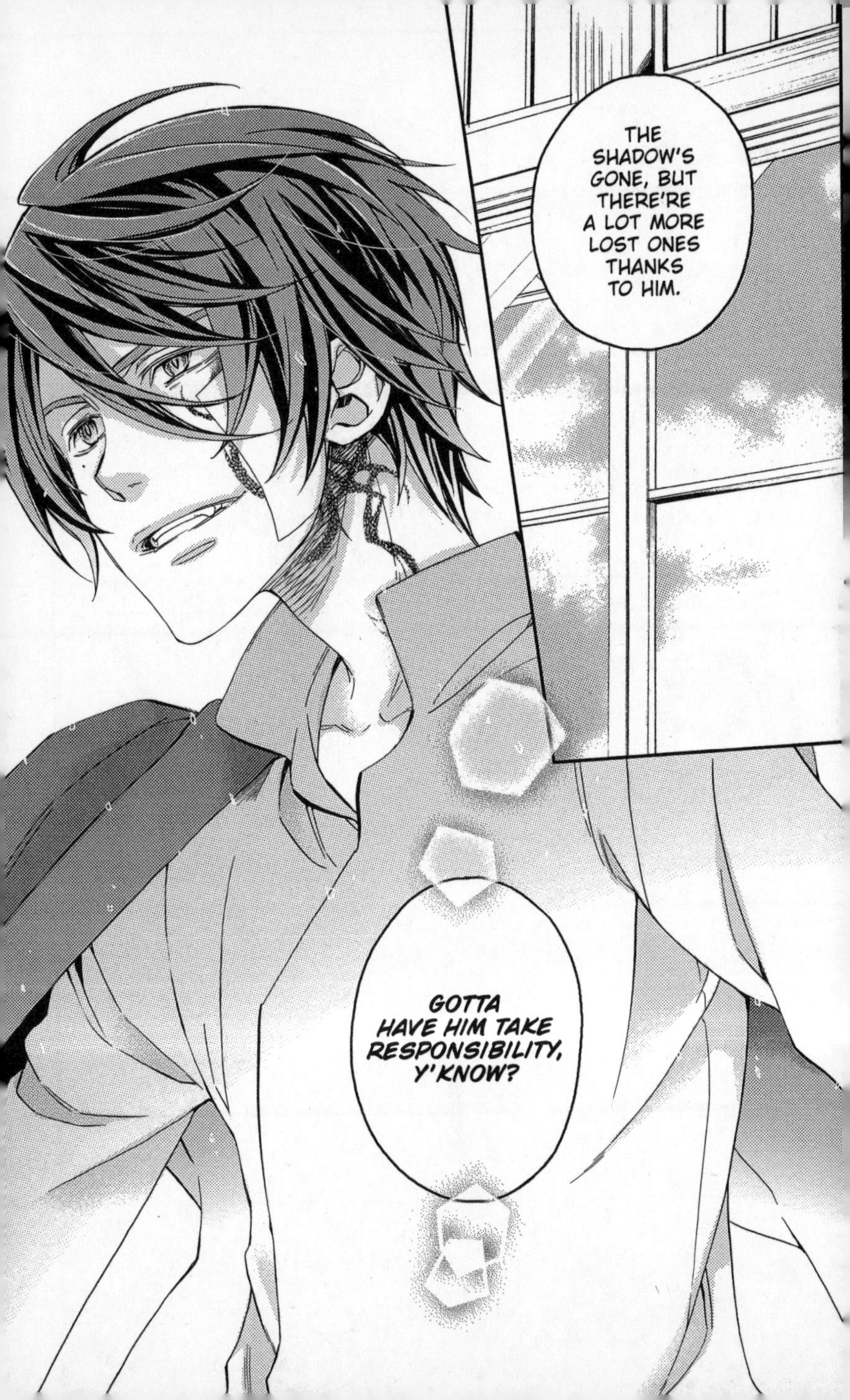
THE SHADOW'S GONE, BUT THERE'RE A LOT MORE LOST ONES THANKS TO HIM.
GOTTA HAVE HIM TAKE RESPONSIBILITY, Y'KNOW?

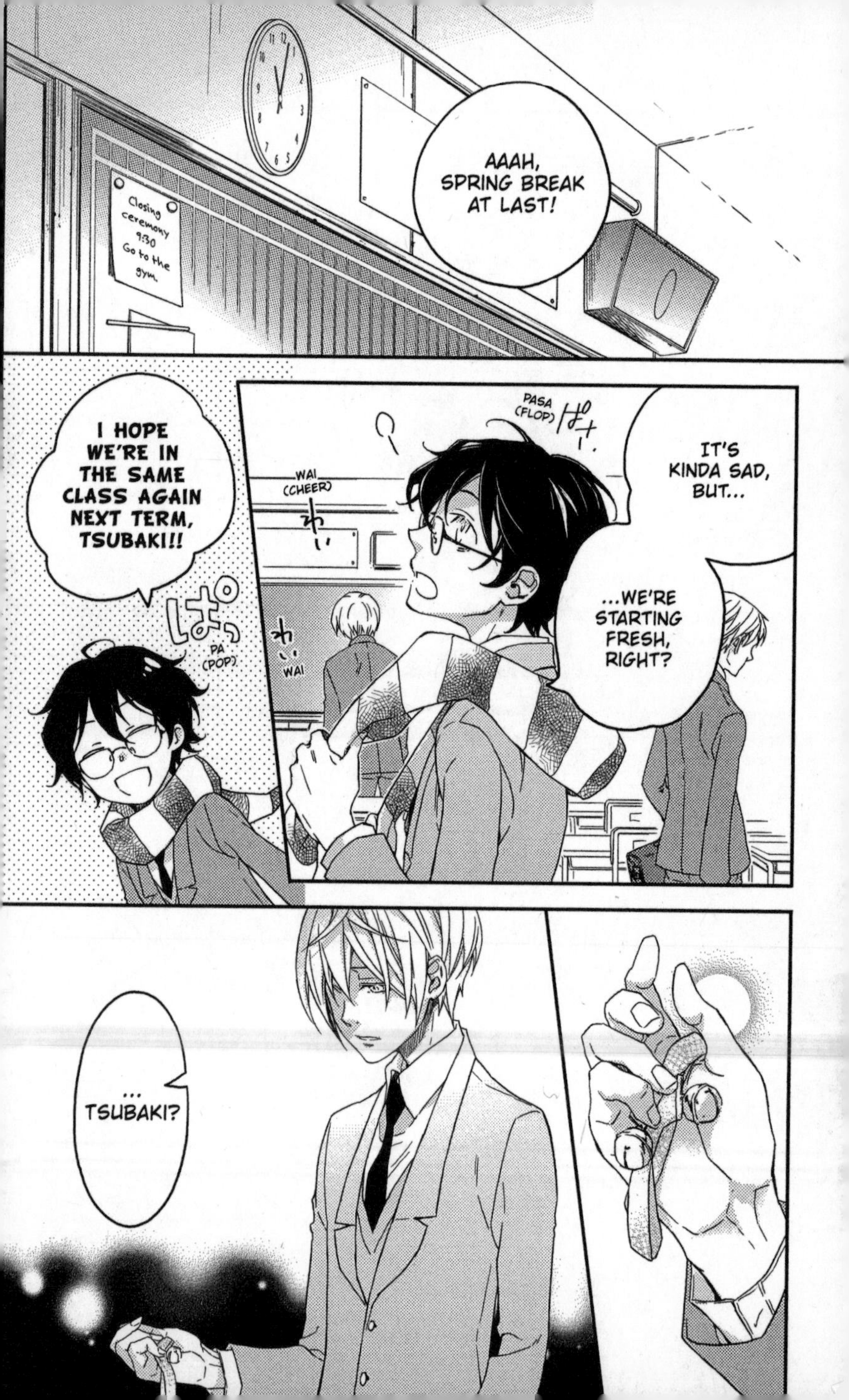
AAAH, SPRING BREAK AT LAST!
Closing ceremony 9:30 Go to the gym.
IT'S KINDA SAD, BUT...
...WE'RE STARTING FRESH, RIGHT?
PASA (FLOP)
WAI (CHEER)
WAI
I HOPE WE'RE IN THE SAME CLASS AGAIN NEXT TERM, TSUBAKI!!
PA (POP)
... TSUBAKI?

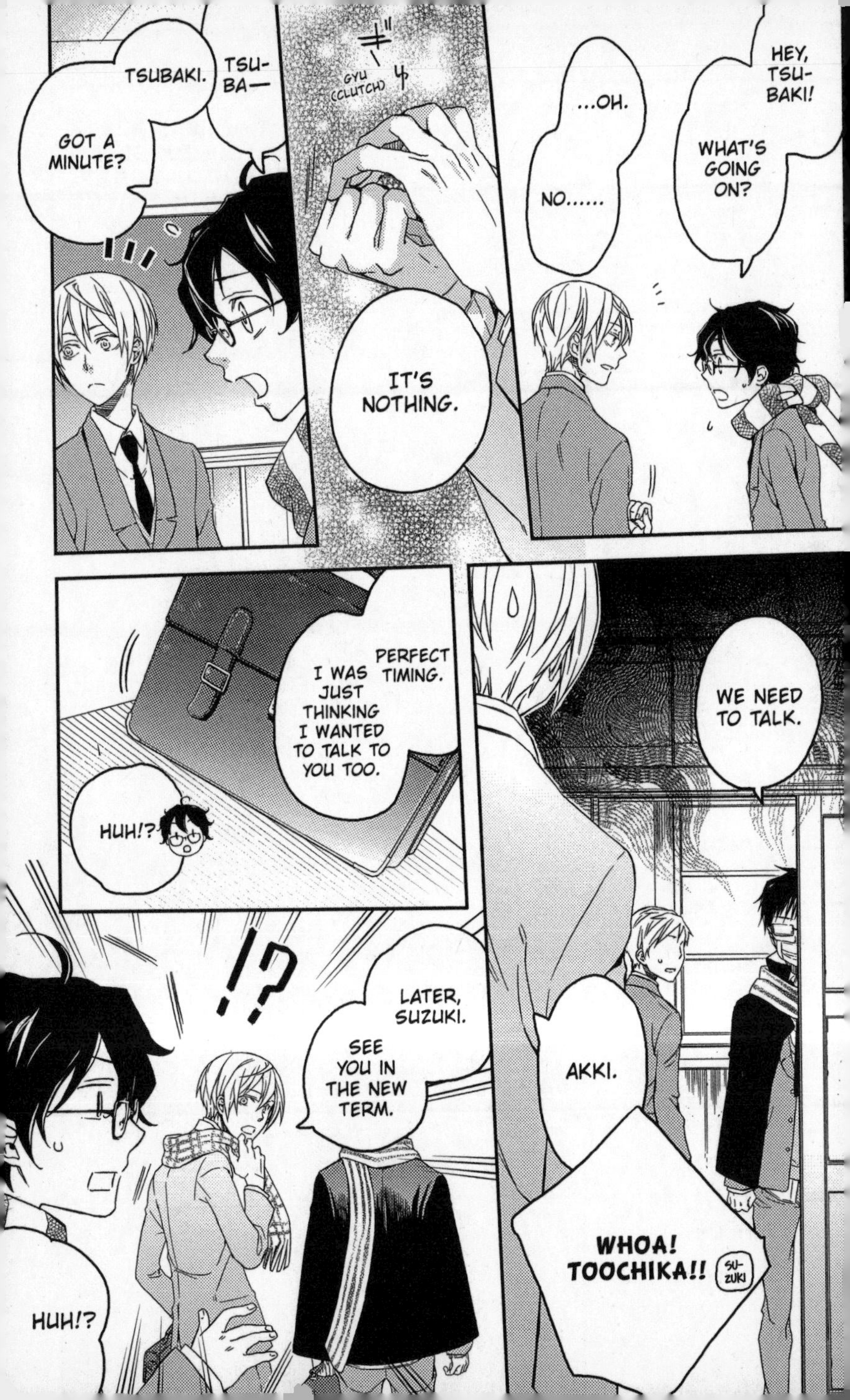
HEY, TSUBAKI!
WHAT'S GOING ON?
...OH.
NO......
GYU (CLUTCH)
IT'S NOTHING.
TSUBA—
TSUBAKI.
GOT A MINUTE?
WE NEED TO TALK.
AKKI.
WHOA! TOOCHIKA!!
SUZUKI
PERFECT TIMING. I WAS JUST THINKING I WANTED TO TALK TO YOU TOO.
HUH!?
!?
LATER, SUZUKI.
SEE YOU IN THE NEW TERM.
HUH!?

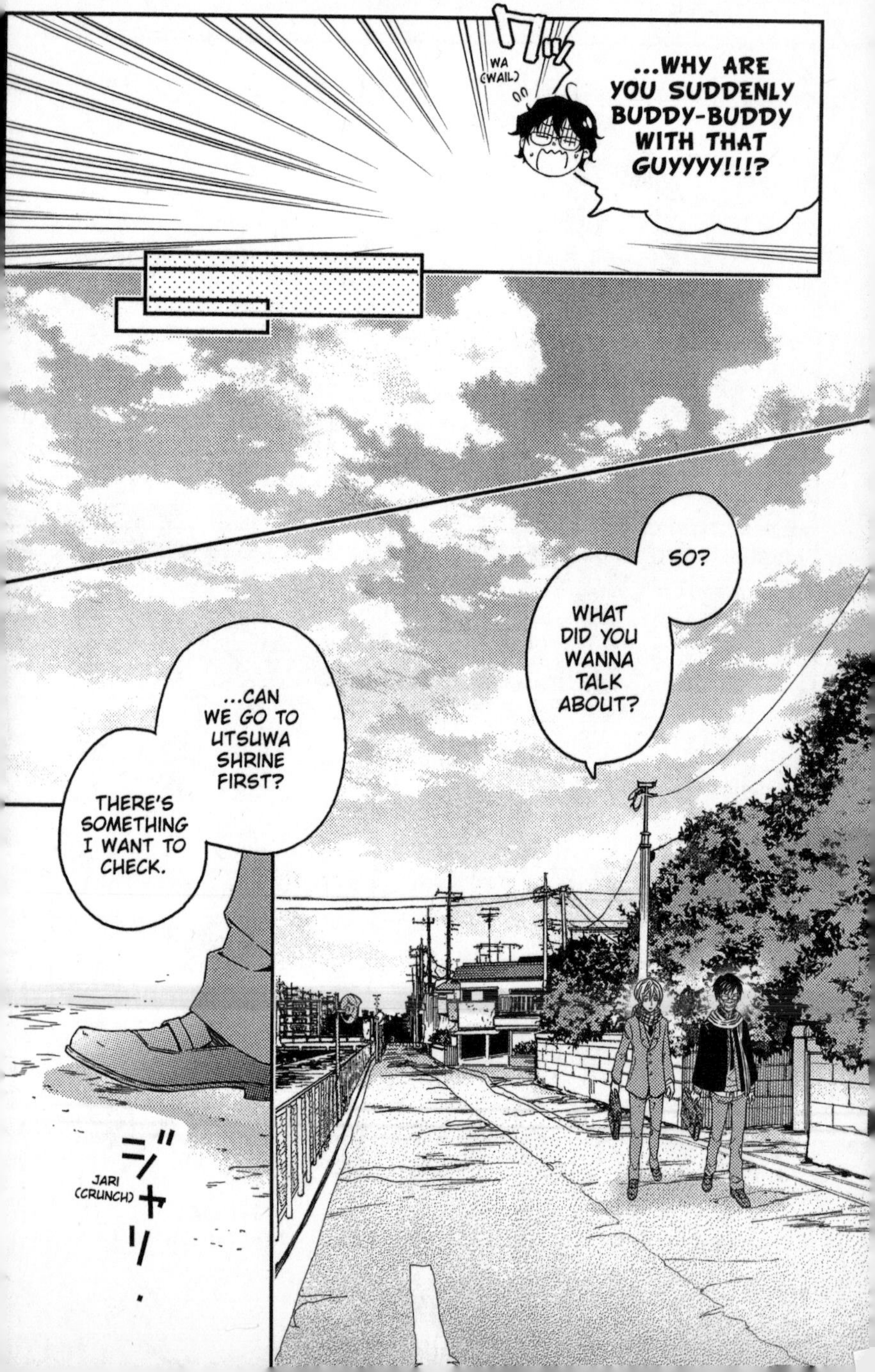

...WHY ARE YOU SUDDENLY BUDDY-BUDDY WITH THAT GUYYYY!!!?
WA (WAIL)
SO?
WHAT DID YOU WANNA TALK ABOUT?
...CAN WE GO TO UTSUWA SHRINE FIRST?
THERE'S SOMETHING I WANT TO CHECK.
ジャリ.
JARI (CRUNCH)

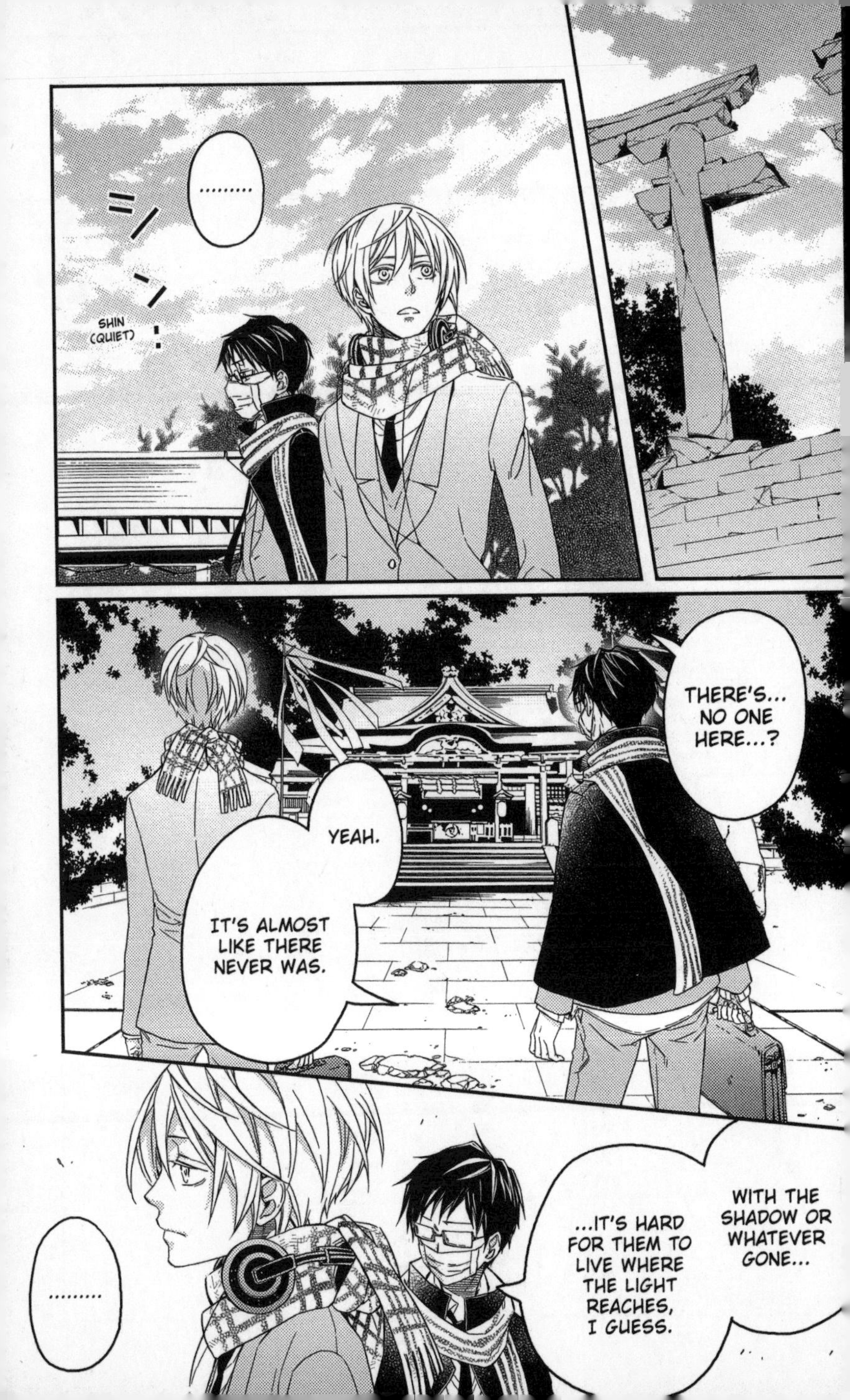
....
SHIN (QUIET)
THERE'S... NO ONE HERE...?
YEAH.
IT'S ALMOST LIKE THERE NEVER WAS.
WITH THE SHADOW OR WHATEVER GONE...
...IT'S HARD FOR THEM TO LIVE WHERE THE LIGHT REACHES, I GUESS.
....

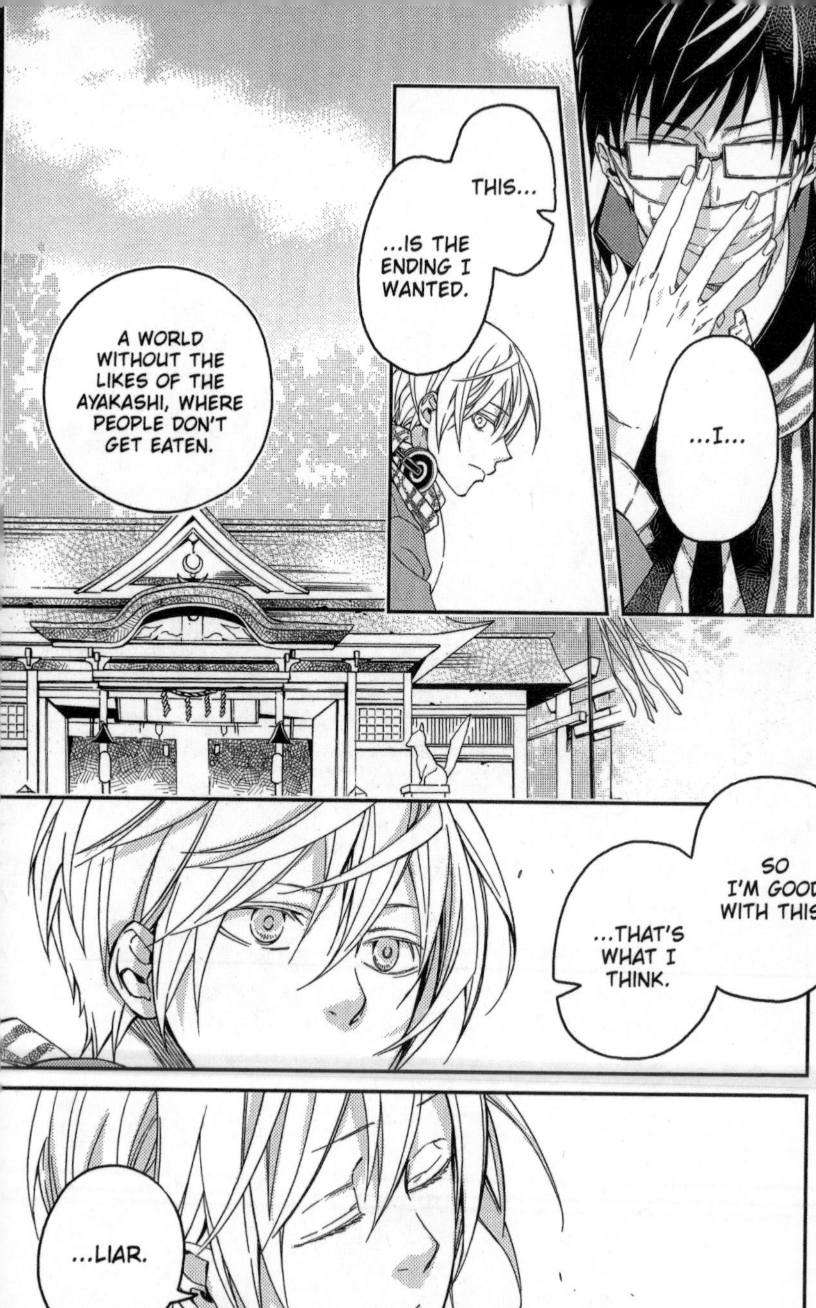
...I...
THIS...
...IS THE ENDING I WANTED.
A WORLD WITHOUT THE LIKES OF THE AYAKASHI, WHERE PEOPLE DON'T GET EATEN.
SO I'M GOOD WITH THIS.
...THAT'S WHAT I THINK.
...LIAR.

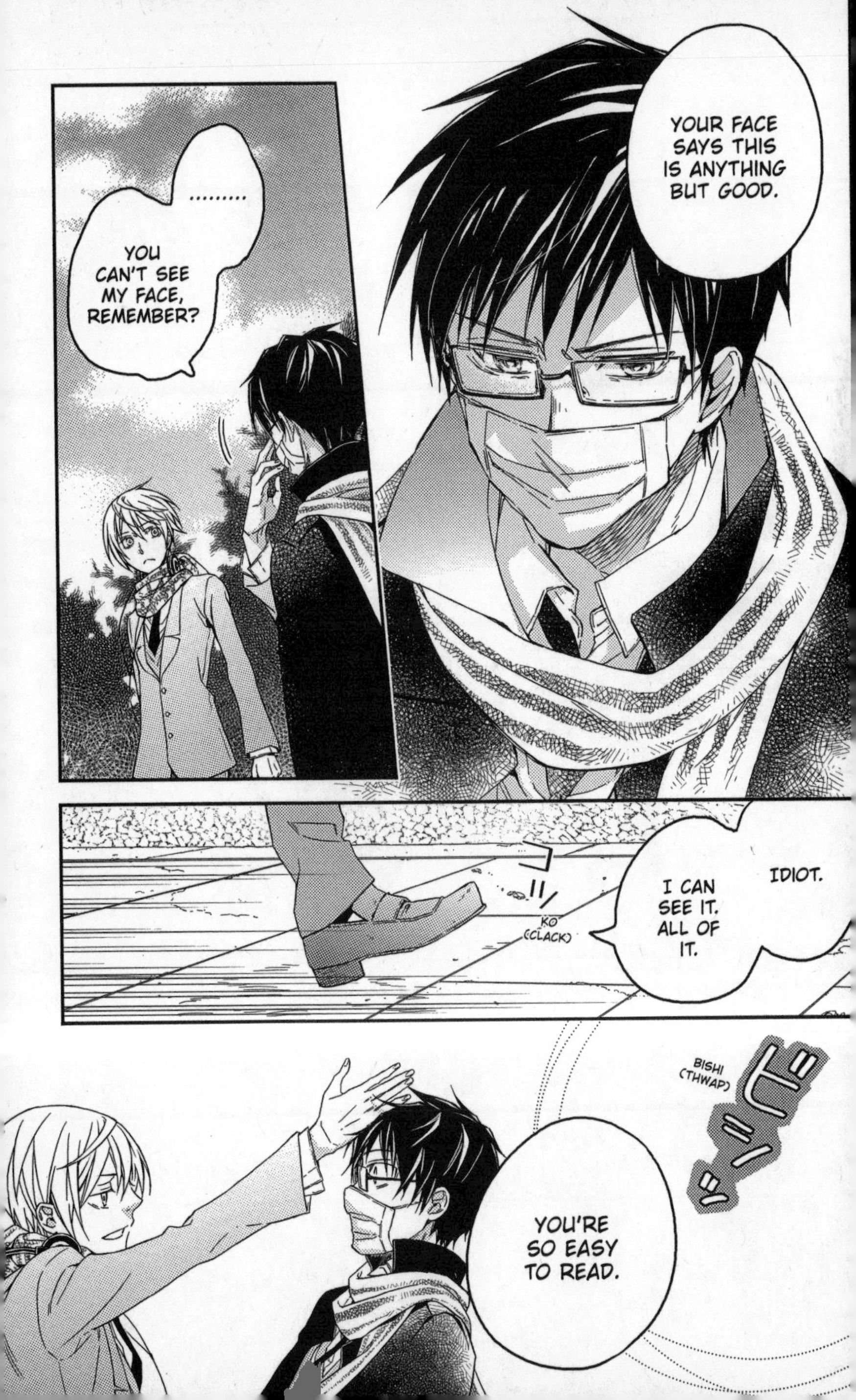
YOUR FACE SAYS THIS IS ANYTHING BUT GOOD.
....
YOU CAN'T SEE MY FACE, REMEMBER?
IDIOT.
I CAN SEE IT. ALL OF IT.
KO (CLACK)
BISHI (THWAP)
YOU'RE SO EASY TO READ.

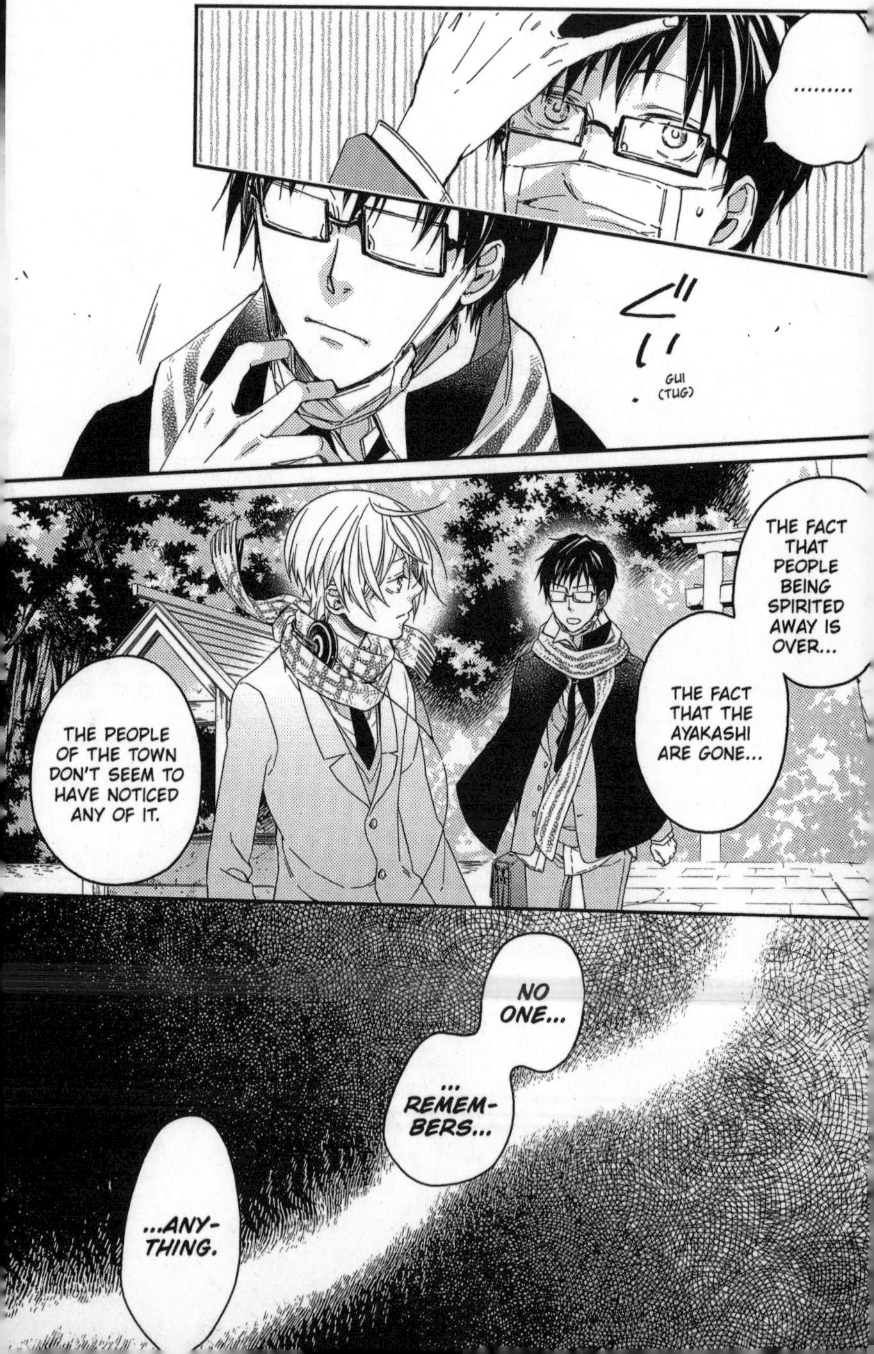
....
GUI (TUG)
THE FACT THAT PEOPLE BEING SPIRITED AWAY IS OVER...
THE FACT THAT THE AYAKASHI ARE GONE...
THE PEOPLE OF THE TOWN DON'T SEEM TO HAVE NOTICED ANY OF IT.
NO ONE...
...REMEMBERS...
...ANYTHING.

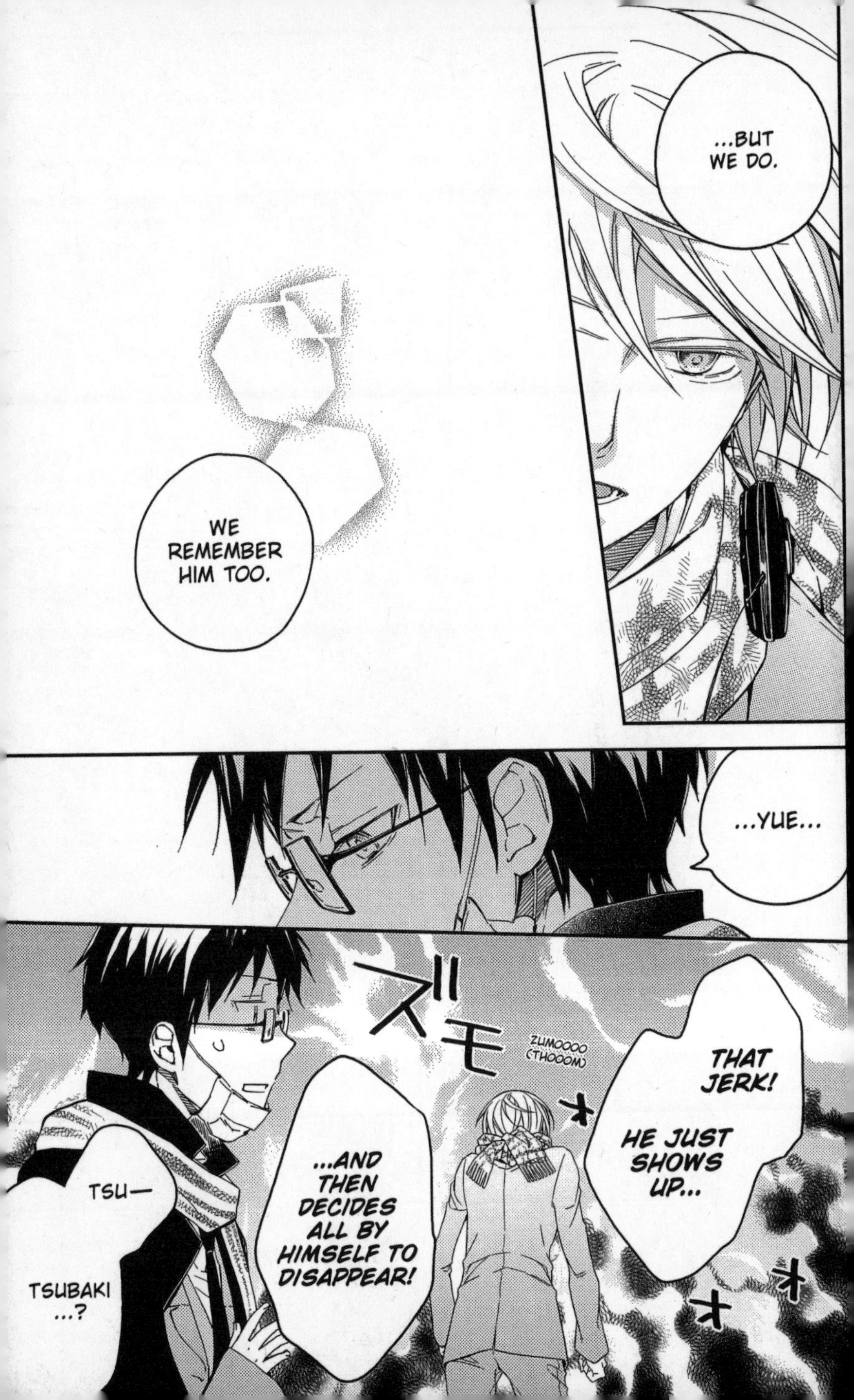
...BUT WE DO.
WE REMEMBER HIM TOO.
...YUE...
THAT JERK!
ZUMOOOO (THOOOM)
HE JUST SHOWS UP...
...AND THEN DECIDES ALL BY HIMSELF TO DISAPPEAR!
TSU—
TSUBAKI ...?

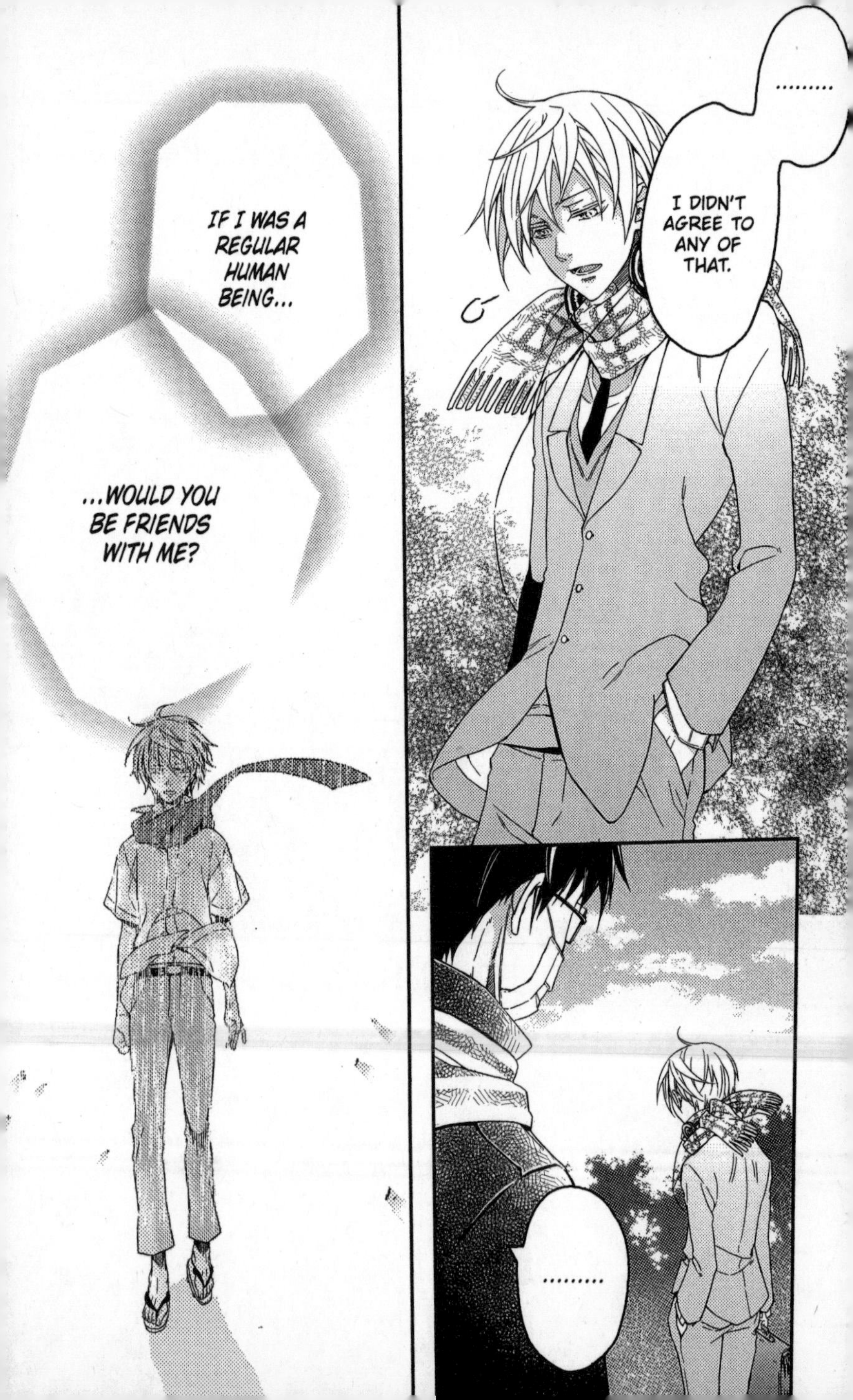
....
I DIDN'T AGREE TO ANY OF THAT.
....
IF I WAS A REGULAR HUMAN BEING...
...WOULD YOU BE FRIENDS WITH ME?

HOW DARE HE RUN OFF ON US WITHOUT HEARING THE ANSWER...

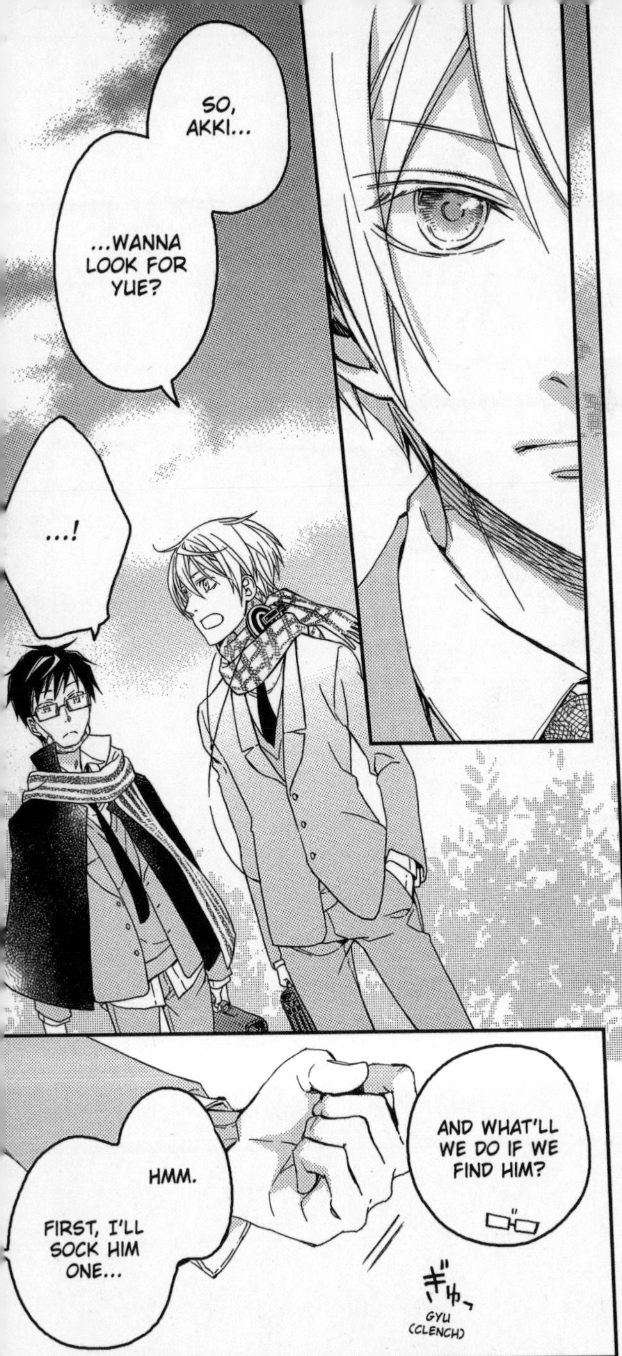
SO, AKKI...
...WANNA LOOK FOR YUE?
...!
AND WHAT'LL WE DO IF WE FIND HIM?
HMM.
FIRST, I'LL SOCK HIM ONE...
ぎゅっ
GYU (CLENCH)

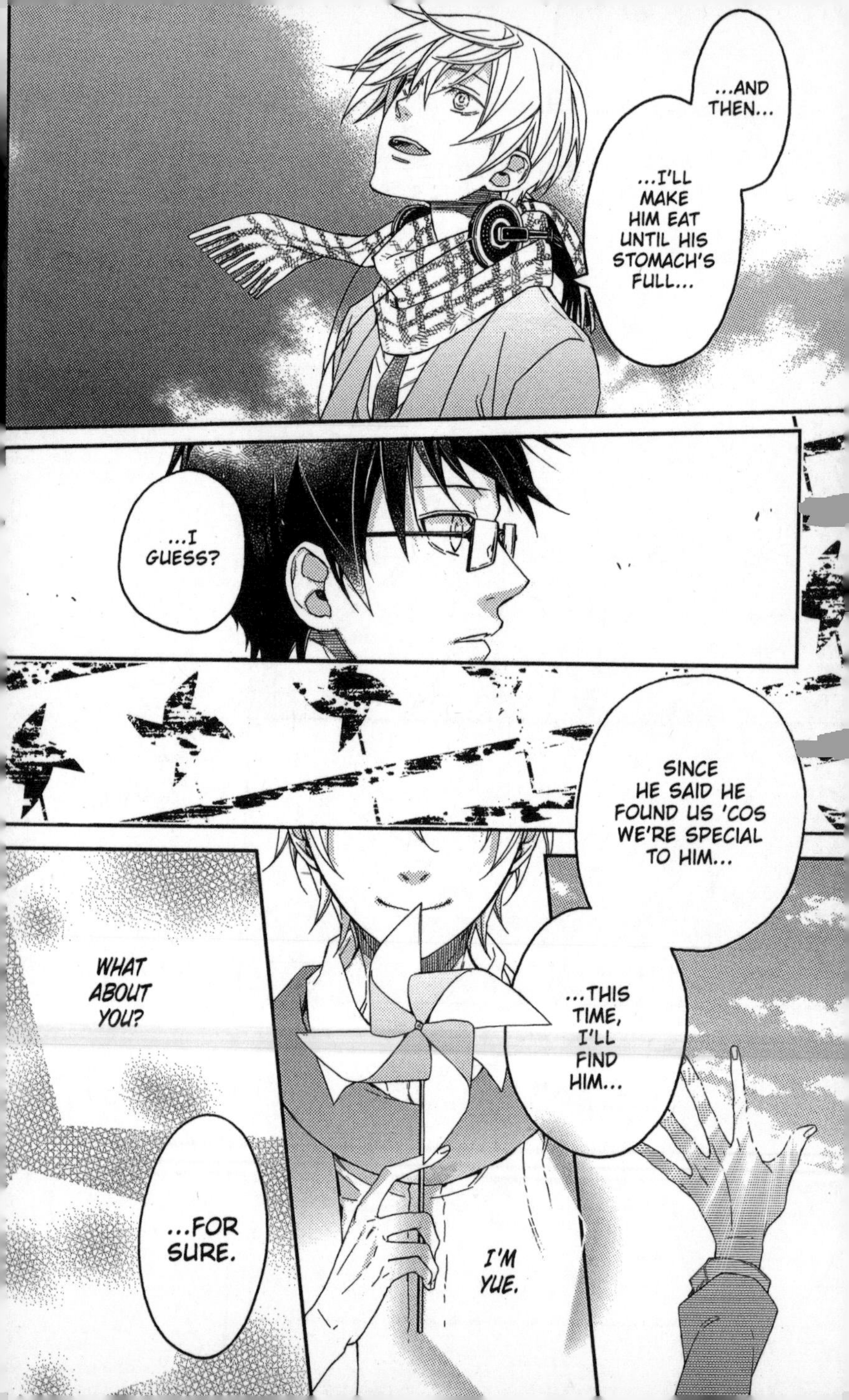
...AND THEN...
...I'LL MAKE HIM EAT UNTIL HIS STOMACH'S FULL...
...I GUESS?
SINCE HE SAID HE FOUND US 'COS WE'RE SPECIAL TO HIM...
...THIS TIME, I'LL FIND HIM...
...FOR SURE.
I'M YUE.
WHAT ABOUT YOU?

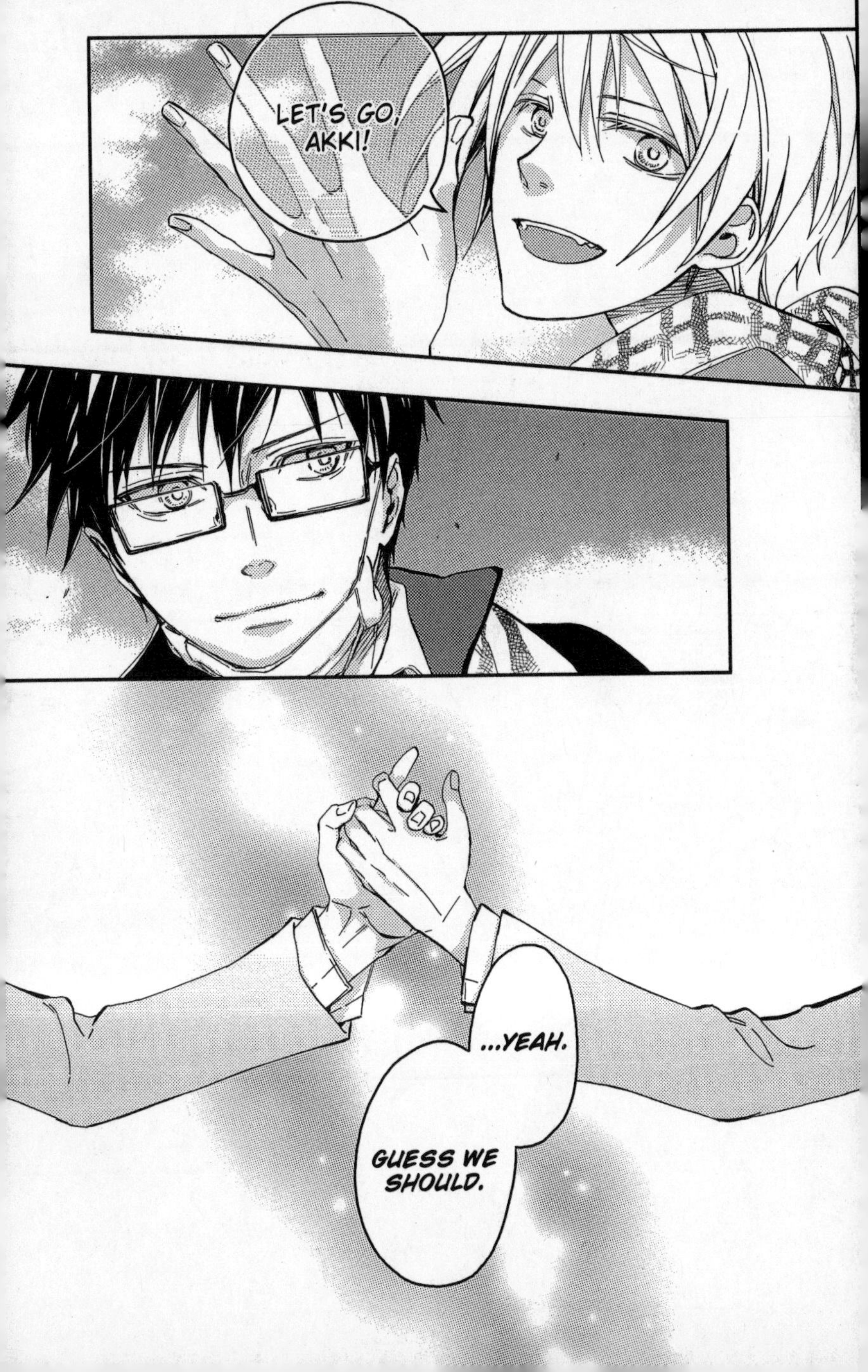
LET'S GO, AKKI!
...YEAH.
GUESS WE SHOULD.

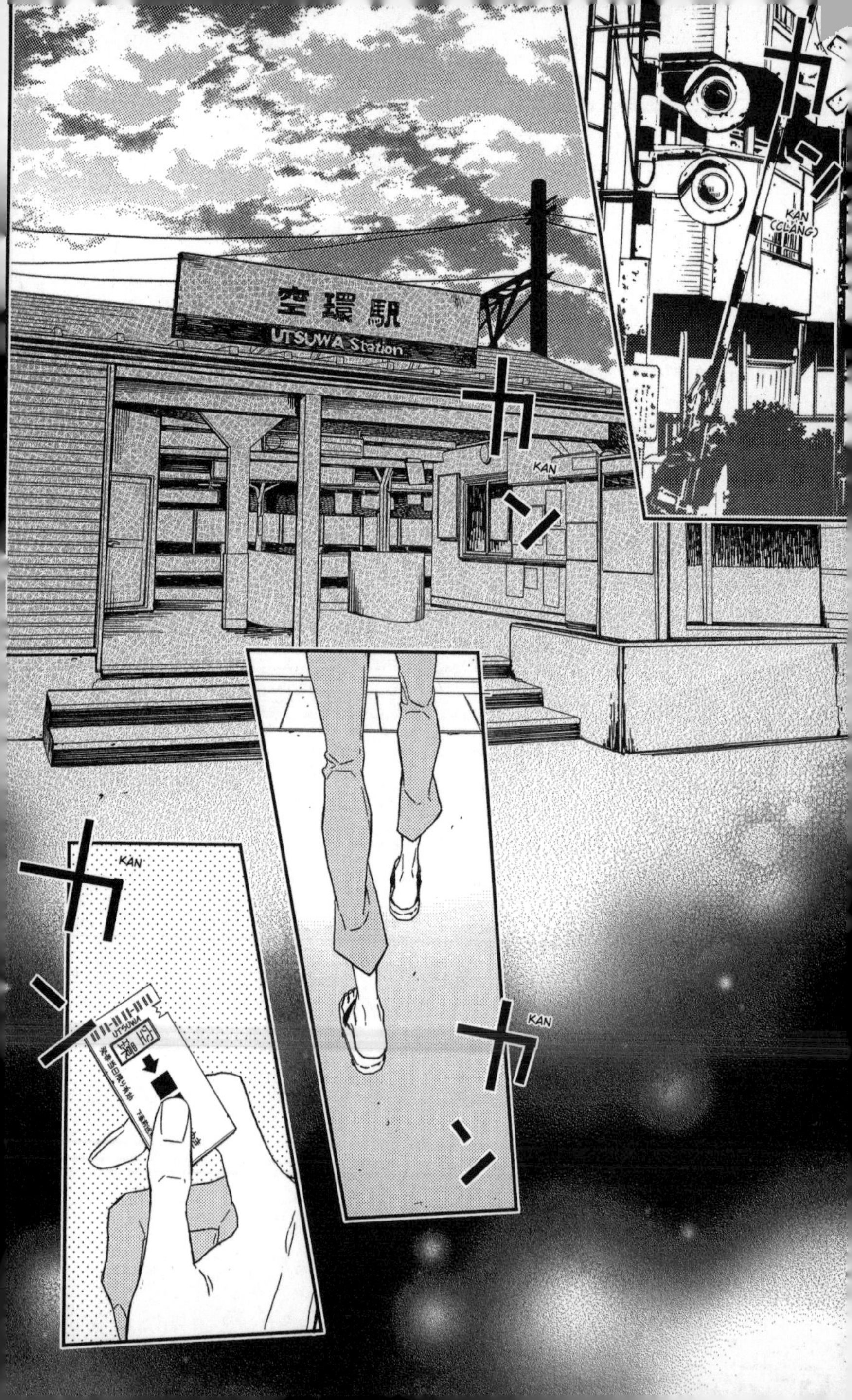
KAN (CLANG)
空環駅
UTSUWA Station
KAN
KAN
KAN
UTSUWA

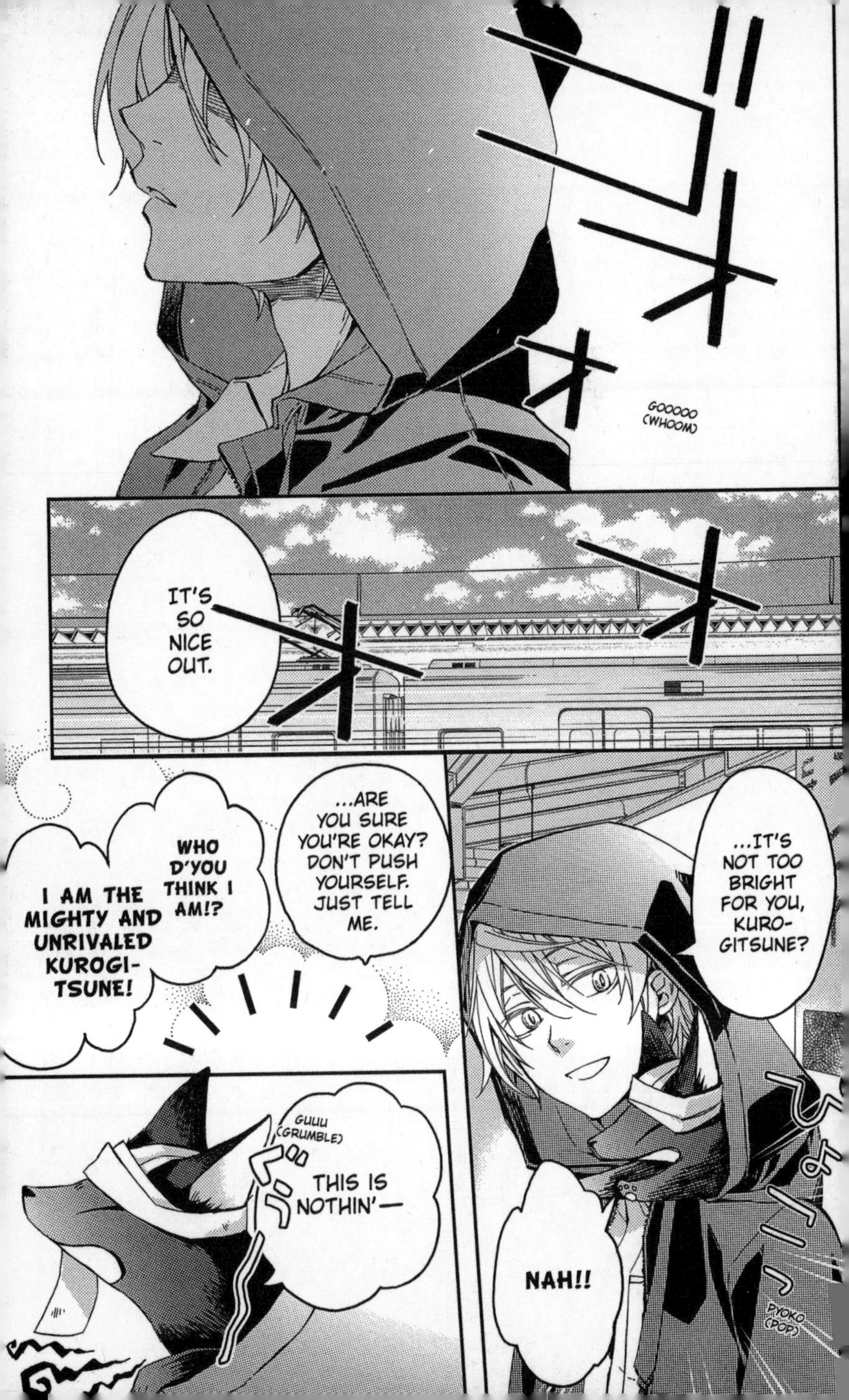
GOOOOO (WHOOM)
IT'S SO NICE OUT.
...IT'S NOT TOO BRIGHT FOR YOU, KURO-GITSUNE?
NAH!!
PYOKO (POP)
...ARE YOU SURE YOU'RE OKAY? DON'T PUSH YOURSELF. JUST TELL ME.
WHO D'YOU THINK I AM!?
I AM THE MIGHTY AND UNRIVALED KUROGI-TSUNE!
GUUU (GRUMBLE)
THIS IS NOTHIN'—

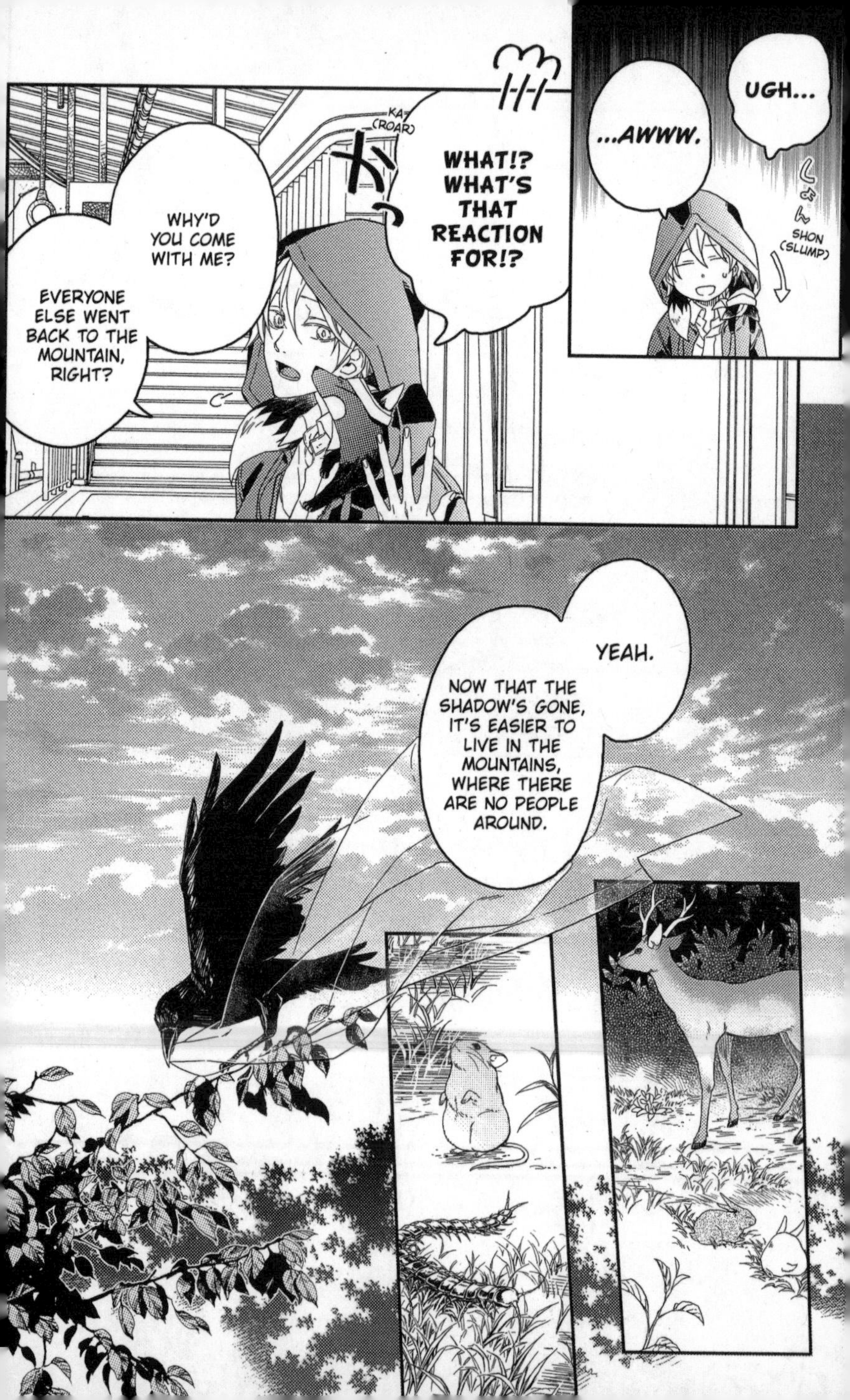
UGH...
...AWWW.
しょん
SHON (SLUMP)
カッ
KA (ROAR)
WHAT!? WHAT'S THAT REACTION FOR!?
WHY'D YOU COME WITH ME?
EVERYONE ELSE WENT BACK TO THE MOUNTAIN, RIGHT?
YEAH.
NOW THAT THE SHADOW'S GONE, IT'S EASIER TO LIVE IN THE MOUNTAINS, WHERE THERE ARE NO PEOPLE AROUND.

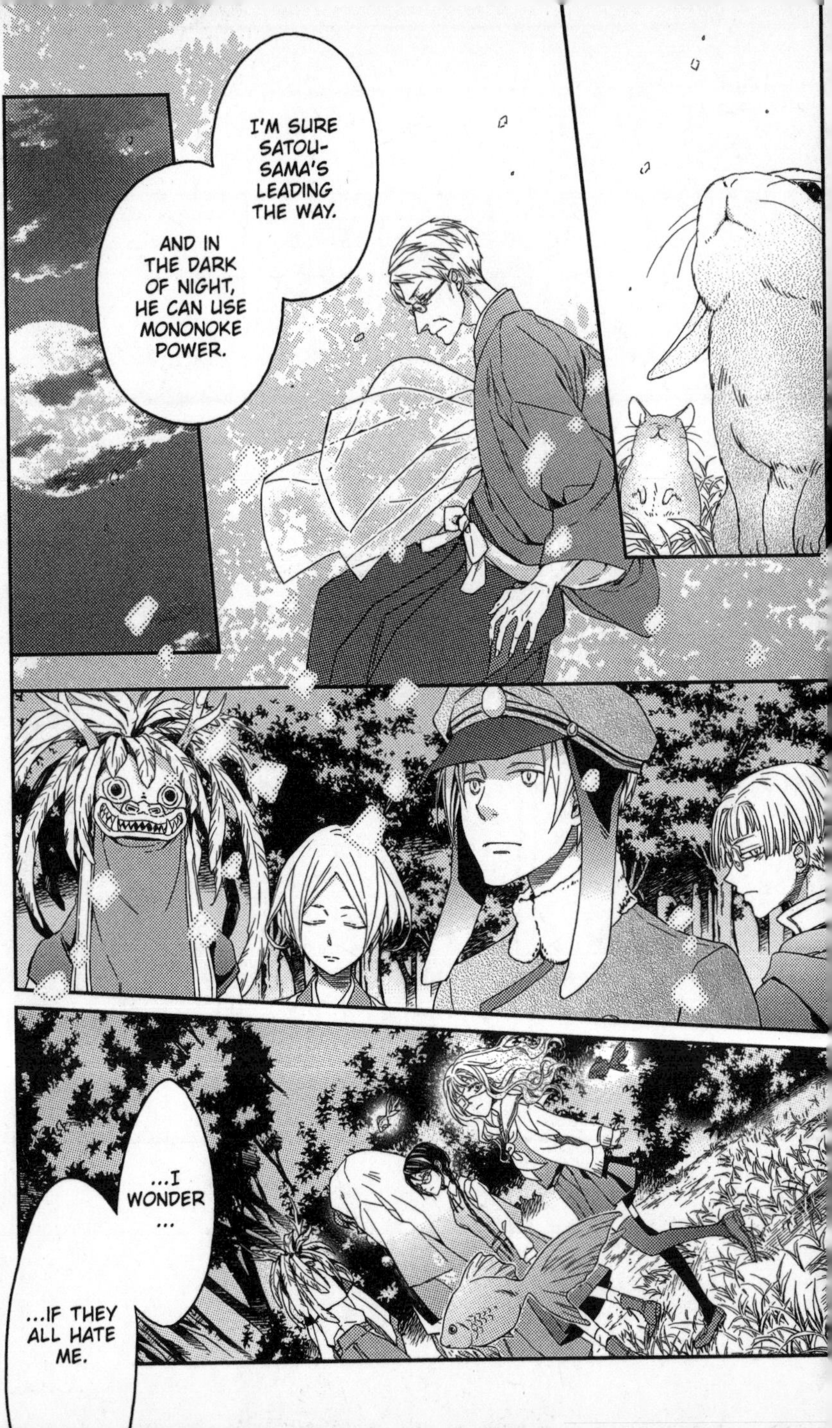
I'M SURE SATOU-SAMA'S LEADING THE WAY.
AND IN THE DARK OF NIGHT, HE CAN USE MONONOKE POWER.
...I WONDER ...
...IF THEY ALL HATE ME.

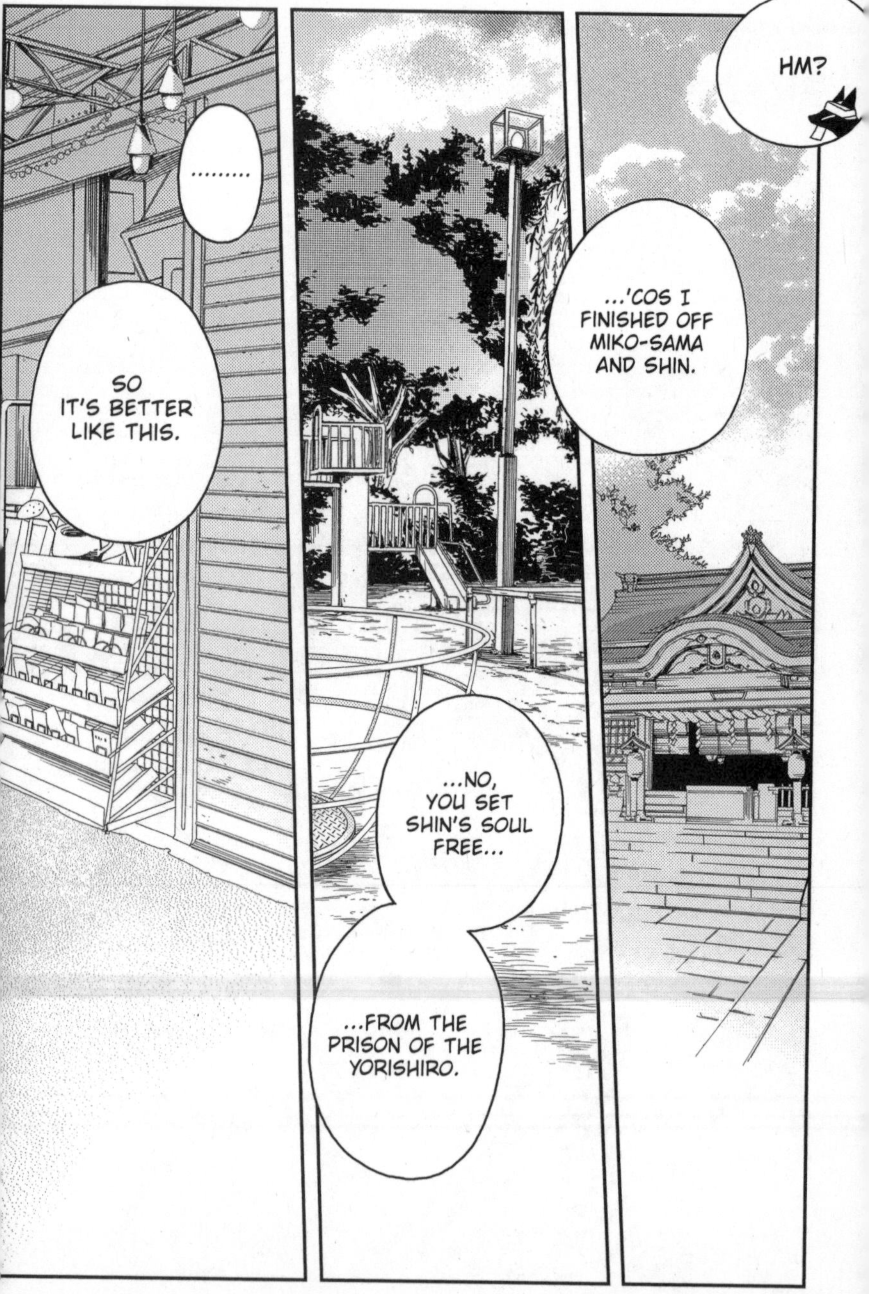
HM?
...'COS I FINISHED OFF MIKO-SAMA AND SHIN.
...NO, YOU SET SHIN'S SOUL FREE...
...FROM THE PRISON OF THE YORISHIRO.
....
SO IT'S BETTER LIKE THIS.

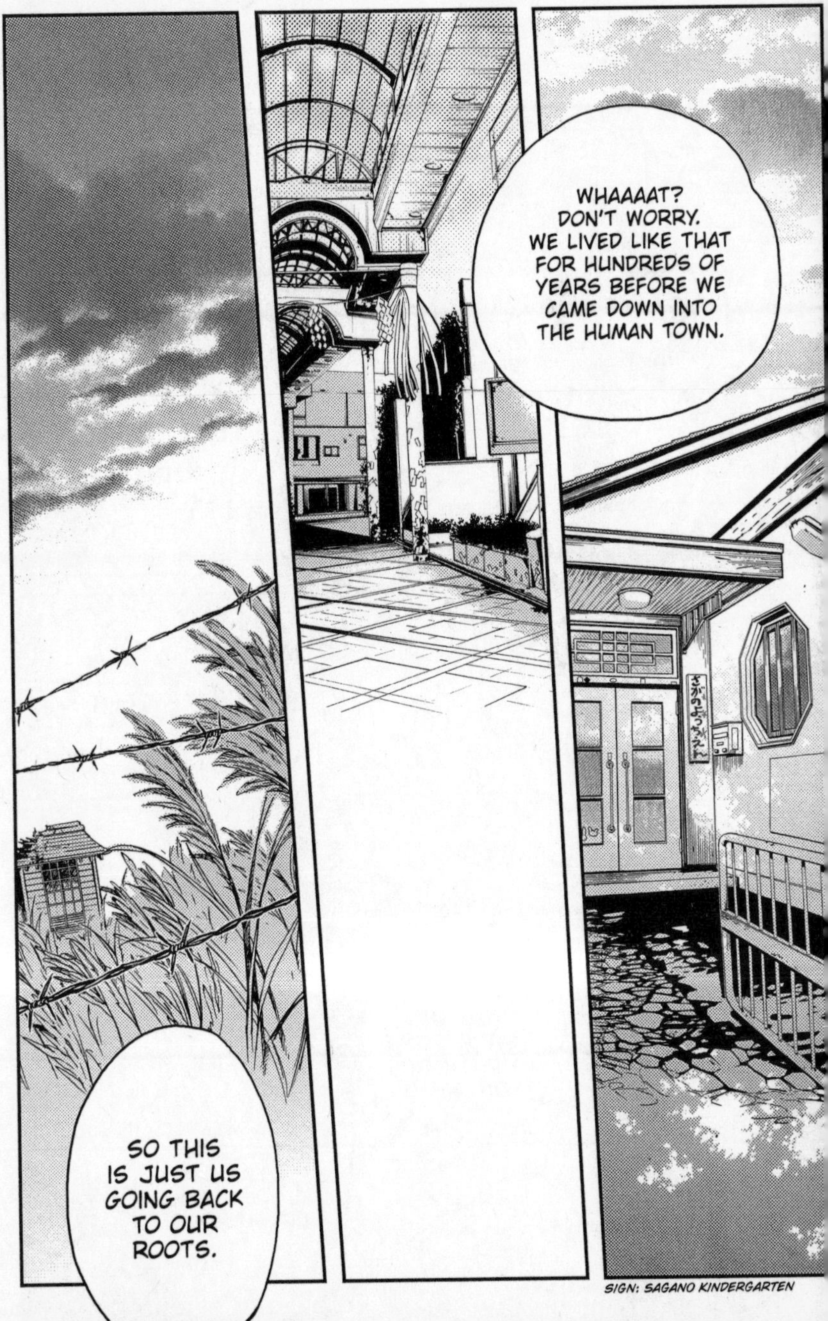
WHAAAAT? DON'T WORRY. WE LIVED LIKE THAT FOR HUNDREDS OF YEARS BEFORE WE CAME DOWN INTO THE HUMAN TOWN.
SO THIS IS JUST US GOING BACK TO OUR ROOTS.
SIGN: SAGANO KINDERGARTEN

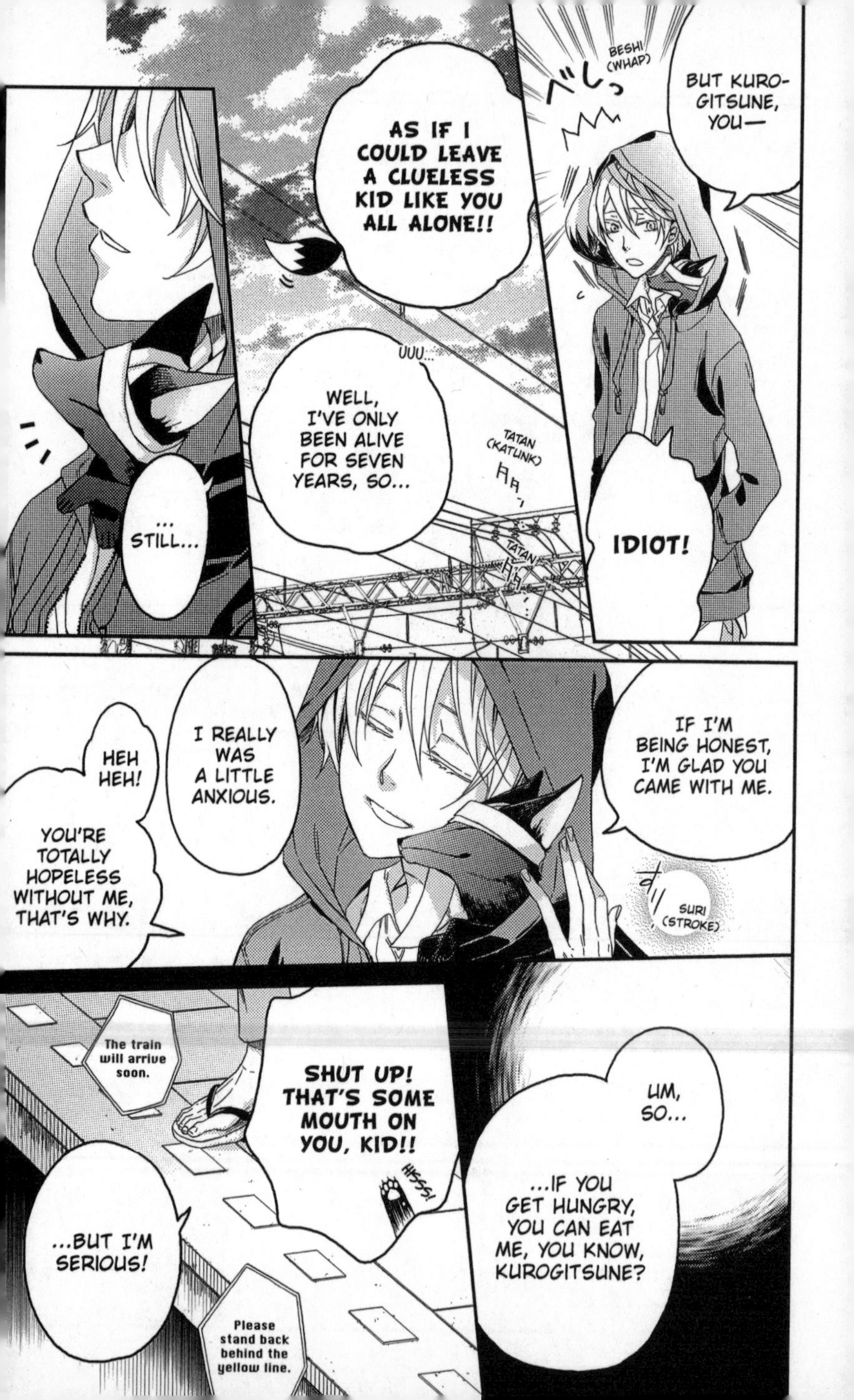
BUT KURO-GITSUNE, YOU—
べしっ
BESHI (WHAP)
IDIOT!
AS IF I COULD LEAVE A CLUELESS KID LIKE YOU ALL ALONE!!
TATAN (KATUNK)
TATAN
UUU...
WELL, I'VE ONLY BEEN ALIVE FOR SEVEN YEARS, SO...
... STILL...
IF I'M BEING HONEST, I'M GLAD YOU CAME WITH ME.
SURI (STROKE)
I REALLY WAS A LITTLE ANXIOUS.
HEH HEH!
YOU'RE TOTALLY HOPELESS WITHOUT ME, THAT'S WHY.
UM, SO...
...IF YOU GET HUNGRY, YOU CAN EAT ME, YOU KNOW, KUROGITSUNE?
SHUT UP! THAT'S SOME MOUTH ON YOU, KID!!
HISSS!
The train will arrive soon.
...BUT I'M SERIOUS!
Please stand back behind the yellow line.

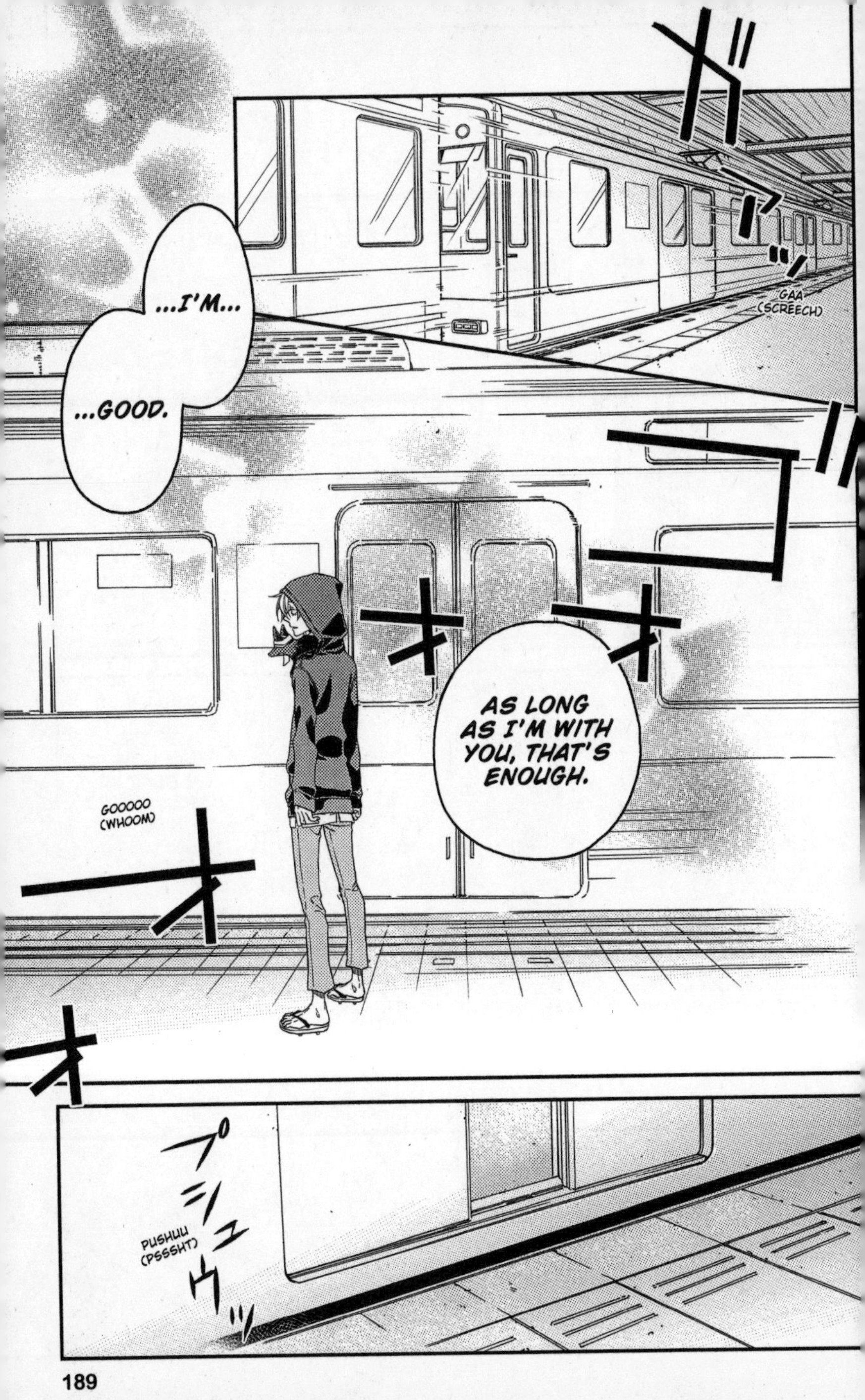
GAA (SCREECH)
...I'M...
...GOOD.
AS LONG AS I'M WITH YOU, THAT'S ENOUGH.
GOOOOO (WHOOM)
PUSHUU (PSSSHT)

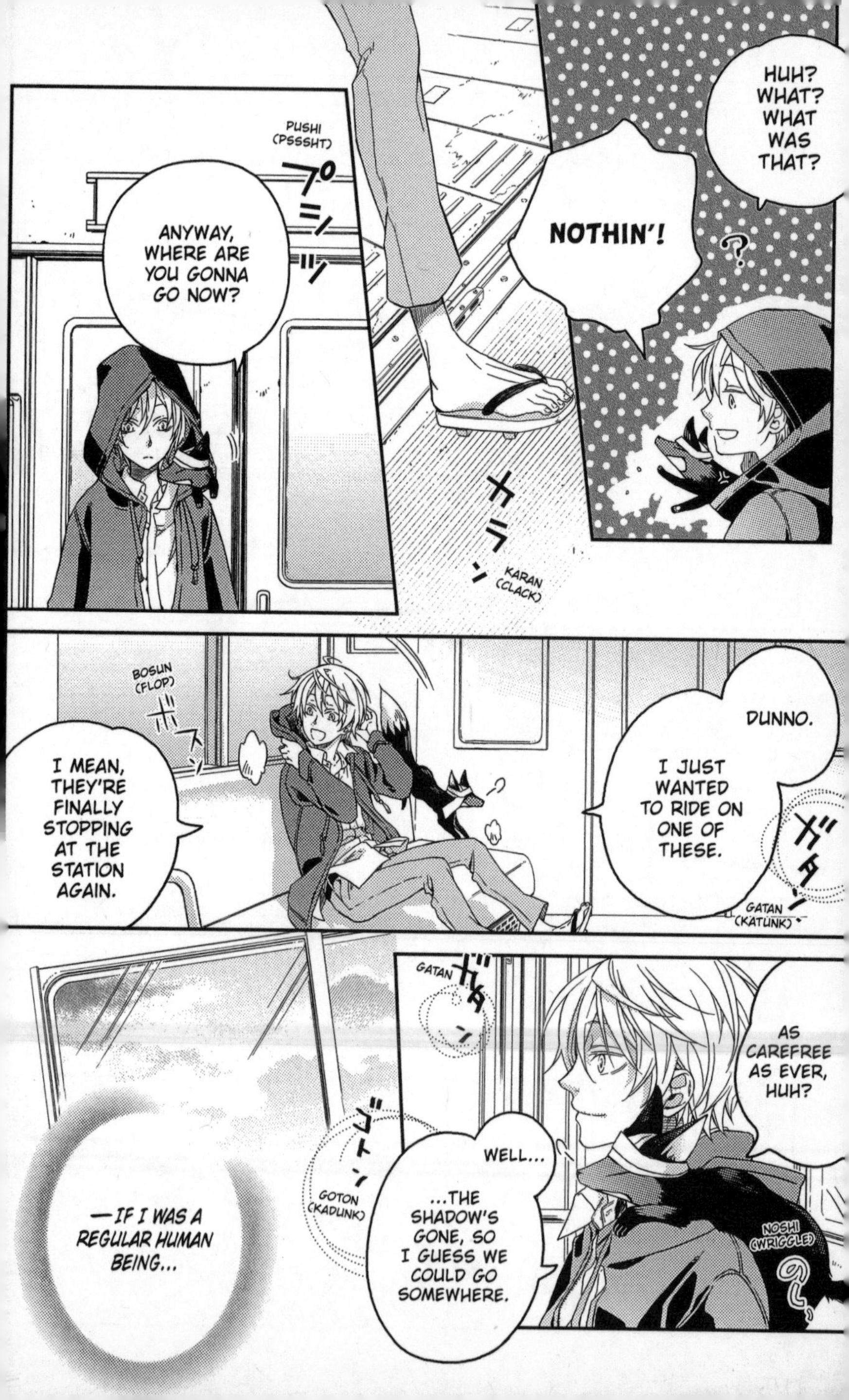
HUH? WHAT? WHAT WAS THAT?
NOTHIN'!
?
KARAN (CLACK)
PUSHI (PSSSHT)
ANYWAY, WHERE ARE YOU GONNA GO NOW?
DUNNO.
I JUST WANTED TO RIDE ON ONE OF THESE.
GATAN (KATUNK)
BOSUN (FLOP)
I MEAN, THEY'RE FINALLY STOPPING AT THE STATION AGAIN.
AS CAREFREE AS EVER, HUH?
NOSHI (WRIGGLE)
GATAN
WELL...
...THE SHADOW'S GONE, SO I GUESS WE COULD GO SOMEWHERE.
GOTON (KADUNK)
—IF I WAS A REGULAR HUMAN BEING...

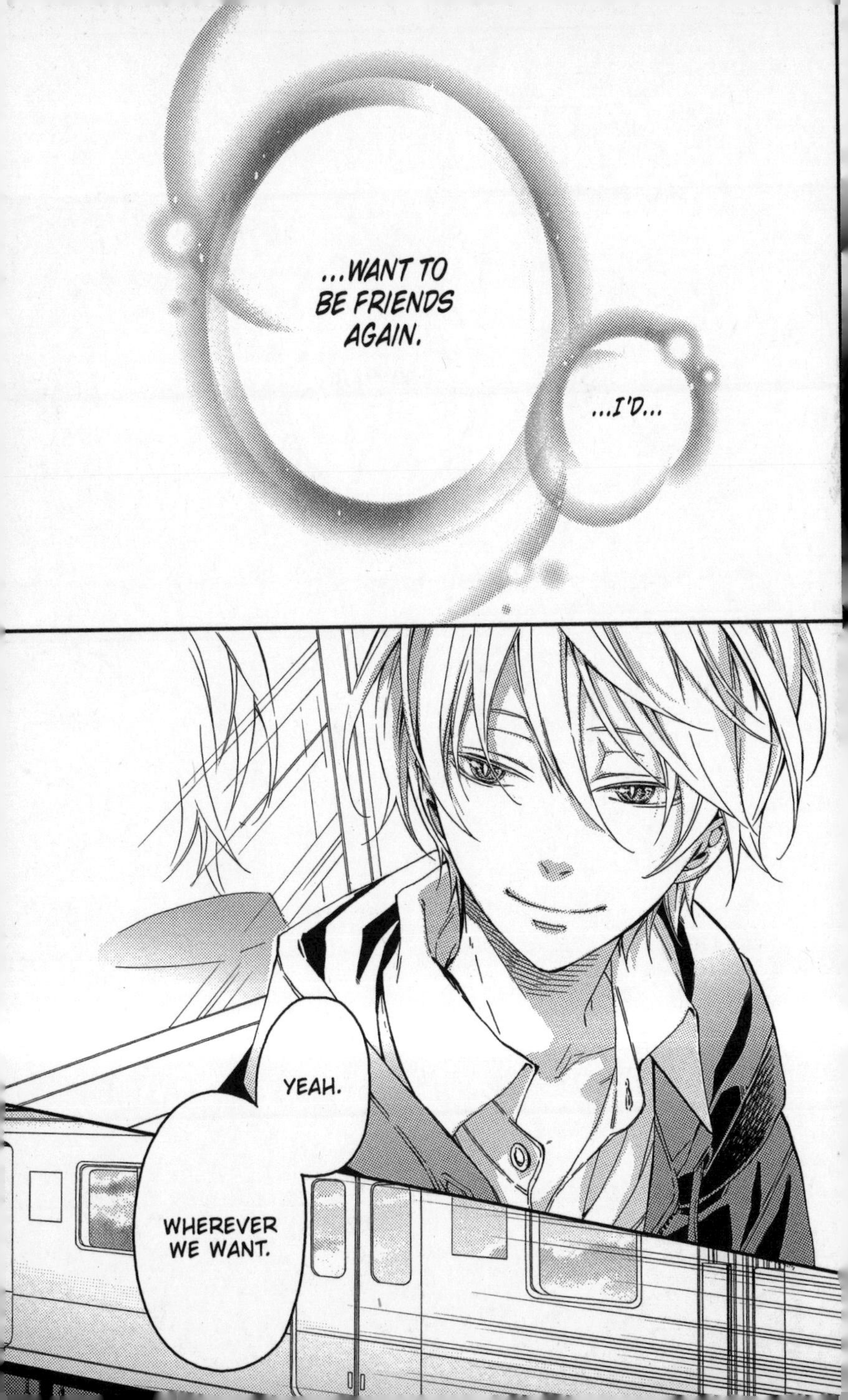
...I'D...
...WANT TO BE FRIENDS AGAIN.
YEAH.
WHEREVER WE WANT.

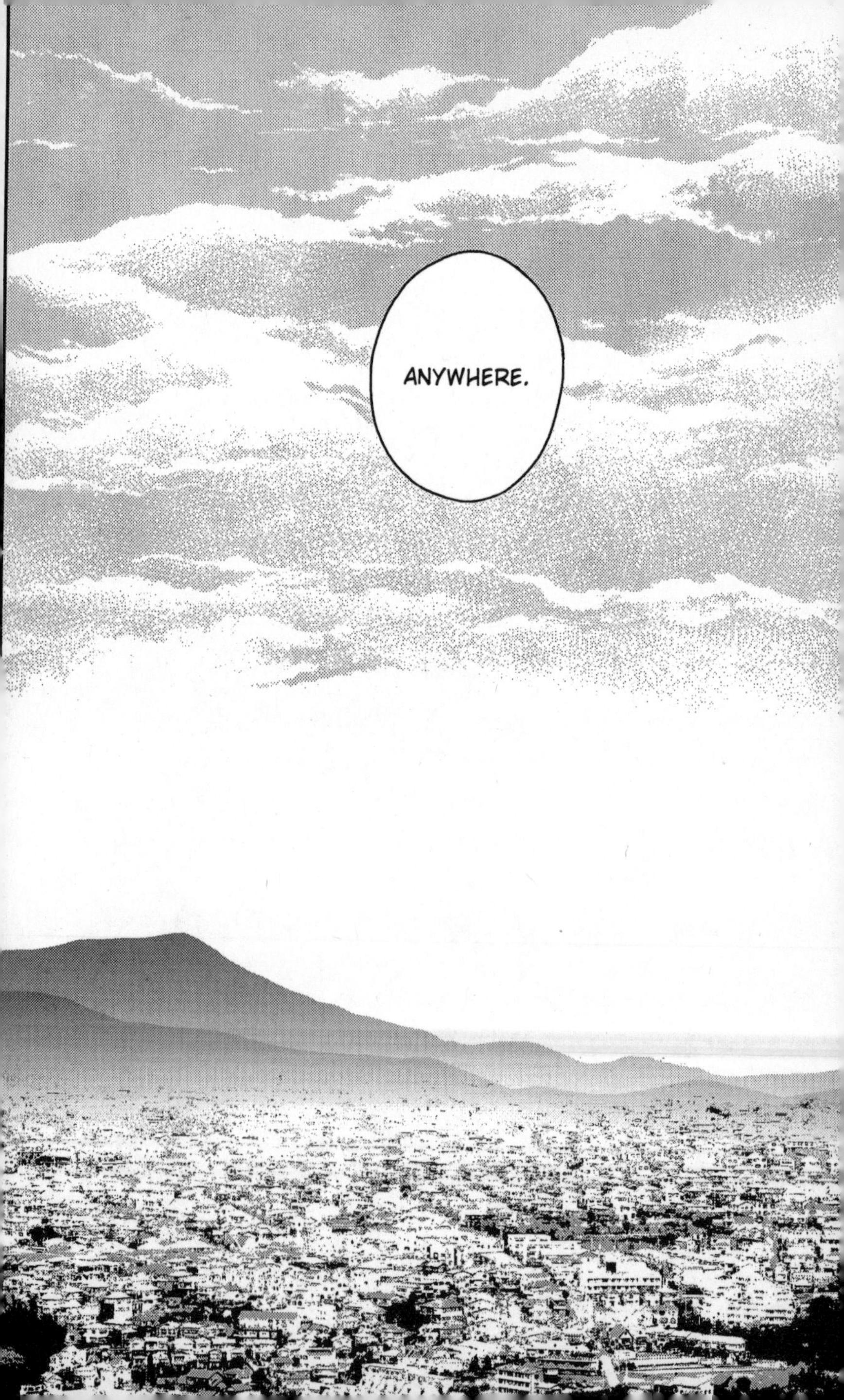
ANYWHERE.

Of the Red,
the Light,
and the
Ayakashi

THE END

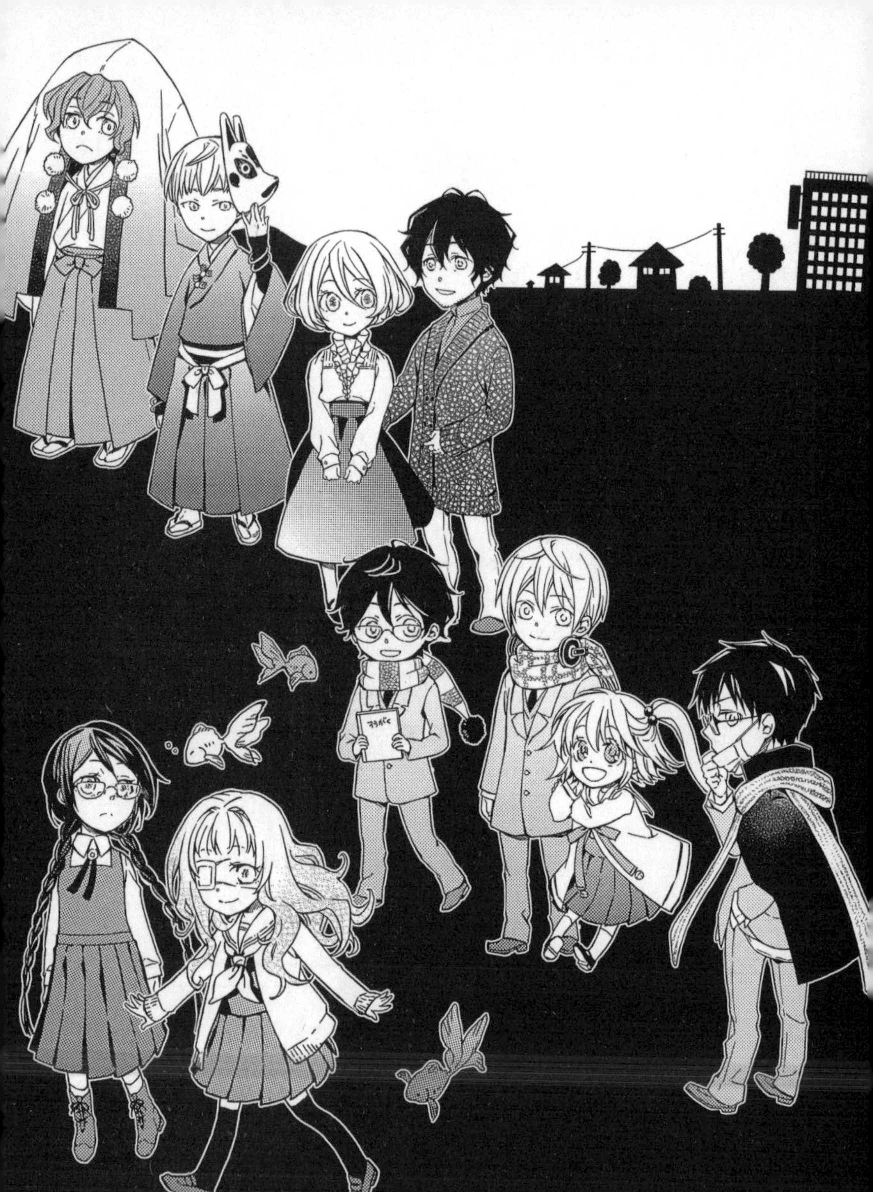
すうがく

This the end of the comic version of *Of the Red, the Light, and the Ayakashi*. Yue-kun and Kurogitsune have set out on a journey together...exactly four years after the first book. Good for you, Yue-kun.

I was able to make it this far with the support of so many people.

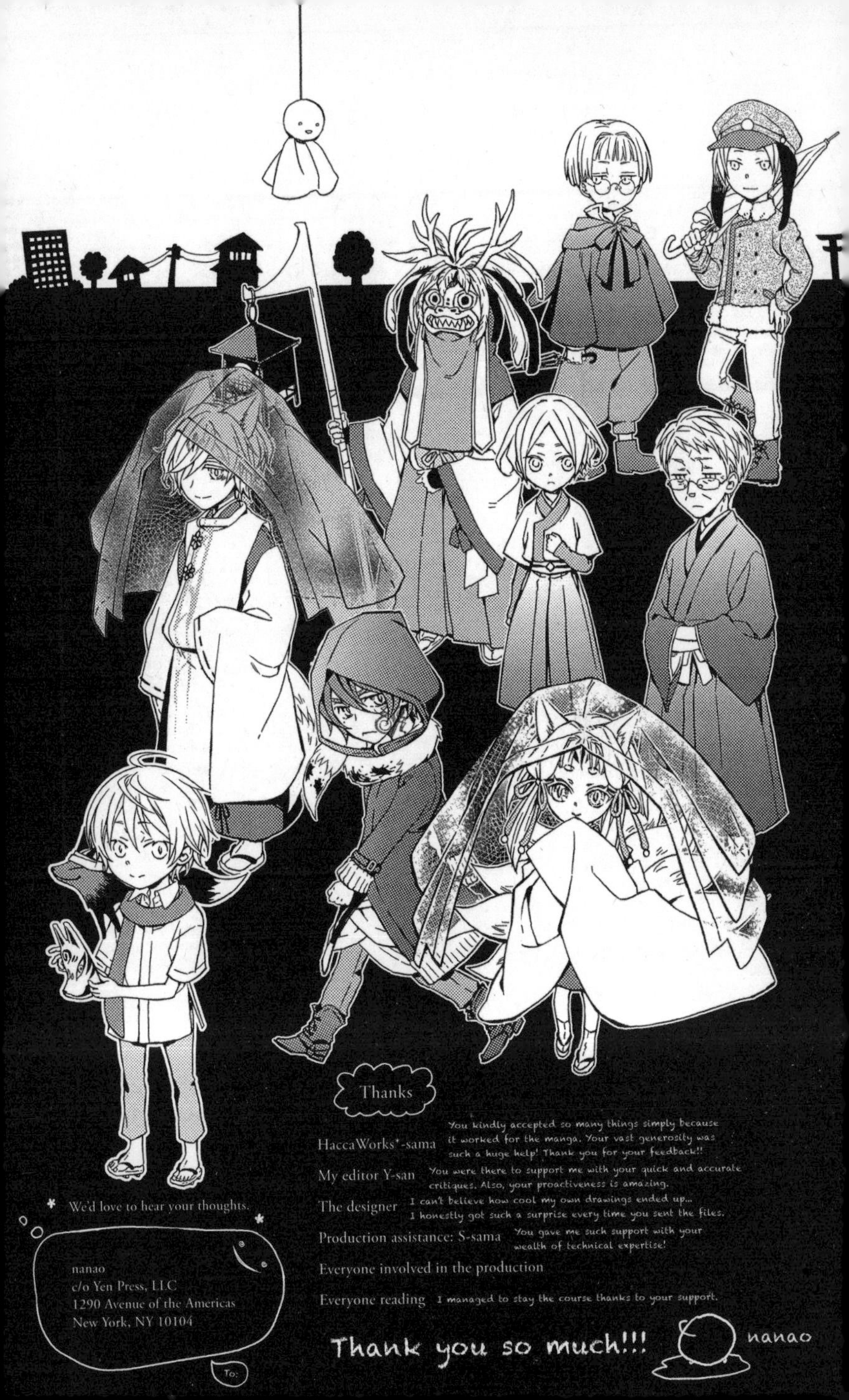

Thanks

HaccaWorks*-sama — You kindly accepted so many things simply because it worked for the manga. Your vast generosity was such a huge help! Thank you for your feedback!!

My editor Y-san — You were there to support me with your quick and accurate critiques. Also, your proactiveness is amazing.

The designer — I can't believe how cool my own drawings ended up... I honestly got such a surprise every time you sent the files.

Production assistance: S-sama — You gave me such support with your wealth of technical expertise!

Everyone involved in the production

Everyone reading — I managed to stay the course thanks to your support.

Thank you so much!!! — nanao

* We'd love to hear your thoughts. *

nanao
c/o Yen Press, LLC
1290 Avenue of the Americas
New York, NY 10104

To:

THANKS FOR YOUR HARD WORK ON NINE VOLUMES OF OF THE RED!

FROM
HaccaWorks*

I got to help out with the latter half of the plot. Nanao-san, the editor, and I managed to arrive at this ending while struggling constantly with how to make sure we kept the worldview in the manga version.

What did you think? I had a lot of fun! If you get the chance, please let us know what you thought. Thank you so much.

Yuta Warabe

As just one reader, I really enjoyed this. I fell in love with everyone all over again. Nanao-san, the editor, everyone involved with the OF THE RED manga, thank you so much!!

—Satoru Mizaki

Nanao-sensei's Yue-kun is just such a good kid that we wanted him to be happy, and this is the result.

I think you only get to see this in the manga version. Thank you so much!

Torika Shimizu

I looked forward to every volume of this OF THE RED that we only get to see in the manga. Before I knew it, nine volumes flew by in the blink of an eye. Congratulations on completing the long journey, Nanao-san, the editor in charge, and everyone reading!

—Misaki Kanan

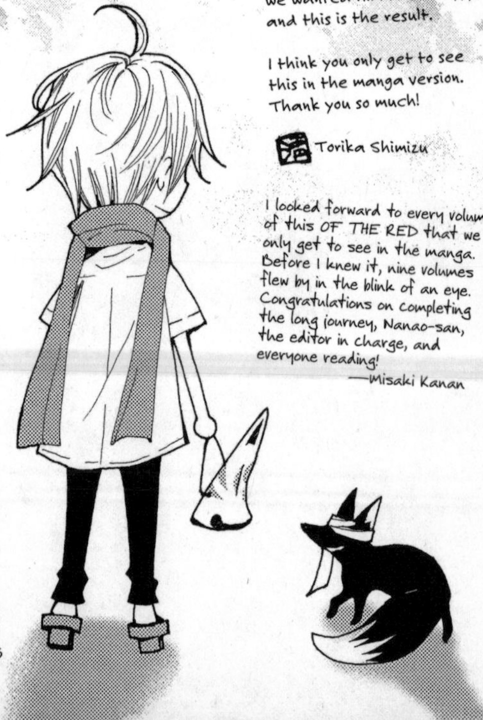

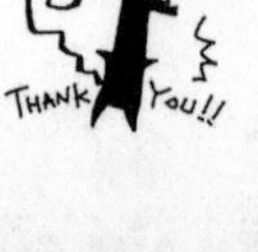
THANK YOU!!

WE WOULD ALSO LIKE TO THANK EVERYONE WHO WORKED ON THE ENGLISH EDITION FOR THEIR CONSIDERATE AND ATTENTIVE EFFORTS ON THIS SERIES!

TRANSLATION NOTES

COMMON HONORIFICS

no honorific: Indicates familiarity or closeness; if used without permission or reason, addressing someone in this manner would be an insult.

-san: The Japanese equivalent of Mr./Mrs./Miss. If a situation calls for politeness, this is the fail-safe honorific.

-sama: Conveys great respect; may also indicate that the social status of the speaker is lower than that of the addressee.

-kun: Used most often when referring to boys, this indicates affection or familiarity. Occasionally used by older men among their peers, but it may also be used by anyone referring to a person of lower standing.

-chan, -tan: An affectionate honorific indicating familiarity used mostly in reference to girls; also used in reference to cute persons or animals.

Ayakashi is a general term for ghosts, monsters, haunted objects, mythical animals, and all sorts of uncanny things from Japanese folklore.

PAGE 12
Nikujaga is a meat and potato stew dish.

PAGE 49
This fortune of **"caution"** tells the receiver to proceed with caution. The signs suggest that they are likely to fail if they rush forward, and they need to proceed in the proper order of things and work hard.

PAGE 163
Takoyaki are fried dumplings with pieces of octopus inside.

PAGE 185
Mononoke is a term sometimes used interchangeably with *ayakashi* and refers to a variety of spirits from Japanese literary and cultural traditions.

The story's not quite over yet!

Want to know what Tougo, Akiyoshi, Yue, and Kurogitsune are getting up to now?

Of the Red, the Light, and the Ayakashi ⑩

Coming in March 2018!

Of the Red, the Light, and the Ayakashi

ART BY Nanao
STORY BY HaccaWorks*

Translation: Jocelyne Allen ✦ Lettering: Alexis Eckerman

AKAYA AKASHIYA AYAKASHINO
© Nanao 2016
© HaccaWorks* 2016
First published in Japan in 2016 by KADOKAWA CORPORATION. English translation rights reserved by YEN PRESS, LLC under the license from KADOKAWA CORPORATION, Tokyo through TUTTLE-MORI AGENCY, Inc., Tokyo.

English translation © 2017 by Yen Press, LLC

Yen Press
1290 Avenue of the Americas
New York, NY 10104

Visit us!
yenpress.com
facebook.com/yenpress
twitter.com/yenpress
yenpress.tumblr.com
instagram.com/yenpress

First Yen Press Edition: December 2017

Yen Press is an imprint of Yen Press, LLC.
The Yen Press name and logo are trademarks of Yen Press, LLC.

Library of Congress Control Number: 2016932691

ISBNs: 978-0-316-47448-1 (print)
978-0-316-47449-8 (ebook)

10 9 8 7 6 5 4 3 2 1

BVG

Printed in the United States of America